AMERICAN
SOCIOLOGY

AMERICAN
SOCIOLOGY

The Story of Sociology in the

UNITED STATES

through 1950

by

HOWARD W. ODUM

University of North Carolina

LONGMANS, GREEN AND CO.

New York · London · Toronto

1951

LONGMANS, GREEN AND CO., INC.
55 FIFTH AVENUE, NEW YORK 3

LONGMANS, GREEN AND CO., LTD.
6 & 7 CLIFFORD STREET, LONDON W 1

LONGMANS, GREEN AND CO.
215 VICTORIA STREET, TORONTO 1

AMERICAN SOCIOLOGY

PUBLISHED SIMULTANEOUSLY IN THE DOMINION OF CANADA BY
LONGMANS, GREEN AND CO., TORONTO

FIRST EDITION

Printed in the United States of America
Vail-Ballou Press, Inc., Binghamton, N. Y.

Contents

PART I. *The Background of American Sociology*

PART II. *American Sociology as American Sociologists: The Presidents of the American Sociological Society*

PART III. *American Sociology as American Sociologists: Authors of Texts*

v

PART IV. *American Sociology on Other Levels*

PART V. *Toward Inventory*

AMERICAN
SOCIOLOGY

PART I

The Background of American Sociology

CHAPTER 1

The Story of American Sociology

The halfway divide of an epochal century normally becomes the occasion for reviewing history, summarizing achievements, viewing with pride, noting with alarm, and generally taking stock of what has gone before, and making reappraisals looking to the future. This is especially true of mid-century 1950 American society, set in its new framework of world leadership. The catalogue of these mid-century achievements and status will include many general historical reviews, the literary history of America, appraisals of scientific and technological progress, the economic contributions to American culture, together with a hundred and one special inventories, and the great American census. All these in time may well constitute a powerful literature in the annals of our changing world.

One of the stories that needs most to be told is that of American sociology. This is true for several reasons. In the first place, just as each epochal period must write and interpret its history in its own terms and establish its own criteria of judgments, so in special areas of new development, such as sociology, there is great opportunity not only to chronicle its story, by having sociologists write for sociologists and for other social scientists, but also by having sociologists write for students and make the story meaningful to all people who read. In the next place, the story of American sociology has never been adequately told, either for its own sake as a dynamic social science, or for its part in the development and interpretation of American society and, in particular, of American education. In these capacities it has been neglected in both the annals of the academic world and of the general literature. Furthermore, the total story of sociology reflects such rich heritage as may well provide a new wealth of source materials from which can be fabricated sociology's part in the warp and woof of a social structure that was the new world of America, "cutting loose and faring forth" from its European mooring, and that is now the America of the new "one world" construct of 1950 and after. The story of sociology can be told, however, only in its perspective to the total American society and its European background and not merely as an isolated discipline or textbook literature.

Sociology's coming of age in America may be likened unto a fiftieth anniversary of hardy pioneering along the frontiers of social science. These fifty years of frontier work, moreover, have coincided with the most dynamic period of American history and have seen the greatest technological, economic, and social changes ever recorded throughout the world. So, too, the rise and development of sociology, its significance to science, its relation to the other social sciences, its increasing application to social practice, and its general cultural implications constitute one of the most interesting of all the aspects of the epic of American university education and its spread to the widening forum of the people.

Knowledge of this record of American sociology is an essential requirement for the thousands of students of sociology in colleges and universities whose introduction to the growing subject cannot be complete without it. Just as the history of American literature is "a history of the books of the great and near great writers in a literature which is more revealing when studied as a by-product of American experience," so the very concepts of American sociology cannot be definitive without an understanding of what American sociologists have written and are continuing to contribute to the new science of society and to the American scene itself. And, again, as in the case of American literature, the emphasis must inevitably fall upon men more than movements, although their work is often reflected in the light of special movements. Looking backward, we can appraise through a review of the work of American sociologists what America has done in answer to Herbert Spencer's first book challenge, "On the Need for Sociology." Looking both ways, the story of American sociology is especially needed now by students and social scientists the world over, when, in contrast to a past era in which America looked abroad for its sociological leadership, the world's expectations must now be found largely in American sociology.

Still more recently important is the double task of appraisal and reappraisal of sociology to the end that it may take its rightful place in the new dynamics of the social sciences from which so much is demanded now by both the natural sciences and humanities as well as by the public, in the ever-pyramiding of the dilemmas of an atomic age. As a dynamic science of society more is expected of sociology than ever before and it may well be that it offers the greatest opportunity of any of the social sciences, in both its scientific capacity for empirical study and for providing a social morale in an age of science. But as a social science itself, in an age pre-eminently scientific, sociology faces its greatest opportunity up to now. For, even as is true of American science in general, in its actual achievements and promise and in its potential leadership of world science, so also American sociology must be counted upon to do a major task or else lose its place in the unprecedented procession of the sciences and humanities. It comes to pass, therefore, that the story of America's sociology up to 1950 is also of the essence of the sociology of tomorrow.

A Product of American Society

Sociology derives its new opportunity and obligation from several sources. One is from its distinctive American heritage of achievement in the last fifty years and its look ahead for the next half century. Another is the extraordinary need in the contemporary world for a social science to seek special knowledge of how men may live together and continue the development of human society and welfare and meet the crises brought on by science and technology, so often out of perspective to human relations, and so to provide the basis for not only a social morale in an age of science but for societal survival as well. A more critical appraisal of the maturity of American sociology is given in Chapters 24 and 25. Sociology's new role in academic freedom and survival processes derives from its capacity for over-all research into the total system of society, seeking balance between the individual and the group, between the human spirit and scientific achievement, between the folk culture and state civilization, and between and among the great institutions and their dilemmas in the changing structure of the modern world.

With reference to sociology's heritage it has been as "American" as American literature, American culture, and the freedoms of the new world democracy. This American quality has been continuous from its beginning with concern for the problems of a growing republic, on through its heritage of European philosophy and learning and its first founding fathers and their successors. Just as it inherited from Europe the fruits of the Industrial Revolution and the great breakdown of European culture at about the turn of this century, so at mid-century America has no choice but to accept the challenge for leadership in the second half. Now, in this setting, sociology has sought no pot of gold at the rainbow's end for universal "solutions" of problems. It has sought knowledge and mastery through the social science approach and through the training of creative social scientists, instead of trying to mold a new society through intellectual ideologies and propaganda.

As for its first pioneers around the turn of the twentieth century, they were vigorous frontiersmen, working hard, living long, dynamic elders in a field newly American. There was Franklin H. Giddings, raised on the discipline and fortitude of a New England rural-village family and coming into sociology from the very symbol of American freedom of the press, the *Springfield Republican*. He was American in his bold frontiering in the upper brackets of graduate university work and in expanding his influence throughout the regions of America. There was Lester F. Ward, often characterized as the archetype of American country boy from the Middle West, working his way up to formal education and scholarship, and blending his work with government and university tasks while preparing a voluminous new literature of dynamic sociology, basic to the new concepts of progress as America saw it. And there were Albion Woodbury Small and William Graham Sumner, typifying early American education in its pattern of moving on from the sacred to the secular. Each came into sociology from the field of the ministry, seeking the truth that should make men free, but preaching powerfully thereafter, on the one hand, of moral dominance, and on the other, of American laissez faire. There was George Vincent, as American as baseball, through his many years as university professor, university president, Chautauqua orator, president of the Rockefeller Foundation. Then there was Charles Horton Cooley, scarcely ever leaving his beloved University of Michigan campus, pioneering in the field of discovering knowledge about persons and society, children and human development, behavior and social psychology; as stubborn as an American individualist, as generous as the most liberal scholar. And Edward Alsworth Ross, striding across a continent and back again, overflowing into our neighboring republics and later dashing into the Orient, seeking to learn and to tell about human society in all its places and cultures. And more: George Howard, writing three volumes on the history of marriage timed with the growth of that American institution, the state university; Frank W. Blackmar, as American as Johns Hopkins, adapting the European learning to the American scene; and Ulysses G. Weatherly, joining with John R. Commons and Richard T. Ely to form an American Society for Christian Sociology.

Nor were their successors as presidents of the American Sociological Society scarcely less American. Their first phalanx came up from the ranks in the hard way of work, learning, and apprenticeship in many fields and from all the American regions. Three were American in the melting-pot pattern of being born outside the borders of the United States, as were four heads of the later departments of sociology at Yale, Harvard, and Columbia universities. Some of the later presidents of the American Sociological Society and their scholar colleagues sometimes inclined toward the ranks of those intellectuals, so culturally and methodologically specialized as to qualify for an isolationism from reality that characterized some of their literary colleagues who fled America for European escape. Others of these were characteristic of the American scene from the 1920's to the 1950's, powerfully influenced by both the ideologies of a broken Europe and some American ideologies and action-agencies seeking new modes of societal accommodation to new worlds.

As is true in the story of American literature, the heart of the American quality is found in the writers and their regions, with, nevertheless, an American over-all; so the contributions of American sociology are found primarily in the personalities and writings of college and university sociologists in all their specialisms, rather than in any abstract conceptual theory that might be called "American." And just as American culture was long conditioned by European culture, so American sociology and sociologists have been doubly conditioned, on the one hand, by the European setting and, on the other, by the American. This is, again, similarly true of American economic thought and theory and of American political science and philosophy and, to a considerable degree, of American education.

This major untold story of American sociology up to 1950 is not, therefore, just a general story of social science and social problems, nor is it merely the history of social thought and philosophy, and of what mankind over the centuries has tried to find out and record about human relationships. Nor is it simply the summary of all those systematic attempts to conceptualize social processes through well thought-out systems of social theory. It is, on the contrary, something much more concrete and definitive. It is the specific story of American sociology from the time it came to be designated sociology, as such, identified through the American Sociological Society in 1905–1906, and growing up among the 1810 accredited colleges and universities under the accurate designation of sociology. It is the story of American sociology in terms of what sociologists have produced in research and writing and what they have done in college and university teaching. Included are cooperative and creative efforts in allied activities and something of the annals of ameliorative efforts in the background of the pre-sociological era from the 1860's to the turn of the century. Although the literature of sociology is rich in its attempts to define the field, even such definitions are valid primarily because they are part and parcel of the contributions of American sociologists themselves who, in contrast to European sociologists, have made their contributions primarily from their faculty positions in departments of sociology in American institutions of learning.

Once again, American sociology is as "American" as American economics or American political science, or American history, in the sense that they are all an integral part of American culture. Sociological thought, like economic thought, can be understood, as Joseph Dorfman says in his notable three-volume *The Economic Mind in American Civilization,* I, p. ix, "only when it is treated in its natural habitat of practical affairs and intellectual endeavor. It grows by constant cross-breeding with other species of learning and speculation."

Compared with American Economics, Political Science, and History

One of the best indexes of the "American" educational character of sociology may be seen from a comparison of the presidents of the American Sociological Society with those of the American Economic Association and the American Political Science Association, as they represented the same universities during the same years and under the same general conditions. These, together with the presidents of the American Historical Association, reflect perhaps the most dynamic personalities in the development of the upper brackets of American culture and education in the first half of the twentieth century. Within this fourfold grouping, American sociologists rank well up toward the top, both in their university status and in their influence upon American education. This comparison is set forth in the catalogue below, starting with the first presidents of the American Sociological Society, but omitting the earlie years of the American Economic Association, some of whose president, like those of the American Historical Association, were men of public affairs. How the biographies of these six score American leaders is the biography of an American epoch may be seen from a look at them and their universities.

Year	American Sociological Society	American Economic Association	American Political Science Association
1906	Lester F. Ward, Brown	Jeremiah W. Jenks, Cornell	Frank J. Goodnow, Columbia
1907	Lester F. Ward, Brown	Jeremiah W. Jenks, Cornell	Albert Shaw, New York, Editor
1908	William Graham Sumner, Yale	Simon N. Patten, Pennsylvania	Frederic N. Judson, Yale
1909	William Graham Sumner, Yale	Davis R. Dewey, Massachusetts Institute of Technology	James Bryce, Harvard
1910	Franklin H. Giddings, Columbia	Edmund J. James, Illinois	A. Lawrence Lowell, Harvard
1911	Franklin H. Giddings, Columbia	Henry W. Farnam, Yale	Woodrow Wilson, Princeton
1912	Albion W. Small, Chicago	Frank A. Fetter, Princeton	Simeon E. Baldwin, Harvard
1913	Albion W. Small, Chicago	David Kinley, Illinois	Albert Bushnell Hart, Harvard
1914	Edward A. Ross, Wisconsin	John H. Gray, Minnesota	W. W. Willoughby, Johns Hopkins
1915	Edward A. Ross, Wisconsin	Walter F. Willcox, Cornell	John Bassett Moore, Columbia

Year	American Sociological Society	American Economic Association	American Political Science Association
1916	George E. Vincent, Chicago	Thomas N. Carver, Harvard	Ernst Freund, Chicago
1917	George E. Howard, Nebraska	John R. Commons, Wisconsin	Jesse Macy, Grinnell
1918	Charles H. Cooley, Michigan	Irving Fisher, Yale	Munro Smith, Columbia
1919	Frank W. Blackmar, Kansas	Henry B. Gardner, Brown	Henry Jones Ford, Minnesota
1920	James Q. Dealey, Brown	Herbert J. Davenport, Cornell	Paul S. Reinsch, Wisconsin
1921	Edward Cary Hayes, Illinois	Jacob H. Hollander, Johns Hopkins	Leo S. Rowe, Pennsylvania
1922	James P. Lichtenberger, Pennsylvania	Henry R. Seager, Columbia	William A. Dunning, Columbia
1923	Ulysses G. Weatherly, Indiana	Carl C. Plehn, California	Harry A. Garfield, Williams
1924	Charles A. Ellwood, Missouri	Wesley C. Mitchell, Columbia	James W. Garner, Illinois
1925	Robert E. Park, Chicago	Allyn A. Young, Harvard	Charles E. Merriam, Chicago
1926	John L. Gillin, Wisconsin	Edwin W. Kemmerer, Princeton	Charles A. Beard, Columbia
1927	William I. Thomas, Chicago	Thomas S. Adams, Yale	William B. Munro, Harvard
1928	John M. Gillette, North Dakota	Fred M. Taylor, Michigan	Jesse S. Reeves, Michigan
1929	William F. Ogburn, Chicago	Edwin F. Gay, Harvard	John A. Fairlie, Illinois
1930	Howard W. Odum, North Carolina	Matthew B. Hammond, Ohio State	Benjamin F. Shambaugh, Ohio State
1931	Emory S. Bogardus, Southern California	Ernest L. Bogart, Illinois	Edwin S. Corwin, Princeton
1932	L. L. Bernard, Washington University	George E. Barnett, Johns Hopkins	William F. Willoughby, Johns Hopkins
1933	E. B. Reuter, Iowa	William Z. Ripley, Harvard	Isidor Loeb, Washington University
1934	Ernest W. Burgess, Chicago	Harry A. Millis, Chicago	Walter J. Shepard, Ohio

Year	American Sociological Society	American Economic Association	American Political Science Association
1935	F. Stuart Chapin, Minnesota	John M. Clark, Columbia	Francis W. Coker, Yale
1936	Henry Pratt Fairchild, New York University	Alvin S. Johnson, New School for Social Research	Arthur N. Holcombe, Harvard
1937	Ellsworth Faris, Chicago	Oliver M. W. Sprague, Harvard	Thomas Reed Powell, Harvard
1938	Frank H. Hankins, Smith	Alvin H. Hansen, Harvard	Clarence A. Dykstra, Wisconsin
1939	Edwin H. Sutherland, Indiana	Jacob Viner, Chicago	Charles Groves Haines, California
1940	Robert M. MacIver, Columbia	Frederick C. Mills, Columbia	Robert C. Brooks, Swarthmore
1941	Stuart A. Queen, Washington University	Sumner H. Slichter, Harvard	Frederic A. Ogg, Wisconsin
1942	Dwight Sanderson, Cornell	Edwin G. Nourse, Brookings	William Anderson, Wisconsin
1943	George A. Lundberg, Bennington College	Albert B. Wolfe, Ohio State	Robert E. Cushman, Cornell
1944	Rupert B. Vance, North Carolina	Joseph S. Davis, Stanford	Leonard D. White, Chicago
1945	Kimball Young, Queens	K. L. Sharfman, Michigan	John M. Gaus, Wisconsin
1946	Carl C. Taylor, U.S. Bureau of Agricultural Economics	E. A. Goldenweiser, Institute for Advanced Study	Walter F. Dodd, Princeton
1947	Louis Wirth, Chicago	Paul H. Douglas, Chicago	Arthur W. Macmahon, Columbia
1948	E. Franklin Fraizer, Howard	Joseph A. Schumpeter, Columbia	Henry R. Spencer, Ohio State
1949	Talcott Parsons, Harvard	Howard S. Ellis, California	Quincy Wright, Chicago
1950	Leonard Cottrell, Cornell	Frank H. Knight, Chicago	James K. Pollock, Michigan

American Sociology, a College and University Subject

The predominance of college and university professors of sociology as presidents of the American Sociological Society constitutes one evidence in favor of defining American sociology primarily as a college and university subject. The presidents of the American Historical Association, organized in 1884, on the other hand, include others besides university men: judges, ministers, representatives of the Army and Navy and of public service. Among them were John Jay, William Wirt Henry, George Fisher, Edward Eggleston, Alfred Mahon, Henry Charles Lee, Simeon Baldwin, Theodore Roosevelt, H. Morse Stevens, Jean Jules Jusserand, Woodrow Wilson. These were alongside, of course, a distinguished succession of notable historians in the same universities from which came the sociologists, economists, and political scientists, as, for instance, Charles A. Beard, James Harvey Robinson, and William A. Dunning from Columbia; Albert Bushnell Hart, Frederick Jackson Turner, and Edward Channing from Harvard, to sample only two universities. The presidents of the American Economic Association and American Political Science Association also included many who were not professors in universities.

In our third chapter, "The American Background and Heritage," in contrast to "The European Heritage," are catalogued the presidents of the National Conference of Social Work, which was, up to 1918, the National Conference of Charities and Correction. This group, again reflecting a powerful battery of dominant Americans in allied fields, represented one of the two parallel breakaways from the old American Social Science Association, of which the other included the American Historical Association, founded in 1884, the American Economic Association, founded in 1885, the American Political Science Association, founded in 1904, and the American Sociological Society, founded in 1905. In contrast to the heads of these academic learned societies the seventy-five presidents of the National Conference of Social Work, begun in 1874, included only a few university professors as connecting links between the "Social Problems" branch and the "Social Science" branch of the original movement. Among these professors were F. B. Sanborn, Cornell, in 1881; Charles R. Henderson, professor of sociology at the University of Chicago, in 1889; Edward T. Devine, sometime professor of Social Economy at Columbia, in 1906; Richard C. Cabot, professor of Social Ethics of Harvard, in 1931; and Edith Abbott, of the University of Chicago, in 1937. Also from earlier social work to later faculty member in schools of social work were Robert Kelso of Michigan and Frank Bruno of Washington University.

How sociology in America is primarily a college and university subject is again indicated by comparing the membership of the American Sociological Society, which is predominantly institutional, with the American Political Science Association and the American Economic Association with approximately 40 per cent of their members nonacademic, and with the American statistical group and the psychological groups with even larger ratios. American sociologists are primarily members of the sociology faculties who are teaching, writing, and doing research in American colleges and universities. This measure of identification not only makes possible the definition of the main stream of American sociology, but enables us to evaluate in perspective other segments that by popular usage are known as "sociology."

Other Segments of American Sociology

Yet, while the story of American sociology is primarily a story of teaching, research, and writing in a special field of American higher education, in reality the totality of sociology, as it has developed and is now known in the United States, may be said to comprehend other important segments. That is, in addition to its being the main facet of a college and university subject, there are at least four other aspects which, from the viewpoint of America's public and general cultural development, must be incorporated into the total picture. The first of the popular concepts of sociology is what is usually termed "practical" and applied sociology, a field of study and action that is relatively the same as envisaged by the public as social reform or social amelioration, and is often confused with social work. This means that, off and on the records, sociology has some standing with the public as an applied branch of knowledge that is calculated to do what the public thinks it ought to do, or is an ameliorative or/and relatively radical subject. A catalogue of notable Americans in this area is given in Chapter 22, on applied social science, practical sociology, and interdisciplinary efforts.

This last segment is another important section representing the work of scholars and writers in allied fields and cooperative interdisciplinary work from which come rich source materials used widely by sociologists. This is of several sorts, namely from psychology, anthropology, economics, and other allied fields; from clinical and social work areas; and from the fields of social interpretation and planning.

Another segment is that part of the American learning and culture which, designated by the *Publishers' Weekly* as "Sociology," contributes its quota to the vast array of learning and miscellaneous American literature, and which includes social interpretation and criticism, as well as "sociological" fiction and drama. And finally sociology, on its own integral merits, is one of the social sciences, striving constantly to become more rigorously scientific. Each of these divisions may be said to have a fair heritage.

Sociology in College and University

First, then, the heart of American sociology is found in its place in the college and university curriculum as a subject, taken by thousands of students, taught by hundreds of instructors using a vast literature of texts and library readings. The development of sociology as an important part of the American college and university curriculum constitutes a major part of the extraordinary expansion of higher education and of the social sciences in particular. Still more specifically, sociology has had more than a proportionate share in the whole rapid development of graduate education in the United States, where its record has been impressive, clear, and cumulative. From meager beginnings scarcely more than fifty years ago, with a very few students, primarily graduates, sociology is now taught as an undergraduate subject, by several thousand instructors to perhaps nearly a half million students in nearly all of the 1810 institutions of higher learning in the United States. In 1947–48 there were 6271 undergraduate degrees with majors in sociology, granted by more than five hundred colleges and universities. Since the 1890's, when such men as W. I. Thomas and George Vincent received their degrees at Chicago, more than one thousand Ph.D. degrees in sociology have been earned in more than 50 universities, Chicago leading with nearly two hundred. Since 1936 when *The American Journal of Sociology* began cataloguing dissertation subjects, 596 degrees were reported from 41 institutions, with Chicago and the Catholic University of America leading with 71 each.

As an index of the growth of college sociology, it may be noted that a single introductory textbook in sociology, one of several best sellers in the 1930–40's, will sell ten times as many copies as all of the texts of the first big four, Ward, Sumner, Giddings, and Small, in those earlier days when their authors were gratified with the sale of a few hundred copies and when the publishers considered 1500 copies a relatively large edition. One of the former students of Giddings could report through his publishers on the sale of his own textbooks in excess of a quarter of a million copies, while a former student of Small could report sales of more than a million copies, if foreign translations are included. And the total sales, by 1950, of the generous "Scotchman," E. A. Ross, were just short of a half million. These sociology books, as "best sellers," may be taken as indices of the expansion of sociology in colleges and universities in recent years. So, in contrast to the turn of the century when the total list of texts was practically limited to Ward, Giddings, and Small, by 1950 more than one hundred introductory texts or "principles" had been published; while perhaps double that number could be catalogued in the special fields of social problems, social pathology, the family, population, race, urban and rural sociology, and the other specialisms. The nature and range of these may be seen from catalogues in Chapters 14–20 of this book.

These texts grew naturally out of the need of class instruction which increased from a very few courses in the early 1900's to the present time when the aggregate sociological offering now affords hundreds of courses in general sociology and social problems and in a score of special areas of the study of society. Thus a sampling of states shows, for instance, that, as reported by T. C. McCormick of the University, the state of Wisconsin in 1950 can list more than thirty institutions cataloguing more than two hundred courses taught by more than fifty teachers. Or, to estimate from actual countings the over-all range and variety of courses offered, L. L. Bernard studied 219 colleges which increased the 815 courses offered in 1909 to 3420 courses by 1944, as reported in "The Teaching of Sociology in the United States in the Last Fifty Years" in Volume 50 of *The American Journal of Sociology*. In Volume

7 of the *American Sociological Review,* Raymond and Ruby Kennedy reported on a study of courses offered by 607 four-year colleges that offered 5541 courses in sociology.

As Allied Social Science and Practical Sociology

Next, sociology has achieved a place of its own as an applied branch of knowledge, laying the foundation for solving problems rather than trying to solve them itself. We have pointed out how the public expects more from sociology in 1950 than it has at any time since its earlier beginnings in the 1900's. This expectation reflects a question that Giddings was wont to ask, namely, "What is sociology and what is it good for?" The implication is that sociology has considerable standing outside the academic world as an applied branch of knowledge capable of doing what the public thinks it ought to do, namely, of helping to solve problems and to set the incidence for reform and corrections. In much of the popular writings and editorials the sociologist is assumed to be one whose judgment is needed. Insofar as this is true and insofar as the sociologist has responded to some of the main needs and expectations, he has contributed largely to the American learning and culture.

This field of sociology is often inaccurately called "applied sociology." It may be more and less than that in particular instances but in general it is not sociology, either in the accurate meaning of "social science" or within the limits of what American sociologists teach, write, or do in American institutions of learning. It must be remembered that it is not possible to have *applied* sociology until sociological theory or science has been developed. Mere work in an area of social problems or action programs or community organization does not constitute sociology unless, first, the special area is being studied as the basis for discovering facts for sociology, or, second, is being utilized as a testing ground for the application of sociology. Perhaps the nearest designation may be that of borderline sociologists and the nearest definition in terms of illustration may be by examples of persons and of activities. The area from which illustrations are selected may be nearer the field of social work or public welfare or in the field of public affairs. Or it may be nearer what is sometimes called interpretative sociology, or it may be nearer intercultural relations not treated as special sociology. Or again, it may be in the region between more than one of the social sciences or in allied fields, such as those of the clinical psychologist, the marriage counselor, the newspaper columnist, or the specialist in population. Or, finally, the borderline sociologist may be defined arbitrarily as the writer whose works have been uniformly utilized and quoted by sociologists as source material or as authentic results of empirical study.

A good example of this popular area of practical and interpretative sociology may be cited in the case of Paul and Arthur Kellogg and the record of *The Survey Midmonthly* and *Survey Graphic* (since 1949, *The Survey*), many special issues of which have often been used as teaching materials in many sociology classes. Another example might be the work of Thomas Jesse Jones as executive of the Phelps Stokes Fund for practical work in race relations, with special reference to the Negro. More specifically, as illustration, the Kelloggs and Jones were faithful members of the F. H. G. Club at Columbia, a notable group of Giddings-ites who met fortnightly and were all Ph.D's in sociology or candidates for such degrees. They were contemporary with Gillin, Tenney, Lichtenberger, Chapin, Gehlke, Ogburn, Hankins, Odum, and others who moved directly into academic sociology. The Kelloggs and Jones were "promising sociologists" and they lived up to their promise in what was, however, borderline sociology rather than university social science. By the same token, *The Survey,* primarily the journal of social work, remains in the field of "practical sociology." Still another example may be cited in earlier days at Chicago where Charles R. Henderson and, more notably, Jane Addams made contributions of great value to sociology.

Of the special studies, Hamilton's 200 married women in New York, or the Gluecks' and Healy's studies of delinquents in Boston were examples. Neva R. Deardorf, who received her Ph.D. from the University of Pennsylvania, did important research in social work organizations in New York, and Sydnor Walker, of the Laura Spelman Rockefeller Memorial, wrote her doctor's dissertation at Columbia on social work which was published by the University of North Carolina Press. O. E. Baker at Washington was prolific in his speaking and writing on population and human resources conservation. Lewis Mumford has been a powerful influence in urbanism, regionalism, and social planning, as well as contributing to the literature of historical continuity of societal evolution. Another illustration may be found by analyzing the range of authors quoted in the eight main source books used by sociologists in which some six hundred authors are quoted with less than one-sixth being sociologists in the definitive sense. These illustrations and others are treated at length in Chapters 15, 22, 24.

The Public's Challenge to Sociology

The classification of a large number of volumes as "sociology" and many editorial challenges to the "sociologists" to "do something about it" and much general "sociological" writing may also be indicative of a growing emphasis upon sociology as the chief of the social sciences from a popular point of view. Next to religion, fiction, and juveniles, books catalogued in the *Publishers' Weekly* as "sociology" are next in order, with "economics" a close second, and sometimes the two grouped together. Yet, there are many other evidences of a different sort of this increasing public interest in sociology. The lawyers and the specialists in government and politics are asking what the sociologists have to say about many of the chief social problems of the day. The newspapers and the public in general keep asking the sociologists about crime, and poverty, and other problems — the same sort of questions they are asking the economists about the economic order: What facts can you give us? What is your science good for and how is it being applied? Is sociology a study of society in the modern world attempting to understand and interpret civilization, as well as being a theoretical and historical study in the classroom? In the United Nations and in international councils, sociology is posited as a standard constituent.

By the same token, there are many challenges and critical notes. What are the sociologists doing? What should they do? Is sociology just a subject for professors to teach and write about in terms of learned jargon? And is it the medium of social agitation for immature minds and restless unadjusted individuals? Is it socialistic in its goals? Is it social service or social work devoted to ameliorative processes? These questions are evident not only among the lay folk. Thousands of prospective students and adult education recruits protest sociology's failure to come to grips with life, and they want to make it more human. And a large public wants to know why sociology can't help them "service" the great multiplications of social science and technology and of social organizations.

So, too, the natural scientists want to know what sociology is and whether it can function more effectively to match the effects of technology. The other social scientists insist upon better definitions and more scientific methodology in the field of sociology. The college president and the university dean want to know more and more what sociology is and what it can do. And those who provide the funds for colleges and universities want to know too. And in the meantime more college departments of sociology have been established, courses have been multiplied, more students have enrolled to insist upon the answer to the questions, What is sociology and what is it good for? What is its part in the great modern task of seeing that men can live together peacefully?

And yet the public has not expected too much of sociology. As a college subject it was practically unknown to students in all the general run of colleges as late as 1900, at the beginning of the American sociological era. Moreover, sociology found little sanction among the early humanists and arts faculties, whose advice to the great body of students was such as to ostracize the new subject. Yet we must remember that in the higher learning up to almost a century ago, as pointed out in relation to economics by Joseph Dorfman on page 503 of Volume II of his *The Economic Mind in American Civilization,* "the physical sciences were generally viewed with suspicion." And so, just as men genuinely interested in the sciences had no place in the college, it being a matter of common sense that the best college teachers would be clergymen, so, even more, sociology was not to loom large in the student's education. There were other reasons why too much was not or should not be expected of sociology. One was that, just as the difference in political theory among those more learned in the business world made little difference in their specific outlook or procedure in business and commerce, so the learned theories about social development had little influence upon any except the professors and a limited number of graduate students. And just as a native systematic literature on economics was long in developing in the United States because the new academic world was not fruitful soil, so for sociology, only that soil was cultivated which was cleared for the interacademic growing of sociological theory. Nor must we forget, as we recall the earlier philosophic backgrounds of American sociology, that even at the beginning of the twentieth century, psychology was still often mental philosophy, ethics was moral philosophy, and economics and sociology were often identified as branches of moral philosophy.

Sociology's Framework for the Science of Society

In the light of these backgrounds sociology's record has been relatively impressive in its quantitative ratio to the total of American education, and accordingly in its cumulative contributions to the higher learning; in its considerable bulk of textbook literature; in the perfection of its own science; and in its place among and contribution to the social sciences themselves. Thus, sociology has become an integral part of the American culture not only through the relevance of interaction with the American environment and its cross breeding with European social philosophy and sociology, but as something "American" in its own right. Yet, finally, if too much has not been expected of sociology, we must not forget that in America the influence of the intellectuals has never exerted so direct an influence and control on social action and political organizations as has been the case in Europe. And yet reasonable expectations that might have been anticipated with some assurance have been realized. The body of sociological literature has reflected many of the characteristics of early and contemporary forces in the framework of the changing structure of a peculiar American society and has developed some basic knowledge to apply to the ongoings of the next fifty years.

So, too, within this framework, sociologists have succeeded in delineating effectively the total field and making sociology a comprehensive science of society. As such, sociology is a part of the fabric of American science, participating in the programs of the American Association for the Advancement of Science, of which it is an integral unit. It functions primarily through its own learned society, the American Sociological Society, originally with its several sections and divisions, and later with its varied topics, seeking to inquire into and to report on the comprehensive study of human society, and its own learned journals. As far as sociology is a comprehensive science of society, it reflects the totality of historical study and of researches and materials which American sociologists have succeeded in gathering together and presenting through all known methods, including the earlier historical and philosophical approach and the later concrete research methods and empirical study. As in the case of other sciences, sociology's main areas of approach and content comprehend the whole sweep of societal relations — its own field — together with an increasing number of specialisms.

Thus, in addition to the historical aspects of social study, the main divisions of American sociology provide an adequate breakdown of the field into such units as general sociology, including principles and elements of sociology, theory, and methodology; and into such special sociologies and sub-sciences as to provide adequate empirical study and the implementation of results. Included among the special areas are the family and institutions, social problems and social pathology, crime and penology, race and ethnic groups, the community, rural sociology, urban sociology, industrial sociology, social psychology, educational sociology, population and demography, ecology, folk sociology and regionalism, together with a varied methodology and statistical approach to scientific research.

Within these fields, sociology has produced a distinctive contribution of books and periodical literature. Perhaps more than three hundred volumes would do credit to specialists in any field, while an index and annotation of journal and monograph contributions, adequately classified, would constitute an amazing bibliography. This richness and variety of fields, however, conforms closely to a similar divisional field in the natural sciences and in other social sciences. Even basic sciences, such as physics and chemistry, have more than a score of divisions and sub-subjects, while the American Association for the Advancement of Science has literally hundreds of subdivisions and sections in its annual and special meetings, the cataloguing of which requires a program brochure of more than one hundred pages.

As early as 1933, L. L. Bernard, editing the papers read at the annual meeting of the American Sociological Society, of which he had been president, and adding other chapters solicited by him, compiled a volume on *The Fields and Methods of Sociology* in which he catalogued some thirty subdivisions of sociology. These included Historical Sociology, Biological Sociology, Demography, Social Geography, Human Ecology, The Community, Rural Sociology, Urban Sociology, Folk Sociology, Cultural Sociology, Social Psychology, Educational Sociology,

Sociology of Religion, of Law, of the Family, of Institutions, Social Ethics, Social Organization, Social Control, Social Work, Social Investigation, Social Statistics.

As late as 1948, the fifth printing of E. B. Reuter's *Handbook of Sociology* catalogued a little more than a score of "areas of specialized studies" in each of which was included a select bibliography to indicate the substantial nature of each area. Included in the classification were some special areas in addition to Bernard's, namely Eugenics, Collective Behavior, Public Opinion. In his "summary of essentials," were also listed some thirty factors as describing the range of study essential to an understanding of sociology. Among these essentials were The Nature and Processes of Sociology; The Nature of Society; The Biological Basis of Human Life; The Geographic Environment; The Growth of Population; Human Ecology; Other Distributional Patterns; Segregation and Class Structure; Groups and Group Life; The Human Community; Community and Society; Human Nature; The Development of Personality; The Individual as the Person; Social Interaction; General Forms of Interaction; Competition and Special Distribution; Conflict and the Determination of Status; Accommodation and the Social Equilibrium; Assimilation and Moral Unity; Culture; Race and Culture; Culture and Original Nature; Social Organization and Institutions; Customs and Conventions; Major Social Institutions; Institutional Control; Social Change and Disorganization; Personal Disorganization; The Disorganization of Personality; Collective Behavior and Social Reorganization.

Meetings and Publications

Other examples of the range of special sociology include the divisions and sections of the annual meetings of the American Sociological Society; the titles indicating the subject matter of the papers presented at the annual meetings of the Society; the titles of Ph.D. dissertations for the last twenty years; and the number and nature of sociology courses taught; the nature of articles contributed to the *American Sociological Review*; and the range and subject of courses in sociology in the colleges.

The sections into which the annual meeting of the American Sociological Society are divided, in addition to illustrating the field of sociology, confirm the definition of sociology in terms of what the sociologists are doing. In addition to the Division on Social Research and the general evening meetings devoted to more general and theoretical subjects, the following sections may be taken as representative, until recent years, of the Society's effort to provide separate programs: Rural Sociology, Social Statistics, Educational Sociology, Political Sociology, The Teaching of Sociology, The Community, The Sociology of Religion, The Family, Sociology and Psychiatry.

In utilizing these classifications as a basis for defining sociology, it is important to note the distinction between *sociology studying society* through these various subdivisions as units of study and workers in the field of social practice involved in these same subdivisions. That is, sociology, like all sciences, must approach its study through units and subjects that are small enough and specialized enough to enable the scientist to be reasonably successful in his study. He studies society through the special aspects of the family or rural society or urban civilization; but his science is not confused with rural programs, or religious organizations, or social work, or education. It is of the nature of modern sociology that it expects to find its laboratory and its social data from the actual field of changing society. The subsequent utilization of sociological findings will be a matter for what may be called social practice. The fact that many students and workers, as well as the public, confuse these two phases does not in any way affect the original sphere of sociology as the scientific study of society. Insofar as all science has the twofold objective of discovering truth and attaining mastery, so sociology emphasizes social research and the actual laboratory of social practice as mutually essential. Social work, for instance, utilizes the results of sociological research and study, but it also provides a changing subject matter and a laboratory wherein sociology may find much of its richest material.

This emphasis upon research and practice is after all common to all the sciences, each of which has developed its own breakdown of special fields. For instance, the American Chemical Society has no less than eighteen professional divisions. These include the divisions of Organic Chemistry; Physical and Inorganic Chemistry; Industrial and Engineering Chemistry; Medicinal Chemistry; Biological Chemistry; Agricultural and Food Chemistry; Petroleum Chemistry; Colloid Chemistry;

Cellulose Chemistry; Rubber Chemistry; Sugar Chemistry and Technology; Microchemistry; Paint and Varnish Chemistry; Gas and Fuel Chemistry; Fertilizer Chemistry; Water, Sewage, and Sanitation Chemistry; the History of Chemistry; Chemical Education.

An analysis of approximately two thousand papers presented in the annual meetings of the American Sociological Society up to 1950 shows that, like the divisional organization of the society's program activities, such papers might tend to group themselves into two classes: the one would tend more nearly to treat of special areas or specialisms sometimes bordering on social practice, the other would feature general sociology, including theory, concepts, and methodology. Taking the titles at random, and listing the subject matter rather than the actual titles, the first core of unit-subjects includes such topics as Americanization, immigration, citizenship, community organization, war and peace, recreation, maladjustments and social personality, public opinion, social institutions, the family, population and food supply, social attitudes, birth rates, status of women, sex and discord, environment as a social factor, human ecology, eugenics, races and nationalities, the Negro, industrial relations, child welfare, public welfare, standards of living, poverty, dependency indices, religion and religions, citizenship, crime and penology, youth and society, intolerance, leadership, legislation, the New Deal and rural life, social planning.

Among the more theoretical subjects, including those on methods and concepts, were: regional planning, regional sociology, culture area, ecology, methodology, social prediction, social analysis, social stratification, structure and function, social conflict, culture conflicts, sociological research, group fallacy and social science, social statistics, teaching sociology, rural sociology, social work, historical sociology, European sociology, social evolution, social control, human progress, social progress, democracy, social mobility, social distance, social psychology, social attitudes, cultural sociology, social isolation, social education, educational sociology, social patterns, culture and culture patterns, social behavior, social measurement, biological factors in society, social consciousness, social revolution, endemics, social ideals, social powers, assimilation, human nature, psychology and culture, socialism, communism.

An unpublished classification by Theodore Wirths, of more than six hundred articles published in the *American Sociological Review* since its first issue, shows the 20 most commonly used titles, somewhat in the following order. Social Theory leads with 236 titles. The others in order are: Marriage and the Family, 95; Social Statistics and Research Methodology, 89; Population Sociology, 68; Social Problems, 65; Social Psychology, 56; Criminology, 35; Race Relations and Ethnic Groups, 30; Ecology, 22; Social Planning, 21; Educational Sociology, 18; Social Pathology, 13; Teaching of Sociology, 12; Housing, 11; Industrial Sociology, 11; Rural Sociology, 11; Urban Sociology, 9; Biographical, 8; Introductory or Principles, 7; Bibliographical, 6; with certain isolated topics not easily classified.

Doctors' Dissertations and Courses in Sociology

Still another index of the nature and range of sociological fields of inquiry may be seen in a classification of Ph.D. dissertation topics from 1936–48 as published in *The American Journal of Sociology*. In numerical order, as tabulated by C. M. Grigg, they are: Social Theory, 115; Race Relations and Ethnic Groups, 82; Rural Sociology, 65; Social Psychology, 55; Sociology of Religion, 53; Educational Sociology, 53; Sociological Statistics and Research Methodology, 53; Social Problems, 49; Marriage and Family, 49; Population Sociology, 42; Urban Sociology, 41; Ecology and Regionalism, 41; Criminology, 40; Cultural Sociology, 39; Industrial Sociology, 38; Community Studies, 27; Social Pathology, 20; Cooperative Movement, 19; Introductory, Principles, and/or Teaching, 12; Recreation, 4.

One answer to the question of what sociology is must be found in the classification of courses taught in American colleges. From a study of course names and catalogue descriptions, Raymond and Ruby Kennedy, in "Sociology in American Colleges" on pages 661–75 of Volume 7 of the *American Sociological Review,* set up 31 categories. A total of 5544 courses were listed by 607 schools. In the order of their rank as percentage of all courses, they are listed from 1 to 31: General Sociology, Social Problems, Marriage and the Family, Social Work, Criminology, Research Methods, Social Psychology, Rural Sociology, Anthropology, Social Theory, Race and Ethnic Groups, Urban Sociology, Public Welfare, Population Problems, Social Processes, Child Welfare, Community Organization, Economic Sociology, Educational Sociology, Social Movements, Social Organization, Statistics, Social History, Social Geography, Social Science Orientation, Religion, Urban-Rural Sociology, Leisure and Recreation, Social Ethics, Leadership, Political Sociology.

Sociology in the Survey of a National Culture

An example of both the theoretical and scientific sociological inquiry alongside a sound practical understanding of American society was the *Recent Social Trends,* begun in December, 1929, by the President's Research Committee on Social Trends. This was both sociological research and social analysis in the sense that most of the authors were sociologists attempting to study a total society through research and diagnosis of the main units of its structure and function. In major areas questions were asked and answered in terms of measurable statistical indices and published in two large volumes with appropriate chapters and a dozen separate monographs. Here are the main divisional questions:

To what extent and how are mechanical inventions and scientific discoveries the causes of social change?

What are the major changes in our economic organization and what are their social consequences?

What of the nature, extent, and social effects of communication, mobility, and the dissemination of news?

What are the population trends in America and what are their social consequences?

What are the trends in the utilization of land and natural resources and what social consequences are involved?

What are the trends in education and what are the chief technical and social problems remaining unsolved in this field?

What are the range and significance of the changing social attitudes of the American people?

What are the changes in the social and economic status of racial and ethnic groups in the United States?

How is the vitality of the American people related to social change and to social welfare?

What is the measure of the changing family and its significance to modern life and culture?

What about the changing status of women in occupations, politics, and other activities outside the home?

What are the measures of progress in relation to the child and youth in society?

What are the occupations of the American people and what are the activities of the unoccupied?

What of the changing role of labor and labor groups in our social structure?

What are the changes in religious organizations and how are they related to other social changes?

What are the developments of associations, leisure time activities, and recreation in the United States?

What is the scope and range of the arts and their influence upon social change?

What are the consumption habits of the American people and how do they affect social life?

What are the changes in rural America and what is their significance to future development?

What are the changes in urban life and what are the trends in the social life of cities?

What are the developments in the extent and nature of crime and the treatment of society's offenders?

What are the changes in law and legal institutions and their relation to social justice and institutions?

What are the trends in American philanthropy and in private social work?

What is the relation of public welfare or public social work to American institutions and social amelioration?

What are the significant elements involved in public health and medicine in their relation to the general welfare?

What is the measure and meaning of the considerable extension of governmental functions?

What are the trends in public administration and what are the social objectives involved?

What is the distribution of the increase in governmental expenditures and their relation to taxation, governmental finance, and citizenship?

What are the facilities for recording, preserving, and utilizing social data for the study of social problems and how are these social resources strengthened?

What is the measure and meaning of this new sweep of the application of social research and the social sciences to the problems of living
and of modern civilization?

The "problems" stated here in the form of questions may be cited
to illustrate the field and methods of sociology in several ways, but
with special reference to the usefulness of sociological inquiry. In the
first place the studies reflected a new range and method of social research,
the first major national inventory ever undertaken under the auspices
of the head of the nation. Next they analyzed the structure of contemporary American society and indicated a type of social analysis and inventory. The sociological emphasis is further reflected in two chief
ways. One is in the systematic arrangement of data basic to a final synthesis of the whole study. The volumes are sociological volumes in the
sense that they are primarily inquiries into social relationships on the
level of human association and institutions. Likewise the point of view
of each of the studies is sociological in its conceptualization and method.
Neither the methodology nor the objectives are those of economics,
or psychology, or anthropology, or political science, even though the
data and personnel of these other social sciences are often drawn
upon. These studies do not inquire into the technique of value, or
business cycles, or standards of living, or price, or gold standards, or into
the general historical aspect of race development, or individual human
behavior, or other technical scholarly subjects in the several fields. They
do, however, frankly inquire into the social facts and implications
through the joint method of analysis and synthesis. These problems also
illustrate the trends of modern sociology in the utilization of the data
of other social sciences, and in the hypothesis that scientific methods
of research must be employed, and that the interpretation of results
involve the social relationships and problems that grow out of actual
changing situations. Sociology, in other words, in this instance becomes the orderly and comprehensive scientific study of society,
when society is synonymous with the American society of the United
States.

Sociology as Tool and as Science

As an increasingly important and dynamic science of society, sociology
has tended to follow two equally important directions: one as a tool and

the other as a science. As a tool, both for liberal education and social practice, sociology frankly assumes the scientific nature of its methods and content and seeks to provide adequate tools for curriculum development, for creative thinking, for the scientific attitude and analysis of problems and situations, for realistic citizenship, and for pre-professional preparation for such fields as social work, public administration, public welfare, journalism, education, politics.

As a science, sociology has tended to focus upon two major objectives. One is research in which the emphasis is upon increasingly more rigorous scientific methods and analysis, and upon increasingly dynamic and realistic concrete empirical study and broader inquiries into both specialized areas and the total societal area. The other is a synthesis of this increasingly large and important body of knowledge with a view to the contribution of sound theory basic to the multiple tasks of social discovery, social interpretation, and social invention. The field of sociology, however, is not limited to the formalized concept of society or human relationships or like-minded groups, but comprehends the totality of the societal process which we call culture and the societal product which we call civilization.

Sociology as Sociologists: The Presidents of the American Sociological Society

Now we return to our starting point for the definitive story of American sociology which begins with the founding of the American Sociological Society in 1905 and the immediate backgrounds of sociology courses and departments in American institutions in the 1890's and at the turn of the century. From these two starting points our story of American sociology gains momentum and moves rapidly in a rising action toward its 1950 achievements, being constantly interrupted by the varying fortunes of the American scene and the changing tempo of American university education. In the pre-sociological period the stream of sociology rises in the springs of a rapidly developing nation with its growing pains and problems and swells into the main current of American civilization headed toward the end of the nineteenth century at which time Henry Steele Commager records, in his *The American Mind,* 1950, the turning point in the nation's intellectual and spiritual outlook. From then on, also, the span of sociology's biography is almost identical with the rise and development of graduate studies and "university" proper in America.

Professional, organized American sociology, then, stems from the founding of the American Sociological Society. The presidents of the Society were the first ex-officio standard bearers of the accelerating sociological movement which was to result in sociology's becoming one of the major units in American college and university education. The earlier presidents were frontiersmen in a new field and, as the full-fledged representatives of the new social science, they set the incidence clearly for the beginning of our story. It was perhaps symbolic of this slow-moving story and of the small number of American sociologists in the earlier days that each of the first five presidents of the sociological society was re-elected for a second term. Each also symbolized maturity, forcefulness, dynamic personality, and a certain distinguished heritage reflected from various universities and origins. As connoting scholarship, almost all of the first forty presidents up to 1950 were members of Phi Beta Kappa and many were Fellows in the American Association for the Advancement of Science, as well as prolific writers and dynamic promoters of sociology. As connoting persistency, continuity, and maturity, all of the earlier ones, old enough by now, average three score years and ten, with the Wisconsin pair, Ross and Gillin, moving beyond the eighty-year limit.

Migrating from the nation's capital, Lester F. Ward had come to Brown University whence he was elected president for 1906 and 1907. William Graham Sumner, stemming from Yale University, guided the society for 1908 and 1909. Franklin H. Giddings from Columbia, 1910 and 1911, and Albion W. Small from the western hinterland of Chicago, for 1912 and 1913. These have often been called the first Big Four who gave most momentum to American sociology and set the stage and the pace for what was to follow.

Following E. A. Ross of the University of Wisconsin, who was the last to hold the office for two years in 1914 and 1915, the tempo speeds up a little and our next ten, each with one-year tenure only, included George E. Vincent of the University of Chicago, for 1916; George E. Howard of the University of Nebraska, for 1917; Charles H. Cooley of the University of Michigan, for 1918; Frank W. Blackmar of the University of Kansas, for 1919; James Q. Dealey of Brown University, for

1920; Edward Cary Hayes of the University of Illinois, for 1921; James
P. Lichtenberger of the University of Pennsylvania, for 1922; Ulysses G.
Weatherly of the University of Indiana, for 1923; Charles A. Ellwood
of the University of Missouri, for 1924.

Like most of the other American expansions, the geographic range
of the Society's presidents was widening and moving westward. For,
since the first Big Four, with the exception of Dealey, no president had
come from the East until 1922 when James P. Lichtenberger came from
the University of Pennsylvania. Now the next ten continued this trend
toward the West with only Howard W. Odum in 1930 from the East.
The others were Robert E. Park from Chicago, in 1925; John L. Gillin
from the University of Wisconsin, in 1926; William I. Thomas, stemming from the University of Chicago, was a professor at large, in 1927;
John M. Gillette from the University of North Dakota, in 1928; William
F. Ogburn from Chicago, in 1929; Emory S. Bogardus from the University of Southern California, in 1931; L. L. Bernard from Washington
University, previously from North Carolina and Tulane, in 1932; E. B.
Reuter from Iowa State, in 1933; and Ernest W. Burgess from Chicago,
in 1934.

This second ten had gone still farther west, to name Gillette of North
Dakota and Bogardus of Southern California. Now for the third ten,
the Society came back East for more, with half from eastern institutions
including New York three times, and Massachusetts and North Caro-
lina once each. From the East were Henry Pratt Fairchild from New
York University, in 1936; Frank H. Hankins from Smith, in 1938;
Robert M. MacIver from Columbia, in 1940; Dwight Sanderson from
Cornell, in 1942; and Rupert B. Vance from North Carolina, in 1944.
Those from the West were: F. Stuart Chapin from the University of
Minnesota, in 1935; Ellsworth Faris from Chicago, in 1937; Edwin H.
Sutherland from Indiana, in 1939; Stuart A. Queen from Washing-
ton University, in 1941; George A. Lundberg from the University of
Washington and formerly from Bennington, in 1943. Finally, of the
last six up to 1950 only Louis Wirth of the University of Chicago, in
1947, was from the West. The others are Kimball Young from Queens
College and later from Northwestern, in 1945; Carl C. Taylor from the
U. S. Bureau of Agricultural Economics and earlier from North Carolina State, in 1946; E. Franklin Frazier from Howard and earlier from

Fisk, in 1948; Talcott Parsons from Harvard, in 1949; and Leonard Cottrell from Cornell, in 1950.

Regional and Institutional Distribution

This preview of the two score presidents of the American Sociological Society from twenty-four institutions from almost as many states gives us a sort of quick introduction not only to the first fifty years of sociology as clearly defined as a college discipline, but it also indicates pretty well the geographic distribution of this particular level of leadership. A look at these presidents indicates a wide distribution in the different regions, states, and major universities, the Middle States overwhelmingly predominating, Illinois alone having ten. Exactly one-half of all the presidents up to 1950 were from institutions in the Middle States. The Northeast was next with fifteen, and the Southeast was third. Although only two were elected president during the time they held positions in southern institutions, there were no less than a baker's dozen of the presidents who at one time or another had taught in the South. The Far West was next with one elected directly and three who were at one time or another identified with the Far West. Finally, there was one from the Northwest and one transferred to the Southwest. Of the presidents, seven were from the University of Chicago, while only eight other universities had more than one, namely, Brown, Columbia, Cornell, Indiana, North Carolina, Minnesota, Washington, and Wisconsin.

This distribution represents the institutions from which each president was elected. Subsequently there was some interregional exchange giving a still wider representation. Thus, James Q. Dealey moved from the Northeast to the Southwest; Charles A. Ellwood, elected from Missouri was later elected to the head of the sociology department at Duke University; George A. Lundberg moved from the East to the Far West to the University of Washington. W. I. Thomas was elected at large from New York, although he came from the Middle States and later sojourned at California. Among others who taught in regions different from those they were elected from were Charles A. Ellwood at Duke University; L. L. Bernard, at North Carolina and Tulane, Carl C. Taylor, at North Carolina State; R. E. Park, E. B. Reuter, and Franklin Frazier at Fisk University. Stuart A. Queen was earlier professor of social technology at Goucher, transferring later to the Middle States, and Louis

Wirth was associate professor at Tulane. In their very early years, Faris and Thomas taught at Texas Christian University and the University of Tennessee, respectively, while Leonard Cottrell taught originally at Virginia Polytechnic. Kimball Young, coming from the Northwest, taught then at the University of Wisconsin, whence he went to Queens from which he was elected president of the Society, following which he transferred to Northwestern University. E. A. Ross, earlier from the Far West and Northeast, later came to the Middle States; Albion W. Small, originally from the Northeast, moved on to the Middle States.

Tested in the Light of Contemporary Society

Many of the subjects of the addresses of the presidents of the Society still appear appropriate and are so timely that if we should omit the date and authors they might appear to be current major themes. For instance, Giddings' "Relation of Social Theory to Public Policy" as early as 1910 ended with an appeal for ways and means for seeking equilibrium of international power. His final sentences were: "The great superiorities that now preclude effective government by discussion throughout the world are: (1) technical proficiency based on scientific knowledge, and (2) concentrated economic power. If we sincerely wish for peace, we must be willing to see a vast equalizing of industrial efficiency between the East and the West. We must also welcome every change that tends to bring about a fairer apportionment of natural resources among nations and within them, and a more equal distribution of wealth. If these conditions can be met, there will be a Parliament of Man."

In 1914 and 1915, E. A. Ross's addresses were devoted to "Freedom of Communication and the Struggle for Right" and "War as Determiner." In this latter, Ross predicted that "a great union" of the world is the only answer. In 1917, George E. Howard discussed crisis in human affairs under the title of "Ideals as a Factor in the Future Control of International Society." Frank W. Blackmar, in 1919, wrote on "A Working Democracy"; Ulysses G. Weatherly, in 1923, on "Racial Pessimism"; Charles A. Ellwood, in 1924, on "Intolerance"; John M. Gillette, in 1928, on "Urban Influence and Selection"; Howard W. Odum on "Folk and Regional Conflict," in 1930; E. B. Reuter, in 1933, on "Race and Culture Contacts"; E. W. Burgess, in 1934, on "Social Planning and the

Mores"; F. Stuart Chapin, in 1935, on "Social Theory and Social Action"; H. P. Fairchild, in 1936, on "Business as an Institution"; Frank H. Hankins, in 1938, on "Social Science and Social Action"; George A. Lundberg, in 1943, on "Sociologists and the Peace."

There were no less than ten addresses devoted specifically to sociology as a subject: Lester F. Ward, 1906, "The Establishment of Sociology"; Albion W. Small, 1912, "The Present Outlook of Social Science"; Edward C. Hayes, 1921, "The Sociological Point of View"; Robert E. Park, 1925, "The Concept of Position in Sociology"; John L. Gillin, 1926, "The Development of Sociology in the United States"; Ellsworth Faris, 1937, "The Promise of Sociology"; Robert M. MacIver, 1940, "Some Reflections on Sociology during a Crisis"; Stuart A. Queen, 1941, "Can Sociologists Face Reality?"; Dwight Sanderson, 1942, "Sociology as a Means to Democracy"; Carl C. Taylor, 1946, "Sociology and Common Sense."

There were also a number of addresses dealing with the theory of social structure and the dynamics of society, each of which projected ample framework for plenty of research and testing; but few have been followed up with the testing. Among the addresses that might be so classified, Lester F. Ward, in 1907, wrote on "Social Classes in the Light of Modern Sociological Theory"; while William Graham Sumner, in 1908, wrote about "The Family and Social Change" and, in 1909, "Religion and the Mores." In 1916, George E. Vincent spoke on "Countryside and Nation," and George E. Howard, as already catalogued, in 1917, on "Ideals as a Factor in the Future Control of International Society." Cooley wrote in 1918 of "A Primary Culture for Democracy," while Frank W. Blackmar, in 1919, discussed "A Working Democracy." Other addresses that posited theoretical reference included those of W. I. Thomas, in 1927, on "The Behavior Pattern and the Situation"; John M. Gillette, in 1928, on "Urban Influence and Selection"; W. F. Ogburn, in 1929, on "Folkways of a Scientific Society"; Howard W. Odum, in 1930, on "Folk and Regional Conflict as a Field of Sociological Study"; Emory S. Bogardus, in 1931, on "Social Process on the Pacific Coast"; L. L. Bernard, in 1932, on "Sociological Research and the Exceptional Man"; Stuart Chapin, in 1933, on "Social Theory and Social Action"; E. W. Burgess, in 1934, on "Social Planning and the Mores"; R. B. Vance, in 1944, on "Social Dynamics"; Louis Wirth, in 1947, on "Consensus and Mass Communication"; Franklin Frazier, in 1948, on "Race Contacts and Social Structure"; and Talcott Parsons, in 1949, on "The Prospect of Sociological Theory."

Regional Sociological Societies

Beginning in 1925 with the organization of the Ohio Valley Sociological Society, the story of American sociology continues with more ex-officio representation and definition in the six regional societies whose combined membership exceeds that of the American Sociological Society. Each holds its annual meetings with programs in which many participants join in the discussion of timely subjects. Some of the regional programs approach in quality and quantity the best of the national annual meetings. The Eastern Sociological Society has had 16 presidents of whom four have been president of the American Sociological Society. The Southern Sociological Society has had 15 presidents, with one former president of the national group; the Ohio Valley Society has had 22 presidents, with one former national president; the Midwest Sociological Society has had 15 presidents; the Pacific Sociological Society has had 21 presidents including two former presidents of the American Sociological Society. The Southwestern Society has had 10. The further story of these regional leaders is told in Chapter 21.

The definition of American sociology in terms of what American sociologists do, however, is exemplified in other groups than the presidents of the American Sociological Society and its affiliate regional societies, for, among the American sociologists who have contributed largely to sociology, there are others who have attained their rating through ex-officio places, as well as through their achievements. These are the heads of departments of colleges and universities where sociology has been featured. Such institutions include the state colleges and universities and denominational and privately endowed institutions. Among these, besides individual institutions of distinction, are certain groups, including Catholic schools in various regions in which more than two hundred sociologists have been listed in their *Who's Who among Catholic Sociologists*. Negro colleges in the South have featured the teaching of sociology and have compiled a list of more than one hundred teachers. Beginning with Atlanta University and W. E. B. DuBois in the 1890's, these institutions have featured such leaders as Charles S. Johnson, Franklin Frazier, Ira Reid, Oliver Cox. Another major group is that of the rural sociologists who are featured in the story of their own Rural Sociological Society and the journal, *Rural Sociology* in Chapters 21 and 23. And finally, the increasing number of younger sociologists who are writing a greater ratio of sociology textbooks than was the case in the earlier days of sociology in America may almost be catalogued as the "promising group." Whereas the great majority of the textbooks in sociology in the first few decades of sociology's formal development were written by presidents of the American Sociological Society, the proportion in the 1940's would be nearer one-third.

The Backbone of American Sociology

Therefore, alongside this first group of scholars and teachers as reflected in the presidents of the American Sociological Society and their regional affiliates would be that larger group whose contributions have made American sociology what it is. More specifically, and including many overlappings, these are the authors of the main textbooks, the contributors to the sociological journals, and the teachers who have done the important routine tasks. First are the authors of texts on general sociology including introductory texts and principles of sociology, as it has been in America, together with those on history, theory, and methodology. A still larger number have made contributions to the special fields of sociology, which may be catalogued as special sociology and specialisms. These include both elementary texts and mature research in such areas as Marriage and the Family, Institutions, Social Problems and Deviation, the Community, Rural, Urban, and Industrial Sociology, Social Pathology, Penology, Criminology, Social Psychology, Population, Demography, Race, Ethnic Groups, Folk, Intercultural Relations, Area Studies, Ecology and Regionalism. A considerable overlapping between and among these groups is natural; yet it indicates that, in the aggregate, teachers, writers, and scholars who have not been ex-officio heads of the American Sociological Society have contributed a greater amount to the total literature of sociology than have the presidents themselves. This list again reflects a wide geographic distribution and university representation throughout the whole nation.

There is, next, what might be likened to an extraordinary sociological panel of younger sociologists, whose contributions can be catalogued and appraised only by detailed analysis of courses being taught, of research being done, of articles contributed to the learned journals, and of the spirit and dynamics of the younger generation of sociologists. Their contributions aggregate a very large amount of material and, while the breadth of their interest and the extent of their knowledge of the broader fields of history, economics, philosophy, and education may be less apparent than that of many of the older sociologists, the composite of their contributions may also be greater. Some of these are already articulate in such catalogues as the Sociological Research Society, which is a body of less than one hundred scholars elected by the group on the basis of research interests and achievements, and in the folkways of American sociologists who by word of mouth feature younger men and women on the horizon even as best sellers are featured among the book-buying public. These will have to wait for the first new decade of the second half century for their ratings although something of their contributions will be subsequently presented in relation to their several places in this story of American sociology. Along with their writings and efforts must be appraised also that considerable output of our borderline sociologists and their segment of the literature of American sociology. All of this literature is distinctive because it reflects the flowering of sociology in the setting of American society. Before presenting the detailed story of the personalities and writings of American sociologists, therefore, we proceed first to tell something more about the European heritage and the American background that produce American sociology for American institutions of higher learning.

CHAPTER 2

The European Heritage of American Sociology

The verdict that the New World as it developed in the over-all society of the United States was so influenced by its European heritage and so conditioned by its American traits that it could not be explained by either, seems peculiarly appropriate to American sociology. And yet, it seems likely that the European influence has been even greater upon American sociology than upon American culture in general. So great, however, has been the impact of European culture and thought upon American political philosophy and institutions and upon educational and general culture patterns of the New World that one major American sociologist, Pitirim A. Sorokin, writing on "socio-cultural trends in Euro-American culture during the last hundred years" in his *A Century of Social Thought,* published in 1939, insisted that there was no essential difference between American and European culture. Sorokin argued that "any contention that American and European cultures are different is wrong." Although there is no agreement on such a sweeping characterization, it was certainly true that in the earlier days Thomas Jefferson and other founding fathers were greatly influenced by European contributions, while, from the days of Benjamin Franklin on, personal contacts with European diplomacy and European visitors continued as a strong influence. Something of the range of visiting, writing, and influence of Europeans in personal media may be noted from Henry Steele Commager's estimate, as quoted in Chapter 1, that more than a thousand Europeans, from Bryce to Brogan, have written about America.

We have already pointed out how the European influence, strangely enough, resulted in contrasting trends, the one toward general social science and its focus upon social problems and the other toward integral sociology and social theory. More specifically, the influence of the British Social Science Association, timed to fit in with America's growing consciousness of its social problems, exerted considerable influence upon the social science movement in the United States in the 1860's. This was both American and European, and the special emphasis was upon a new social science that would study and discuss the main questions related to the increasing number of social problems in the United States. Alongside this, it was logical for the associationist movement, looking toward Utopian solutions, to develop and afford experimentation in the laboratory of the New World.

Then, subsequently, the influence of sociological literature from Europe, beginning with Comte, changed the setting for American sociology, so that the emphasis shifted to European social thought which continued to influence college and university sociology throughout its entire development, including a new tendency in the 1940's and continuing into 1950 to re-explore certain sources of European sociology as valuable supplements to the greater stream of American sociology. This total influence may be seen by observing the stream flow of European sources into American sociology a decade before, and about the time of the founding of the American Sociological Society, in which the influence of Spencer, Comte, Darwin, Ratzenhofer, Durkheim, Adam Smith, and others was powerful enough to dominate the pioneer American sociologists. Yet, fifty years later there was considerable revivification of the European influence through Durkheim, Simmel, Max Weber, Tönnies, Mannheim, von Wiese. And in the decades between, in the teaching of historical sociology, which was mostly cataloguing European sociologists, and in the study of "principles" and "theory" there was never a time when the American sociologists were not only calling the roll, but answering the roll call of multiple European sociologists.

European Scholars and American Sociology

The Bernards' *Origins of American Sociology* featuring the American backgrounds, with nearly a hundred pre-sociological Americans, listed more than two score Europeans as main conditioning authors for the American development. Among others, there are listed in order: Bacon, Bastiat, Bentham, Branford, Buckle, Carlyle, Comte, Condorcet, Cousin, Darwin, De Tocqueville, Galton, Guizot, Haeckel, Hegel, Hobbes,

Hume, Huxley, Lieber, Locke, Malthus, Martineau, Marx, Mill, Montesquieu, More, Proudhon, Quételet, Ricardo, Rousseau, Ruskin, Saint-Simon, Smith, Spencer, Turgot, Tylor, Vico, Voltaire.

And Harry Elmer Barnes featuring more of the theoretical foundations of sociology, catalogues a special gallery of Europeans whose work is commonly accepted as basic. These included Bagehot, Buckle, Comte, Condorcet, Darwin, Durkheim, Fiske, Fouillée, Ginsberg, Gumplowicz, Hobbes, Hobhouse, Hegel, Kidd, Le Bon, Le Play, Locke, Novicow, Oppenheimer, Pareto, Ratzenhofer, Schäffle, Simmel, Spencer, Stein, Tarde, Tönnies, Wallas, Max and Alfred Weber, Westermarck, von Wiese, Znaniecki, Wundt. These are major threads in the fabric of sociology as Barnes chronicles it in *From Lore to Science, Contemporary Social Theory, Introduction to the History of Sociology, Historical Sociology.*

Yet, after all, it was American sociology that was important. And back again to Vernon Parrington's *Main Currents in American Thought,* his dictum that America, being the child of two continents, can be explained in its significant traits by neither alone, is an excellent characterization of American sociology. We have already pointed out how the origins and development of American sociology, even as American culture itself, reflected a sort of contemporaneous parallel force, the one development of American life breaking away from its European heritage and the other, a later development, flourishing from the double meanings of American problems and European writings. This parallel between American cultural development and American sociology gives us also the basis for a clear concept of the structure of American society within which sociology was to grow up and come of age. The stream to European influence was composed essentially of three currents. The first of these was the continuous flow of the European heritage of tradition, philosophy, political and economic factors, setting the stage for both the rise of sociological interests and for determining the actual social field. The second was the direct influence of the British Social Science Association upon the American social science movements. And the third was the very great influence of the earlier and later European sociologists upon American sociologists. We may look at each of these briefly.

Multiple Nature of European Influence

There are several currents to the stream flow of general European heritage. One of these is clearly delineated by Parrington in his estimate of the dichotomy of systems of European thought that have "domesticated themselves in America," and, cross fertilized with American indigenous growths, have resulted in what is accepted as "American." "In broad outline," says Parrington, on page iii of his Introduction to Volume I, "those germinal contributions were the bequests successively of English independency, of French romantic theory, of the industrial revolution and laissez faire, of nineteenth-century science, and of continental theories of collectivism." These, taking root in American soil, grew into such luxurious flowering of thought and Utopian concepts as might well be compared with the abundance and denseness of America's natural resources.

In particular, the successive development of English independency and French romantic theory and their conflicting ideologies set the stage for earlier American liberalism in conflict with New England reactionary theology. But there were new beginnings "from the raw materials of European immigrants" in other regions spreading westward that created the American yeomanry that was to remake America and set the incidence for the changing social structure of American society that was to be the laboratory of American sociology as well as of political science. Parrington thus indicates something of the rise of the new American liberalism which was, for instance, to set the frame of reference for William Graham Sumner's foundation for his sociology. Accordingly, as he observes on page v of his *Main Currents in American Thought,* "while French romantic theory was spreading widely through the backwoods of America, providing an intellectual justification for the native agrarianism, another philosophy, derived from English liberalism of the later eighteenth century, was taking possession of the commercial towns. Realistic and material rather than romantic and Utopian, it was implicitly hostile to all the major premises and ideals of the French school. It conceived of human nature neither as good nor bad, but as acquisitive; and it proposed to erect a new social and political philosophy in accordance with the needs of a capitalistic order.

It was concerned with exploitation and the rights of trade, rather than with justice and the rights of man." Here was perhaps one of the best illustrations of the principle of laissez faire, and the doctrine of the economic man which was to influence the American culture economy of the future. According to Parrington, on page vi of the same reference, this "would reduce the political state to the role of policeman, to keep the peace. With humanitarian and social interests, the state must not intermeddle — such functions lie outside its legitimate sphere. An expression of the aspirations of trading and speculating classes, it professed to believe that economic law — by which term it glorified the spontaneous play of the acquisitive instinct — was competent to regulate men in society, and that if freedom of trade were achieved, all lesser and secondary freedoms would follow."

Literary Parallels

Returning again to the parallelism between the general European influence upon American letters and culture and upon the sociological climate in America, Van Wyck Brooks cites Lester F. Ward, "the founder of American sociology," as one of the notable Americans along with Melville and Whitman whom Americans have forgotten all too soon. Ward, according to Brooks, on page 404 of his *The Times of Melville and Whitman,* "shared in the Darwinian controversies of the eighteen-seventies and gradually developed his own sociological system. An American member of the family of minds that included Spencer, Huxley and Comte, he greatly admired Condorcet and his faith in the future, although he knew it would require a longer time than Cordorcet thought for the world 'to get its growth.' All the races of men must first be blended into one race, and for this a millennium might be necessary, or ten thousand years, — 'but not as long as it took to develop the horse,' — for he was an ardent believer in evolution, though he never supposed that this was automatic. Far from regarding it as a merely natural or unconscious process, he thought of it rather as voluntary, according to law, a conscious striving for a higher goal, for the individual as well as the race, a great continuous flow of human effort. The idea of continuity was central in his thinking. As an equalitarian, with a lifelong sympathy for the submerged, he attacked monopolistic privilege and

the laissez-faire system, and his *Dynamic Sociology* was the only American book that was ordered to be burned officially in the Russia of the
czars."

Parrington points out vividly certain surprising contrasts between
the influence of Spencer and of Comte on American life. "One would
have supposed," he wrote, on page 197 of Book II of *Main Currents in
American Thought,* "that Positivism would have appealed to American
intellectuals, as it appealed to liberal English thinkers like Mill and
Spencer. Not only has the American mind taken kindly to sociology,
but the history of America, as Woodbridge Riley has pointed out, offers
too pat an illustration of the Comtean law of progress to be overlooked.
The three centuries of American existence — the seventeenth with its
theocracy, the eighteenth with its abstract theories of political rights
and its faith in constitutions, and the nineteenth with its industrialism
based on science — would seem to be pages out of the Positivist philosophy of history. That Comte made so slight an impression on the
mind of New England was due, no doubt, to the current influence of
transcendentalism with its metaphysical backgrounds. Although eager
young intellectuals like John Fiske might accept it while awaiting a
more adequate evolutionary philosophy, the country was not yet ripe
for Positivism. When that time came it was Spencer rather than Comte
who became the master of American intellectuals — Spencer and in a
lesser degree John Stuart Mill. Both Spencer and Mill had come under
the influence of the French sociological school, and it was through their
writings that the new social philosophy penetrated America."

The Frontier Breaks Away from Europe

Another way of exploring the relation of the European heritage to
what was primarily American is to recall Frederick Jackson Turner's
identification of American culture as that which became different from
European culture, as a result of America's frontier life in its ever western expansion. In *The Frontier in American History,* pp. 2–3, Turner
writes that America was "continually beginning over again on the frontier. This perennial rebirth, this fluidity of American life, this expansion
westward with its new opportunities, its continuous touch with the
simplicity of primitive society, furnish the forces dominating American

character." This was the transitional period when Americans, being both isolated from European sources and too busy to be concerned with them, began the more integral American culture.

There are, however, variations of the Turner concept and differing opinions as to its validity, each reflecting the earlier geographic cultural basis for the development of American diversity and unity, the summary of all, however, agreeing that the evolution of American culture has occurred as a series of shifting frontiers. The physical frontiers, giving opportunity for the free functioning of the folk culture, developed social frontiers different from the European, as, for instance, the role of women in societal development, the classless American democracy, the state university. The economic, social, and psychological demands upon the pioneers thus resulted in the creating of new culture patterns that progressively became more American and less European. These, however, would again be greatly influenced later by European scholarship and education and would again be remolded partly as protest of the American folk and partly by the sheer force of American character and trends.

Laurence M. Larson says, in his *The Changing West and Other Essays,* that "while the 'old west' was characterized by its Americanism, democracy, and Protestantism, the 'new wests' emerging after 1850 were dominated by alien groups, different in racial type, intellectual interests, religious and moral standards, and temperament from the earlier pioneers. The development of these newer frontiers was the slow process of Americanization of these alien groups." In similar reference, William Allen White, in *The Changing West,* page 12, says: ". . . out of those two, tiny, rude, primitive edifices, the little white church and the little red school-house, rose liberty of action, which was the architect of the spiritual structure of our western civilization."

In three other main ways more specific than its general influence upon American culture, European influence had a large part in the growth and development of American sociology. One was the influence of the British Social Science Association upon the development of American social science; another was the influence of certain classical writers, such as Condorcet, upon American leaders such as Thomas Jefferson; and a third was the specific influence of European sociology upon early American sociologists.

The Social Science Associations

In Chapter 3 we trace more of the influence of the British Social Science Association in the United States in its special emphasis upon the "social problems" background of American sociology. Perhaps the Bernards' interpretation of the rise and nature of the British national association for the promotion of social science, founded in 1857, will give the clearest picture of its influence upon American social science. This influence was not the definitive one but was cumulative, even as was the American movement. First, the problems background and the purposive nature of the new social science were similar in both instances. L. L. and Jessie Bernard stated that it was the British Social Science Association that sought to set the incidence of the new movement in the wake of the Industrial Revolution, for the problems and results came earlier in England than in the rest of the world. Like many another country, England, being the pioneer, had no ready-made remedies for problems that arose. The Bernards, on page 536 of *Origins of American Sociology,* quote F. J. C. Hearnshaw as saying, "The creation of riches proved an easier task than their equitable distribution. The countryside still shudders at the memory of the hungry forties; but the plight of many of the workers in the industrial towns which sprang up like mushrooms was no better. Professor Clapham assures us that their condition was not quite so bad as it has been painted by the Hammonds and other investigators, but there is plenty of evidence that masses of the population, of both sexes and of all ages, were hideously overworked and underfed. The birth rate rose by leaps and bounds during the first half of the century, and the deathrate was increased by the herding of the industrial armies in the slums. Foresight is among the rarest of human qualities, and the country, absorbed in the production of wealth, allowed a condition of affairs to arise which disgraced the richest nation in Europe. Byron had declared in the House of Lords that even in Turkey he had never witnessed such scenes of squalid degradation as in the land of his birth. Engels' grim survey of the working classes in 1844 suggested that the situation was as bad as ever, and Karl Marx based his *Kapital* mainly on the experience of England."

Just as there was considerable distance between the origins and development of the social science movement and the later crystallized discipline of sociology, so there was a great gap between the general influence of the British Social Science Association upon American sociology and the later concrete influence of European sociology upon American sociologists. Both, however, were important and both had their cumulative effect upon the total picture of early sociological developments. Yet, it was the specific influence of particular European sociologists upon American sociologists that gave character to much of earlier American sociology. Something of this influence has already been indicated as it affected American thought and letters in general. We now turn to the story of American sociology itself.

There are three main bodies of evidence indicating the influence of European sociologists upon American sociology. The first is the direct influence of particular European sociologists upon American sociologists in the earlier days of the American pioneers. This may be illustrated simply by reference to the first presidents of the American Sociological Society and their writings. The second is the continued influence through the uniform study by practically all departments of sociology, of "historical sociology" consistently cataloguing and interpreting European authors in required courses. Third, the continued emphasis upon European authors and the retapping of European sources in the 1940's by many of the later leading sociologists is significant. This may well be illustrated by the work of Tönnies, the Webers, Mannheim, von Wiese, and the wide use of Gurvitch and Moore's *Twentieth Century Sociology,* in which American sociology is often treated primarily in its non-American perspective.

Gillin's Estimate

Now returning to the earlier American sociology and the direct influence of European sociology, John L. Gillin cites three authors who had much to do with its founding. As he points out in his chapter on Giddings, pages 191 and 192 of Odum's *American Masters of Social Science,* Auguste Comte, the inventor of the word sociology, published his *System of Positive Politics* between 1851 and 1854 with Harriet Martineau's condensed translation in 1853, followed by the second edition in 1875, and a new edition in three volumes in 1896. Herbert Spencer's *Study of Sociology* was published in 1873, and in 1874 appeared the first volume of his *Principles of Sociology.* Then, in 1869, appeared Bagehot's

Physics and Politics, published in the United States in 1898. "These three men, then, Comte, Spencer, and Bagehot, the one a French-man and the others two Englishmen, whose writings were available in English, furnish one group of influences which explain the origin of sociology in the United States. That the measure of their influence was great, especially that of the first two, is evidenced by the writings of almost every one of our early American sociologists."

Gillin quotes Professor Small of the University of Chicago as remem-bering at least fifteen important scholars of the United States who, hav-ing studied in the German universities in the seventies, returned to the United States inspired by a new spirit and by the methods of their Ger-man teachers. The list of a few of the early epoch-making names in the development of the social sciences in the United States was almost iden-tical with the catalogue of those who had taken their graduate work in Germany. William Graham Sumner had studied in Germany in the sixties and, returning to Yale, announced a course in sociology in 1876. Herbert B. Adams, head of the Department of History and Politics at the newly established Johns Hopkins University, selected as his associate Richard T. Ely who had received his Ph.D. degree at Heidelberg in 1879. President Gilman, who was one of the pre-sociological Americans inter-ested in social science, had drawn thither a galaxy of these German-trained professors when he organized the university. Others included Albion W. Small, who in 1893 became head of the Department of So-ciology at the newly organized University of Chicago, and Professor John W. Burgess, at Leipzig and Berlin from 1871 to 1873, who was called upon to organize the Faculty of Political Science at Columbia University. Besides these leaders, the roll should include Henry W. Farnum of Yale, Frank J. Goodnow of Columbia, later president of Johns Hopkins, Arthur T. Hadley, president emeritus of Yale, George E. Howard, early head of the Department of Political Science and So-ciology at the University of Nebraska, Edmund J. James of the Univer-sity of Pennsylvania, E. R. A. Seligman, noted economist of Columbia University, Professor William M. Sloane of Columbia, and Frank W. Taussig of Harvard.

Perhaps enough has already been said to indicate the European influ-ence upon Ward's great works. Even though it is often said that much of Ward's sociology was developed in the framework of antagonism to

Spencer and others, nevertheless the influence was dominant on the genesis of his "system." Further than that, two simple examples will perhaps suffice for added illustration. First, although Ward's training, background, and notable achievements in his pre-sociological days had been the results of his field work and observation as a scientist, not once in his new comprehensive sociologies does he venture into the realm of field work and away from the literary sources he adopted from his wide readings and high motivation in his new love, sociology, with its European backgrounds. Another illustration may be found in his *Psychic Factors of Civilization* in which he does not utilize the newer approaches of American psychology but rather makes a philosophical (mental philosophy and historical reference) approach with an abundance of European citations.

The Giddings Background

In the case of Franklin H. Giddings, in addition to the bibliographies he utilizes in his earlier books, two simple evidences may be cited. In the first place, by his own testimony, it was his reading of Darwin, Spencer, Huxley, and others that set him on his way toward what came to be a sort of Dean of American University Sociologists. Giddings himself had described this period. He says, quoted by Gillin, as above, on page 197, "My interest in sociology, as I have on various occasions told, began while I was yet a youth, when accidentally a copy of the first number of the *Popular Science Monthly* fell into my hands a few days after its publication, and I read the first chapter of Spencer's *The Study of Sociology*. Before I entered college I had read a lot of Darwin, Tyndall, and Huxley, and nearly half of what Spencer had then printed. At college, and during ten subsequent years of newspaper work, I kept up my interest and my reading in sociology and was ready to improve the first chance that offered to teach it after I went to Bryn Mawr."

Among the special readings in European sociology cited by Giddings in his first article on "The Province of Sociology," in the *Annals* of the American Academy of Political and Social Science, Volume I, number 1, July 1890, are Mill's *Logic*; Spencer's *Principles of Sociology*; Schäffle's *Bau und Leben*; De Greef's *Introduction à la Sociologie*; Gayau's *L'art au Point de Vue Sociologique,* and also his *Éducation et Hérédité, étude sociologique*; Gumplowicz's *Der Rassenkampf,* Combes de Kestrade's *Éléments de Sociologie*; the works of Darwin and Haeckel; and De Roberty's, *La Sociologie*. In the next place, the influence of Adam Smith upon Giddings' main earlier theory of *The Consciousness of Kind* may be cited as a complete definitive influence.

In his preface to the third edition of his *Principles*, pages x–xi, Giddings wrote: "Were I now re-writing the sketch of the development of social theory, I think that I should indeed claim for Adam Smith the first place among sociologists. The recently recovered notes of Smith's lectures on 'Justice, Police, Revenue, and Arms' show that Smith had sketched a complete system of social science. The system is structurally weak, however, because this great but always cautious philosopher was evidently never quite sure in his own mind whether the prime cause of social relations should be sought in that generic sympathy which is discoursed of in 'The Theory of Moral Sentiments,' or in the advantages of mutual aid which are described in 'The Wealth of Nations.' In the years that have passed since Adam Smith's death, thought has been busy with the logical organization of the social sciences, and it is possible for us now to shun some errors that he did not avoid. The most important claim, then, that I make for the sociological theory that is here presented, is that I have throughout insisted that fellow-feeling is a cause in social phenomena, and that mutual aid is an effect. It is upon this fundamental position that I find myself in disagreement with those who hold that mutual aid is primary. Rightly or wrongly, I believe that the true point of departure for sociology is found in 'The Theory of Moral Sentiments' rather than in 'The Wealth of Nations.' The stone that the builders of political economy rejected will, I believe, become the head of the corner for sociology."

Clarence H. Northcutt, in his chapter on Giddings in Barnes' *Introduction to the History of Sociology,* ascribed much of Giddings' work to the influence of his sociological predecessors somewhat as follows: From Comte, he accepted the need for a basic social science and his culture of main stages in the history of civilization. From Darwin and Spencer, he found his momentum on evolutionary thinking and was influenced by Spencer's "system" of sociology. His consciousness of kind was adopted from Adam Smith's "sympathy," and his early psychology stemmed from Tarde as did his methodology from Mill, Jevons, and Pearson.

Small and European Scholars

Hayes says of Small, on pages 153–154 of Odum's *American Masters of Social Science,* that "More than any other American sociologist, Professor Small has mediated to us the results of European scholarship." Following the three years ending in 1879 when he was a student at Newton Theological Seminary, Small spent two years in study abroad, one at the University of Berlin and one at the University of Leipzig. While there, he had married Fräulein Valeria von Massow and so maintained a lifelong intimacy with German life and thought. He not only reflected the teachings of the sociologists but also the influence of other notable European social scientists, listed by Hayes on page 158, such as the historians Guizot, Taine, Lamprecht, and Laurent of Belgium; the political scientists Bagehot, Bluntschli, and Stein — forerunners of Wallas, Kohler, and Max Weber of Heidelberg; the economists Schmoller, Wagner, Dietzel, Brentano, Boehm-Bawerk, Phillippowicz, Alfred Marshall, and John Stuart Mill; and the philosophers Wundt, Simmel, Durkheim, and later Dewey and Hobhouse. "For a time it seemed as though the contributions toward the developing movement that has taken the name of sociology which were being made by German social scientists were at least as notable as the hostility toward it that was common among social scientists in our own country."

Small's magnum opus, *General Sociology,* devoted perhaps a half of its 700 pages to an interpretation of Ratzenhofer, Schäffle, and Spencer. And it is often said that this book was the chief medium through which these outlooks became familiar to readers in the United States. His *Adam Smith* and *Modern Sociology,* published in 1907, like Giddings, gave Adam Smith great credit for much that influenced his own work. Yet, with all this European background and reading, it is doubtful if any of the earlier sociologists were more distinctively "American" than Small, as editor for over thirty years of *The American Journal of Sociology.*

Ross, Cooley, and Others

Continuing the story of the earlier American sociologists, both Ross and Cooley, of the special American heritage, found much of their beginnings of sociology in European sources. Ross was a graduate student at Johns Hopkins University where the European influence in the earlier days was great, having been introduced by G. Stanley Hall and perpetuated by Daniel Coit Gilman. Then he studied in Berlin and later, in his pioneering work on social psychology, he featured the analysis of planes and currents according to Tarde's conventionality and custom much of which was based upon Le Bon's psychology of crowds. Cooley's readings in the earlier formative years were heavily weighted with Comte, Spencer, Darwin, Gumplowicz, Tarde, Westermarck, and Schäffle. Charles A. Ellwood, following the advice of Small, studied at Berlin under Schmoller, Simmel, Paulsen and, in later years, was influenced by Hobhouse and Marett. In 1927–28, he spent most of his leave of absence in France, Italy, and Austria, and later was president of the International Institute of Sociology in 1935–36. W. I. Thomas, the Tennesseean, studied at Berlin and later, while teaching English at Oberlin, he studied the works of Spencer and some of the German graduate students' theses. Still later Florian Znaniecki was to exert a greater influence upon his American sociology through his collaboration in the *Polish Peasant*.

Of the later and younger presidents of the American Sociological Society, Talcott Parsons of Harvard, president in 1949, reverts to the earlier pattern of being directly conditioned by European authors. It is a long way from Small, the first, and Ellwood and Hayes, the last of the early sociologists primarily schooled in German sociology and philosophy, to Parsons. The roll call in between shows a rather distinctively American band, Gillette and Taylor, Kimball Young and Cottrell, Queen and Burgess, Vance and Bernard, and the others, as American as a great body of American writers in literature and history. Parsons' main work, however, stems from the special field of Max Weber at Heidelberg, following his contacts with Ginsberg and Hobhouse in the London School of Economics. Although Max Weber died in 1920, Parsons had considered his work of sufficient importance for it to dominate his own contributions up to 1949 when he was chairman of Harvard's Department of Social Relations, and president of the American Sociological Society. All of this was during the world's period of greatest tensions in the aftermath of World War II and the atomic bomb, and yet, isolated from both the intercultural world of conflict and America, Parsons' influence was enough to call forth a great deal of enthusiasm and to command a large following among the sociologists in the United States. Nevertheless, much of Parsons' theory stemmed from the recognition of the defects of Marxism and of Weber's study of capitalism, both of which were supreme social issues, and Parsons sought to develop from these interacting sources a more scientific sociological theory geared to sociological research.

Although there is no way to assess accurately the total influence of European sociologists and social philosophers upon American sociology, there can be no doubt that it was great. Howard Becker, who has devoted a great deal of study to this field, in response to a special query, estimates that the most lasting influences have been those of Max Weber, Znaniecki, Tönnies, Durkheim, Pareto, and von Wiese. Harry Elmer Barnes, in his encyclopedic *Introduction to the History of Sociology* treats the European group as consisting of thirty-two, presented in as many chapters, as compared with a baker's dozen of American sociologists. The Barnes catalogue of chapter treatments of Europeans includes Comte, Spencer, Gumplowicz, Wundt, Tönnies, Simmel, von Wiese, Max Weber, Alfred Weber, Troeltsch, Sombart, Oppenheimer, Freyer, Ratzenhofer, Spann, Stein, Kovalevski, Fouillée, Tarde, Le Bon, Durkheim, De Greef, Pareto and four other Italian sociologists, Kidd, Hobhouse, Westermarck, Briffault, Geddes, Branford, and Wallas. Of the American sociologists, besides his listing of Henry Lewis Morgan, the anthropologist, he features Ward and Sumner as the pioneers, along with Spencer, Comte, and Gumplowicz. As other exponents of "Sociological Theory in America" he lists Giddings, Small, Thomas, Stuckenberg, Ross, Cooley, Ellwood, Hayes, and Sorokin.

Further estimates may be made of the influence of particular European sociologists upon particular American sociologists in subsequent chapters on historical sociology and social theory and in the sketches of American sociologists in Chapters 4 to 13 and again in Chapters 24 and 25. So, too, the European influence is powerfully reflected in the transitional period that we next discuss in Chapter 3.

CHAPTER 3

The American Background and Heritage

We return again to our earlier characterization of American sociology as conforming to the general American pattern of part European and part American. In the case of sociology the dichotomy is especially marked. Starting with the general European culture and philosophy, then finding itself propelled by an American high motivation, and then again being conditioned by the European sociologists, the new science moved quickly into a main place in the college and university curriculum. Here was a contradiction: American sociology became so dominant that it took the European sociology, so prejudiced against sociology as an integral social science, and utilized its contents and methods to create a distinctive American sociology. At the same time that the European sociologists set the incidence for what American sociologists would teach, American sociologists were setting the incidence for something quite different and American in total framework and influence.

A part of this was due to the influence of the British Social Science Association upon the American Social Science Association in its objective of establishing a social science that would "solve" America's growing problems. A part was due to the leadership of many Americans active in the amelioration of the lot of the underprivileged. Another part was due to the American university movement and in particular to the great universities of the Middle West. But also a great part, too often overlooked by sociologists, was American society itself, with the powerful interactions between the New World and the Old, between American white settlers and American Indians, and between the people and the extraordinary regional range and variety of American resources and geography. Thus the United States was continuously in process as of a transitional society in which culture and institutions adapted themselves to social change more than they dominated the process of change. Sociology was no exception to this rule.

The American Heritage and Promise

The expansion of the old world of European society which became the America of the New World and the setting for American sociology, in the light of contemporary world events, may well reflect the most distinctive epoch in the history of human society up to now. The founding fathers envisaged a new world that was later to be characterized as the American Dream, while European observers marveled and doubted. America was to be a world apart, sufficient unto itself, and related to the rest of the world primarily for its example. Yet, in its major achievements, America has, of course, surpassed even this dream and exceeded the wildest imaginations of its founders and even of the later apostles of progress. But in the fabulous changes, America was no longer the isolated society but became both direct participator and leader in another new "one-world" society.

American sociology as a part of this epochal development has a number of facets. In the first place, it stems from the never-ceasing quest of mankind to know more about human society, and it followed the European heritage and methods of inquiry. In the second place, it flowered and fruited in the American soil, enriched by the American spirit and character. In the American adaptation, as well as developing its own science and supplanting European leadership, American sociology has exerted considerable influence upon the normal processes of societal development in the New World, with special reference to higher education and culture. It is noteworthy that the rise of American sociology started at about the same time that European culture was beginning to break under the impact of the fruits of the Industrial Revolution and technology. Thus American sociology had inherited a double obligation of building upon the European backgrounds at the same time that its maturing methodology and range multiplied its opportunity to study American society in the setting of the changing structure of the modern contemporary world.

An understanding of this American society is necessary not only, then, as a background of American sociology but most particularly to interpret the nature and range of the contributions of American sociologists up to 1950 and to indicate the promise of American sociology in the future. Here in American society is, in practical reality, the capital of the new world of intercultural relations and the practical leadership of the scientific and economic world. The student of sociology, interested primarily in the specific study of his own science, often overlooks the significance of the development of his own American society from its relatively simple folk culture, first, of the American Indian and then, of the frontier America, on through the quick-moving development into a society reflecting not only the most advanced stages of civilization yet attained by man, but also, at the mid-twentieth-century mark, the most dominant civilization in the world. To understand American sociology, therefore, its achievements and its defaults, it is necessary for the sociologist to understand the structure of American society and to recapture something of the powerful processes that have been going on.

Reference materials for the understanding of American society are so abundant as to constitute almost limitless resources for the sociologist. Yet the sociologists need only examine adequate samplings of three sorts. One is the literary and historical verdicts of those who have written about America, at home and abroad. Another source is found in the cultural and physiographic picture of America, while a third is revealed in the results of statistical research and cultural analysis of American society. The historian, Henry Steele Commager, has examined scores of writings and has recorded them in his *America in Perspective,* which reflects "The United States through Foreign Eyes," while America's own historians have recorded faithfully the development of the American society as they interpret it close up. Of the commentators who looked at America through the perspective of the Old World, there were several thousand, while at home in America other thousands have sought the meaning and promise of the new society.

Early Questioning and Later Answers

Yet, the sociologist is interested primarily in those characterizations that indicate the distinctive character of American society as the soil from which his European-planted sociology has grown into American sociology. Thus, the incomparable De Tocqueville wrote that he saw in America much more than America, namely, democracy and the key to the future. Here was a situation interesting not only to the United States itself but to the whole world; "it concerns not a nation but all mankind." This, citing Commager, pages xiii–xiv of *America in Perspective,* was no idle comment, for "all mankind was, perforce, interested in the American experiment. Here was the largest, the best equipped, of all laboratories, and one whose findings were compulsory, as it were. What would be the consequences of political democracy, of social equality, of universal free education, of the intermixture of peoples and races, of new standards of material well-being? Could a democracy avoid degenerating into a tyranny of the majority? Could the arts and the sciences flourish in a society that was committed to the doctrine of equality? Could morality prosper without an established Church? The answers to these, and to scores of questions no less momentous, were to be found, it was thought, in America."

A little more than a hundred years after De Tocqueville, after the New World society had gone far toward experimenting in its laboratory, D. W. Brogan wrote in *The American Character,* page ix, "Above all, I have tried to make plain that there is no parallel in history to the experiment of free government on this scale." And again, writing on pages 3-4, "The settlement of North America, the filling-up of its vast empty spaces, is the most remarkable extension of one society over an ocean barrier of which we have any knowledge. Century after century, tens of millions of Europeans have crossed three thousand miles of ocean, leaving behind them an old, reasonably adapted society in a familiar and, on the whole, friendly physical environment. They have brought with them European ideas, European techniques, European bodies and physical habits. They have brought these to an empty continent and it has taken them centuries not merely to fill that continent, but to create ways of life adapted to a different climate, to a different set of economic possibilities, and to a society held together at its beginnings by imported political and social habits, and only slowly and with repeated crises creating American political and social habits to replace the European importations that, with each decade, wore thinner and thinner like an old carpet. In this process the modern American has been created; the interplay of geographic, biological, historical forces has made him."

In his own society the American sociologist finds a suitable laboratory for answering the question why so many cultures are different in so many different environments and why all cultures differ as they change in the time cycle. In his *The American People,* Geoffrey Gorer has at-

tempted a summary of some of the ongoings of this American laboratory. He says on page 245, "During nearly two centuries men, women,
and children have abandoned their homes and countries and crossed
the oceans to the United States of North America, carrying with them
the hope of finding there some freedom or opportunity that their country of birth could not or did not give them. They made the journey as
individuals, at most as small families, united only negatively by their
rejection of the countries they had left behind. The original settlement,
made by loyal Englishmen and by Englishmen who had rejected English
tyranny, succeeded in unparalleled fashion in assimilating these millions
from all over the world, giving their children a common American
character and unwittingly, almost inadvertently, forming a nation. The
advance of democracy in the old world involved the lessening of the
rights of the state and the increase in the rights of the individual.
Uniquely, America did not start as a state, but as millions of individuals
seeking their own advantage."

Finally, to take a single example of our American historians, Werten-
baker writes about "An Old World in a New Mould" when, on page 1
of his *The Founding of American Civilization*, he says, "The most stu-
pendous phenomenon of all history is the transit of European civilizations to the two American continents. For four and a half centuries Europeans have been crossing the Atlantic to establish in a new world their
blood, languages, religions, political institutions, agriculture, commerce,
industries, literatures, arts, customs. This movement, involving many
nations and millions of men and women, has been termed the expansion
of Europe, or the creation of a new Europe in America." For the American sociologist, this was the first big breakaway from the European
anthropology that set Europe as the creator of modern western culture
and European man as the subject of anthropology.

For sociology, then, America *had to be* the supreme living social laboratory, challenging the new science to set its frame of reference not only for
the study of American society and for the attainment of a democratic
order, but for initiating new scientific ways of measuring societal phenomena, analyzing results, and testing them in a new world laboratory.
This might set the incidence for new reaches in the dynamics of a more
realistic sociology of knowledge. The extraordinary sweep of science and
technology and the tremendous impact of all this on the people, together

with the new impact of intercultural and international relationships, constituted the obligation and opportunity for American sociology to become the most advanced in the history of human society.

American Transitional Society as Laboratory

Perhaps, however, America as the laboratory for the study of *transitional society* in the framework of a rapidly changing social structure became the central base for American sociology's new participation. This problem of transitional society, with the increasing complexity of the American experience, is reflected not only in social change or studies in *Recent Social Trends* but also in the past history of the nation as well as in the current dilemmas that condition future economic and social arrangements. To pass over theoretical premises of the continuity of the social process in all society and come directly to the United States, there was first of all the transition from the Jeffersonian small nation of rural states, of one or two regions of simple motivation, of homogeneity of people, of few occupations, with small individual fortunes centered chiefly in farm and forest, in land and homes, of simple and religious culture, to the present very large nation of urban and industrial majorities, in greatly differing regions with complex motivation and heterogeneity of population, with hundreds of varied occupations, with large individual fortunes, with fabulous salaries, with corporate holdings and wealth not only in farm lands and commodities, but also in city real estate, factories, railroads, traction and steamship lines, coal and iron, stores, banks, utilities, amusements, food, tobacco, textiles, furniture, rubber, leather, glass, machinery, automobiles, metal, petroleum, power, soap, drugs, and innumerable consumers' goods.

In "Orderly Transitional Democracy," in *The Annals* of the American Academy of Political and Social Science for July, 1935, I have enumerated some of the levels of transition. There was a transition from slaves to free men in sectional realignment, in a disorderly war of brothers stranger than fiction, which set the incidence for national expansion, corporate wealth, uneven distribution of wealth, and for class and regional conflict. There was a transition from agrarian culture and rural folk to industrial life and urbanization; from isolation to international contacts and back to nationalism; from lack of education to universal education; from illiteracy to a new literacy fearfully and wonderfully fabricated. There was the gradual but sure transition from the sacred to the secular. Again, there was the transition from the rule of the few to the dominance of the many; from a man's world to a new world in which women assume increasingly larger influence; from the authority of the elders to the questioning of youth; from state and local priority to federal centralization and back to regional structures; from the human, man-land, man-labor emphasis to technology; from ideologies to science; from a producers' to a consumers' technological world where "the better you live the more oil you use." And there was the greatest of all transitions to be made between primary individuation and primary socialization in the setting of peace to war, to war to peace, to atomic war, to the processes of societal survival.

The Bernard and Barnes Recordings

But to return to the earlier period of American sociology and its dichotomy of European and American backgrounds, the two leading historians of the sociological movement in America, L. L. Bernard and Harry Elmer Barnes, agree upon the general European influence but with different emphasis upon the American incidence of the new science.

The Bernards, in *Origins of American Sociology*, find the beginnings in a series of movements and organizations that combined a spirit of reform and a zeal for scientific study drawn from European philosophical and scientific currents. The first stage of this process is identified as the Associationist Movement of the 1840's, which was a transplantation of Fourierism. When the Comtean influence began to be felt, mainly through the writings of J. S. Mill, Buckle, and Spencer, the impetus for an American Social Science Association in 1865 was established. The Association derived from the Massachusetts Board of State Charities in 1863, which was concerned with facts as well as with melioration. The "problem" emphasis, however, was not continued for long, being diverted into special channels, leaving the main stream to develop into a powerful academic social science movement, of which sociology was one of the main tributaries. In 1870, the National Prison Association broke away. In succeeding years were formed the American Historical Association, the American Political Science Association, the American Sociological Society, the American Economic Association, the Philadelphia Social Science Association developing into the notable American Academy of Political and Social Science which reflected autonomous movements in the wider social science movement. Considerably weakened by this development, the Association experienced a final split between the social work aspect and the theoretical aspect in the emergence of the National Conference of Charities and Correction (later the National Conference of Social Work) on the one hand, and in academic social science on the other. From this point on, sociology, as one of the integral social sciences, has been nurtured in the college and the university soil of a rapidly growing republic.

How uniformly the separation of social work from sociology has gone on may be seen from an examination of the current schools and departments of social work in the United States. It is notable that the trend in social work, even as in sociology, has been almost completely toward academic status, since no school affiliated with the American Association of Schools of Social Work now is not identified with a college or a university. At the same time, with one or two possible exceptions, the deans, directors, and heads of departments are no longer sociologists, nor are the courses in social work under the administration of departments of sociology. Of the fifty-three member schools of the Association all are organized as "schools," except for ten "departments" and one "institute." Twenty of the member schools are in state universities. In the total fifty-three are representatives of no less than thirty-six states. Of those who went from sociology to social work, as administrative heads, are Niles Carpenter of Buffalo, J. J. Rhyne of Oklahoma, Coyle E. Moore of Florida State, Arthur Beely of Utah. On the other hand, in place of Bogardus at Southern California is Arline Johnson; in place of Gillin at Wisconsin, Arthur P. Miles; in place of Chapin at Minnesota, John C. Kidneigh; in place of Odum at North Carolina, Arthur E. Fink; instead of Steiner at Washington, William McCullough; instead of Cutler at Western Reserve, Margaret Johnson. No less than twenty of the administrative heads are women, most of whom came to their tasks from the professional field of social work.

Barnes, in his *Introduction to the History of Sociology,* does not concern himself primarily with the origin of American sociology or directly with its American problem-origins. However, he seems to build his discussion of American sociology around the process of sociological European borrowing. Both Ward and Sumner are described as interpreters,

Sumner as "Spencerianism in American Dress." They are the "pioneers of [American] sociology," according to Barnes, though a great deal of their work derives from the work of Comte, Spencer, Darwin, Wundt, Ratzenhofer, and Gumplowicz. Later American sociologists — Ross, Giddings, Small, Cooley, Thomas, Ellwood, Stuckenberg, Hayes — are also presented as being influenced, not by an indigenous movement, but by such European thinkers as Mill, Karl Pearson, Durkheim, Darwin, Adam Smith, Sombart, and others.

Three American Developments

Three main American developments, however, must not be overlooked, as contributing greatly to the channeling of American sociology into its ultimate course. One of these was no more nor less than the normal and logical development of American education and American literature to include an increasing emphasis upon matters of social concern, with a sort of wholesome merging of the literary, the religious, and the philosophical ideologies into the American Dream. This influence has been consistent all the way along and runs as a thread through the later development of sociology as it contributed to the university curriculum and the social consciousness of the nation. Needless to say that the same tendency has been recorded in the history of American economics and political science.

Another development was clearly one which featured the moral emphasis and motivation, in which social ethics tended to be incorporated into education, literature, and the social sciences, concerned especially with social conduct, justice, morality. This trend can be relatively clearly defined in the later story of the beginnings of sociology in the various American institutions. More indirectly, the attempt on the part of certain economists and industrialists to apply sociology to rationalize economic behavior and especially classical economics and slavery with the subsequent contrary ideologies may well be listed as a part of the earlier sociological movement. Representative of the earlier simpler forms of this was John R. Commons' and Richard T. Ely's move to found an American Institute of Christian Sociology. Perhaps the third factor was the most direct conditioning influence, however, namely, the emphasis and the writings on many social problems in America, such as immigration, urbanism, poverty and dependency, and the increasing dilemmas of adjustment of European immigrants to a new world of Americans, to a changing economic nation, with the resulting tendencies toward crime, delinquency, and group conflicts.

How American sociology developed from this point on may be indicated in two ways. The first is to note the earlier beginnings of sociology as a study of social problems and to trace that movement as it led to the development of the National Conference of Charities and Correction, which became the National Conference of Social Work in 1918. Within this conference there grew up a score of subdivisions with their special problem areas, such as child welfare, delinquency, community problems, and family case work. All this was in great contrast to the subsequent split-off from the general "problems" approach and to the university departments of sociology as described above. The second way in which this problem approach may be noted is in the charter statements of the earlier departments of sociology, which give their reasons for establishing this new discipline of sociology. In these, the stated problem-basis of the origin and nature of sociology was somewhat in contrast to the later developments of the departments that featured primarily social theory.

The Columbia University Statement

An example may be cited in Columbia University, which for many years had little to do with social work or social problems. In 1894, in announcing its chair of sociology, the following statement gives emphatic evidence of the problem-situation backgrounds. "It is becoming more and more apparent," the statement reads, "that industrial and social progress is bringing the modern community face to face with social questions of the greatest magnitude, the solution of which will demand the best scientific study and the most honest practical endeavor. The term 'sociology,' however it may be defined, includes a large number of the subjects which are most seriously interesting men at the present time. The effective treatment of social problems demands that they be dealt with both theoretically and concretely." More of the prospectus is quoted in Frank L. Tolman in "Study of Sociology in Institutions of Learning in the United States," *The American Journal of Sociology*, Vol. 7, 799–838, "The trustees have recently appointed a special professor of sociology, whose function it shall be to develop the theoretical teaching of sociology proper, and to direct the students in practical sociological work."

Here Giddings, who prepared the statement, was foreshadowing sociology's dichotomy of *General Sociology* and *Special Sociology,* so much epitomized in the story of American sociology. The statement continues, "This newly established chair will provide for a thorough study of philosophical or general sociology and of the practical or concrete social questions in their relation to sociological principles. By the term 'general sociology' is meant the scientific study of society as a whole, a search for its causes, for the laws of its structure and growth, and for a rational view of its purpose, function, meaning, or destiny. This will lead up to the more particular study of the phenomena of modern populations and their concentration in great cities. Of such phenomena none are of greater concern, from either the theoretical or practical point of view, than the growth and characteristics of the dependent, defective, and delinquent classes. Special courses of instruction will, therefore, be offered on pauperism, poor laws, methods of charity, crime, penology, and social ethics.

"It is in the city that the problems of poverty, of mendicancy, of intemperance, of unsanitary surroundings, and of debasing social influences are met in their most acute form. Hence the city is the natural laboratory of social science."

Thus Columbia University's argument on behalf of sociology may well serve as preview to the study of the problem-basis upon which American sociology was founded, which is discussed more critically in Chapter 16. In the first place, it coincides with our definition of sociology as primarily a college and university discipline and our "take-off" may well be from this vantage point. But, in the next place, it sets the framework of American sociology in the logical needs of both university education and of American society as it grew apace. And it is symbolic of that normal development of a new field which led Albion W. Small, in "Fifty Years of Sociology in the United States," in the May, 1916, issue of *The American Journal of Sociology,* page 724, to insist that the sociological movement was a child of its time like every other thought movement. "It was," he said, "not an isolated, alien, detached curiosity. It was a part of the orderly unfolding of native conditions." And the Columbia statement serves as a marker on the road, looking both ways:

backward to those general and specific situations that contributed to
sociology's growth, and forward to those developments that were to be
both prophetic of the future and somewhat contradictory to its main
premises.

Sociology and the Enlightenment in a Changing America

Returning now to the rise of sociology in the United States as a logical
development in the new American society, we note again something of
the parallel between sociology and the literature of liberalism and of
criticism. Thus Vernon L. Parrington, in his *Main Currents of American Thought,* in 1927 comes logically to what he calls "Sociology and
the Enlightenment" from a review of "Changing America," Volume
III, page 189, "Another world of thought and experience was rising
above the horizon," and again he refers to this as "a world in which
the divinities were science and the machine." Parrington points out
further how "for six generations the pattern of life had been woven
by the impulse of dispersion that in scattering men along a wide frontier
had disintegrated the philosophies and rejected the social order brought
from the old world, transforming America into such a society of free
men as the Enlightenment had dreamed of — decentralized, individualistic, democratic. Dispersion, disintegration, individualism, anarchism
— such was the inevitable drift under the compulsions of a fluid economics and frontier ways, of which the ultimate philosophical expression
had been Thoreau at Walden Pond, discovering in his bean patch the
same anarchistic principles that Godwin had learned of the French na-
turists — of which the prophet had been Walt Whitman, dreaming
amidst the formless crowds of Manhattan his generous dreams of the
democratic brotherhood — and of which Jay Gould the sordid wrecker
in Wall Street was the prosaic reality."

How the Industrial Revolution, whose new machines had created
great cities, was "to undo in a few brief years the long work of the dispersion, repudiate the ideals of the Enlightenment, and provide a new
pattern for a consolidating urban society," has been reflected in sociology's dichotomy of rural and urban sociology and its later studies of the
universal processes of development from the folk society to state civilization. Thus appeared the tendency toward concentration, "with its compulsions to reintegration and conformity — the imperious subjection of

the individual to a standardizing order, the stripping away of the slack frontier freedoms in the routine of the factory, the substitution of the ideal of plutocracy for the ideal of Jacksonian democracy."

How the need for sociology to fathom the problems of America paralleled the development of American civilization was illustrated by Parrington when he pointed out how the "work of the machine was hastened by the new spirit of science that spread silently through the land, effecting a revolution in men's thinking as great as the machine was effecting in men's lives. Provincial America had been theological — and political-minded; but with the staying of the dispersion and the creation of an urban psychology, the ground was prepared for the reception of new philosophies that came from the contemplation of the laws of the material universe."

It is profitable to compare Lester F. Ward's challenge of sociology to do something about societal planning with the authentic history of American culture. Thus Parrington again, on page 189, says, "The incoming of science had two immediate results: the application of technology to industry that was to further the Industrial Revolution; and the impact on speculative thought of the newly discovered laws of science that was to create a new philosophy. In the second of these twin influences lay an intellectual revolution that was to disintegrate the old theological cosmos, push far back the boundaries of space and time, reorient the mind towards all ultimate problems, and bring into question all the traditional faiths — political and social as well as theological and philosophical. Out of science was to come a new spirit of criticism and realism that was to set the pattern for later thought."

How the changing structure of American society set the incidence for sociology's attempt to evolve sound theory for the solution of current problems is also paralleled by the later application by European sociologists to the problems of a complex civilization and to social planning. In the United States, Van Wyck Brooks, in his *Times of Melville and Whitman,* on pages 465 and 466, tells of the great change from rural to urban life, using Lester F. Ward's growing up as a boy in what was then the Middle West as a sort of "ideal type" in America, namely, "the sociologist who began as a Western farmhand." "But," he continues, "the life-hungry natives of the backwoods communities, the sons and daughters of the farms were pouring by hundreds of thousands into the cities, caught by their glamour and their lights, their crowds and shows. The rural life, like the life of the sea in Cooper and Melville and Dana, had lost its pre-eminence and its magic in the minds of the masses. With the growth of the cities the power of money had also grown in a sinister way and poverty was increasing along with this."

How these developments created the field and the method both for the new liberalism and sociological emphasis was pointed out, as ". . . Meanwhile, New York was becoming the almshouse of the poor of half the planet, and foreign countries were deliberately dumping their paupers and criminals in the United States, their blind, their crippled, their insane. Several of the continental nations were making the town a penal colony, and its slums were rapidly approaching the European level," with "hordes of peasants a thousand miles removed from the educated freemen who had founded and maintained the republic."

The American Literary Parallel

Walt Whitman, described as the Poet of American Democracy and Equality, and forerunner of the twentieth century sociological inquiry into the newer problems of intercultural and ethnic relations, "disturbed by the spread of poverty in the United States, was shocked by something he saw in 1879, two good-looking young Americans carrying bags and iron hooks, plodding along spying for rags and bones. It astonished him as similar sights astonished the novelist Howells in a country where Thomas Jefferson had never seen a pauper, where few had ever thought of a pauper existing, and he felt that if, like the countries of Europe, we grew vast crops of desperate nomads it would mean that our republican experiment had utterly failed." So, too, in American literature as in American sociology, as reflected by Van Wyck Brooks on pages 467 and 471 of his *Times of Melville and Whitman,* of the "many writers [who] were alarmed by the growing division of classes and the spread of poverty along with the increase of wealth, Melville, for one . . . had been deeply aware of the poverty of England in *Redburn* and was one of the first to be aroused in the United States. In *The Tartarus of Maids* he had attacked the horrors of the industrial system in one of the paper mills of the Berkshire region, as he had satirized in *The Confidence-Man* the growing greed for money, which made fools or knaves of most of the people in the book. Sidney Lanier who, like Melville and Whitman, would have preferred an agrarian system, was up in arms against the regime of trade, and Mark Twain, capitalist that he was, said that the unionized workman was the greatest of all the births of the greatest of ages."

It is important to note here that Lester F. Ward, along with Henry George and Thorstein Veblen, was recognized by the literary historians as a dynamic force in the new inquiry into American life. Thus Van Wyck Brooks points out on page 471 of the *Times of Melville and Whitman* that ". . . meanwhile, Lester F. Ward, who never became a socialist, was also obsessed with the problems of the submerged and the poor, attacking monopolistic privilege and dwelling on the need of education as the chief hope of the masses and the underman. Lester Ward, like Henry George, had something in common with Thorstein Veblen, who was to acknowledge him later as a precursor of his own, and George himself acclaimed a work that Lester Ward's brother, who was also a printer, had written and set up in type with his own hands. Cyrenus Ward's *The Ancient Lowly* was a vast untidy pioneer book on the life of the working classes of the ancient world, presenting an astonishing body of facts, suppressed or ignored by historians and scholars, on the organizations and strikes of the workers of old."

Influence of Sociologists on American Life

We have already pointed out in Chapter 1 how the concern for social justice and the multiplying problems in American social structure became the field for a vast American literature of criticism and "sociological" emphasis. In Chapters 24 and 25 we indicate measures of the influence of American culture on sociology and of sociology on American culture. It seems likely that American sociologists have rarely been credited with much of the background and motivation for a large part of this literature. It might well be assumed that teachers of sociology had been responsible for about the same amount of sociological emphasis and form in literature as, let us say, teachers of English were responsible for distinguished writing on the level of fiction and biography. Yet, perhaps the quest for justice and equality as a part of the American Dream, alongside the search for ways of solving problems of poverty and dependency, may have been reflected in the Walt Whitman general dream of a world of small owners, a country of homesteads without poverty or wealth. But neither Whitman nor the other liberals could be pinned down to specific workable programs. A part of this was no doubt due to the rise, experimentation, and failure of the Utopian or Associationist Movement which never caught on with American sociology, although a part of the American background.

Utopian Approach to American Culture Economy

Of and by the Utopian ideology and practice, the Bernards estimate on page 104 and following, of *Origins of American Sociology,* that there were no less than thirty-three colonies organized in the United States along the lines of Fourierism. They quoted Waterman as giving the number at forty and Noyes at thirty-four. Bernard points out that the West Roxbury Community, founded by George Ripley at the suggestion of Dr. Channing, became the most famous of all, under the name of the Brook Farm Phalanx, and the center of the whole Association movement in the United States. The total number of phalanxes were distributed somewhat as follows: eight in Ohio; six in New York; six in Pennsylvania; three in Massachusetts; three in Illinois; two in New Jersey; two in Michigan; two in Wisconsin; and one each in Indiana and Iowa. The enthusiasm and high motivation reflected in the earlier stages were manifest in the first annual convention of "The Friends of Association based upon the Truths of Social Science," whose resolution Bernard quotes. They resolved: "that with a solemn sense of our responsibilities as advocates of the cause of Universal Unity, with an earnest desire to secure consistent cooperation among the Associations of the United States, and to prevent in the outset all possibility of those disunions among Associations, which waste the resources and paralyze the energies of existing Society, we hereby declare that, in our opinion, the time has arrived, when it becomes the imperative duty of the several Associations in our country, which are based upon the truths of Social Science as announced by Fourier, to take measures for the immediate formation of a Union of Associations."

All of these efforts constituted a series of interesting chapters more in American history than in the story of American sociology yet they were apparently essential stages as witnessed by their influence upon many American scholars, such as the economists John Bates Clark, John R. Commons and Richard T. Ely. All the experimental phalanxes were ultimately disbanded, and they therefore constituted more of a background than an integral part of sociology or economics. There were several reasons why they failed. The chief one was that they represented a movement of isolated intellectuals and moralists too far afield from reality to become an enduring part of the rugged American folk society irresistibly forging its powerful frontier society, even as many of the 1950 intellectual and moral isolationists could not sense the dynamics and complexity of contemporary state civilization. The ideologies that were projected were far and away beyond any organizational and community specifications capable of building enduring societies. Their demands exceeded the capacity and experience of their constituents. So, too, isolated units and phalanxes were in no way integrated with the realistic whole of American society, nor did they ever provide for the total elements of human society in their specifications.

A part of the failure of the Utopias is explained by A. E. Bestor, Jr., in his 1950 *Backwoods Utopias,* on the ground that the communities did not succeed in the communitarian point of view and practice. That is, the first failures were simply those of each individual community and had no cumulative effect upon others that followed. This premise, however, does have considerable bearing upon later situations insofar as the complexity of society and the interrelationship with big-time corporations and centralized government would make unlikely the culture-economy of communitarianism. It also gives focus to the trends toward community organization and autonomy as substitutes for too much mechanization of control in the contemporary state civilization.

The American Social Science Association

Now, returning again to the "problem" backgrounds of early American sociology, the situation can probably best be described by citing the language which summarized what progressive education was later to call the "felt needs" of those leaders who were seeking to make articulate the new social science from which later branched off sociology, social work, and to some extent certain special aspects of political economy. The circular for the organization of a social science group was issued, according to pages 540–41 of *Origins of American Sociology,* by the Massachusetts Board of State Charities on August 2, 1865. This was indicative of the backgrounds as were the leaders who signed the call, namely, Nathan Allen, Edward Earle, H. B. Wheelwright, F. B. Sanborn, Theodore Metcalf, J. C. Blaisdell, and S. G. Howe. The circular itself read as follows: "Our attention has lately been called to the importance of some organization in the United States, both local and national, whose object shall be the discussion of those questions relating to the Sanitary Condition of the People, the Relief, Employment, and Education of the Poor, the Prevention of Crime, the Amelioration of the Criminal Law, the Discipline of Prisons, the Remedial Treatment of the Insane, and those numerous matters of statistical and philanthropic interest which are included under the general head of Social Science. An association for the consideration of these questions has existed in Great Britain for several years, including among its members many of the most eminent philanthropists and statistical writers of that country. Its published proceedings have been of great service to England and to the world."

The Bernards' researches indicate this call was answered by about three hundred people who met on October 4, 1865, and organized the American Association for the Promotion of Social Science. The further nature of the organization may be seen through an examination of the final wording of the constitution. The original constitution, as finally adopted, stated the objectives of the American Social Science Association, according to the Bernards, on page 562, as follows: "to aid the development of Social Science, and to guide the public mind to the best practical means of promoting the Amendment of Laws, the Advancement of Education, the Prevention and Repression of Crime, the Reformation of Criminals, and the progress of Public Morality, the adoption of Sanitary Regulations, and the diffusion of sound principles on the Questions of Economy, Trade, and Finance. It will give attention to Pauperism and the topics related thereto; including the responsibility of the well-endowed and successful, and the wise and educated, the honest and respectable, for the failures of others. It will aim to bring together the various societies and individuals now interested in these objects, for the purpose of obtaining by discussion the real elements of Truth; by which doubts are removed, conflicting opinions harmonized, and a common ground afforded for treating wisely the great social problems of the day."

Science and Reform

The enthusiastic movement toward the establishment of a social science was "sociological," as measured by the later developments of American sociology in two or three ways. That is, it sought measurement in the study of society and it sought to delineate problems that might be isolated, studied, and described for subsequent "solution." The Bernards, on page 845, estimated the movement as transitional, ending "by seeking (1) to construct a theory of social organization and evolution which would provide an adequate blue print for detailed human betterment and (2) to work out through a careful application of scientific methods, largely quantitative in character, those concrete steps in social reform, mainly through legislation and cooperative private endeavor, which would fill out this larger abstract pattern of an ideal social order. In the end, the movement was both systematic and opportunistic or piecemeal."

How the two main elements that characterized the American social science movement came to the parting of the ways has been indicated in Chapter 2 on "The European Heritage." The Bernards have pointed out, on pages 845–46, how the "two ruling motivations were a passion for social reform and an adoration of science. The first of these was by all odds much the more emphasized in the early period. When, however, half a century later Social Science emerged from a period during which the ideas of Comte had seethed and bubbled throughout the intellectual world, the passion for reform was, for the time being at least, somewhat spent. It was becoming decidedly secondary to the growing worship of science. Indeed, in our day there are sociologists who wish entirely to repudiate the reformistic tradition in their science."

Personalities in the American Scene

How the earlier American "problem" and popular backgrounds of sociology contrast with the later European and theoretical sociology may be seen from a study of those individuals who were most articulate in the pre-sociological era as well as from an examination of the presidents and addresses of the National Conference of Social Work as contrasted with those of the American Sociological Society. There is here little common ground of the meeting of ideas and persons and little overlapping of personalities. On the other hand, the personalities who most influenced the American sociologists themselves were the European social theorists listed in Chapter 2.

Of those whose work and influence appeared to be worthy of recording, the Bernards list approximately a hundred. Many of these are not well known to American sociologists, although the names of a few are recognized as prominent in American life. Among these would be Bancroft, Barnard, Brisbane, Carey, the Channings, De Bow, Fairbanks, Finley, Fitzhugh, George, Gilman, Greeley, Howe, the Owens, the Walkers, and Andrew White. Among others cited by Bernard are: J. T. and John Adams, J. H. and Nathan Allen, Stephen Andrew, Edward Atkinson, Lyman Atwater, Alexander Bain, Adin Ballou, John Bascom, W. F. Blackman, Calvin Blanchard, Francis Bowen, Jeffrey Brackett, George H. Calvert, John W. Chadwick, James Freeman Clarke, Stephen Colwell, George W. Curtis, Alexander Delmar, John W. Draper, Henry Edger, William Elder, George H. Evans, Octavius Brooks Frothingham, Parke Godwin, William Godwin, Robert S. Hamilton, W. T. Harris, David Hartley, Richmond L. Hawkins, Samuel Hazard.

Not all of the list, however, is merely a catalogue of names. Amos G. Warner was to help found a university department of sociology. Carroll D. Wright was to write a sociology text utilizing census data. Frank B. Sanborn was forerunner of a new Cornell. Still others listed included George F. Holmes, Edward Howland, Marie Howland, Freeman Hunt, E. J. James, Edward Jarvis, Lawrence C. Johnson, John Koren, Karl H. Lashley, George H. Lewes, John McClintock, James McCosh, Edward D. Mansfield, Lewis Masquerier, John Monesca, Oliver S. Munsell, H. C. Murphy, S. N. D. North, Josiah C. Nott, John Humphrey Noyes, James O'Connell, Thomas Paine, William Paley, Theodore Parker, A. P. Peabody, Arthur L. Perry, Timothy Pitkin, George Ripley, Frank B. Sanborn, Edwin J. Schellhous, E. Peshine Smith, Goldwin Smith, Simon Stern, Dugald Stewart, Augustus H. Strong, William Strong, Robert Ellis Thompson, George Tucker, Henry Villard, Horace B. Wallace, Amos G. Warner, Josiah Warren, Francis Wayland, David A. Wells, Francis Wharton, Theodore D. Woolsey, Carroll D. Wright, R. J. Wright, and E. L. Youmans.

The National Conference of Social Work

Perhaps, of the university men, only Richmond Mayo Smith and Carroll D. Wright of the pre-statistical sociological era, and Andrew White of Cornell and Daniel Coit Gilman of Johns Hopkins are very well known to the later generations of sociologists, although Sanborn of Cornell and Adams of Hopkins are sometimes featured. So, too, the early notable leaders who became presidents of the National Conference of Charities and Correction and the National Conference of Social Work seem to have been relatively little acquainted with or known by the leading American sociologists, although by 1950 at least a half dozen of the presidents had been professors in universities.

However, something of the relation between social work and emerging sociology may be seen from a comparison of the presidents of the National Conference of Social Work with the presidents of the American Sociological Society. Only one of the presidents of the National Conference from 1874 to 1950, C. R. Henderson in 1899, might be classified as a sociologist, although Bruno and Kelso came near enough to work closely with them, while Hastings Hart and Jane Addams were perennial bridges between the two groups. The roll of presidents included, on the contrary, primarily workers in the field: ministers, educators, social workers, publishers, newspaper people, philanthropists, lawyers. The mere roll call of the presidents of the National Conference of Social Work, nearly twice as many as of the American Sociological Society, constitutes an exercise in the understanding of the background of American sociology. The personalities of these leaders, together with the gallery of their photographs set in the time schedule becomes an elemental part of the essential record.

1874—J. V. L. Pruyn	1883—Fred H. Wines
1875—John J. Bagley	1884—William P. Letchworth
1876—Samuel J. Tilden	1885—Phillip C. Garrett
1877—J. V. L. Pruyn	1886—William Howard Neff
1878—R. M. Bishop	1887—H. H. Giles
1879—G. S. Robinson	1888—Charles S. Hoyt
1880—Roeliff Brinkerhoff	1889—George D. Gillespie
1881—F. B. Sanborn	1890—A. G. Byers
1882—Andrew E. Elmore	1891—Oscar C. McCulloch

1892—Myron W. Reed
1893—Hastings H. Hart
1894—Lucius C. Storrs
1895—Robert Treat Paine
1896—Albert O. Wright
1897—Alexander Johnson
1898—William R. Stewart
1899—C. R. Henderson
1900—Charles E. Faulkner
1901—John M. Glenn
1902—Timothy Nicholson
1903—Robert W. De Forest
1904—Jeffrey R. Brackett
1905—Samuel G. Smith
1906—Edward T. Devine
1907—Amos W. Butler
1908—Thomas M. Mulry
1909—Ernest P. Bicknell
1910—Jane Addams
1911—Homer Folks
1912—Julian W. Mack
1913—Frank Tucker
1914—Graham Taylor
1915—Mary Willcox Glenn
1916—Francis H. Gavisk
1917—Frederic Almy
1918—Robert A. Woods
1919—Julia C. Lathrop
1920—Owen R. Lovejoy
1921—Allen T. Burns

1922—Robert W. Kelso
1923—Homer Folks
1924—Grace Abbott
1925—William J. Norton
1926—Gertrude Vaile
1927—John A. Lapp
1928—Sherman C. Kingsley
1929—Porter R. Lee
1930—Miriam Van Waters
1931—Richard C. Cabot
1932—C. M. Bookman
1933—Frank J. Bruno
1934—William Hodson
1935—Katharine F. Lenroot
1936—Robert F. Keegan
1937—Edith Abbott
1938—Solomon Lowenstein
1939—Paul Kellogg
1940—Grace L. Coyle
1941—Jane M. Hoey
1942—Shelby Harrison
1943—Fred K. Hoehler
1944—Elizabeth Wisner
1945—Ellen C. Potter
1946—K. L. M. Pray
1947—Arlien Johnson
1948—Leonard W. Mayo
1949—Ralph Blanchard
1950—Martha M. Eliot

The titles of presidential addresses read before the National Conference indicate the varied, yet consistent fields of interest, often in contrast
to those of the sociologists as given in Chapter 1. Among the earlier subjects were: "State and National Registration of the Dependent, the Defective, and the Delinquent Classes"; "The Relation of the National
Conference of Charities and Correction to the Progress of the Past
Twenty Years"; "The Empire of Charity"; "The New Philanthropy";
"The Mother-State and Her Weaker Children"; "The Duty of the State
to the Erring and Dependent"; "The Relation of Philanthropy to Social
Order and Progress"; "Twentieth-century Alignments for the Promotion of Social Order"; "The Worker: Purpose and Preparation"; "The

Dominant Note of the Modern Philanthropy"; "The Burden of Feeble-Mindedness"; "Disaster Relief and Its Problems"; "Charity and Social Justice."

From 1918, when the National Conference of Charities and Correction became the National Conference of Social Work, the titles of the presidential addresses indicate more of the professional and scientific approach to social work and its evaluation as a part of the democratic process. Among the titles were: "Child Welfare Standards: A Test of Democracy"; "The Faith of a Social Worker"; "Does Social Work Promote Social Progress?"; "Changing Fundamentals of Social Work"; "Prevention Succeeds"; "Public Protection of Children"; "What Is Social Work?"; "Who Needs Social Service?"; "Social Work: Cause and Function"; "Philosophical Trends in Modern Social Work"; "The Social Consequences and Treatment of Unemployment"; "Social Work Objectives in the New Era"; "The Social Worker in the New Deal"; "Social Work and the Social Order"; "Democracy at the Crossroads"; "Public Assistance — Whither Bound?"; "The Test of American Democracy."

Earlier in this chapter we pointed out the essential nature of contemporary society as being peculiarly transitional at a time when America approached the mid-century mark of 1950. Bernard had noted a similar situation in the rise of the social science movement and its struggle in the transitional period following the Civil War. The social science movement was transitional in a triple sense: "first in its emphases, second in its concept of science in general, and, finally, in its concept and method of approach to social reform. In spite of the complete transformation in both the scientific and the reform aspects of the new discipline, Social Science remained throughout its history more of a vision and an aspiration than a scientific reality." In some ways the earlier social science movement reminds one of the same sort of dilemma described by Gunnar Myrdal in his *American Dilemma,* as the problem of distance between the American Dream and American fulfillment. As Bernard put it, there was the same situation, "Whether blue-printing Utopias in the clouds or puttering with babies in the slums, whether appealing to Utopian natural law or to idealized science, Social Science epitomized always the tough hard strain of idealism which, from the beginning of the Republic, has characterized the American people. A very noble impatience with social and economic injustice, and an earnest determination to do something about it — that was Social Science."

The two ideals, science and reform, however, became divorced and went their separate ways. One became academic sociology, economics, political science, and the other social work and "philanthropy." The American social science dream was transcended by the European influence, which later developed into the American method, which was still again greatly influenced by the revivification of European theory in the 1940's. In the earlier transitional era was the beginning of the American blend, which by 1950 was to supersede the European form and tradition. And in between, an epochal half century recorded the phenomenal "market" for college and university sociology in a growth from a quarter million college students in 1900 to more than two and a half million by 1950 with national educational leaders predicting double this enrollment by 1960. By 1950 there were more than fifty American universities offering the Ph.D. degree in sociology and 1810 accredited institutions eligible for undergraduate sociology.

PART II

American Sociology as American Sociologists: The Presidents of the American Sociological Society

CHAPTER 4

The First Big Four, 1906–1913: Ward, Sumner, Giddings, Small

In the beginning of the American blend of sociology, the work of the few earlier sociologists was different from that of the many later sociologists in somewhat the same way in which the pioneering of the frontiersmen was different from those who followed to consolidate gains and to attain specialization. A biography entitled "Franklin Henry Giddings, American Fontiersman" would not be out of place. Lester F. Ward would not only be "The American Aristotle" but a pioneer in academic sociology blazing new trails. William Graham Sumner, commonly designated as exponent of laissez faire, nevertheless trod over unbroken new grounds of broad research in virgin territory like some Paul Bunyan's Blue Ox. And Albion W. Small devoted most of his later life to the task of justifying his pioneering in sociology, and, like a Frederick Jackson Turner in history, to defining American sociology as a new frontier. These men were frontiersmen, breaking new grounds, clearing new vistas, blazing new trails, discovering new areas, defending themselves from attack, pushing on again and founding new dynasties with their students and followers.

This means, of course, that the range and nature of their work were different from that of those who would come later to mature the new science and to emulate the other sciences. It means that they had to budgetize their time and energy for the felling of trees and the building of cabins with little leisure time for the refinements of research and the empirical study of more pretentious mansions. There was still another way in which the early pioneers were occupied that was different from the way in which the later generations worked. This was in their role of establishing the subject of sociology in the curriculum, identifying it with a department, popularizing it with administration, faculty, and students, attending conferences to give weight and dignity to the new subject, and making contributions to the general morale of the growing American college and university. Also, since there had been no instruction in formal sociology, there were none who came to the new social science with academic sociological preparation except through European sources. Theirs was to create and to achieve where none had gone before and with no distinguished academic heritage, except what they got from European and philosophical backgrounds.

We have characterized Ward, Sumner, Giddings, and Small as the first Big Four for several reasons. In the first place they were not only pioneers but each came quickly to achieve his own full-grown prestige in the university world of sociology at Brown, Yale, Columbia, and Chicago, although Ward's university status was more the product of his contributions than the medium for developing his work. These four were also chronologically the first four in the hierarchy of the presidents of the American Sociological Society. Their published works quickly assumed the proportions of the foundations of sociology which were to become required readings and "classics" in the bibliographies of American sociology. Their immediate contemporaries, Ross, Vincent, Blackmar, Howard, Weatherly, Cooley, Thomas, and Ellwood achieved their leadership through the slow, long, and hard way of working gradually through other fields up to major university status while a few of these, although doing yeoman service to sociology, never achieved major contributions to the literature of the new science. Each of the Big Four held the office of president of the American Sociological Society for two years. Each ranked high in the councils of his own university and in public esteem, and each lived beyond his three score years and ten. Yet each was so different from the others as to defy comparison on the same levels except in their ex-officio top places in early sociology in the United States.

Nevertheless, there has often been good-natured rivalry among their admirers over which one should be called the "Dean of American Sociology." Evidence and arguments have been put forth to indicate the rela-

tive influence and contributions of each which might justify his designation as "America's First Sociologist," measured by his permanent
place in the total story of sociology in the United States. Sometimes
these estimates have been presented primarily simply as vivid ways of
interpreting the work of each to students, and sometimes as an effort to
define the field of early sociology by identifying each as "first" in certain
aspects of sociological work. Sometimes the claims have been based upon
a sort of composite index of their influence upon students and sociology's
development, alongside their scholarly contributions to the subject. The
several evidences cited as plausible arguments on behalf of each are also
exercises in the history of American sociology.

For instance, Harry Elmer Barnes in his treatise, *An Introduction to
the History of Sociology,* without apparent contradiction, gives each of
the four a first ranking. Thus, on page 173, he says it can be said that
among American writers, Lester F. Ward "produced the most impressive and comprehensive system of sociology and was also the earliest
systematic American sociologist. . . . it is certain that no other sociologist approached the subject equipped with a body of scientific knowledge
which equalled that possessed by Ward." Again, on page 155, "Among
the sociologists of America there is little doubt that the late William
Graham Sumner of Yale University was the most vigorous and striking
personality . . . the most inspiring and popular teacher that . . .
American social science has ever produced." Then on page 763, he says
that "Franklin Henry Giddings was probably the ablest sociologist that
the United States ever produced, and among sociologists abroad perhaps
only Durkheim, Hobhouse, and Max Weber would rank with him." Of
Small, Barnes wrote on page 787, that he was "the most voluminous
American contributor of his generation" as a historian of social thought,
and "No other American writer devoted so much attention and energy
to the program of justifying the existence of sociology as a subject of
academic standing and professional importance."

As a matter of record, it might very well be accurate to rate each of the
four in high priority ratio on the basis of given selected premises. Small's
early establishment of a great Department of Sociology, his founding
and editing of *The American Journal of Sociology,* and his influence in
setting the stage and training of the largest number of doctorates who
were placed in a greater number of colleges and universities than those

of any other university marks him without a peer. On the other hand, Giddings' pioneering in a similar department, his influencing of an extraordinary number of sociologists who achieved distinction in so many capacities, his part in editing *The Annals* of the American Academy of Political and Social Science, *The Political Science Quarterly,* and *The Proceedings* of the American Economic Association, and his part in founding *Social Forces,* together with his superior and original contribution to the theory and methodology of sociology, might well place him first in any total category. Likewise, Lester F. Ward's pioneering as "Founder" and his sheer quantity production of sociological treatises, and by the same token his contribution to the new dynamic sociology in such powerful array of original works, constitute evidence to lead perhaps a majority of present-day sociologists to place him first as "the Nestor" of American sociologists. Finally, to select a single exclusive item, Sumner's *Folkways* and his contribution of the *folkways* and *mores* have been more universally accepted as a permanent contribution than anything offered by any of the other three. The total story of each of these, as will be the case with each sociologist treated, will not be alone in this chapter, but throughout the book wherever areas of sociology, in which they made contributions, are discussed. In methodology, in theory, or race and ethnic groups, or in whatever fields, their place in American sociology will be cumulatively studied.

Lester F. Ward: 1841–1913

We begin with Lester Frank Ward as the first president of the American Sociological Society in 1906 and re-elected for a second term in 1907. Like the other three he lived to a ripe age exceeding the three score years and ten, having been born in 1841 and living up to 1913. About Ward, as about the other pioneers, we write briefly the story of his part in American sociology within the general multiple framework of his background and how he came into the field of sociology; of his ex-officio positions and varied activities and influence upon students and sociology in general; of his approach and methods and what he produced; of the general rating of his sociology as it appears in the contemporary scene. The theme of his presidential address and some of his specialisms are logical components of the story.

Often called the "Nestor of American sociology," Ward has also been described as the typical American with a boyhood background in the rural Middle West from which point, long without formal education, he worked his way to the top. Like many another American, Ward's life was consistently and paradoxically both ordinary and exceptional in that he followed the pioneer trail westward, moved back eastward; worked his way up from the farm, moved quickly from the farm to teaching, study, then to scientific endeavor. With little schooling for either science or social science, he attained distinction in both; with little financial backing of any sort and no fellowship or endowment, he achieved a rare mastery through the long, hard road of year-by-year progress. He was representative of the American struggle in other ways, one of which was that he married, went to war, was wounded, came back to set himself to work again in the fields to which his love of nature on the prairies and his early reading of a few books had pointed the way.

He was in still another way both consistent and paradoxically American in that he became a governmental worker earning his necessary livelihood for forty years yet equipping himself with rare distinction through scientific study and the reading of great books in philosophy which would become basic to his future work in sociology. Thirty-five years after he entered government service he acted as a special agent for the United States Bureau of Education in a report on "Sociology at the Paris Exposition in 1900," as told by James Q. Dealey in Chapter III of Howard W. Odum's *American Masters of Social Science*. His Washington connections also gave him opportunity to follow another American custom, namely, to do part-time study in evening classes, achieving, besides the bachelor's degree, a diploma in medicine, a law degree, the master's degree and the honorary doctor's degree. Alongside all this preparatory work he was a considerable "joiner" of many societies and, strangely enough, became president of the Institut International de Sociologie from 1900 to 1903, to be followed then by his election as first president of the American Sociological Society.

This amazing record of preparation and action was paralleled only by the extraordinary output of scientific talks and articles followed, then, by the large and impressive number of volumes that he produced without university support or research assistance. In some ways, Ward appears suddenly to the new sociological world as a full-grown sociologist and becomes a professor of sociology in a department prepared by James

Q. Dealey who was to be not only his colleague in Brown University from 1906, but also a fellow president of the American Sociological Society seven years after Ward's death. Dealey was thus his successor as well as his predecessor at Brown University. Ward's two presidential addresses were representative of his approach and general methods and were both published in *The American Journal of Sociology*. His first address, "The Establishment of Sociology," was published in Volume XII, March, 1907; it discussed the value of sociology and its progress as a science in the face of obstacles. His second address, "Social Classes in the Light of Modern Sociological Theory," was published in Volume XIII, March, 1908. In this address Ward held that classes and castes are based to a large extent upon military conquest of one race by another. But this does not necessarily mean that the conquered group is inferior. There are "natural inequalities of men" but these do not correspond to existing classes. It follows that artificial inequalities (classes) are a hindrance and should be abolished.

Ward's main books were *Dynamic Sociology,* 1883; *The Psychic Factors of Civilization,* 1893; *Outlines of Sociology,* 1898; *Pure Sociology,* 1903; *Textbook of Sociology* (with Dealey), 1905; *Applied Sociology,* 1906; *Glimpses of the Cosmos,* 1913–18. This last work, according to Dealey, on pages 70–71 of Odum's *American Masters of Social Science,* originally planned by him to be issued in twelve volumes, was "reduced to six after his death owing to lack of funds for publication. This series is rather unique in that it presents a chronological arrangement of everything Ward ever published, 'great and small, good, bad, and indifferent,' exclusive of books and large illustrated memoirs and monographs. Ward's thought was that by such an arrangement the development of his intellectual life might best be traced, from the callow productions of early youth to the matured reflections of later manhood."

Ward's methodology and approach was consistent with that of Giddings and Small of his contemporaries and with the European sociologists before him. That is, although he had done distinctive work in the natural sciences, when he came to study sociology, it was rather through the avenue of reading great books than through any field work or empirical research. And although he had been librarian of the United States Bureau of Statistics, he made no special use of the statistical method; Dealey, writing of him on pages 67–68, as above, described him as "an intellectual worker . . . the very embodiment of order and system. From 1860 to the time of his death he kept a diary, writing down scrupulously at the end of every day its chief events, especially those that bore upon his literary life. He kept a careful record also of the facts respecting his numerous writings and in addition a complete scrap-book system of twenty-three volumes, classified under the headings, *Reviews and Press Notices, Autograph Letters* and *Biography*. . . . he read systematically, noting important passages or thoughts and indexing them with cross references in his filing system, for, in order to be able to locate any item easily, he made a thorough card index of every name, subject, or important key work contained in his diaries or scrapbooks, or noted in his reading. A series of supplementary letter files systematically arranged completed his filing system. Whenever possible he worked standing at a high desk and in doing his literary work he used the pencil or the pen, not a typist or a typewriter, these being made use of only in official business. In *Glimpses of the Cosmos* he explains the methods he used in writing each of his several sociological works . . ."

Dealey pointed out further, on page 72, that "Throughout this period of formal education he had no scientific studies of any value and his interests were largely in the field of philosophy and education. He started the next decade (1871–1881) with a clear conviction that education was the great panacea for human progress and began systematic reading in philosophy, religion and the sciences, being especially attracted by the works of Francis Bacon, Kant, and Draper, and of Agassiz, Lyell, Haeckel, Comte and Spencer. Meanwhile, he devoted himself to the study of botany, and later of anthropology and geology, and during the whole decade devoted himself to the preparation of the manuscript that ultimately became *Dynamic Sociology*. In Washington itself he was in contact with a large intellectual and scientific circle of kindred minds and in this cultural atmosphere, through discussion and the presentation of papers at literary and scientific gatherings, he broadened out in his attainment and in his world view of life."

Finally, Ward's sociology stands the test of the contemporary scene in many ways. His concept, which foreshadowed social planning, was a pioneer construct; his thesis that woman can make a new contribution to mankind's progress still challenges; his emphasis upon education was paramount to America's major outlines of progress. His faith in the technical and artificial was prophetic of what has happened but inconsistent with the newer construct of balance between the natural and technical. Yet these and other limitations are but commensurate with the magnitude of Ward's efforts and with the limitations of all students and writers who undertake the task of social analysis and direction.

Perhaps Dealey's appraisal will not overestimate Ward's place in American sociology. What Dealey says on pages 90–91, as above, is that "In due time the blunders he made will pass into oblivion but the truths he taught should place him in Comte's list of the immortals. In his system of sociology it is obvious that his conclusions are not usually based on personal studies of concrete facts. In his scientific studies of some thirty years his work was almost entirely of that sort, as shown in his botanical and geological monographs. In his generation, however, comparatively few inductive studies had been made in the field of social phenomena and to some the methodology of those few seems defective in these days. Nor had he the time nor the inclination to make such studies himself. To Ward it seemed more important in his day to master the best thought of the time, including the newer scientific teachings of the nineteenth century, and then to synthesize all into a coherent whole, supplemented by his own thought-contributions wherever he found gaps or defects in this synthesizing philosophy. These contributions he was able to make because of his marvellous grasp of the several fields of science in their interrelations, a grasp much broader and deeper than that held by his immediate predecessors, Spencer and Comte, and also because of his keen, logical intellect and his deep insight into the inner unity of this monistic universe. He is the first great sociologist to indicate scientific bases for sex equality, for democracy and racial unity; the first to mark out the roads to social meliorism and progress, and the first to stress the place of psychic factors in a civilization becoming telic."

Finally, on pages 91–92, Dealey estimates that Ward's teachings which, in their original form, *Dynamic Sociology,* have been before the reading world for over forty years, have now become common property. ". . . numerous authors have taken his ideas, often unconsciously, and elaborated them, sometimes thereby gaining credit for the thought itself. His works are a treasure house of living thought and this will survive, perhaps long after the books themselves have grown musty on neglected shelves. Yet in future years, when another generation with a larger perspective estimates the scientifically based social philosophies of the past and passing generations, Lester Frank Ward will surely be ranked high among America's masters of social science."

William Graham Sumner: 1840–1910

Continuing in chronological order, William Graham Sumner of Yale as second president of the American Sociological Society becomes our next pioneer in this early story of American sociology. Maurice Davie in his preface to *Sumner Today*, sponsored by the William Graham Sumner Club at Yale, wrote about Sumner that he was one of the greatest pioneers in the scientific approach to Sociology through the "problem" aspects of the Study of Society. Sumner also was representative, in his background, of the multiple approach through training in religion and philosophy and through the emphasis upon economics and political science. His was also an "American" career in the making in that his immediate family background was both European and American, he was educated in high school and college, then further conditioned by study in Germany and England and by the reading of European contributions. Born in New Jersey in 1840, educated in New England and abroad, preaching in New York and New Jersey, and finally working out his own "Science of Society" at Yale, from 1872 to 1910, Sumner wrote about himself, on page xvi, "I began to interest men in this important department of study, and to prepare them to follow its development, years before any such attempt was made at any other university in the world. I have followed the growth of the science of sociology in all its branches and have seen it far surpass all the hope and faith I ever had in it." Thus, Sumner typified again the college and university foundations of American sociology, himself coming into the field from non-sociological training but staying by his work at Yale faithfully and laboriously until the end of his career in 1910. At twenty-seven he had been ordained deacon, at Yale, at twenty-nine he was priest at New York and assistant at Calvary Church in New York, and at thirty he was rector of the Church of the Redeemer at Morristown, New Jersey. After two years, however, he was offered the chair of political and social science at Yale which he accepted, saying, "I had always been very fond of teaching and knew that the best work I could ever do in the world would be in that profession; also, that I ought to be in an academical career." Of Sumner in this career, Harry Elmer Barnes estimated that among the sociologists of America, he was "the most rigorous and striking personality" and "the most inspiring and popular teacher."

Sumner's main books were *Problems in Political Economy*, 1885; *Folkways*, 1907; *Earth Hunger and Other Essays*, 1913; *War and Other Essays*, 1913; *The Challenge of Facts*, 1914; *The Forgotten Man*, 1918; *What Social Classes Owe to Each Other*, 1883; *The Science of Society* (with A. G. Keller), 1927. Yet, unlike Ward, his contact with students, as the most popular teacher at Yale for so many years, was more important for sociology in the United States than his books. And unlike Giddings and Small his influence was upon college generations of undergraduates rather than graduate students. Unlike the successors of Giddings, Sumner's successors at Yale "carried on" his work through Keller's prodigious labors in bringing out the four volumes of *The Science of Society* and through the allegiance of the Yale sociology faculty and the William Graham Sumner Club which celebrated the centenary of his birth by sponsoring the book *Sumner Today*, edited by Maurice Davie, the William Graham Sumner professor of sociology, successor to A. G. Keller who had been professor of the science of society and a militant follower of Sumner.

Sumner's rating in American sociology seems clearly based upon four special considerations rather than upon his general contributions to sociology or his own qualifications as a sociologist. First, was his ex-officio rating, namely, distinguished pioneer in the study of the science of society and his presidency of the American Sociological Society. Yet, Small at Chicago was astonished that a man who had done so little in sociology should be proposed for president. Nevertheless this election set the incidence for his major achievement, which was the contribution of the *folkways* and *mores*, terms not only universally accepted but made popular in the common language of the public. The other distinction that sets him apart as pioneer was his blazing a new trail in research on the cultural-anthropological level and his amazing quantitative recording of traits of folk whenever he could find them in any language or any place. His facility in and knowledge of a baker's dozen languages was scarcely equaled unless by Franz Boas of Columbia a little later. Sumner might very well be called the forerunner of the anthropological tradition and the cross-cultural index of the Institute of Human Relations at Yale. Sumner had no financial research assistance and almost no help, yet his impressive cabinets and files compare favorably with the work of many later individuals supported by many thousands of dollars although, of course, the methodologies were not comparable in terms of kind. The nearest comparable basis would be to contrast Murdock's excellent 1949 *Social Structure,* widely reviewed as notable, with Sumner's *Folkways.* Yet of the two and in the light of pioneering, of sound theory, and of the final construct of the folkways, Sumner's contribution remains, for the present, more permanent.

Sumner's other special claim to a major role, in addition to his influence upon students, he owed partly to the loyalty and hard work of A. G. Keller who saw to it that much of Sumner's life work was presented in *The Science of Society.* Of his works, then, *Folkways* and *The Science of Society* are all that need to be recorded in his favor as one of the first Big Four, his other works being something like the old "chips from a German workshop" of a Max Müller and full of random but penetrating considerations of many situations.

No one can fully appreciate the range and prodigious amount of systematic study that Sumner did without examining at first hand the records as Keller has presented them. Concerning Sumner's methods, Keller emphasized this point on page xxiii of Maurice Davie's *Sumner Today.* "To anyone," wrote Keller, "who has made intimate acquaintance with *Folkways* or *The Science of Society,* Sumner's methods are outstandingly apparent. They consist, in essence, in the assembling of a large body of verified and re-verified facts of experience, and then in letting these facts tell their own story, under the application of what Huxley called 'trained and organized common sense,' that is to say, the inductive method of science."

Keller refers to Sumner's longer works as "colossal industry." Multiplying his fifty-two boxes of 3000 sheets each gives an idea of the work done. Keller continues, "The brute bulk of Sumner's materials is a silent witness to the labor which he devoted to investigation. No one who has ever cast his eye over them has failed to be staggered by their sheer quantity. There were, when he ceased to collect, fifty-two drawers and boxes of close-packed notes, averaging some three thousand sheets of uniform size to the receptacle. No one helped him gather these materials; they were all out of his own reading and many of them in his own handwriting, the majority being excerpts marked by him for a copyist. He had no 'shop,' and his single copyist cost him about twenty dollars a month during the academic year.

"These notes reveal a knowledge of some thirteen languages. Sumner's insistence upon getting to sources may be illustrated by the fact that what set him to learning Russian was a determination to get to the truth about the Russian *mir,* or village community; and it may be added here that he spent one summer reviewing his college mathematics and taking lessons in calculus in order to see for himself whether there was anything for him in mathematical economics. His life-reading, in all lines, including history, theology, metaphysics, and general literature, is but poorly represented by the combined bibliographies of his several works. He was quite a novel-reader, and used to contend that fiction was an outstanding agency for apprehension of the mores of a period and for diffusion of culture within the international range."

Sumner's pioneering volume, *Folkways,* has for its subtitle: "A Study of the Sociological Importance of Usages, Manners, Customs, Mores, and Morals." His study was based upon the assumption that the first function of life is to live, and that in the struggle for existence the ability to adapt and change is vital. Through trial and error and experimentation, through pain and struggle, through the constant meeting of new needs, society itself not only has survived, but has developed its cultures. In this work, Sumner, as pointed out by Murdock in the preface to *Social Structure,* was, with Keller, the first to emphasize the importance to sociology of the study of comparative societies, which was much later to be featured in *group* concepts, although Cooley a little later featured the primary group, and the study of comparative societies was the last feature of Giddings' published work.

Franklin H. Giddings: 1855-1931

The third president of the American Sociological Society, Franklin Henry Giddings, 1910 and 1911, was about as different from Ward and Sumner, his predecessors, as it would be possible to be. Yet the similarities in American backgrounds and in the manner in which he came to be a sociologist are marked. Born and educated in New England, reading deeply and widely in European philosophy and sociology, having six years experience in journalism and six years experimental teaching at

Bryn Mawr and Columbia, then being full-fledged professor of sociology and the history of civilization at Columbia for a third of a century, he both typified the American pioneer and symbolized the emergence of American sociology as a college and university subject. The calendar of his sojournings, oversimplified, would be: Born in Sherman, Connecticut, in 1855, began his teaching at Bryn Mawr in 1888, lectured at Columbia 1892–94, was appointed to what is estimated the first full professorship of sociology in America in 1894, was assigned also the endowed professorship of sociology and the history of civilization in 1906, became emeritus professor in 1928, and died in 1931. Like his two predecessors and Small, who followed him, he lived beyond his seventy years and remained vigorous and active all the way along.

His ex-officio status was fixed, not only by the records of his college and university work but by a number of other distinguished achievements. Like Ward, he was president of the Institut International de Sociologie. He was fellow of the American Statistical Association and of the American Association for the Advancement of Science. Holding no graduate degree from any college or university, he received a number of honorary degrees including the Ph.D. and the Litt.D. from Union, and the LL.D. from the University of North Carolina, Columbia, and Iowa. His influence upon sociology was measured in terms of his textbooks, his lectures and teachings, and the continued extension of his work by more than fifty Ph.D. graduates who held top positions in college, university, publishing, and public affairs.

I have pointed out in Chapter I of *American Masters of Social Science* that Giddings represents a type whose achievements take on the proportions of the heroic, if measured by energy, thoroughness, comprehensiveness and scholarship. For, starting without the usual academic degree, like Ward, he produced monumental contributions, directing his own studies and readings with remarkable effectiveness, taking a vigorous part in the formation of American ideals, all the while teaching, writing, editing, publishing.

The framework and background of his "theory" are illustrated by his broad interest and varied activities. Thus, his newspaper apprenticeship was continuously reflected in his vigorous style; his decade of editorial work on *The Independent,* and his co-editorship at one time or another of the *Annals* of the American Academy of Political and Social Science, the *Political Science Quarterly*, and of the *Publications* of the American Economic Association in turn reflect a very great influence upon much of his writings — his *Responsible State*, the politico-juristic part of his earlier theory, his earlier writings on the sociological nature of political economy, his later *Democracy and Empire*, and at least two chapters in his *Studies in the Theory of Human Society*. The influence was even more marked in his later Teachers College lectures and in his *Civilization and Society*, in his discussions of democracy, patriotism, and social legislation.

His status as scholar and professor may be measured by his books and periodical literature and by his special public lectures and stimulation of research and publication among others. His bibliography included no less than fourteen books and over two hundred articles, a list of which may be found in the *Bibliography of the Faculty of Political Science*, of Columbia University, published in 1931. His main books include: *Principles of Sociology*, 1896; *Elements of Sociology*, 1898; *Democracy and Empire*, 1900; *Inductive Sociology*, 1901; *Readings in Description and Historical Sociology*, 1906; *The Responsible State*, 1918; *Studies in the Theory of Human Society*, 1922; *Scientific Study of Human Society*, 1924; and *Civilization and Society*, 1932.

Giddings' priority as a pioneer in American sociology, like Sumner's, must rest, not only on his profound theoretical contributions and their application to public affairs, but also on his methodologies and his tremendous labors in searching sources for details and in pioneering in the statistical method. For the first part of his career his methods were very much the same as those of the others, namely, the extensive and careful examination of sources from books and his prolific readings and recordings, together with his critical comments and revisions through cross-fertilization of ideas. We have already indicated the influence of European writers upon his work, so that there is no need for further emphasis upon this. His pioneering in the statistical and analytical method, especially in what was really his latest book, *Scientific Study of Human Society*, first published serially in *Social Forces*, and later by the University of North Carolina Press, constituted a new era in American sociology. As forerunner of this, however, he had long been working on the fringes of such a new methodology, first with Mayo-Smith and later in his excellent *Inductive Sociology*, certainly one of the first and best texts on systematic sociology ever produced. The measure of Giddings' rank in statistics was not in the ultimate definitiveness of his statistical methods and contribution, but in his setting the stage and actually contributing something to the science and in his influence upon others, such as Ogburn, Chaddock, and then through the sweep of an almost universal adoption by sociologists in the later years to make the statistical method a standard requirement in sociology as in all sciences.

With reference to his status and the sum total of his work as a sociologist, final estimates must be made from an examination of the composite works and influence that he exerted. In order to present his story vividly, it seems possible to present a broad general assumption that the matured sociology of Giddings, as it was from the beginning, and as it was continuously and progressively developed during the later years of his active work, approximated a realistic and rigorous science of society. Such an appraisal is based upon the whole framework and picture of Giddings' life and work. It takes into consideration such basic factors as the historical, theoretical, methodological, realistic, and factual aspects, as well as the testing field of current civilization and, as he was wont to call it, the "ongoings of society." It takes into consideration the quantity and quality of his contributions, the breadth and variety of his work and interests, the all-pervading unity of his philosophy, and the influence of his personality upon his students and upon the university world wherever he touched it. And it takes into consideration, also, alongside the remarkable consistency of the quality and range of his work, some inconsistencies on different levels and in his dogmatic emotional approach to certain problems.

It seems possible to characterize the later Giddings' sociology as a scientific study of human society, constantly seeking more rigorous scientific methods and more effective applications to the end that society may attain a better selection, preservation, and development of a superior mankind. Or it envisages the mastery of a society considered as a means to an end which is the attainment of a greater human adequacy, such adequacy to comprehend elements of endurance, health, reproductive vigor, intelligence, self-control, ability to make adjustments, happiness, and the sum total of human welfare. Such a science, Professor Giddings insisted, must achieve a more adequate body of societal facts but also a more realistic facing of facts, twin motivations of genuine science. This purposive nature of sociology was exemplified in his observation that "facing the facts that the physical and biological sciences have made known to us has enabled us to live more comfortably and longer than men once did. Facing the facts that the social sciences are making known to us, and will make better known, should enable us to diminish human misery and to live more wisely than the human race has lived hitherto." (*The Scientific Study of Human Society*, pp. 37-38.)

This purposive nature of the science was exemplified further in Giddings' "social telesis," which may serve as a theoretical testing field for much of the practical application of his sociology to such objectives as democracy, education, social welfare. "The visualized ends of telic activity in human society and by it," Giddings wrote on pages 170-71 of his *Scientific Study of Human Society*, "are amelioration of the human lot, by security and material abundance; the survival (which security and abundance make possible) of variates from a standardized human type in whom lie our hope of discovery, of invention, and of experimentation; the socialization of entire populations, with elimination of the antisocial; and that individuation which is an evolution of intelligent, responsible, self-determining personality — of adequate man. And these ends, for which we strive, we have perceived and found desirable, because a societal evolution which we did not plan produced us, produced them, and enabled us to see them!"

This concept of society and its achievements implies an "explanatory sociology" which Giddings held to be the final achievement of the sociologist. Such a sociology was the "chief concern" of his *Scientific Study of Human Society* whose purpose was further "to indicate wherein and to what extent Sociology is indubitably a *scientific* study of Human Society, and how it can be made more rigorously so." This concept, I think, too, was consistent with an earlier classification of sociology on page 8 of his *Inductive Sociology* into General or Fundamental Sociology and Special Sociology and, with his still earlier "Principles," as well as with his later "Intensive Sociology" with its units of comparative societies, which he described in his last published article in *The American Journal of Sociology*. It was consistent with his claim that sociology must use all known scientific methods and it was consistent with his latest definition of sociology and its framework as set forth in *Civilization and Society*, which he called an "account of the development and behavior of human society." His first purpose as stated, on page 385, "is to present an elementary account of the dynamics and the psychology and of the development and functioning of human society, which may also serve as a sort of introduction to the history and theory of civilization. A second purpose is to present a number of important elementary aspects of the continuing development of modern society as they are reflected in certain social problems and processes. A third purpose is to point out certain practical applications of sociology to our education, public policy and entire cultural development. And a fourth purpose is to indicate the importance of sociology as the scientific study of human society, and to stimulate more rigorous scientific methods and attitudes and more effective applications to the end that society may attain a better selection, preservation, and development of a superior mankind."

Giddings pointed out that he had come to these general conclusions after many years of considering sociology as the scientific study of the human society. He insisted that he was trying to get away from complexities and abstractions and that he was emphasizing the concrete things of reality more and more. During the later years he was constantly reviewing his own varied definitions of sociology, those of many European scholars and those of his American colleagues, in order to make clearer in a single definition the meaning and implications of sociology. "Sociology," he wrote in *Civilization and Society,* page 263, "is the study of the behavior of human beings with, to, and for one another, and of the resulting arrangement of relationships and activities which we call human society." He reminds us that it ought not to be necessary to state in so many words that this human society comprehends all the human beings and their social behavior, their organizations and groups, all of their churches, all of their business organizations, as well as the state and all that it does. These institutions are "arrangements." Thus, more and more, Professor Giddings tended to comprehend society in terms of the people and their behavior measured in terms of societal achievement.

We have characterized Giddings' sociology as being realistic. A part of the realism is found in the sound theory and authentic historical accuracy of his illustrative material and inductions. Giddings used to emphasize a distinction between theory and mere subjective theorizing in the dictum that "it isn't theory, if it won't work." We have already called attention to a certain realism in Giddings' interests and theories in the sense that they grew out of active experience and observation. We have yet to indicate in subsequent sections of this chapter something of the reality of his sociology as may be tested in relation to public policy, current social problems, and to what might be termed prediction exercises, as well as in his methodological contributions.

There is, however, another test of reality that may be submitted at this point as background upon which to envisage his general sociology. This is the test of relationship to historical and theoretical sociology and to the various "schools" among present-day American sociologists. Like Small's, Giddings' early theory was greatly influenced by the earlier European sociologists. Unlike Small, Giddings did not attempt synthesis and summary from which to develop his own theory. Rather, powerfully stimulated and with great zest, he sought to evolve his own theory as a result of his dissatisfaction with what he found in these masters.

When we come to examine the validity of our assumption concerning the "scientific" nature of Giddings' sociology, we may best utilize Giddings' own language to a large degree. There appear to be three aspects to be examined. One is Giddings' characterization of "science," "scientific," "scientific study," "scientific scrutiny," "scientific activity." Another is the motivating power of his teaching and his insistence that scientific methods be utilized in sociology. The third is the nature of his own theory and methodology.

"The scientific study of any subject," Giddings insisted on pages 41–42 of his *Scientific Study of Human Society,* "is the substitution of business-like ways of 'making sure' about it for the lazy habit of 'taking it for granted' and the worse habit of making irresponsible assertions about it. To make sure, it is necessary to have done with a careless 'looking into it' and to undertake precise observations, many times repeated. It is necessary to make measurements and accountings, to substitute realistic thinking (an honest dealing with facts as they are) for wishful or fanciful or other self-deceiving thinking and to carry on a systematic 'checking up.' " So also there must be kept in mind the importance of right methods. "At every step we must make sure that the methods which we use and rely on have been accredited by exhaustive criticism and trial, and are applicable to the investigation in hand." In another place, page 404 of his *Civilization and Society,* Giddings reminds us that "it ought not to be necessary, but it is necessary, to tell the general public that science is nothing more or less than getting at facts and trying to understand them." Therefore, he concluded, on page 42 of his *Scientific Study of Human Society,* "the discovery of facts *which prove to be facts* is initial scientific activity. In the nature of things it continues more or less fortuitously, however systematic we try to make it. The *scrutiny* of alleged facts to determine whether or not they *are* facts, is the fundamental *systematic* work of science."

From his earliest writings to his latest, Giddings emphasized as basic to "explanation" the systematic observation and recording of likenesses and differences. In his *Scientific Study of Human Society,* Giddings gives vivid verdicts: on page 189, "A true and complete description of anything must include measurements of it," and on page 5, "Every something is a lot of somethings." Finally, to turn to another phase of his "testing fields" of scientific method, he concludes on page 182 that "A scientific scrutiny of facts and a scientific interpretation of relations are not complete until we have asked the question, as old as human apprehension and desire, as old as curiosity, 'What else?' What else is, or happens? What else was or happened? What else will be, or will happen?" So much did he insist on checking up that his final conclusion that the habit of asking what else happens — what else is likely to happen — is in my judgment the most important of all the teachings of sociology.

A. A. Tenney, who was Giddings' colleague at Columbia for a quarter century, summarizes Giddings' construct of discovering society and the resulting concept of *consciousness of kind.* On pages 321–22 of the September, 1931, *Columbia University Quarterly,* writing on "Franklin Henry Giddings, 1855–1931," Tenney said, "The most important question in sociology, as Professor Giddings saw it, was to explain the fact of society. This problem apparently exercised a fascination for him from first to last. Discussion of it appeared in his earliest sociological articles and statements of it are given in all of his more important writings. It runs as follows: By observation we note that the individuals of many forms of organic life both animal and human are formed in groups. The common bond of association running through all of these groupings is not primarily, as economists and some sociologists — especially Ward — have held, that the individual recognizes the utility of association and division of labor. Groups are found far down in the scale of life among organisms to which none can impute mental capacity to recognize utility of any sort. The bond of union, Professor Giddings found in what he first called 'consciousness-of-kind.' Later he placed greater emphasis on 'like-mindedness,' and still later on 'collective response to the same stimulus or similar stimuli,' as the fundamental reason for the formation of groups. The existence of the group — the fact of society — is thus explained and along with the discovery comes the explanation of any type of sub-group that may arise in any larger group."

Albion W. Small: 1854–1926

The fourth president of the American Sociological Society was Albion Woodbury Small for 1912, and selected for a second term in 1913, completing an extraordinary succession of Ward, Sumner, Giddings, all living and working vigorously beyond seventy years and all symbolizing the rise of American sociology as a college and university subject rapidly gaining its major place in the curriculum. Like his predecessors, Small came from New England ancestry; like Giddings, he was the son of a minister; like Sumner, he himself was trained for the ministry, and, like them all, he came relatively late into sociology, without special training in American sociology, although he had two years in Germany, one at Johns Hopkins University, and three as professor and president of Colby before coming to Chicago in 1892 to set up the first and largest department of sociology in the world at that time.

His ex-officio leadership was the greatest of any of the Big Four in several ways. In the first place, half of the presidents of the American Sociological Society came from the University of Chicago Department of Sociology, either as faculty members or Ph.D. graduates of later distinction. By 1950, there were nearly two hundred Ph.D. graduates, representing every state in the union, teaching in more than a hundred colleges and universities throughout the land, and contributing the greater portion of the texts and special works in American sociology. In the next place, Small's founding of *The American Journal of Sociology* was epochal and this, together with his editorship and contributions for over thirty years, undoubtedly constituted his greatest contribution to American sociology. His treatise on "Fifty Years of American Sociology," published in the *Journal* in 1916 is still the standard reference, practically equivalent to a monograph. So, too, no one equaled Small in insuring the publication of the Proceedings of the annual meetings of the Society in the earlier days when problems of publishing were not simple.

Nevertheless, Small's books, while not approximating those of Ward and Giddings, were substantial contributions to the sociological literature of the times. His main books included *Introduction to the Study of Society* (with Vincent), 1894; *General Sociology*, 1905; *Adam Smith and Modern Sociology*, 1907; *Meaning of Social Science*, 1910; *Between Eras: From Capitalism to Democracy*, 1913; *Origins of Sociology*, 1924. Of special and distinctive importance was Small's *General Sociology* and his *Origins of Sociology* in interpreting German sociology to the new sociology of the United States. In this respect he might well be likened unto Talcott Parsons in the later era in that, having sojourned in Germany and been stimulated to the special study of Ratzenhofer and others, he published his own adaptations as compared to Parsons, whose study in Europe resulted in his special interpretation and adaptation of Max Weber and others, and who then proceeded to construct his structure-function theory, thus reviving the influence of German sociology fifty years later. Yet with all of his varied activities Small insisted that "If you consent to tell the world anything about me, do not mince matters at all in telling the plain, blunt truth that I spent my life insisting that there *is* something at the far end of the sociological rainbow," as quoted by Hayes on page 184 of Odum's *American Masters of Social Science*.

In some ways the heart of Small's methodology might be summarized in just that, namely, the presentation of historical sociology from whatever sources possible to an American audience. In all this Small was not so much interested in methodology as in results. In Chapter 3 we have quoted Small at length on the origins of sociology and in Chapter 15 on his methodology. Edward Carey Hayes, an early student and contemporary, wrote of Small on page 187 of *American Masters of Social Science* that "while his works will perpetuate his contributions to sociology, . . . [they] cannot convey to his successors an adequate understanding of the . . . man. . . ." Barnes estimated, on page 777 of his *Introduction to the History of Sociology*, that "Small exercised an influence upon American sociology greater and more salutary than any other individual except, perhaps, Giddings." Barnes has made an excellent summary of Small's contributions on page 787. He gives "first place to his work as a historian of sociological thought" in which he was "the most voluminous American contributor of his generation. He rendered a real service in interpreting the development of Germanic social science in such a fashion as to be of great utility to American readers. This was an achievement of the highest importance and, in all probability, was one which would not have been performed at all if Small had not executed it."

Although more lengthy references to Small than to Giddings, Ward, and Sumner have been made in previous chapters, two special aspects of Small's work need to be emphasized here as indicative of the timeliness of some of his work as appropriate to certain contemporary situations. One is his assumption that life is pervaded by ethical realities and problems. The other was Small's constant pleading for the social sciences to work together. Concerning the former, Hayes estimated, on page 187 of *American Masters of Social Science,* that adequate recognition of the two facts of ethical realities and the unitary character of life constitutes the sociological point of view of Small. Concerning the cooperation of the social sciences, Small wrote so vividly and plausibly that he might well have been writing for the Social Science Research Council in the 1920's and again in the 1940's. See especially more about Small in the sections on Faris, Burgess, Reuter, and in Chapters 14, 15, and 23.

CHAPTER 5

The Next Four, 1914–1918: Ross, Vincent, Howard, Cooley

In the story of the next four senior sociologists, following the first Big Four, such continuing roles as that of pioneer, promoter, defender of the faith, enthusiastic advocate, and builder of departments, must necessarily have a larger place in any appraisal of the part they played in the rising tide of American sociology than would be the case with their successors. For these leaders, Ross, Vincent, Howard, and Cooley, representing four major universities, Wisconsin, Chicago, Nebraska, and Michigan, were practically synonymous with the major stream of westward-moving sociology during this period of development. They represented the Middle West of the United States and, with the exception of Vincent of Chicago, who became president of one of the great western state universities, each was in the way of building a strong department of sociology. And Vincent, perhaps more than any other sociologist except Small, wrote and campaigned about what sociology should be. What manner of men were these early pioneers? How did they differ from the first Four? From what fields did they come to sociology? What were their special interests and the nature of their high purposes? What personalities and writings influenced them most? What did they teach? What did they write? How did they do it and what part did they play inside their own universities? What kind of participation did they reflect in sociological meetings and organizations? What contributions did they make? What evaluations have been made of them by others? What were their judgments of their own work? What limitations did they set for the new social science? And, first, what of the dynamic Ross who in his presidential address in 1915, contemplating new technological weapons of war, new world conflicting cultures, new rationalization for wars of defense, proclaimed a "great union" as the only guarantee of peace and insurance of survival?

E. A. Ross: 1866—

Edward Alsworth Ross was the fifth president of the American Sociological Society, and the last to be re-elected for a second year. He was a prolific writer of books, his texts selling in the aggregate nearly a half million copies; he was an entertaining teacher, an enthusiastic and generous supporter of the American Sociological Society and of his colleagues, striding across a continent back and forth, and finally settling down at the University of Wisconsin where he produced most of his works. And he has even excelled his predecessors in the length and vigor of his years. Born just after the Civil War in 1866, he hastens to help celebrate the approaching half-century mark with the publication of his *Capsules of Social Wisdom* at eighty-two years of age. And in between he has been the most traveled of all America's sociologists, moving hither and yon outside his America, to Mexico, to China, to Russia, to Sweden, to India, and many other places. Barnes concludes that "no other American sociologist has had so interesting and colorful a life as has Ross." Next to Sumner he has been the most popular teacher of undergraduates and for thirty years he headed one of the most distinguished departments of sociology in America.

Like Ward, Ross came from the American Midwest but unlike Ward, he went to get his formal education more directly in college and university. He was graduated from Coe College in 1886, studied at Berlin 1888–89, went on to Johns Hopkins and received his doctorate there in 1891 about the time Small was getting ready to go to Chicago. None of this training, however, was in sociology, and even after his year at Indiana, he accepted a chair in economics and commerce at Cornell University and did not function as professor of sociology until 1893 at Stanford University. Ross's zeal as reformer got him in trouble there and so in 1891 he went as professor of sociology at Nebraska until 1906, whence he moved permanently to the University of Wisconsin where he remained for a third of a century and as emeritus professor gives promise of celebrating fifty years of service at a single university.

In a statement prepared especially for *American Sociology*, Ross tells how he came to specialize in the field of sociology: "In my postgraduate study in the Universities of Berlin and Johns Hopkins, 1888–1891, I took courses in philosophy and economics but nothing in sociology, for nothing was offered. As soon as I held a university chair (1891), however, I began teaching it for it had a fascination for me. While preparing the series of papers that became *Social Control,* 1901, it was borne in upon me how unsettled was everything about the new would-be science and for at least eight years I gave my spare time to such studies as 'The Scope and Task of Sociology,' 'Social Laws,' 'The Unit of Investigation in Sociology,' 'The Properties of Group-Units,' 'The Social Forces,' 'The Factors of Social Change,' and 'Recent Tendencies in Sociology.' These and other like papers were brought out in 1905 under the title *The Foundations of Sociology.*

"These years of critical examination of sociological writings left me exceedingly dissatisfied with the way in which the development of sociology so far had been affected by reigning religious, ethical, or philosophical ideas. I realized that I needed a much broader knowledge of society than I had. In those days no funds were available for 'social research,' but I found that by teaching two summer sessions without pay I could, once in every three years, have a summer and a semester *with* pay, for social exploration. I saw now the possibility of educating myself into a real sociologist by studying different societies 'on the spot,' and I seized it."

Ross's main books are *Social Control,* 1901; *The Foundations of Sociology,* 1905; *Sin and Society,* 1907; *Changing America,* 1908; *Social Psychology,* 1908; *Latter Day Sinners and Saints,* 1910; *Changing Chinese,* 1911; *The Old World in the New,* 1914; *South of Panama,* 1915; *Russia in Upheaval,* 1918; *What Is America?* 1919; *The Principles of Sociology,* 1920, 1930; *The Russian Bolshevik Revolution,* 1921; *The Social Trend,* 1922; *Social Revolution in Mexico,* 1923; *The Social Revolution in Mexico,* 1923; *The Soviet Republic,* 1923; *Roads to Social Peace,* 1924; *Civic Sociology,* 1925; *Readings in Civic Sociology,* 1926; *Standing Room Only?* 1927; *The Outlines of Sociology,* 1933; *Seventy Years of It,* 1936; *New Age Sociology,* 1940. Of these books, *Social Control, Foundations, Principles* and *Social Psychology* represented Ross's more scientific work, while most of the others reflect his popular interest and methodology.

Ross's contributions to American sociology rest upon several bases. He was a pioneer, unafraid in the early days when he was needed. He wrote the first book on social psychology. His *Social Control* was new. He encouraged hundreds of sociologists who were never in his classes, including Sorokin. His texts were teachable, his treatment of social processes is the best classification of any. Yet Ross's popularity was due to the dynamics of his personality as well as to the range and quality of his work. According to Barnes, Ross was distinguished by "his ability to present his ideas in a manner which attracts the lay reader as well as the professional sociologist." On page 819 of his *Introduction to the History of Sociology,* Barnes says that "Although his tendency to popularize has at times led Ross into the pitfalls of overeasy generalization, it must be recognized that sociology owes a great deal to Ross for arousing public interest concerning certain of its problems and methods." His emphasis on getting ideas across to the general reader, still popular in 1950, according to Barnes "seems to be the result of a fusion of a genuine scientific interest in societal phenomena with a strong desire to aid in solving the problems which the peoples of the world have been called upon to face. It is possible to trace the presence of this combination of interests in Ross from his graduate days at Johns Hopkins through his periods of teaching at Indiana, Cornell, Stanford, Nebraska, and finally, Wisconsin."

Ross's principles or theory may be found in the four books that were written primarily from the scientific point of view: *Social Control, The Foundations of Sociology, Social Psychology,* and *Principles of Sociology.* Barnes estimated on page 823 that "although chronology would indicate that the works be taken up in the order listed, a clearer conception of his system can be developed if we start with *The Foundations of Sociology.* The chapter on 'The Unit of Investigation in Sociology' presents a comprehensive map of the field of study for the sociologist as Ross conceived it." Barnes quotes Ross to the effect that "The basic unit of sociological investigation, although not the sole unit, is the social process." And on pages 90–91 of his *Foundations of Sociology,* "The five units so far favorably considered — groups, relations, institutions, imperatives, uniformities — are *products.* They precede the individual and survive him. To the onlooker they appear as gods or fates, moulding the lives and disposing upon the destinies of ordinary men. Nevertheless, they have all risen at some time out of the actions and interactions of men. To understand their genesis we must ascend to that primordial fact known as the *social process.*"

Tested in the light of contemporary 1950 society, Ross rates reappraisal on many counts: (1) his early protest against bigness and exploitation; his sensing of the diversities of world cultures; (2) his uneasiness on the population question; (3) his appeal for world organization and peace; (4) his sensing of the power of communication and psychological currents; (5) his emphasis upon process; (6) and later his powerful urge to give the world the benefit of his "Folk Wisdom."

Ross tells us personally his impressions of sociology as late as 1948. In his statement prepared for this book he says, "Among the effects upon me of all my studies carried on through twenty years were:

"1. I saw that sociology must go forward on its own, not as a mere offshoot of some other science.

"2. I lost confidence in the value of analogies between social processes and other processes.

"3. I ceased to trust the hypothesis that there is *one dominant trend* in the development of all societies, whatever their geographic environment, make-up or history.

"4. I rejected the idea that there is a single underlying pattern for each class of social process and each order of social institution.

"5. I arrived at the conviction that the actual character of a given society is best revealed in the two or three score of major *social processes* that go on within it. These *processes,* the *factors* determining each of them, as well as the products — institutions, groupings, and interactions — to which they give rise, are the principal things the sociologist has to study and set forth.

"As I review the course taken by sociological thinking and research in the fifty-seven years since I began to teach the subject, I am well-contented. Less and less is arm-chair thinking relied on; stronger and stronger is the demand for honest to goodness *social research*. There is great difference of opinion as to the best techniques of research, but never have I met with a suspicion that the methods followed are 'rigged' in advance in order to insure the emergence of certain desired results.

"I do feel, however, that our sociological treatises and journals are *far more optimistic* than they are justified in being. They take little notice of the fact that *natural selection* has been almost put out of business insofar as it pertains to human beings, and that in scores of ways the hereditarily *inferior,* the constitutionally *less fit,* are being helped to survive and multiply. Unless more attention is given to the significance of biology for human beings, it is easy to foresee the plight of our posterity after three or four centuries!"

Ross is still worried about the earth's population, and says, "Again, sociologists are ceasing to hold the complete confidence of the higher intellectual circles by their neglect of what is happening in the field of population growth and population pressure."

Ross, like his contemporaries, was called upon to undertake many tasks and he participated in a wide range of activities. He was director of education on "The Floating University," 1928–29, and lectured at Harvard, University of Chicago, Northwestern. He was secretary of the American Economic Association 1892–93, was a member of the Institut International de Sociologie. He gave the Weil Lectures on Citizenship at North Carolina in 1924, and was advisory editor of *The American Journal of Sociology,* and until very recently he "never missed a meeting" of the American Sociological Society.

The two presidential addresses of Ross now appear peculiarly timely and might well, from their titles only, be on the program of tomorrow's most important conferences. In 1914 he talked on "Freedom of Communication and the Struggle for Right." This was printed in *The American Journal of Sociology* for February, 1915. His 1915 address, printed in the *Papers and Proceedings* of the Tenth Annual Meeting of the American Sociological Society, Volume X, page 1 ff., pointed out that the destinies of civilization have been determined by battle and by the techniques and invention of warfare. The role of population pressure, of improved communication, of unequal economic and social conditions in the civilizations of the world are powerfully affecting peace. In the light of his assertion that it was easy for a nationalistic government to convince the people that "a war of defense" is necessary, and of what has happened since 1915, his remedy seems prophetically powerful. What Ross saw was that a "great union" of the world is the only answer.

George E. Vincent: 1864–1941

George E. Vincent, sixth president of the American Sociological Society, was another one of the earlier sociologists who was born about the time of the beginnings of the social science movement in the United States and later contributed definitely to the development of sociology as a university subject. Interestingly enough, he was one of the very first to receive the Ph.D. degree at Chicago, this degree being conferred upon him and W. I. Thomas as the only recipients in 1896, the year following the first two degrees conferred upon Frederick W. Sanders and Jerome H. Raymond. An interesting coincidence also was the fact that David P. Barrows was the only recipient of the Ph.D. degree the following year, and Barrows went on to become president of the University of California as Vincent later became president of the University of Minnesota.

Vincent was, along with George Howard, U. G. Weatherly, C. H. Cooley, and Lester F. Ward, a native of the Middle West. He was born in Rockford, Illinois, in 1864. He went east and to Europe for his earlier education, receiving his A.B. degree from Yale in 1885, studying in Europe in 1886–87, and returning to Chicago for his Ph.D. in 1906. Previous to this he had been fellow at Chicago in 1892–94, assistant, 1894–96, instructor, 1895–96, assistant professor from 1896–1900, and associate professor from 1906 to 1908. Thus he worked his way, university fashion, up to the full professorship about the time he received his Ph.D. degree, and conformed to the general pattern of the day in getting his doctor's degree at a relatively mature age and moving directly then into his professorship of sociology at the University of Chicago which he held for seven years until 1911, when he was elected president of the University of Minnesota.

In all, Professor Vincent was in the department of sociology for almost twenty years in which he had time to establish himself as one of the few mature American sociologists. As a matter of fact, his main text on sociology was in collaboration with Professor Small; while Vincent was assistant in sociology, they brought out the *Introduction to the Study of Society,* in 1895. His ex-officio top rating as president of the American Sociological Society came in 1916 after he had become president of the University of Minnesota. Vincent's main contribution was in the way of general sociology, teaching and promotion, rather than as author or in the field of research. His *The Social Mind and Education* was published in 1897. On the other hand, Vincent had been dean of the College of Arts and Sciences at Chicago from 1907 to 1911, had been president of the Chautauqua Institution from 1907 to 1915 and honorary president thereafter until 1937. As president of the University of Minnesota and one of the most popular and eloquent lecturers in the United States, he reflected honor upon and gave leadership to the American Sociological Society as its president, and he was consistently devoted to the field in supporting the work of sociology at Minnesota.

Vincent's presidential address, published in the *Papers and Proceedings* of the Eleventh Annual Meeting of the American Sociological Society in 1917 represented in some ways a timely contribution. Devoted to "Countryside and Nation," it was a discussion of the economic and social condition of America's farms and rural areas, prophetic of what was later to become a separate and dynamic Rural Sociological Society, with its own journal, some twenty years later. Vincent emphasized, among other factors, the increase in farm tenancy, inefficient management, loss of soil fertility, and suggested the extension of the factory system to farms, cooperatively owned farms, and other arrangements for the enrichment of American country life. Vincent's collaboration with Small in the *Introduction to the Study of Society* was also a pioneer book in that this was perhaps the first elementary textbook in sociology prepared for popular use as a college text. Here the attempt was to chart the field of sociology and to catalogue some of the main problems of sociology somewhat after the manner of Ellwood's later and more widely used *Sociology and Social Problems.* Even as a pioneer book to which Barnes refers as "an archaic curiosity at the present time," it was set in the framework of a quite modern construct of the trend from rural life to urban civilization with some ventures into social psychology. It naturally reflected the influence of the European organic analogies that were contributed by Small with a few chapters in "Books" III and IV. But whatever the nature of the book, it must be recorded as a definite pioneer influence in the teaching of American sociology as a college subject.

Yet Vincent, alongside Small, was a dynamic apostle of the new sociology and was a prolific writer of articles in the new *American Journal of Sociology.* As early as January, 1895, Vincent wrote a major article in the *Review of Reviews* entitled "Sociological Study in College." This article sets forth a plan of instruction for persons in college who intend to take a major in sociology. It is a plan of instruction springing from the concept of society as "a whole which has been naturally produced by the continuous action of innumerable forces that are still operative, effecting unceasing changes in social structures and activities."

Vincent's special interest in sociology was significant in the light of his

PRESIDENTS

of the

AMERICAN SOCIOLOGICAL SOCIETY

and

EDITORS

of the

SOCIOLOGICAL JOURNALS

LESTER F. WARD
President, 1906, 1907

WILLIAM GRAHAM SUMNER
President, 1908, 1909

FRANKLIN H. GIDDINGS
President, 1910, 1911

ALBION W. SMALL
President, 1912, 1913
Editor, *The American Journal
of Sociology,* 1895-1926

E. A. ROSS
President, 1914, 1915

GEORGE E. VINCENT
President, 1916

© *Rentschler's Studio, Ann Arbor, Mich.*

GEORGE E. HOWARD
President, 1917

CHARLES HORTON COOLEY
President, 1918

FRANK W. BLACKMAR
President, 1919

JAMES Q. DEALEY
President, 1920

EDWARD CARY HAYES
President, 1921

JAMES P. LICHTENBERGER
President, 1922

ULYSSES G. WEATHERLY
President, 1923

CHARLES A. ELLWOOD
President, 1924

ROBERT E. PARK
President, 1925

JOHN L. GILLIN
President, 1926

WILLIAM I. THOMAS
President, 1927

JOHN M. GILLETTE
President, 1928

WILLIAM F. OGBURN
President, 1929

© *Samuel Kravitt, New Haven, Conn.*
HOWARD W. ODUM
President, 1930
Editor, *Social Forces,* current

EMORY S. BOGARDUS
President, 1931
Editor, *Journal of Applied Sociology*
(later became *Sociology and Social Research*)

L. L. BERNARD
President, 1932

E. B. REUTER
President, 1933

ERNEST W. BURGESS
President, 1934
Editor, *The American Journal of Sociology,*
1936-40

F. STUART CHAPIN
President, 1935

HENRY PRATT FAIRCHILD
President, 1936

© *Koehne*

ELLSWORTH FARIS
President, 1937
Editor, *The American Journal of Sociology*,
1926-36

FRANK H. HANKINS
President, 1938
Editor, *American Sociological Review*,
1936-37

EDWIN H. SUTHERLAND
President, 1939

ROBERT MORRISON MacIVER
President, 1940

© *Edward H. Goldberger, St. Louis, Mo.*

STUART A. QUEEN
President, 1941

DWIGHT SANDERSON
President, 1942

GEORGE A. LUNDBERG
President, 1943

RUPERT B. VANCE
President, 1944

© *Eugene L. Ray, Evanston, Ill.*
KIMBALL YOUNG
President, 1945

CARL C. TAYLOR
President, 1946

LOUIS WIRTH
President, 1947

E. FRANKLIN FRAZIER
President, 1948

TALCOTT PARSONS
President, 1949

LEONARD S. COTTRELL, JR.
President, 1950

HERBERT BLUMER
Editor, *The American Journal of Sociology,*
current

MARTIN NEUMEYER
Managing Editor,
Sociology and Social Research

KATHARINE JOCHER
Editor, *Social Forces,*
current

READ BAIN
Editor, *American Sociological Review,*
1937-41

JOSEPH K. FOLSOM
Editor, *American Sociological Review*,
1942-45

ROBERT COOLEY ANGELL
Editor, *American Sociological Review*,
1946-48

© *Greystone Studios, Inc.*

MAURICE DAVIE
Editor, *American Sociological Review*,
current

© *U. of Minn., Photographic Laboratory*

LOWRY NELSON
Editor, *Rural Sociology*,
1936-40

© *Walter R. Fleischer*

CARLE C. ZIMMERMAN
Editor, *Rural Sociology,*
1941-42

CHARLES P. LOOMIS
Editor, *Rural Sociology,*
1943-47

© *Adam Pepiot, Lexington, Ky.*

HOWARD W. BEERS
Editor, *Rural Sociology,*
current

© *The Anderson Studio, Gainesville, Fla.*

T. LYNN SMITH
Former Managing Editor, *Rural Sociology*

© *Siddell Studio, Raleigh, N. C.*

C. HORACE HAMILTON
Current Managing Editor, *Rural Sociology*

E. GEORGE PAYNE
Editor, *Journal of Educational Sociology*,
current

© *S. Gordon, Chicago, Ill.*

RALPH A. GALLAGHER, S.J.
Editor,
American Catholic Sociological Review,
current

later educational efforts at the "top of the ladder" at Minnesota from 1911 to 1917, and later as president of the Rockefeller Foundation from 1917 to 1929, when he directed the expenditure of millions of dollars for research and demonstration. He was also a member of the General Education Board from 1914 to 1929. He lectured in Scandinavian universities in 1933 and was a member of various international committees and foundations. He was awarded the honorary degree of LL.D. by Chicago in 1911, Yale in 1911, the University of Michigan in 1913, and the University of Minnesota in 1930. Even with his extraordinarily varied and successful life, he continued a long and active career, even as did his fellow presidents of the American Sociological Society with quieter academic ways of living. When he died on February 1, 1941, he was nearing his seventy-seventh birthday.

George E. Howard: 1849–1928

Following Ross's and Vincent's terms as presidents of the American Sociological Society, perhaps it may be said that American sociology had been well launched and followed a more or less routine development. One phase of this development was the part our presidents of the American Sociological Society played in the development of universities and the way in which their work coincided with logical processes through which sociology grew into a major discipline and accumulated a substantial body of literature. There were relatively few sociologists with full professorships in colleges and universities who had achieved distinction sufficient to rate election as president of the Society. If there had been more such universities, our assumption is that John R. Commons would have continued to teach sociology and would have become a distinguished sociologist. Chicago, Wisconsin, Nebraska, Michigan, Kansas, Indiana, Illinois, Missouri were the leaders and constituted the main stream of the westward dominance of sociology in the United States.

There was another situation, characteristic of graduate degrees and graduate instruction in colleges and universities that was characteristic of sociology. It was that candidates for the doctor's degrees, as achieved, let us say, at Hopkins or in Germany, or even later at Columbia, accepted positions to teach either their major or minor subjects according to the most desirable opportunities that appeared in the then limited field. This was also true of the classical scholar majoring in Latin and minoring in Greek, who would accept appointment in a new department of Greek, if no suitable opportunity appeared in Latin. Especially was this true of economics or political economy, political science, history and later sociology. And since even at Hopkins there was no sociology training as such and positions in sociology were ordinarily developed within the university departments of economics, history, or political science, it happened that the expansion of sociology in the middle western universities was due to the leadership of those scholars in the social sciences who sensed the need and were faced with the opportunity for establishing first new courses and then new departments.

Thus George Howard at Nebraska was first and for many years professor of history and political science before sociology. Weatherly at Indiana was first professor of history and then economics. Blackmar was first professor of history and economics before he was professor of history and sociology. Hayes was first professor of economics and sociology before coming to Illinois, although he was one of the first to receive a degree in sociology from Chicago. Cooley's doctor's degree was in economics, and we have already seen how Ross entered the field from economics. James Q. Dealey's department was one of political science to which Lester F. Ward was invited later as professor of sociology.

All this is of considerable importance in appraising both the work and rating of these leading sociologists in the decade from 1910 to 1920 which was in reality the second main stage of development of American sociology. In the first place, the work of these leaders reflects vividly and accurately the ways in which sociology was maturing. In the second place, it explains the nature and limitations of the sociological contributions made by men who were teachers of more than one subject, organizers of new departments, and still pioneers in writing and contacts in sociology. So, too, it explains both the multiple activities and the lack of research on the part of those professors who had come to their professorships in a few short years and yet advanced to the top of the American Sociological Society's leadership with little or no competition.

The first of this new style of pioneers, within the range of the first eight in sociology's second era, was George Howard, president of the Society in 1917. Like Small, he came from the Northeast to grow up and remain in the Middle West throughout his professional career. Like his predecessors he lived a long and rigorous life nine years beyond his three score years and ten, from 1849 to 1928. Like his predecessors he worked his way up the long hard way of procession and succession. At twenty-seven he got his A.B. from Nebraska and at forty-four his Ph.D. degree from the same institution, and in the meantime he had studied some history and Roman law at Munich and Paris in 1876 and 1878. From this point he became professor of history at Nebraska from 1879 to 1901, professor and lecturer at Chicago in 1903, then back to Nebraska in 1904 as professor of institutional history from 1904 to 1906 and finally as professor of political science and sociology from 1906 to 1928.

An understanding of the range and nature of courses taught indicates that the basic foundations for teaching and for developing a new subject were grounded in the reading of the classical books in each field and in being conversant with the current literature of economics, political theory, social philosophy, and, subsequently, sociology. Thus Howard's two main books were in the field of constitutional history and the American revolution. Yet his presidential address before the American Sociological Society, published in the *Papers and Proceedings* of the Twelfth Annual Meeting of the Society in 1918, reflected the sociological synopsis upon what was then, even as in 1950, a very grave problem of human relations set in the incidence of social change. Discussing "Ideals as a Factor in the Future Control of International Society," he said, on page 1, that "crises in human affairs clear the way for change, often with a view to preventing . . . future crises." To what extent did World War I show the need for a change in values? The "nation-state" must safeguard the welfare of its citizens and that of other men as well. The function of war and militarism as forces in human progress must undergo change. An ideal of democracy must arise. Education is the most efficient instrument of social control and should be used to bring about these changes.

As early as March, 1891, Howard was writing in the *Atlantic Monthly* on the theme of "The State University in America" in which his central theme of education finds focus in state education. In this article Howard criticizes the wasteful expenditure of moneys for public education through uncritical multiplication of routine courses. He recommended a revision of the educational program to include a two-year or three-year general course for people who do not wish professional training. This of course was prophetic of what was and is recommended. The larger universities would then provide professional and graduate training for those persons who wanted it. He decried also the lack of quality extant in so many of the institutions and hoped that a new approach and setup would improve the quality of scholarship. His reasons for favoring state education were because of its excellent success historically and because it achieved better and more usable results than any other system. In support of this he gave historical references showing the development of state financed education in the United States. Howard ends with a combined hope and prophecy that the future of state education will result in consolidation of schools, with better undergraduate education and better facilities and quality in graduate work and instruction.

Like Blackmar, Howard is featured in the *Cosmopolitan* with a photograph, "Portrait, George E. Howard." Accompanying is an article by Harold Bolce on "Polyglots in the Temple of Babel" in which Howard is severely censured for advocating sex instruction in the home and university. This was as early as 1909 and was in the June issue of *Cosmopolitan,* page 61 ff. The references were, of course, to Howard's pioneering and, for the time, monumental three-volume *A History of Matrimonial Institutions,* published in 1904. This was, of course, Howard's magnum opus and it set the incidence for American sociology's scientific study of marriage and the family as a special area of sociology. Although particular reference is made to Howard's work in Chapter 18, we need to record here something of the framework and methods utilized by Howard. Ernest R. Groves and Lee M. Brooks have summarized Howard's general observations and criticisms from Chapters I and IV in his Volume I in their *Readings in the Family,* page 11. The substance of this summary is that Howard holds that since marriage is a product of social experience the only way to understand its modern aspects is to study the general sociological facets surrounding its origin and early history among the races of mankind. And he feels that at last [in 1904], in the laboratory of science, there is some prospect that man may come to know himself. Yet Howard protests that perhaps nowhere is there rasher inference and more sweeping generalization. Especially he felt that many psychological factors were being overlooked as well as economic and evolutionary laws. In the light of what has developed and as described in our Chapter 18, Howard seemed to be on the right track of both query and complaint.

Sociology has done a great deal in this sub-science of the family, and the early assumptions of universal progress were not well founded.

Charles Horton Cooley: 1864–1929

Some students of American sociology have been inclined to add Ross and Cooley to the roster of Ward, Sumner, Giddings, and Small as the "fathers of sociology" because of the dynamics and range of the Ross and Cooley books. This is clearly not the case, although as authors these two rank high and their work may very well be commensurate with that of the first four. As we point out in a number of places, Cooley's work has been more nearly accepted by a larger number of sociologists than perhaps any other. Their work and contributions, however, were on a different time sequence and on a different frontier. This may be indicated by Ross's long and painful rise to the attainment of a department of sociology and the fact that, when Cooley's examination for the doctor's degree at Michigan required a minor in sociology, the examination questions were sent to Michigan by Giddings from Columbia. So, too, Cooley's dissertation on transportation and his studies of children as well as his pioneering work in social psychology were in the second era of American sociology. Cooley was always bantering to the effect that perhaps neither Giddings nor anyone else ever read his examination.

Cooley, like Ward, Vincent, Ross, and Weatherly, was native to the Middle West, but unlike them he never left its domain except once for a short interval abroad, and once with the United States Bureau of the Census. Born in 1864 at Ann Arbor just at the ending of the American Civil War, by the time he was twenty-three he had been graduated from Michigan and at thirty, in 1894, he had received his Ph.D. at Michigan in economics with a minor in sociology. He was assistant in political science from 1892 to 1895, assistant professor of economics from 1899 to 1904, and professor of sociology after that until his death in 1929.

In some ways Cooley as a sociologist might be said to resemble Giddings in what he did and the way he did it more than any of the other older pioneers. For instance, his deep and wide reading covered much of the same ground as Giddings', and his keen analysis, discrimination, adaptation of his reading to his own work, and his critical interpretation reminded one somewhat of Giddings whose work influenced him greatly. Then again, he was early interested in political science, as was

Giddings, and much of his best work was on the level of the psychological approach as also was Giddings'. Also, his ability to systematize his work and to create new terminology were comparable to much that Giddings did.

Concerning his background of reading and the sociologists who influenced him in turning to sociology Cooley wrote on pages 5 and 6 of his *Sociological Theory and Social Research,* edited by Robert Cooley Angell, that "as regards the academic possibilities of sociology I had been awakened by the papers of Professor Giddings which appeared about 1890, dealing with the province of the subject, its relation to political economy and its suitability for university study. I may add that I had made the acquaintance of Giddings, probably at the 1890 meeting of the American Economic Association at Washington, where, at least, I remember hearing him speak, and that he had given kindly encouragement to my sociological aspirations. It was he more than any other who led me to believe that sociology might become a university subject, and myself a teacher of it.

"Lester F. Ward was also at the Washington meeting and was most courteous to me, complimenting me on a paper that I read on what would now be called the ecology of street railways, and giving me a ticket to the Cosmos Club, which, however, I neglected to use. I knew hardly anything of his works at that time but read later, with profit, what I found to be the more readable of them, and had an interesting correspondence with him regarding Galton's views on genius. I had and have the greatest respect for Ward, and concur heartily as to the high rank assigned to him in American sociology, but it would be untrue to say that his writings had any large part in forming my own conceptions of the subject.

"With this preparation, and a very ardent purpose to share in that new development of social knowledge that seemed about to begin, I offered sociology as one of my minor subjects for the Doctor's degree, and set myself to study the accredited authors. I read enough of Comte to give me a general idea of his system, Ward's *Psychic Factors of Civilization* and part of his *Dynamic Sociology,* Darwin's *Origin of Species* and *Descent of Man,* and more or less in Gumplowicz, Quételet (statistics was my other minor), Sir Henry Maine, Morgan, McLennan and Westermarck; also in Jane Addams and other philanthropic writers. But

more time and labor than I put on any of these went to an arduous pe-
rusal of the first volume of Schäffle's *Bau und Leben des socialen Körpers*.
I was looking for a view of the social system that should be more satisfactory than Spencer's and it seemed to me that Schäffle offered the best
prospect of it. Indeed, from my recollection of it, I have no doubt that
his was in many respects a very good view indeed, but just how much it
helped me in working out my own conceptions I am unable to say."

Cooley's main books include his *Personal Competition*, 1899; *Human
Nature and the Social Order*, 1902; *Social Organization*, 1909; *Social
Process*, 1918; *Life and the Student*, 1927; *Sociological Theory and Social
Research*, 1930. In addition to his books his bibliography contains some
twenty-five articles of which twelve were republished in his last book,
Sociological Theory and Social Research.

Barnes, ranking Cooley high in his catalogue of American sociologists,
page 835, points out that Cooley's "generalizations, keen and scholarly as
they are, were derived chiefly from books perused thoughtfully in the
comfortable setting of the library. His own books draw quite as much
upon the great monuments of general literature as upon technical treatments of sociology." Perhaps no other sociologist, unless it was Giddings,
has shown such mastery of the art of dignified expression as to give his
writings a high degree of literary merit not only in content but also in
the form of expression.

Two broad fundamental assumptions characterize Cooley's approach
to social phenomena. The first was his comprehensive and practical view
of the organic nature of history and society. The second was the organic
view of the social process, in which the central theme of Cooley's psychological sociology is the doctrine of the inseparable and complementary nature of society and the individual. This elucidation of the
interaction and interrelationships of the individual and society, Barnes
pointed out in Chapter XLIII of his *Introduction to the History of Sociology,* entitled "Charles Horton Cooley: Pioneer in Psychosociology,"
furnishes the subject matter of Cooley's books and constitutes a coherent
system of social philosophy.

Cooley's methodology is discussed and quoted at length in Chapter
15 of this book. From our inquiries it seems clear that perhaps no other
sociologist has been and is still quoted with such generous commenda-
tion as Cooley. In both the number of references in some fifty textbooks

and in selections in source books, Cooley leads, the details of which are given in Chapter 15. It is often said, too, that his great trilogy, *Human Nature and the Social Order, Social Organization,* and *Social Process,* presented the most acceptable socio-psychological theory yet evaluated on that level of study. And certainly no sociologist or other social scientist has presented the public such a literary gem: he "left himself in imperishable form in *Life and the Student* as it is the fortune of few mortals to do." One of the best ways to compare Cooley's concepts, style, methodology, with those of Ross is to compare Cooley's *Life and the Student* with Ross's *Capsules of Social Wisdom* published for him by *Social Forces* in 1948, and upon which Ross was still working in 1950. Cooley's work is also further evaluated in Chapters 16, 17, 18, and 22. It is pointed out that while Cooley is most often quoted for his primary face-to-face groups and for his "looking glass self," he estimates in his *Sociological Theory and Social Research* that his main contribution was in the field of what he sometimes called organic sociology in which the frame of reference was the inseparability of the individual and the group, the interaction processes between society and the individual. Cooley would have agreed, however, that his realistic studies of behavior through the observation of children, his special exposition of the social processes, and his foundations of social psychology were all part and parcel of his contributions which, still in 1950, are required readings of several sub-areas of general sociology as well as in general sociology.

Cooley's presidential address in 1918, printed in the *Publications of the American Sociological Society: Papers of the 13th Annual Meeting,* Volume XIII, was on "A Primary Culture for Democracy." For Cooley, "culture means the development of the human and social, as distinct from the technical, side of life." His concept of culture was functional in a different way from that posited by some of the later anthropologists. That is, culture was necessary to democracy, and especially at the post-war 1919 period when the new sweep of technology and economic advance challenged society anew.

CHAPTER 6

From 1919–1922:
Blackmar, Dealey, Hayes, Lichtenberger

Among the notable epochs in American higher education was the founding of the Johns Hopkins University and the introduction to America of German scholarship. G. Stanley Hall envisaged a new dynamics of "University" in what he hoped would be the blending of German scholarship with America's new dynamics and limitless freedom of learning. First he introduced this mode of scholarship in Johns Hopkins and later as president of Clark University he followed within the special field of psychology, attracting to his university such men as Boas and Dewey, and introducing to the United States many of the German psychologists, including Freud. Of the sociologists who were associated with Hall in the formative stages of the new borderline — sociology, psychology, anthropology, history — were Harry Elmer Barnes and Frank H. Hankins.

Of the earlier sociologists greatly influenced by Johns Hopkins were Albion W. Small, E. A. Ross, and Frank W. Blackmar. The particular influence at Hopkins, however, was that of Herbert B. Adams, who received his Ph.D. degree in political science in Berlin in 1876, came to Hopkins as fellow in the fall of the same year that Hopkins opened, and grew up with Hopkins, beginning the notable *Studies in Historical and Political Science* in 1882. From that point on Adams was the dominant figure in the field of American social science, along with Richard Ely, at Hopkins. He was leading man in the founding of the American Historical Association, of which he was secretary and executive officer for twenty-five years. The work of Adams has been described in Chapter IV of *American Masters of Social Science,* edited by Howard W. Odum, and published in 1927. The important emphasis here is twofold. First, Adams reflected the influence and methodology of the German scholarship, especially in history and political science and, second, he influenced many young Americans who were to become leaders in American social science, and he was broad enough not to prejudice his students against sociology and social philosophy in his teachings as was evidenced by Ross, Small, and Blackmar. This constitutes a link in the chain of successions in American sociology as Small continued the influence of European sociology through Hayes and others.

Frank W. Blackmar: 1854–1931

In Frank W. Blackmar, ninth president of the American Sociological Society, American sociology finds a peculiarly representative leader of its second stage of development. In almost a dozen ways he may be said to recapitulate the nature and processes of sociology's early development. Although beginning in mathematics and receiving his Ph.D. degree from Johns Hopkins in history and economics, he is recorded as starting one of the major departments of sociology some years before Small established his own great department. Blackmar was one of the Johns Hopkins trilogy, Small, Ross, and Blackmar, who, although stimulated and inspired by Herbert Adams, broke away from their Hopkins general social science training to go more specifically into sociology. He was also one of the pioneers who, like Small, Hayes, Ellwood, came from the Northeast to build sociology in the middle western universities. Like Small, Vincent, and others he also carried on his sociological work alongside being a dean in the university. And like Weatherly of Indiana, Hayes of Illinois, Ellwood of Missouri, Gillin of Wisconsin, and Taylor and Odum of North Carolina, he realigned sociology with social work as president of his State Conference of Social Work — in his case the Kansas State Conference of Charities and Corrections, later, the Conference of Social Work. Also like those of his fellow pioneers, Ward, Sumner, Giddings, Small, Vincent, Howard, Hayes, Weatherly, his long lifetime, from 1854 to 1931, represented an extraordinary span of years many of which reflected a wide experience and influence upon the development of sociology.

Born in Springfield, Pennsylvania, on November 3, 1854, Blackmar received his Ph.B. and A.M. degrees from the University of the Pacific, 1882–84. He followed the early pattern of coming to sociology from history and economics, being professor of history and sociology for ten years, 1889 to 1899, and of economics and sociology for another ten years.

at the University of Kansas before he was professor of sociology from 1912 to 1931. He was dean of the graduate school from 1896 to 1922. Blackmar also followed the early pattern of taking his Ph.D. degree relatively late, following a varied experience, being fellow and graduate student at Hopkins from 1886 to 1889. He was professor of mathematics at the University of the Pacific from 1882 to 1886, receiving his Hopkins Ph.D. degree in 1889 at thirty-five years of age. So, too, in later years he was not only professor and dean but was an elector in the Hall of Fame. He was awarded the honorary LL.D. degree from Southern California, 1921; from Southern Pacific in 1924; and from Baker University, 1929.

Yet in the midst of this he managed to write a considerable number of books as well as articles, including his *Elements of Sociology* in 1905 and one of the most widely used and influential textbooks, *Outlines of Sociology,* with Gillin in 1914. He had previously produced *The Study of History and Sociology* in 1890 and *The Story of Human Progress* in 1896. Subsequently, thirty years later, in 1926 he published his *History of Human Society,* and his excellent little *Justifiable Individualism* in 1922. These followed his earlier non-sociological works *The History of Federal and State Aid to Higher Education in the United States* in 1890, his *Spanish Colonization* and *Spanish Institutions of the Southwest* in 1890 and 1891, and his *Economics* in 1907.

As president of the American Sociological Society in 1919 his address before the Fourteenth Annual Meeting was devoted to "A Working Democracy" and was published in the *Publications of the American Sociological Society* in Vol. XIV, 1920. His premise reminded one of one of Giddings' later warnings, namely, that society must take stock of some things that are happening "or pass off this earth," a theme especially timely in 1950. What Blackmar had said was that new situations had made it necessary for us to take stock of our democracy. His discussion also reminds one of Gunnar Myrdal's thesis in 1947 in his *American Dilemma,* in which he points out the vast distance between America's credo and its practices. What Blackmar said was that Americans were sentimental and idealistic regarding democracy and liberty but must adopt positive realistic theories that must be implemented through education. The nature of Blackmar's general sociology may be estimated from composite definitions as given in Blackmar and Gillin's *Outlines of Sociology.* "Sociology has for its subject matter the life and behavior

of human beings in groups and it seeks to formulate the laws governing group behavior. In its broadest sense it includes the study of the
nature and history of man, the formation and behavior of family,
community, and national groups, and the evolution of all that we
call civilization." And again on page 23, *we may say that the purpose of sociology is, first to understand society; then, to enable us to
formulate a scientific program of social betterment.*" In his earlier *Elements of Sociology,* on pages 13 and 25, Blackmar said, "Sociology treats
of the phenomena of society arising from the association of mankind
and is the most recent of the coordinating social sciences, created for a
special purpose and standing on an independent basis."

Blackmar published a score of articles relating to economics and so-
ciology and to the historical aspects of Kansas, including the life of
Charles Robinson. Among his articles were those in *The Forum* for
July, 1906, August, 1897, June, 1896, January, 1899; *Dial,* March, 1903,
October, 1890, February, 1892. Others were in *Harper's Weekly,* August,
1899; the *Review of Reviews,* June, 1892, September, 1901, October, 1902.
Still others were published in *The Political Science Quarterly, The
American Historical Review, The World Today, The American Journal
of Sociology, The Annals* of the American Academy of Political and
Social Science, and *The Nation.* Like other sociologists of his day, he
was considered "radical." In the *Cosmopolitan* for May, 1909, there was
published "Portrait, Frank W. Blackmar" by Harold Bolce and further
entitled "Blasting at the Rock of Ages," denouncing Blackmar for his
teaching that values change from generation to generation.

James Q. Dealey: 1861–1937

James Q. Dealey typified another of those attributes that have characterized sociology in the United States as "American." He was born in
Manchester, England, in 1861 but developed quite in accord with the
American college and university pattern — receiving the A.B. at Brown
University at twenty-nine years of age, the M.A. at thirty-two, and the
Ph.D. degree at thirty-three in 1895. In this respect his case resembles
that of Louis Wirth of Chicago who, born abroad, developed through
similar stages at the University of Chicago. In something of the same
way, Parsons of Harvard resembles Small of Chicago in that each got his
first major momentum in Germany and followed it with writings greatly

influenced by German sociologists. Dealey's high place in American sociology is due to three technical, "ex officio" achievements. He was president of the American Sociological Society in 1920; he had established at Brown a Department of Political Science that set the incidence for Ward's professorship of sociology and his continued contribution to sociology from the college vantage point; and he made his own contribution to the textbook field with his *Text Book in Sociology* in 1905, with Lester F. Ward; his *The Family in Its Sociological Aspects* in 1912; and *Sociology: Its Development and Application,* 1921. In his political science field of interest he had produced *The Growth of State Constitutions* in 1912, *The State and Government* in 1921, and *The Foreign Policies of the United States* in 1927. After his retirement as professor of sociology and political science in 1928, he was editor of the *Dallas News* until his death in 1937.

For his presidential address, printed in the *Publications of the American Sociological Society,* Volume XV, in 1921, he prepared a paper on "Eudemics, The Science of National or General Welfare." In this address the emphasis upon world crisis appears in 1950 peculiarly timely although it featured the national in contrast to the most common denominator of the international or world order in 1950. What Dealey said was that in this period of world crisis, it would be well to consider the many principles and processes that underlie national improvement. To this end he defines *Eudemics* as a subdivision of social progress. Order should accompany social process and a nation must adapt itself to changing environment and so react to this change that further changes will be more favorable. The factors to be considered include population, the inherent potentialities of the nation, group struggles within the nation. The goal should be national happiness.

The sequence of Dealey's succession to Ward at Brown is in contrast to that of Keller at Yale. At Yale, Keller would have nothing to do with sociology or the American Sociological Society or surely he would have been a unanimous selection for president. Yet he devoted prodigious labor to seeing that Sumner's contributions were preserved and published with an incomparable loyalty and fidelity to Sumner, both personally and professionally. At the same time Keller was relatively prolific in his writing if we consider his books and his articles in which he had a most readable style. Keller's protest was against the term "sociology" for which he adamantly substituted "The science of society." At Brown, Dealey succeeded Ward as president of the American Sociological Society and reflected whatever sociological glory was to be had from Ward's distinguished work and followed with a textbook on sociology of his own some years after Ward's death.

From Dealey's texts it is possible to arrive at an approximation of his sociology. In his *Sociology: Its Development and Application,* page 49, the science of sociology "must seek to make a complete survey of social conditions and problems and to work out empirically improvements in the situation. It must study as completely as possible the processes in the development of social groups and institutions. But, in order to do so intelligently, there is necessarily involved an analysis of the social order, structure, or organization of society, as well as a study of the social forces or psychic factors at work and their resultant social functioning or activities under varying conditions of environment. Finally, it must work out applications of these teachings to present situations, thereby developing the applied science of sociology." From his *Text Book in Sociology,* with Ward, we gather that sociology is "The Study of Human Association including whatever conduces to it or modifies it." Yet in his admirable chapter on Lester F. Ward on page 75 of Odum's *American Masters of Social Science,* 1927, he wrote that "in the sociological world there is no definite agreement as to what constitutes the field of sociology. The field is becoming highly specialized and each specialist tends to assume that his is the real field." Upon his retirement Dealey might be said to have become the practical sociologist, attempting to channel his sociology through the press even as Giddings and Park had come to sociology through the press. By 1930 he had been awarded an honorary doctor's degree by Baylor University as symbol of his success.

Dealey's contributions to American sociology may be catalogued in four categories. His texts on introductory sociology contributed to a needed tools-resource for teaching. His *The Family in Its Sociological Aspects* was, with Howard's three volumes, the main evidence to that date of sociology's contributions to this sub-science of sociology. His contribution to a second special area, namely political sociology, is a part of the third; and his continued support of sociology, his interpretation of Ward, and his presidency of the Society, indicated his place in

American sociology. His *The Family in Its Sociological Aspects* is discussed at length in Chapter 18, so that it is only necessary here to note its priority in setting the premise that marriage and the family were neglected special fields of sociology that offered new opportunity to American sociologists.

Edward Carey Hayes: 1868–1928

Edward Carey Hayes, the eleventh president of the American Sociological Society, in 1921, again followed the pattern of the early pioneers in several aspects. In addition to his coming to sociology from another field of interest, having studied in Germany, and thus taking his doctor's degree relatively late at thirty-four years of age, and, although a New Englander, gaining the leadership of sociology in the Middle West, he was trained in the ministry, as were Small, Sumner, and Vincent before him and Lichtenberger, Ellwood, Gillin, and Steiner after him. Like Vincent, Thomas, and Ellwood, he was a student of Small at Chicago who not only guided him considerably toward the special field of sociology, away from philosophy and the ministry, but also sent him for a year to Europe for special study.

Born in Lewiston, Maine, in 1868, he was graduated from Bates College in 1887, went to Cobb Divinity School for two years and was ordained minister in 1893. He was pastor at Augusta, Maine, from then until 1896, when he went to Keuka College, New York, for two years as dean. From there he went to Miami University in Ohio as professor of economics and sociology for five years, from which position he went to the University of Illinois where he was professor of sociology and head of the department until 1928. He was elected president of the American Sociological Society from his position at Illinois.

Hayes continued, after settling down at the University of Illinois, to participate in a wide range of activities in the places where he worked and in broader fields of action, as well as to produce substantially in the field of sociology, publishing many articles as well as two books that ranked well up in the lists when published in 1915 and in 1921. He had also built up a large undergraduate Department of Sociology at Illinois and had taught in summer sessions at Harvard, Columbia, Chicago, Pennsylvania, and Colorado. Thus, in all his work and contacts he represented sociology in such ways, at learned societies, on and off the campus, as to give prestige to sociology in this second major stage of development.

From the founding of the American Sociological Society to his death, this wholesome influence of Hayes was manifest. He was present in 1905 when the Society was started, and thus became a charter member. His name appeared frequently in the Proceedings of the Society until the time of his death. He was a member of the Committee of Ten appointed by the American Sociological Society to outline the subject-matter of the fundamental course in sociology. He was appointed to represent the American Sociological Society on the Joint Commission on Presentation of Social Studies in the Schools. He was second vice-president of the Society for 1919, first vice-president for 1920, and president for 1921. He was secretary of the Social Psychology Section of the World's Congress of Science in the St. Louis Exposition in 1904. He served as president of the Illinois Conference of Charities and Corrections and was a member of the Illinois Welfare Commission. He was advisory editor of *The American Journal of Sociology,* and cooperating editor of the *Journal of Applied Sociology* (later *Sociology and Social Research*). He was editor of the Lippincott series in sociology, of which the first volume appeared in 1922. He was a member of the German Sociological Society, a member of the Institut International de Sociologie (Paris), and a member and former vice-president of the Instituto Internazionale di Sociologia (Rome). He organized the Family Welfare Society of Champaign.

His presidential address, printed in the *Publications of the American Sociological Society* in the *Papers and Proceedings* of the sixteenth Annual Meeting, Volume XVI, was devoted to "The Sociological Point of View." Like most of the earlier sociologists he wrote plausibly about the need for research from the sociological point of view, which, to him, might well be the greatest possible contribution toward the interpretation of life, for human life derives its content from human society, the subject matter of sociology. Although Hayes defined no methodologies or approaches, he discussed areas of evolution, social structure, social function, social causation, and he made social process the heart of his sociological system.

Hayes contributed more than twenty-five main articles to *The American Journal of Sociology, Social Forces,* and *Sociology and Social Re-*

search. His main books were his comprehensive textbook *Introduction to the Study of Sociology,* in 1915, his *Sociology,* in 1918, his edited, *Recent Development in the Social Sciences,* in 1927, and his *Sociology and Ethics,* in 1921. In this last book Hayes showed both originality and conformity to his great teacher, Small, whose ethical emphasis was always present. In this book he also resembles Ellwood's moral and religious emphasis in his later books. The ethical inferences are ever present also in his *Introduction to the Study of Sociology,* where, summarizing page 8, Sociology is (1) ethical, regarding the weal and woe of all men as facts to be accounted for; (2) it views the facts of human experience as belonging to the orderly course of nature; (3) the essence of life in sociology is seen to be made up of a functional process of conscious activities; (4) sociology sets itself to the task of synthesis; (5) in the study of these facts it aims to dissolve all bonds of party, sect, and prejudice.

Other of Hayes' definitions include the following composite: "Sociology is an intellectual movement resulting from the insistence of the mind that the methods of science shall be carried out in the realm of human activities." And again on page 28: "Sociology is the study of groups of living beings and of the life of such groups, as affected by natural, by artificial physical environments, by the psychophysical traits of the members of such groups, and above all, by relations of conditions and consequences between the activities of the members of such groups." On page 31, sociology is described as "the attempt to study in a truly scientific spirit and by a broadly comparative method that conscious life of man which is also the life of society and which can evolve as it does only in society and as the life of society." Finally, Hayes says on page 43 that "The term 'sociology' celebrates the thoroughgoing adoption of the scientific method in the study of human life."

Harry Elmer Barnes, in his *Introduction to the History of Sociology,* rates Hayes a place in American sociology as one of eleven to whom a chapter is devoted. Chapter XLV is entitled "The Sociological Theories of Edward Carey Hayes." The other American sociologists include, of the presidents of the American Sociological Society, Ward, Sumner, Giddings, Small, Thomas, Ross, Cooley, Ellwood. Two of these — Ward and Sumner — were designated "Founders." Barnes, on page 871, estimated that Hayes was "primarily interested in the organization and interpretation of sociological data rather than in esoteric and minute social research. He wished, above all else, to make sociology clear, coherent, and socially useful. In Hayes' opinion, the prime object of sociological study is the social process." Again, on page 874, Hayes's sociological writings were, on the whole, "characterized more by a large amount of practical common sense than by special profundity or brilliant powers of generalization. He wrote in a very clear and readable style, and — to compare him with two of his best-known contemporaries in middle western institutions — his work stands midway between the erudition of C. A. Ellwood and the brilliant phraseology of E. A. Ross."

Hayes had developed a large Department of Sociology at Illinois but remained constantly a supporter and helper of Small in the editing of *The American Journal of Sociology*. In his chapter on Small in Odum's *American Masters of Social Science* may be found something of the manner of man he was. About Small he writes on page 149 that anyone who wishes to form a mental picture of Small must imagine "the ideal of a gentleman," and that "the fundamental element of his life has been always the ethical element," and that "He has been interested in scholarship as a means of solving life's puzzles."

And so we come to record Hayes' special contribution as his *Sociology and Ethics*. Hayes also, however, had a great deal to say on the relations of government and sociology and so was, along with Dealey, following Giddings and Sumner, one of the forerunners of political sociology. He reflected the critical attitude toward social theory in his article on "The 'Social Forces' Error" in the March, 1911, issue of *The American Journal of Sociology,* and in his July, September, November, 1911, articles on "The Classification of Social Phenomena."

James P. Lichtenberger: 1870–

Lichtenberger, the twelfth president of the American Sociological Society in 1922, reversed the more recent order of regional priority. Like Ward, he was born and raised in the Middle West but moved ultimately to the Northeast where, in 1950, he could celebrate a half century of his eighty years of active life. He was also the only other president of the Society in this decade, except Dealey, who was not from one of the great universities of the Middle West, two being from Chicago and one each from Illinois, Michigan, Wisconsin, Indiana, Kansas, Nebraska, Missouri. He was born at Decatur, Illinois, June 10, 1870, was graduated from Eureka College, took an A.M. at Hiram College, Ohio, at thirty-two, and his Ph.D. at Columbia in 1909 at thirty-nine years of age.

Lichtenberger, like Small, Hayes, Gillin, and others, had started his professional career as a minister and was pastor at Canton, Illinois, from 1896 to 1899, at Buffalo, New York, from 1899 to 1902 and in New York city from 1902 to 1908. Also in New York, while working for his Ph.D. degree at Columbia, he was fellow in the New York School of Philanthropy, later the New York School of Social Work; also he taught one semester in political science in 1908 in Columbia's extension division. After receiving his degree at Columbia, he came to the University of Pennsylvania as assistant professor of sociology in 1909, where he remained for thirty-one years until his retirement as emeritus professor in 1940. He was made full professor in 1914. He was also secretary of the American Academy of Political and Social Science from 1912 to 1950.

Lichtenberger applied himself more to general teaching and contacts with other universities and travel in vacations than to research and writing. He taught in summer sessions at Illinois, Western Reserve, Oregon, Virginia, and was exchange professor at the University of Washington for one quarter in 1929. Lichtenberger made it a point to visit every state in the Union, every province in the Dominion of Canada, with trips to every continent on the globe. He was active in Philadelphia affairs, being president of the Contemporary Club, The University Club, member of The City Club.

Lichtenberger's two volumes were his *Development of Social Theory,* in 1925, and his *Divorce: A Study of Social Causation,* in 1931. The volume on divorce was first published in 1909 as his doctor's dissertation in the Columbia University "Studies in History, Economics and Public Law." His *Development of Social Theory* was long a standard requirement in courses on social theory and the history of social thought, being in reality a text on the history of social thought more nearly than a treatise on theory, as defined in later sociology. This book, along with those of Bristol, Sorokin, House, and Bogardus, constituted a sort of minimum requirement or reference shelf for students during the late 1920's and early 1930's. Lichtenberger's contribution here is discussed subsequently in Chapter 15.

The subject of his presidential address in 1922 was "The Moral Dualism of Machiavelli"; it was published in the *Papers and Proceedings* of the Seventeenth Annual Meeting of the American Sociological Society in 1923, Volume XVII. In this address Lichtenberger stressed an important point that Machiavelli was the product of his time and reflected a double standard of what might be in the ideal type and what was real in society, featuring the conflict between idealism and practical necessity. In his *Thoughts of a Statesman* Machiavelli stressed moral idealism and, in his *The Prince,* he described what men do under the circumstances.

Lichtenberger's contribution to American sociology may be found in his two books and in his presidential address, which, like his books, began at Columbia. In addition to these, his ex officio influence at the University of Pennsylvania, on the American Sociological Society, and on the American Academy of Political and Social Science were a part of his work. Lichtenberger continued his interests begun in special study under Giddings at Columbia when his text on theory was developed in the traditional historical way. His political science interest was interpreted through Machiavelli, and his interest in practical studies through the study of divorce. Lichtenberger and Carl Kelsey worked closely together and reflected the development of sociology at the University of Pennsylvania where Kelsey had published his *Physical Basis of Society* following a special study of the Negro farmer.

CHAPTER 7

From 1923–1926:
Weatherly, Ellwood, Park, Gillin

It has been a common complaint that sociology in these earlier days did not have university support and did not afford enough positions for all new scholars who might have been recruited for sociology and therefore did not have an equal opportunity with economics, history, and political science. As evidence in support of the assumption that sociology would have forged ahead if it had had opportunity, the rapid rise of sociology after the 1920's in more accelerated ratio is cited. An example of where sociology lost an opportunity and a prospective "great" is the career of John R. Commons. Seeking a post from which to carry on his highly motivated and often dissenting work in the field of human relations, he went to Oberlin where he taught sociology as an associate professor of political science at $1200 a year, after teaching social science and failing to be reappointed at Wesleyan in 1890. A year later he moved to Indiana where his chief interest was still, as Joseph Dorfman reports, in "The Saga of John Rogers Commons," on pages 276–94 of Volume III of his *The Economic Mind in American Civilization,* "in the implications which science had for the social and spiritual life of the people." The rest of the story is well-known history. When a professorship in sociology was offered him at Syracuse University, he accepted it, and planned a fifteen-year program in which he would feature law and society, so much neglected, as he thought, by Giddings and other sociologists, but because of his radical views his chair of sociology was declared vacant. After five years of free-lance work including the New York Bureau of Economic Research, which folded up, Commons got his chance and, at the age of forty-two, returned to the University of Wisconsin where he made that institution a leader in American thought and where with Ely he paved the way for Ross to achieve leadership in sociology. It was in this period that the emerging sociologists, Weatherly, Ellwood, Park, and Gillin, had similar difficulties but emerged as sociologists.

Ulysses G. Weatherly: 1865–1940

If U. G. Weatherly, thirteenth president of the American Sociological Society in 1923, was not noted for his large written contributions to sociology, neither was his contemporary, Carl C. Plehn of the University of California, who was president of the American Economic Association the same year, or Edwin F. Gay of Harvard, president a little later, who never published a book and scarcely an article, yet ranked as one of the most influential of Harvard's nine presidents of the American Economic Association. Weatherly's status and place in the University of Indiana was in line with a distinguished succession that pioneered in Indiana's Department of Economics, in which, like Cooley at Michigan, Weatherly began his work.

Strangely enough, about the time Small was organizing his department at Chicago, John R. Commons, the prospective great economist, started sociology at Indiana as professor of economics and social science with a salary of $2000 a year and, with the noted Ely, organized in 1893 an American Institute of Christian Sociology, mentioned earlier in Chapter 1, for the purpose of studying American social problems from both the scientific and Christian standpoint. Weatherly was professor of economics and sociology from 1899 to 1940 although he was assistant professor of history from 1895 to 1898 and was associate professor for a year preceding his taking over sociology in 1899. Here again it must be recalled that positions in the social sciences in universities were hard to find and that a man like John Bates Clark was forced to transfer back and forth from East to West, and West to East, from small college to university, before finding himself. It is an important part of the record of American sociology that so many of the earlier sociologists carved out for themselves a place in sociology which they in turn developed to fuller stature.

Weatherly was following this early American pattern of coming to sociology from history and economics after studying in Heidelberg and Leipzig although he had received his Ph.D. at Cornell as early as 1894. Like several of the other pioneers in sociology he was born just after the civil war in Newton, Indiana, in 1865 and although receiving his A.B. at Colgate, he came back to his own native region to remain until his death in 1940 at seventy-five years of age. During these years he devoted himself primarily to teaching and contacts, mostly at Indiana, but also to teaching in summer sessions at Colorado, Columbia, Cornell, Oregon, Southern California. He received honorary degrees from his Alma Mater, Colgate, in 1910, and from Indiana in 1911. He was president of the Indiana Conference of Charities and Corrections, Chairman of the Indiana Child Labor Commission, and member of the Indiana Commission of Industrial Education. In his earlier years he was joint editor of the *Economic Bulletin.*

In 1927 his *Social Progress: The Dynamics of Social Change* was published. Something of the negative aspects of progress was reflected in his presidential address in 1923 and published under the title of "Racial Pessimism" in *The Publications of the American Sociological Society,* Volume XVIII, 1924. Weatherly estimated that skepticism concerning the permanence of western civilization had been growing. One question he asked was whether civilization was bankrupt in the light of the deterioration of race under increasingly complex cultures. He thought that while the white race will be declining in number, the aggressive color consciousness endangers it. Culture interests have not yet attained their proper place as a basis of organization and control. Social science should give more attention to loyalty. This was in line with the ethical emphasis placed upon sociology by Small and Hayes.

James E. Moffat, emeritus professor of economics at the University of Indiana with whom Weatherly worked, is preparing a biographical sketch, in which he places emphasis especially upon Weatherly's qualities of teaching and interpersonal relations on and off the campus. He has compiled a bibliography of more than eighty titles, of which no less than fifty are book reviews. Among the notable books of his day which Weatherly reviewed were those of Sumner, Durkheim, Ross, Morgan, Park, Wissler, Veblen. Weatherly's bibliography included a dozen titles on race and a few on women in industry. One of his articles, "The Racial Element in Social Assimilation," published in *The American Journal of Sociology* for March, 1911, indicated a special interest in a field partly discussed in his presidential address more than a decade later. Earlier, in the May, 1909, *American Journal of Sociology,* Weatherly had asked a question that was to be repeated over and over again for the next two decades. This was, "How does the access of women to industrial occupations react on the family?" Here his viewpoints and methods were similar to those of Howard and Dealey which are discussed in Chapter 18. Still earlier in 1900 he published an article on pages 521–34 of *The American Historical Association Report* on "Stein's German Policy at the Congress of Vienna." Weatherly also, from its organization, was a regular attendant and participator in the meetings of the American Sociological Society. A typical example of those earlier discussions was one in 1911 when Weatherly, Ross, Hayes, and Small, in addition to Maurice Parmelee and Jerome Davis, all discussed F. W. Blackmar's paper on "Leadership and Reform." That would be the perfect picture of American sociology as reflected by American sociologists, in that midwestern segment at that time.

Charles A. Ellwood: 1873–1946

The fourteenth president of the American Sociological Society, Charles A. Ellwood, in 1924, might very well be selected as one of the three of the first presidents who had a thorough education in sociology, although he, too, had minored strongly in economics and had been influenced by Ely. In addition to starting with the dynamic Ross at Cornell, he also worked with W. F. Willcox and J. W. Jenks. But his real training was with Small, Henderson, Thomas, and Vincent at Chicago, from which point on he was a full-fledged sociologist. In his background in general, however, he conformed to the patterns of the early years of twentieth-century sociology. He was born in New York, January 20, 1873, and was graduated from Cornell University in 1896; yet thereafter he became an exponent of the Middle States, first with his studying at Chicago, then in his transitional efforts to get located at Nebraska, then finally at the University of Missouri where he became one of the leading American sociologists for thirty years, before building another department at Duke University for still another fifteen years.

Like Small, Blackmar, Hayes, and Weatherly before him, he also studied in Europe and returned to receive his Ph.D. degree under Small at Chicago in 1899. Like them, he also received considerable momentum from certain economists, particularly Ely and Jenks, but, unlike his predecessors, he received his doctor's degree at the earlier age of twenty-six, and was the first of the presidents who came all the way up through university training in sociology. His experience was similar to that of others of his contemporaries in sociology, as well as in economics and political science, in that it was difficult to find a position in sociology in any university. He thus went directly as secretary of a charity organization society at Lincoln, Nebraska, where he could also lecture in sociology at the University of Nebraska, all for perhaps less than a thousand dollars a year. Then there was an offer of a professorship of sociology at the University of Missouri at $1500 which he accepted with his characteristic eagerness and to which he devoted himself powerfully for three decades.

Ellwood was like his earlier contemporaries in that he devoted himself to much work, many contacts and varied teaching, having taught in perhaps a baker's dozen institutions during the summer or on leave of absence from Missouri or Duke. Among others, he was visiting professor, largely in summers, at Columbia, Chicago, Colorado, Southern California, Utah, Wisconsin, Harvard, Northwestern. In addition to his prominence in the American Sociological Society, he, like Hayes and Weatherly and Howard, was president of the State Conference of Charities and Corrections as was his colleague Howard Jenson after him. He traveled and studied in Czechoslovakia, France, Italy, Austria, Germany, England, and in other places beyond his own nation. Among the many other activities and honors, the following may be listed: Chairman of the Section on Social Psychology, International Congress of Arts and Sciences, St. Louis, 1904; Fellow of the American Association for the Advancement of Science; Corresponding member, Deutsche Gesellschaft für Sociologie; Honorary member, Masaryk Sociological Society of Czechoslovakia; Honorary member, Société de Sociologie de Genève; National President, Pi Gamma Mu, 1931–37; President, International Congress of Sociology, Brussels, 1935; President, International Institute of Sociology, 1935–36; member of National Education Association and director of the Department of Social Studies, 1922–24. In connection with publications, Ellwood was advisory editor of *The American Journal of Sociology* and an associate editor of the *Journal of Criminal Law and Criminology*. He served on the editorial staffs of the *Journal of Educational Sociology, Sociology and Social Research* (formerly *Journal of Applied Sociology*), *Social Science,* and *World Affairs Interpreter.* He received the LL.D. degree from Bethany College in 1922.

His main books included *Public Relief and Private Charity in England,* 1903; *Sociology and Modern Social Problems,* 1910; *Sociology in*

Its Psychological Aspects, 1913; *The Social Problem,* 1915; *Introduction to Social Psychology,* 1917; *The Reconstruction of Religion,* 1922; *Christianity and Social Science,* 1923; *The Psychology of Human Society,* 1925; *Cultural Evolution,* 1927; *Man's Social Destiny,* 1929; *Methods in Sociology,* 1933; *A History of Social Philosophy,* 1938. In addition to these, Ellwood collaborated in a dozen other books, wrote approximately a hundred and fifty articles, and contributed nearly two score articles to encyclopedias and brochures. The aggregate sale of his books, he estimated, ran into more than a million copies, including foreign translations of several.

Ellwood's presidential address was devoted to "Intolerance" and was published in the *Papers and Proceedings* of the Nineteenth Annual Meeting of the American Sociological Society, Volume IX, 1925. His address was an attempt to give sociological interpretation to certain trends that followed in the wake of World War I. It was, therefore, an American sociologist's reaction and was set in the national framework and would appear peculiarly appropriate in the light of much discussion of the same subject after World War II. Ellwood was concerned that intolerance seemed to be growing in every form of American life and he concluded that intolerance was a handicap to social progress. Intolerance breeds separation, misunderstanding, and hostility between groups, which may lead to civic disorder and revolution. Repression that suppresses intercommunication also breeds revolution. Intercommunication is the organ of adjustment for conscious social change. His remedy was to convert the people to a scientific attitude of mind.

Howard Jensen, long-time colleague and successor of Ellwood at Duke, considers Barnes's estimate of Ellwood as authentic in that it had Ellwood's general approval. Barnes says on pages 855–56 of his *Introduction to the History of Sociology,* "one may say that his deep and abiding interest in social reform, the meliorative undercurrent in all his social philosophy, and his belief in the possibility of rational social progress through education in the social sciences were derived from his reading of Lester F. Ward and Auguste Comte and from the teachings of his mentor, Albion W. Small. His interest in, and command of, functional psychology and his application of it to sociology came mainly from his studies under Dewey and Angell. His later shift to an anthropocultural approach to social problems was due mainly to the influence of L. T.

Hobhouse and R. R. Marett. In the reconstruction of his psychological sociology in the twenties, Ellwood was influenced not only by Marett and Hobhouse, but especially by C. H. Cooley. He was particularly impressed by Cooley's synthesis and restatement of his psychological sociology in his *Social Process."*

Barnes sees, on pages 864–65, "in the development of Ellwood's sociological outlook . . . what has been a characteristic trend in contemporary sociology, namely, a recognition of the fact that psychological sociology is a branch of cultural sociology — that psychic forces are more of a cultural, than a biological, product. Ellwood's attitude toward culture has been evolutionary. In approaching cultural evolution his thought is in harmony with that of Comte, Ward, and Hobhouse, namely, that the course of cultural evolution can be brought under the control of the human mind and can be consciously directed in harmony with the teachings of social science.

"Ellwood has succeeded Ward as the main protagonist in his generation of the idea that sociology should be a normative and ameliorative social philosophy, justified mainly by its aid in improving society and the well-being of mankind. He has fought valiantly against a sterile 'objectivism' in social science."

Presentation of other aspects of Ellwood's work may be studied in Chapters 14, 15, 16, 19, 22.

Robert E. Park: 1864–1944

Park, the fifteenth president of the American Sociological Society for 1925, followed the earlier pattern of coming to sociology relatively late in life and of living and working actively throughout a long life, in his case a span of eighty years. He was contemporary with that considerable group already described as being born just after the Civil War and moving into sociology from a new American epoch. He was born in Pennsylvania in 1864 but moved immediately west and graduated at the University of Michigan in 1887. Like Giddings he got much of his experience in the newspaper world and showed his genius and initiative by preferring to become secretary to Booker T. Washington at Tuskegee, Alabama, to a teaching position at Chicago. Consistently enough, he later became professor of sociology at Chicago and after his retirement there, he taught at Fisk University where he recaptured, as it were, that part of his work which led E. C. Hughes to say of him, in the preface to the 1950 *Robert Ezra Park: Race and Culture,* that "Park probably contributed more ideas for analysis of racial relations and cultural contacts than any other modern social scientist."

Park's own estimate of his approach, methods, and contribution, prepared especially for this book, is characteristic of the man and his work. Pointing out that he was "one of the first and humbler muckrakers," he recalled that his first studies in the field, which he later called sociology, came from services as a newspaper reporter. He continued, "my experience as a reporter led me to study the social function of the newspaper, not as an organ of opinion but a record of current events. In fact, with a group of others of the same mind I started out to reform the newspaper, by making it more accurate and scientific, something like *Time* and *Fortune.* I spent six years at home and abroad at that task. Out of that grew my thesis on the crowd and the public (*Masse und Publikum*) and my interest in collective behavior. I think my principal theoretic interest is still the newspaper as a social institution. One thing that I discovered in the course of my studies was that there was no adequate and no precise language in which to describe the things I wanted to study, 'collective behavior,' for example. As a reporter I had learned a good deal about the city and I had used my position as city and Sunday editor to make systematic studies on the urban community. During my connection with Booker Washington and Tuskegee, I had learned a great deal about the Negro. It was from these two sources mainly that graduate students found materials for the researches which I directed after I went to Chicago.

"It was these researches that revealed to me that we had in sociology much theory but no working concepts. When a student proposed a topic for a thesis, I invariably found myself asking the question: what is this thing you want to study? What is a gang? What is a public? What is a nationality? What is a race in the sociological sense? What is graft? etc. I did not see how we could have anything like scientific research unless we had a system of classification and a frame of reference into which we could sort out and describe in general terms the things we were attempting to investigate. Park and Burgess' *Introduction* was a first rough sketch of such a classification and frame of reference. My contribution to sociology, has been, therefore, not what I intended, not what my original interest would have indicated, but what I needed to make a systematic exploration of the social work in which I found myself. The problem I was interested in was always theoretic rather than practical. I have been mainly an explorer in three fields: Collective Behavior; Human Ecology; and Race Relations."

In the new volume, *Race and Culture* by Robert Ezra Park, edited by Everett C. Hughes and published in 1950, there is an autobiographical note in which he had dictated a more intimate account of how he came to sociology.

Park was author of *Introduction to the Science of Sociology* (with E. W. Burgess), 1921; *Old World Traits Transplanted* (with Herbert A. Miller), 1921; *The Immigrant Press and Its Control,* 1922; *The City — Suggestions for the Study of Human Nature in the Urban Environment,* 1925; and the editor of *An Outline of the Principles of Sociology,* 1939. *Race and Culture* was edited by E. C. Hughes and published in 1950 in order to put together in one place the best things Park had done in this field. In an article in the *American Sociological Review,* June, 1944, pages 322–24, "Robert E. Park, 1864–1944," Ellsworth Faris said that Park would rather "induce ten men to write ten books than to take time off to write one himself."

While at the University of Michigan, according to E. W. Burgess, in "Contributions of Robert E. Park to Sociology" in *Sociology and Social Research* on page 256 of Volume 29 (March–April, 1945), Park was in a circle that included John Dewey, George H. Mead, and Franklin Ford, each of whom was seeking to understand human nature and society as a basis for building a better world. And, of course, during their decade of association, Park was much influenced by Booker T. Washington. Park was very much impressed by the Negro educator and often expressed his indebtedness to that able leader. Others with whom Park was in contact were William James, Royce, Münsterberg, Santayana, Simmel, and Windelbandt.

Professor Burgess estimated that Park made several original contributions. He was a pioneer in originating and developing the field of human ecology; he gave new concepts and methods to the study of race relations; he introduced a realistic and vital approach to the study of news and newspapers in relation to public opinion and popular education. Park, along with W. I. Thomas, seemed to have given major impetus to the movement which shifted sociology from social philosophy to an inductive science of human behavior. His originality is accredited by the fact that he had such an intimate acquaintance with human beings and social situations and by his freedom from conventional ways of looking at behavior. Bogardus has estimated that it is rather well recognized that Park was the father of human ecology: "Not only did he coin the name but he laid out the patterns, offered the earliest exhibit of ecological concepts, defined the major ecological processes and stimulated more advanced students to cultivate the fields of research in ecology than most other sociologists combined."

Another of his colleagues, Ellsworth Faris, on page 323 of the above reference, says that "a partial list of the fields in which he made significant contributions would include: social psychology and the theory of personality; studies on the community; the city; human ecology (he coined the term); the newspaper (as an institution); the social survey (again as an institution); crowd and public — the field of collective behavior; and chiefest of all, race relations and the conflicts of cultures. In the field of method he made valuable contributions as to the use of life histories, guided and unguided, for the investigation of personality."

Earle Fiske Young, one of his students and later professor at the University of Southern California, writing of Park as "a sociological explorer" on page 439 of Volume 28 (July–August, 1944) of *Sociology and Social Research,* says of Park's contributions that "the robustness, virility and independence of Robert E. Park, operating in a wide variety of social research fields — race relations, the community, personality development, social pathology, human ecology, institutional organization, collective behavior, sectarianism, as well as technical methods and the logic of the social sciences — have stimulated such widely different persons and groups that no single appraisal of his meaning for sociology and sociologists can tell the whole story." He goes on to say that more than any other American sociologist, Park demonstrated the breadth of the social fields that lie ready for sociological exploration, the variety of methods available for their cultivation, and the wider implications of the findings of scientific sociology.

Park's presidential address, published in *Papers and Proceedings* of the Twentieth Annual Meeting, Vol. XX, was entitled, "The Concept of Position in Sociology," and was a contribution to the relatively new concept of human ecology. In fine, the sociologist's interest in human ecology is in man's relation to other men as found in definite and typical patterns. Insofar as social structure can be defined in terms of position, and social changes in terms of movement of the population, social phenomena are subject to mathematical measurement. The growth of a city is more than a mere aggregation of people, but involves many changes which are measurable. Not all social phenomena can be measured in terms of location, position and mobility, for the true unit of social interaction is a changing attitude. Nevertheless social relations are often correlated with special relations and hence are measurable in a certain degree.

Other aspects of Park's work are presented in Chapters 14, 19, 20, 21.

John L. Gillin: 1871–

John Lewis Gillin, the sixteenth president of the American Sociological Society for 1926, followed the double pattern of both the earliest presidents and the later ones. On the one hand, Gillin came to sociology relatively mature from another field; yet on the other, he came with the prestige of a Gidding's doctor's degree, earned through persistence and continuous academic work and residence. Thus he continued the new pattern typified by Ellwood and begun still earlier by Thomas, Vincent, and Hayes, namely, a record of academic professional graduate training with the Ph.D. degree in sociology rather than in some other field. Of all the subsequent presidents up to 1950, only Faris of Chicago, whose degree was in psychology, Parsons of Harvard, and MacIver of Columbia did not hold the Ph.D. degree in sociology.

Gillin was still another of the presidents who belonged to the Middle West, being born there in 1871 and remaining there most of his life except for his sojourn in New York for the four years necessary for his M.A. degree in 1903 and his Ph.D. in 1906, and his leaves for educational direction of Home Service in the American Red Cross. The record of his residence in the West included his preparatory school work and the A.B. degree from Iowa College, now Grinnell, in 1895 at twenty-four years of age. Following his graduation, he served six years as minister, then after receiving his doctor's degree at Columbia he went to Ashland

College in Ohio, first as professor of social science and then as president. From there he went to Iowa State, first as assistant professor and then as professor and finally in 1912 to Wisconsin to team up with E. A. Ross where he was, first, professor and, after Ross's retirement, head of the department until 1943 when he became professor emeritus rounding out a span of seventy-nine years by 1950. His Alma Mater, Grinnell, conferred upon him the LL.D. degree in 1930.

Like most of the earlier sociologists, the range of his activities was wide and he devoted much of his time and energy to applied fields of work so that a part of his influence and his rating must rest upon this. Thus, as director of the Department of Civilian Relief of the American Red Cross from 1917 to 1919 and as director of their Education Service from 1921 to 1922, he visited many institutions in various regions and was always advocating the upraising of standards of public welfare and the training of social workers. He was a good "advocate," for instance, in visiting the University of North Carolina in the formative stages of its rapidly growing sociology department and he greatly supplemented the distinguished work which Steiner had done in the National Red Cross and was then doing at the University of North Carolina. Later on, Gillin was president of the Wisconsin State Conference of Charities and Corrections being one of several presidents who headed their state conferences of social work. Besides Gillin, others were Blackmar, Weatherly, Hayes, Ellwood, Bogardus, Odum, Taylor, Chapin, Queen, all of whom influenced the new realignments of sociology with social work.

Gillin's background, his persistent and consistent growth and development in the field of sociology, and his capacity for developing sound theory and methods out of his practical work and research provide one of the best contributions in this total story of American sociology. First, is his own interpretation of how he came into the field and how Giddings was setting the stage for American sociology. As Gillin tells it, in his statement prepared for this book, he was in his last year at Grinnell College where an ex-Congregational preacher by the name of Herron was giving a course he called sociology. "I took it and found it interesting because he tackled some of the problems about which I as a green country boy had been wondering, such as why some people behaved as they did, especially the 'big boys' in finance. Also, President Gates in his chapel lectures stirred my interest in people's behavior. Then near the close of the year a grad of a year or two before returned and told about his year with Giddings at Columbia with great enthusiasm. I noted in my mind, but with little hope that I should ever be able to take graduate work in sociology. I was about to become a minister and pastor of a church. However, after six and a half years as pastor, I decided that I wanted to study sociology with Giddings in the hope that other problems presented in the relations between church members in my parish would be illuminated. Human nature was becoming ever more intriguing. So my wife and I took our courage in our hands and about $400 we had saved and took the train for New York. Giddings opened up things for me. He did not have all the answers but led me to believe that by searching for myself I could find some more answers. Living in New York opened up a lot more problems some of which I had never thought about. I was caught for life. With the suggestions he gave and the constant reiteration that we look for facts about human relationships, and fit those facts into a logical formulation I was ready to attempt to find out for myself answers to the problems that intrigued me. I've been at it ever since. It gave me a philosophy of life that is satisfying and stimulating to this day. I still have a lot of unanswered questions, but for some I have an answer that is satisfying to me."

Gillin's principal contributions to sociology have been in the general field of social pathology, with special emphasis on criminology and penology, although his popular texts on pathology and criminology were supplemented by three introductory textbooks in sociology. The first, in collaboration with Blackmar, was *Outlines of Sociology,* in 1915, with a revised edition in 1923. The last two have been a father-son partnership with John P. Gillin, professor of anthropology in the Department of Sociology and Anthropology at the University of North Carolina, out of which came *An Introduction to Sociology* in 1942, and *Cultural Sociology* in 1948, which is a revision of the 1941 textbook. In his special field, Gillin was also senior author of *Social Problems,* which has had three editions. His *Social Pathology* in 1933, written as a general treatment of social problems, has also had three editions and has been the most popular text in the field. Among his other works are *The Wisconsin Prisoner,* 1946, *A History of Legislation for the Relief of the Poor in Iowa,* 1914 (with F. W. Blackmar), *Poverty and Dependency: Their Relief and Prevention* in 1920, *Taming the Criminal,* 1931, and

Criminology and Penology in 1925. He contributed more than forty articles to learned journals, mostly in *Social Forces,* the *American Sociological Review,* and *Sociology and Social Research,* three of which were on education and training for social work.

Gillin's own estimate of his work, prepared by special request for *American Sociology* is illuminating. "I hesitate to point out," he writes, "what seem to me have been my own rather limited contributions. I'm not sure that I have selected for mention any that are strictly my own. I owe so much to suggestions from others. But I think that some of the matters I have emphasized are in part some that resulted from my observation that other sociologists either neglected or treated in an inadequate way. Let me try to name a few. (a) Growing out of my interest in religious organization, especially my own church, I attempted to discover how it originated, and the social complex out of which it grew. That led me to write my Ph.D. thesis on *The Dunkers: A Sociological Interpretation.* Giddings thought this was the best piece of work I had done up to the time he died. He often urged me to work it over and publish it as a book. (b) Out of that grew my wonder whether the sociologists had given adequate attention to religion as an element in the whole cultural complex. I was not satisfied with Spencer's 'Ecclesiastical Institutions' in his great work on sociology. In the first book I wrote (on the basis of Blackmar's *Elements*) I developed a theory of the part religion played in the development of social organization and life, noting both its constructive and divisive functions. (c) As I gradually worked over into the field of social pathology, I became conscious that the 'social reformers' had done most work there, but had not attempted to apply strict scientific methods to a study of the various aspects of social disorganization. In only one part of that large field have I done what I consider careful scientific work. That is in the field of criminology. I studied the reports of others — the Italian School, the German School, the French School — but I did not feel that they had meticulously gone to the source of information as to why criminals had become criminals. Hence I undertook to interview 486 of the inmates of the Wisconsin State Prison, to check what they told me with information from people in the communities from which they had come and who knew them and their backgrounds. I then compared events in their history with that of their non-criminal brothers. The results appeared, so far as I got reliable results, in my latest book, *The Wisconsin Prisoner,* published in 1946 by the University of Wisconsin Press. In that I made my most strictly scientific contribution."

Gillin comments on his matured estimates of sociology. First, he says, "As I see it sociology beginning as a social philosophy did an important service to the social sciences in calling attention to phases of social life, ignored by history, by political science and economics. Its analysis of forms of social organization, of the social processes and of the social pathology created by change broke ground for a better understanding of the nature of social relationships in all the fields of social activity. But too often its methods, if one judged them by the papers read at the meetings of the American Sociological Society and the discussions heard there, are methods in logic and too often we have been a bunch of logic-choppers, dealing with what might by a stretch of imagination be called the prolegomenon of sociology. 'The definition of definition,' 'operational definition' and such abstruse subjects have diverted and confused a good many promising young scholars from the real job of sociology. Above almost everything else we need research to justify or refute the many hypotheses that some have mistaken for 'gospel truth.' Theory is all right, and by that I mean hypotheses about how individuals and groups in a society interact, the pattern of behavior they form, etc. But those hypotheses must be tested by actual study of social interaction and the products thereof by scholars who know what science means. That we are beginning to get. A small but increasing number of our younger men are attacking various aspects of social life in the scientific spirit. Much more needs to be done along that line to bring our theories in line with the facts. I have seen that growing, and therefore I'm not pessimistic about the future of sociology. Some of our theories have been substantiated, others refuted."

Concerning the greatest opportunity before sociologists in 1950, Gillin feels that careful research is first. He suggests that this "research need not be limited to statistical methods. The anthropologists have something to teach us there. They study the cultures of various primitive peoples. The sociologists in this atomic age should be studying the cultures of our so-called civilized societies. Are the sociological processes that we have assumed to be universal really so? We have already a good deal of knowledge about the primary institutions in civilized societies, such as the family, business organizations, and political institutions. But what do we know about the underlying psycho-sociological motivations of the various civilized societies? We talk about a Latin culture, an Anglo-Saxon, a German, a French, a Chinese, a Japanese culture. Max Weber wrote about "sacred" and "secular" societies. Toynbee has his categories of different civilizations. But what we need, it seems to me, is a much more meticulous study of the underlying psycho-social factors that account for the German, etc., pattern of national behavior, and of the various groups that make up the German and other peoples.

"What challenges are presented to young sociologists in the field of international likenesses and differences in cultural patterns! Every institution should be studied in each culture — studied intensively. In my own field we have some comparative penology, but we have done little in trying to understand why we have the differences and similarities in penal and correctional theory and practice."

Finally in his presidential address and in one or two articles Gillin himself has attempted a general summary of the progress of sociology. His address, published in the *Papers and Proceedings* of the twenty-first Annual Meeting of the American Sociological Society, Volume XXI, was devoted to "The Development of Sociology in the United States" in which he characterized the work of Ward, Sumner, Small, Giddings, Cooley, Ross, and Thomas, and discussed sociology as a university subject.

Gillin's influence has been greatest perhaps through his textbooks of which more than a quarter million have been sold. Like Ross, and many of his earlier contemporaries, he supported well the American Sociological Society and created good will and confidence in the new field.

Other aspects of his work will be discussed in Chapters 14 and 16.

CHAPTER 8

From 1927–1930:
Thomas, Gillette, Ogburn, Odum

The next four presidents of the American Sociological Society from 1927 to 1930 round out the first half, and with the next four represent a sort of median group in the curve of the forty presidents up to 1950. This group continued the dominance of the West with only Odum from an eastern university, although Thomas was a native of Tennessee, and Ogburn, like Odum, was from Georgia. The first two were products of Small at Chicago, while the latter two were of the vintage of Giddings at Columbia. Each, while receiving his Ph.D. degree in sociology, had also specialized in an allied field. Thomas and Odum had a minor background of psychology, Odum having received the Ph.D. at Clark with G. Stanley Hall. Ogburn had minored in economics and was president of the American Statistical Association. Gillette went from theology into sociology, and was a pioneer in what later became the Rural Sociological Society. Each of the four set the incidence for what appeared to be a new strand in American sociology — a new methodology in the case study and life history approach; the establishment of rural sociology in the university; the statistical method and the role of invention in social change; and folk sociology and regionalism.

William I. Thomas: 1863–1947

With F. H. Giddings, E. A. Ross, C. H. Cooley, C. A. Ellwood, and Ellsworth Faris, W. I. Thomas, the seventeenth president of the American Sociological Society in 1927, belonged to what was often called the earlier psychological school of sociologists. Faris received his Ph.D. degree at the University of Chicago in psychology. Ross's *Social Psychology* was the first text published anywhere under that title. Cooley has been commonly credited with much of the beginnings of social psychology in the sociological framework. As one index of how these men were credited with special psychological contributions, Harry Elmer Barnes' chapters on Cooley and Ellwood in his *Introduction to the History of Sociology* had the respective subtitles of "Pioneer in Psychosociology" and "Founder of Scientific Psychological Sociology." His subtitle for the W. I. Thomas chapter was "The Fusion of Psychological and Cultural Sociology."

Of the earlier pioneers with whom Thomas may be compared in his psychological emphasis, besides Giddings and his *consciousness of kind* and *pluralistic behavior,* William Graham Sumner in America and Wilhelm Wundt in Germany were pioneers in cultural psychology, a field long since neglected by the psychologists. Next to Sumner was Ward whose *Psychic Factors of Civilization* was, in its day, a pioneer work of distinction. Of the later presidents of the American Sociological Society, Emory S. Bogardus as early as 1917 had published his *Social Psychology;* Bernard in 1924 and 1926 had published his *Instinct* and his *Introduction to Social Psychology,* and Kimball Young brought out his *Social Psychology* in 1930.

Thomas' presidential address was entitled "The Behavior Pattern and the Situation" in which, among other things, he discussed attitudes, values, forms of adaptation, together with the total situation and all their implications. This might well be compared with the development of Gestalt psychology in Germany and was one of the several contributions that led Barnes, in Chapter XI, to say that Thomas was "regarded by many students of sociological theory as the most erudite and creative of American social psychologists. In his later years Thomas extended his conceptions and methods to what might be called a 'psycho-cultural' approach to social phenomena. Certainly, no other sociologist excels Thomas in his mastery of the subject or in a firm command of the auxiliary sciences essential to the successful exploitation of the field of ethnic and psychological sociology. Unfortunately, Thomas confined his systematic exposition of psychological sociology to his university lectures, which were never published. His published contributions to the subject are relatively few and fragmentary, woven into extensive documentary studies. But his general position and method can be reconstructed and summarized with relative confidence and accuracy" (page 793).

Few sociologists had such long and varied experiences as did Thomas who, with George E. Vincent, received his doctor's degree in 1896, the second year in which Small's new Department of Sociology founded in 1893 had awarded the Ph.D. degree. So varied and different was his work that it was thirty-one years after receiving his Ph.D. that he was elected president of the American Sociological Society at a time when he was, even while living, almost revered by many of his younger sociologists, following the Chicago influence of both older and younger groups. A measure of the extraordinary esteem in which he was held may be seen from the tributes paid to him by his contemporaries: Faris in *The American Journal of Sociology* for March, 1948, and *Sociology and Social Research* for the same date; Burgess in *Sociology and Social Research* for March–April, 1948; Kimball Young in the *American Sociological Review* for February, 1948; Florian Znaniecki in *Sociology and Social Research,* March–April, 1948; and others.

Thomas was a fellow at Chicago in 1895, received his degree in 1896, was assistant professor in 1897, associate professor in 1900, and professor from 1910 to 1918 when he went to New York to do research independently of a university. In the light of his Chicago experiences and his powerfully individualistic personality it was perhaps not surprising that he never became identified permanently with any university, although a number of universities were looking for such a distinguished sociologist to head their departments. He was lecturer at the New School for Social Research in New York from 1923 to 1928 and was a guest lecturer, holding a series of seminars, at Harvard in 1936–37. His marriage to Dorothy Swaine Thomas and his collaboration with her led him to spend his final years from 1940 to 1947 at Berkeley, California, where he died on December 5.

Like many of his contemporary sociologists, Thomas' background and experiences were varied in closely related fields. He came to sociology from the field of language and philosophy, having spent a year at the universities of Berlin and Göttingen after which he taught English for three years at Oberlin. He was an associate editor of *The American Journal of Sociology* from the first issue in 1895 until he left Chicago in 1917. He was later a member of the American Academy of Arts and Sciences, was representative for sociology in the Social Science Research Council from 1928 to 1932, and later was secretary of the Committee on Personality and Culture of the Council. He also represented the American Sociological Society on the American Council of Learned Societies.

He had visited Europe after receiving his Ph.D. at Chicago and became interested in folk psychology through Wilhelm Wundt and sought some new methodology of studying nationalities and culture. As early as January, 1896, Thomas had written an article in *The American Journal of Sociology,* page 434 ff., on "The Scope and Method of Folk Psychology." In America it seemed likely that George Meade at Chicago, as well as Cooley, exerted some influence upon him although his was an independent way of doing whatever he did.

His own estimates of what he did and the primary emphasis of his work, prepared for *American Sociology up to 1950,* reflect a fair and modest appraisal. He reduced his main lines of interest to two: first, "The sociopsychological aspects of culture history, or otherwise stated, social psychology as examined in relation to races, nationalities, classes, interest groups, etc., in different cultural situations and historical epochs; and second, personality development in normal, criminal and psychopathic individuals in relation to cultural situations and particular trains of experience as seen through their life-histories, which may be in the form of autobiographies, case studies, continuous and organized interviews, etc. (I do not say 'psychoanalysis' because of the meaning which this term has acquired.)"

Thomas wrote further, "I do not feel that I have been greatly influenced by any of my teachers of sociology. My interests, as I have indicated, were in the marginal fields and not in sociology as it was organized and taught at that time, that is, the historical and methodological approach of Professor Small and the remedial and correctional interests of Professor Henderson."

His principal works were: *The Polish Peasant in Europe and America,* 1918–21 (with Florian Znaniecki); *Primitive Behavior,* 1936; *Source Book for Social Origins,* 1909; *Sex and Society,* 1907; *The Child in America,* 1928 (with Dorothy S. Thomas). He also contributed nearly a score of articles to *The American Journal of Sociology,* a half dozen to the *American Magazine,* and perhaps a dozen miscellaneous articles elsewhere.

John M. Gillette: 1866–1949

Still another of the presidents of the American Sociological Society who lived and worked beyond the eighty-year mark was John M. Gillette, the eighteenth president in 1928. Like Sumner, Small, Hayes, Weatherly, Gillin, Lichtenberger, he came into the field of sociology from the ministry, and like many of the others the span of his life coincided with the rise and development of sociology following the Civil War and moving on up to the mid-point of the twentieth century. Born in Missouri in 1866, he received an M.A. degree from Princeton Theological Seminary in 1895 and a Ph.D. at Chicago Theological Seminary in 1899. He had been ordained a Presbyterian minister in 1895 and had preached in rural churches in Kansas and later in the frontier town of Dodge City. After receiving his degree at the Chicago Theological Seminary he transferred to sociology at the university where he received his Ph.D. two years later. For six years after that, he was president of the Academy for Young Women in Illinois and professor of psychology and the social sciences at the Valley State Teachers College in North Dakota. Then in 1907 he went to the University of North Dakota and the following year established the new Department of Sociology which he headed for forty years.

And like most of his contemporaries his life reflected a wide and varied experience. Besides being vice-president and president of the American Sociological Society, he was an associate member of the International Institute of Sociology and an advisory member of the Academy of Agriculture of Czechoslovakia. He was, at home, a member of the North Dakota State Welfare Commission, and of the advisory committee of the National Child Labor Committee and of the National Committee on Prisons and Prison Labor, as well as of the advisory committee of the State Workmen's Compensation and Unemployment Insurance Division. Still nearer home, at Grand Forks, he was vice-president and president of the Charity Organization Society and the City Council. As indicating public recognition he received two honorary degrees, the Doctor of Laws from Park College and the Doctor of Humanities from the University of North Dakota. Gillette blazed new trails not only in a frontier American society itself but in rural sociology. James M. Reinhardt points out in tributes in the *American Sociological Review* and *Social Forces,* Fall, 1949, that he "was often referred to as the dean of rural sociology because of the formative influence that his pioneer works in the field had in this and other countries. A review of college catalogue offerings in sociology for a considerable period following the appearance of his *Constructive Rural Sociology* in 1913, and the first edition of his *Rural Sociology* in 1922, reveals the pre-eminence of his position in this expanding field, over many years. His early works in rural sociology attracted wide attention throughout the world, and translations of his books were used in various European universities and in the Imperial University of Japan."

Reinhardt continues, "Dr. Gillette's intellectual interests ranged far and wide. In addition to his work in rural sociology, he wrote books in such related areas as general sociology, education, the family, and social problems. He also published numerous articles and pamphlets on a variety of subjects, including anthropology, regionalism, and weather. His intellectual activity and mental acuity showed no signs of impairment right up to the time of his death. His outstanding investigations showing a definite scientific relation between variable weather conditions and the economic status of a people, as well as a number of other researches, were done after his 80th year." In fact, "He was actively engaged during the last year of his life on several projects including a sociological interpretation of the life and times of the Great Plains during his 83 years."

His main books include *Vocational Education,* in 1910; *Constructive Rural Sociology,* in 1913 and revised in 1916; *Rural Sociology,* in 1922 and revised in 1936; with James M. Reinhardt, *Current Social Problems,* in 1933, revised in 1937. From his main field of endeavor, rural sociology, we may gain an idea of his concept of sociology. Thus from pages 6 and 7 of his *Rural Sociology,* he says, "If by sociology is always meant a rigidly scientific attempt to account for group phenomena, and if, further, the attempt must be dissociated from utilitarian motives, then the title 'rural sociology' is incompetent to express the scientific import of sociological studies of rural communities."

Gillette's presidential address, "Urban Influence and Selection" was published in Volume XXIII of *Papers and Proceedings* of the Twenty-third Annual Meeting of the American Sociological Society. In this address he pointed out that, as creators and centers of culture, cities dominate greater and greater areas of outlying populations, due to multiplication of kinds of cultural goods and increase in agencies of distribution. The psychosocial effects of this urbanization are seen in the molding and directive influences which urban centers manifest. Psychophysical effects appear in population movements and redistribution in quantity and quality. The city is accumulating more educated leaders as well as pathological and subnormal classes. The rural areas have a larger proportion of normal but unexceptional persons.

More about Gillette will be presented in Chapter 17.

William F. Ogburn: 1886–

Going directly to graduate work at Columbia University with Giddings in 1908, three years after his graduation from Georgia's Mercer University in 1905, William F. Ogburn, the nineteenth president of the American Sociological Society, was the first to make sociology his first and last field of professional work. That is, after his excursion into secondary-school teaching, as was customary with most graduates of Georgia colleges who expected to go into professional work, Ogburn began his studies in sociology and was still going strong at the 1950 mark. His only transitional excursion away from sociology was as instructor at Princeton University in economics, politics, and history while he was working for his Ph.D. degree in sociology at Columbia, unless his year of postwar economic studies in France or his presidency of the American Statistical Association could be so designated.

Born in Butler, Georgia, in 1886, and having received the B.S. degree from Mercer University at Macon, Georgia, and the M.A. degree in 1909 from Columbia University and the Ph.D. in 1912, he was professor of sociology at Reed College, Portland, Oregon, for four years where he did what he sometimes estimates his best teaching. Following the Reed College tenure he was for two years, 1918 and 1919, in World War I, examiner and head of the cost of living department for the National War Labor Board and special agent for the United States Bureau of Labor Statistics. Following this service he came back to Columbia University as professor of sociology in 1919 where he remained until 1927 when he was called to Chicago to serve in a similar capacity. In 1933 he was appointed to the Sewell L. Avery distinguished service professorship and has remained there continuously except for leaves of absence granted to undertake special work. He received the honorary degree of LL.D. from his Alma Mater and from the University of North Carolina.

Like his predecessors among the presidents of the American Sociological Society, he has been called on to cooperate in many ventures and to undertake much in allied fields. Although Giddings had been the sociological pioneer in insisting that statistics be given a major role in sociology, and although he had been a fellow in the American Statistical Association, Ogburn was a president of the Association and editor of its journal. So, too, although several of the presidents of the American Sociological Society have been fellows in the American Association for the Advancement of Science, Ogburn has been the only vice-president up to 1950. And again, Ogburn has been the only sociologist to be president of the Social Science Research Council and chairman of its Problems and Policy Committee. Other related scientific associations included the International Statistical Institute, the Population Association of America, the Sociological Research Association. His active and advisory services to outside agencies have also been numerous. He was chairman of the United States Census Advisory Committee, director of the Consumers Advisory Board of the National Recovery Administration, special adviser to the Resettlement Administration and research consultant to the National Resources Committee, 1935–43.

His most distinctive cooperative research effort, however, was his directorship of the President's Research Committee on Social Trends established by President Herbert Hoover and running from 1930 to 1933. Ogburn not only was mainly responsible for the outlines and arrangements for this study but the appropriation of more than a half million dollars for the study by the Rockefeller Foundation was facilitated by Ogburn's directing the study. Another president of the Society, Howard W. Odum, who had initiated the request for the appropriation, was assistant director of research, while the other members of the committee were Wesley C. Mitchell of Columbia, chairman, Charles E. Merriam of Chicago, vice-chairman, Shelby Harrison of the Russell Sage Foundation, and Alice Hamilton of Harvard. The results of this cooperative research program were published in two main volumes of thirty-four chapters by almost as many collaborators, in addition to the 200-page summary and thirteen separate monographs. Ogburn himself contributed two of the main chapters dealing with science, invention, and social change, and with marriage and family relationships.

In this work Ogburn was able to urge upon the committee one of his major indices of methodology, namely, that research be undertaken in no area unless statistical data were available for objective measurement.

And in those cases where the major authors had not had access to or experience in statistical research, it was the policy of the Committee to provide statistical assistants. Thus, Samuel Stouffer, subsequently to go as professor of sociology and director of the research laboratory of social relations at Harvard, collaborated with Jesse F. Steiner in his excellent chapter on the community and recreational activities, and Clarence Heer, professor of finance at North Carolina, collaborated with Howard W. Odum in his chapter on public welfare.

Ogburn's main books and brochures included *Progress and Uniformity in Child-Labor Legislation: A Study in Statistical Measurement*, published as his Ph.D. thesis, 1912; *Social Change with Respect to Culture and Original Nature*, 1922; *The Social Sciences and Their Interrelations*, edited jointly by Ogburn and Alexander Goldenweiser, 1927; *American Marriage and Family Relationships* with E. R. Groves, 1928; *The Economic Development of Post-War France: A Survey of Production*, with William Joffé, 1929; Social Changes, edited for *The American Journal of Sociology* and published each year, 1927 to 1935. *Recent Social Trends*, 1933, Director of research; *Sociology* — a textbook, with Meyer F. Nimkoff, 1940; *American Society in Wartime*, edited 1944; *The Social Effects of Aviation*, 1946. A revised edition of *Social Change* appeared in 1950.

In addition to these books a number of smaller pamphlets have been published. Most important of these are: *Living with Machines*, 1933; *You and Machines*, 1934; *Social Characteristics of Cities: A Basis for New Interpretations of the Role of the City in American Life*, 1937; *Technological Trends and National Policy*, 1937; *Machines and Tomorrow's World*, 1938; *War, Babies and the Future*, 1943; *The Politics of Atomic Energy*, 1946.

Few men in American sociology have equaled Ogburn in sheer quantity of output of articles for journals. Not including book reviews, approximately a hundred and seventy-five such articles have appeared, in addition to approximately twenty chapters written for and published in books edited by others. According to the chief subject matter and to journals carrying them, these journals have been divided into two groups in an unpublished paper in 1948, (1) learned and technical journals and (2) popular magazines. The number of articles appearing in the learned and technical journals include fifty-three from sociological journals, including *The American Journal of Sociology, Social Forces, Publications* of the American Sociological Society, *Annals* of the American Academy of Political and Social Science, *Sociology and Social Research.*

The range of his contributions is indicated by some eighty-five articles in other journals, including *Public Management, Journal of the American Statistical Association, Survey Graphic, Monthly Labor Review, Political Science Quarterly, Scientific Monthly, Journal of Political Economy, American Political Science Review, American Economic Review, State Review of Literature, Journal of Adult Education, American Labor Year Book.* There have been some fifty articles in popular magazines and newspapers, including the *New York Times,* the *Berliner Tageblatt, Air Affairs, American Magazine, Ladies' Home Journal, Nation's Business.*

Although Ogburn may not be as noted as his teacher Giddings was for the creation of a great many sociological terms and concepts, his term *cultural lag,* defined sociologically for the first time in his book *Social Change,* has become a classic. As Ogburn defined it on page 196 of this book, "The thesis is . . . that the source of most modern social changes today is the material culture. The material-culture changes force changes in other parts of culture such as social organization and customs, but these latter parts of culture do not change as quickly. They lag behind the material-culture changes, hence we are living in a period of maladjustment."

Ogburn writes, "I think we have made a good deal of progress in the scientific method in sociology since you and I were in the graduate school together at Columbia University, and I think the United States is far ahead of any other country especially continental Europe, in scientific sociology. But at best the movement will be slow. I think much too much attention is given to systematization and not enough to verification. On the other hand, I am not a perfectionist. If I were, I would advocate a restriction of effort to a narrow field such as statistical surveys, population studies, and vital statistics. I think the degree of accuracy and the extent of verification is contingent upon the need in laying out work, and I am not disposed to be critical particularly of failures to obtain perfection. Rather I would welcome approximations provided the author knows that they are approximations and knows what science is. I would rule out, however, some approximations where the goal for the author is philosophy, persuasion, propaganda, ethics, or the essay. I am not adverse to the sociologist writing essays or propaganda providing he does this merely as a human being and not as a scientist."

When urged to indicate the nature of some of his own contributions Ogburn wrote: "I claim that the problem of social evolution is solved and that I have played a considerable part in solving it. By solving I mean solving in the sense that Darwin solved the problem of biological evolution. Darwin did it by pointing out three factors: variation, natural selection, and heredity. Darwin added the factor of natural selection. The problem of social evolution is solved by four factors: invention, exponential accumulation, diffusion, and adjustment. My contribution has been largely in the factor of exponential accumulation and also in the development of the factor of invention. I also think that my role has been significant in the adjustment of one part of culture to another (cultural lag). There will no doubt be refinements in the analysis and measurements just as there have been in Darwin's three factors which explain biological evolution.

"One other contribution of mine I'm rather fond of is the observation verified by measurement that trend lines seldom change their direction very sharply or quickly although the fluctuations about a trend line often do. The development of the reasons why trend lines do not change their direction sharply is interesting, but this discovery rests upon its significance for planning and for the recognition it gives to social stability."

Although Ogburn's many contributions have been indicated as in the field of statistical method, the influence of technology upon society, the family, and population, he writes that "I suppose I would be classed by most of my colleagues as in the field of social change although I don't like to be fenced in." And with reference to sociology's great opportunities in the future, he wrote, "I think the greatest opportunity in sociology lies in getting away from bias and prejudice and contributing reliable information. You will recall that the idea which you and I had in carrying through together the *Social Trends* study was to rule out all opinion unsupported and to accept nothing but reliable conclusions. The idea was that as a multiplication table should be reliable both for the Tory and the Communist, so the conclusion of social trends should be valid alike for the radical and the conservative. I think the almost universal acceptance of the social trends study was a tribute to a measure of success

in making it reliable. If we succeed in building up a respect for the reliability of social science among statesmen, responsible educators, and capable congressmen, and among business and social leaders, universities
and the students will follow. One of the biggest hindrances to the attainment is the distorting effect of bias and emotion. Another practical
obstacle to research I have come to think is the prestige which goes to
the advisory function in public affairs and the prestige of committee work
with agencies such as federal government and the special wartime
agencies. It is impossible to do research work and committee work in
Washington at the same time, and nowadays sociologists run away
from the long, hard, slow tasks of research for the quicker, easier prestige
of counseling in public affairs. Such counselors I call committee bums."

Ogburn's presidential address in 1929 was in character when he spoke
on "The Folkways of a Scientific Sociology." In substance it was what he
wrote later in *The Scientific Monthly,* for April, 1930. "In the past the
great names in sociology have been social theorists and social philosophers. But this will not be the case in the future. For social theory and
social philosophy will decline, that is, in the field of scientific sociology.
Social theory will have no place in a scientific sociology, for it is not built
upon sufficient data. Of course, certain syntheses of broader researches
may be called theory, a new meaning for an old term. But such syntheses
will be based on evidence. Social theory in good part is the product of
wishful thinking, taking form in the Zeitgeist in which it is developed."

More about Ogburn will appear in Chapters 14, 15, 18, 20.

Howard W. Odum: 1884–

Like his immediate predecessor, W. F. Ogburn, Howard W. Odum,
the twentieth president of the American Sociological Society in 1930,
was born in Georgia, was graduated from a denominational college
about the same time as Ogburn, taught for a few years, and applied at
Columbia University for his Ph.D. degree under Giddings at the same
time that Ogburn was a student there. Odum was graduated from
Emory in 1904, received his A.M. from the University of Mississippi in
1906, and his Ph.D. degree from Columbia in 1910. But unlike Ogburn,
he had come into sociology not quite so directly and completely, having
majored in Greek and minored in Latin and Shakespeare at the Uni-

versity of Mississippi for his A.M. in 1906, and on his way to Columbia's Giddings had stopped over for his Ph.D. in psychology in 1909 with the eminent G. Stanley Hall at Clark University at Worcester, Massachusetts. Incidentally, he took his first course in sociology, utilizing the Giddings *Principles* under Frank H. Hankins, then an instructor at Clark and a recent Ph.D. in sociology from Columbia, who was to become, also, president of the American Sociological Society eight years after Odum. In 1908, Odum had applied for a fellowship at Columbia, eager to start on his sociology degree at once. But, with such men as Ogburn, Ghelke, Chapin, and others already on the ground, he didn't have a chance. When, therefore, G. Stanley Hall, having seen some of his work on the folk songs and poetry of the southern Negroes and his community studies, offered him a fellowship at Clark, he accepted eagerly and was to find in Hall first, and in Giddings later, as he saw them, the two greatest teachers in America at that time, and rarely ever excelled at any time. At Clark, Odum had the benefit of Hall's pioneering in bringing over Freud and other German psychologists, his insistence upon clinical observations in psychiatry, as well as the beginnings of anthropology under Alexander Chamberlain, a disciple of Boas.

Odum's original conversion to sociology and his invitation to Clark came through a devoted colleague at the University of Mississippi, Thomas P. Bailey, professor of psychology and a Ph.D. graduate from Clark. But even before that, his work in the classics was more in the field of ancient society than of language and literature. His M.A. thesis was on "The Religion of Sophocles"; his prepared manuscript for the Latin minor was on "The Life of the Roman Boy"; and his Shakespeare paper was on "The Women of Shakespeare." In other words, he was more interested in culture than language. When, therefore, Professor Bailey proposed that he make the first concrete study of the Negro in southern towns, Odum began immediately and devoted all his spare time to it during his last two years as instructor in Latin at the University of Mississippi. Naturally, such a survey would begin with Oxford, Mississippi, where he recalls well the Faulkner family, one of whom was later to produce the most accurate portraiture of any writer of certain aspects of southern life.

The incidence and sequence of these studies were basic to the work and publications of later years. The studies themselves grew out of the observation that there had been practically no scientific studies of the Negro in the South; that the South itself was amazingly ignorant about the Negro; that practically no one was interested in the subject; and that nevertheless this was the distinctive field of inquiry where knowledge must be had before progress in other respects could be made. In the wake of the community studies themselves it soon became evident that, in the folk character of the Negroes and their relationship with the whites, in their folk songs and sayings, in their folk beliefs and folk cultures were to be found an extraordinary untapped mine of information that was not only essential to the understanding of the Negro and the South but that would soon be passing beyond the point where it could be recovered. To the community studies, therefore, were added the subsidiary inquiries into the folk society of the Negro that existed and has always existed within the white "state society" and that has been responsible for much of the vitality and surviving powers and progress of the Negro in the United States.

Odum's doctoral dissertation at Clark was on "The Folk Songs and Poetry of Southern Negroes" featuring the importance of folk culture and folk psychology. Parts of this study were published in *The American Journal of Religious Education* at Clark and in two issues of *The Journal of American Folk Lore,* under the editorship of Franz Boas. All were later incorporated into two volumes, in collaboration with Guy B. Johnson, namely, *The Negro and His Songs* and *Negro Workaday Songs,* in which the legendary John Henry was discovered and presented to the public in a number of variants in ballad song and story. From these beginnings in the study of the Negro, Odum continued up to 1950 both in research and study, and in active programs in the field of Negro-white relationships. Subsequent study and publication included a two-year study of the Negro in Philadelphia some twenty years after Du Bois's, *The Philadelphia Negro.* This Philadelphia study followed immediately the Ph.D. degree at Columbia. Subsequently, Odum published, in 1928, 1929, and 1931, in addition to articles and the two volumes on Negro songs, his trilogy, *Rainbow Round My Shoulder, Wings on My Feet,* and *Cold Blue Moon,* a study of the black man in a white man's world; and his *Race and Rumors of Race* in 1943.

The sequence of Odum's academic degrees begins with his A.B. at Emory in 1904; A.M. at the University of Mississippi in 1906; Ph.D. at Clark University in 1909; Ph.D. at Columbia in 1910; LL.D. at Emory University in 1931; Litt.D. at College of the Ozarks in 1935; LL.D. at Harvard in 1939; L.H.D. at Clark in 1941. The sequence of his professional positions, following his instructorship at the University of Mississippi from 1905 to 1908, showed him as "research expert," Bureau of Municipal Research in Philadelphia, from 1910 to 1912; director, Whittier Center, Philadelphia, 1912–13; associate professor and professor at the University of Georgia, 1913–18; director of Civilian Relief Southern Division, American Red Cross, 1918; professor of sociology and dean of the College of Liberal Arts, Emory University, 1919–20; Kenan Professor of Sociology and head of department, University of North Carolina since 1920, director of the School of Public Welfare, 1920–32; founder and director of the Institute for Research in Social Science, 1924–44. He was the founder of *Social Forces* and has been editor since 1922. In pursuit of regional first-hand acquaintance, he was visiting professor at the University of Illinois for the second semesters in 1934 and 1935; Walker Ames professor at the University of Washington, winter, 1942; visiting professor and Silliman Fellow at Yale University in 1946–47. He was also visiting professor in summer sessions at Southern California, Columbia, and Utah.

Like most of the others before him, he was called upon for various activities in related fields. He was chief of the Social Science Division of A Century of Progress World's Fair, 1930–32, where he planned a Hall of Nations and Cultures; assistant director of research of the President's Research Committee on Social Trends. He was fellow and member of the executive committee of the American Association for the Advancement of Science, vice-president and member of the executive committee of the National Conference of Social Work. He was a member of P.E.N. He was president of the Commission on Interracial Cooperation, 1937–44; of the Southern Regional Council, 1944–46. Nearer home, he was president of the North Carolina Conference for Social Service, 1936–37; the North Carolina Interracial Commission, 1930–31; chairman, North Carolina Civil Works Administration, 1933–34; chairman, North Carolina Emergency Relief Administration, 1933–35. Outside the university field he had been president of the North Carolina Jersey Cattle Club in 1942–44, and in 1948 received the Master Breeder Award by the American Jersey Cattle Club for the United States that year for his work in twenty-five years of genetic line breeding.

In the order of publication his books include *Social and Mental Traits of the Negro*, 1910; *Systems of Public Welfare* (with D. W. Willard), 1925; *Southern Pioneers*, 1925; *Sociology and Social Problems*, 1925; *The Negro and His Songs* (with Guy B. Johnson), 1925; *Public Welfare and Social Work*, 1926; *Negro Workaday Songs* (with Guy B. Johnson), 1926; *American Masters of Social Science*, edited, 1927; *Man's Quest for Social Guidance*, 1927; *Rainbow Round My Shoulder*, 1928; *Wings on My Feet*, 1929; *Introduction to Social Research* (with Katharine Jocher), 1929; *An American Epoch*, 1930; *Cold Blue Moon*, 1931; *Southern Regions of the United States*, 1936; *American Regionalism* (with Harry Estill Moore), 1938; *American Social Problems*, 1939, revised edition, 1945; *American Democracy Anew*, 1940; *Race and Rumors of Race*, 1943; *The Way of the South*, 1947; *Understanding Society*, 1947; *American Sociology*, 1951. He was editor of the Henry Holt "American Social Science Series" and the University of North Carolina "Social Study Series." His bibliography of articles and editorials totaled approximately one hundred and fifty and he has collaborated in more than a score of volumes.

Odum's presidential address in 1930, published in the *Publications of the American Sociological Society* in 1931, was on "Folk and Regional Conflict as a Field of Sociological Study." The address was a challenge to utilize the approach of comparative sociology in the search for sound theory useful in the conflicts of the world of technology and the breaking up of old cultures. Here he attempted distinctive definitions of the folk and of regionalism as basic to folk sociology and the integration of cultures.

From the study of authentic theoretical sources and from empirical studies and observations of folk societies, there had emerged the construct of folk sociology as a theory of the continuum of society developing from the folk culture to the state civilization. As corollaries for analysis, measurement, and societal direction, regionalism, technicways, and social planning were posited as tools of both research and planning programs in the framework of understanding society and of so analyzing the total situation as to effect empirical study and planning that would be effective for both survival and social progress and adequate for both the individual and the group in isolated situations and in the mass phenomena. Further references to Odum's work may be found in Chapters 14, 16, 19, 20, 23.

CHAPTER 9

From 1931–1934:
Bogardus, Bernard, Reuter, Burgess

In some ways the twentieth and twenty-first presidents of the American Sociological Society not only represented the median point in numbers of the first forty presidents up to 1950, but may also be said to mark a sort of special era in the regional development of sociology in the United States, expanding it into two new major regions. Emory S. Bogardus as the twenty-first president was the first to be elected from the Far West in recognition not only of his contributions to sociology over the years but also of the distinctive regional pioneering he had done in establishing one of the largest departments of sociology, even as Odum had been elected the year before from the Southeast more because of his pioneering in that region than for actual contributions made.

Emory S. Bogardus: 1882–

Emory S. Bogardus, twenty-first president of the American Sociological Society, was born near Belvidere, Illinois, February 21, 1882, received his A.B. degree from Northwestern in 1908, A.M. in 1909, and Ph.D. from Chicago in 1911. He went directly from receiving his University of Chicago doctorate to Southern California as assistant professor in 1911 and became professor and head of the department of sociology shortly thereafter. He came into the field of sociology after the usual preliminary trial-and-error method of working in business, in newspaper reporting, on the farm, and in boys' clubs in the city. In Northwestern University he was first interested in mathematics and in philosophy from which he became interested in the experimental aspects of psychology. Then, from his experience in boys' work at the University Settlement, he became interested in problems of maladjustment and alleviating human misery. His next step was to go to the University of Chicago directly from Northwestern where he had majored in psychology. At Chicago

he found the exact persons and fields through which to continue his interests as basic to his specialization in sociology. Small emphasized social
process, Henderson featured social organization, Vincent and Thomas
both came near to social psychology, Mead continued the philosophical
interest, and W. I. Thomas featured the methodological emphasis upon
research. All these added up logically to influence Bogardus' later work.

Bogardus must be recorded as one of the most prolific writers among
all the American sociologists. His total bibliography, beginning in 1898
and continuing for more than fifty years, added up to 275 titles of which
he catalogued some 41 as being in the field of general sociology, 15 on
leadership, 27 on social distance, 52 on race and ethnic groups, 30 on
social psychology, 17 on social research, 16 on cooperatives. Many of
these were minor contributed notes or short articles in *Sociology and
Social Research.*

In a tribute paid to Professor Bogardus by his colleagues and distinguished guests in 1937, in token of twenty-five years of leadership, it was
pointed out that more important even than his editorial work and the
many articles he has contributed to this and other journals, were his
widely used books. Among these were *Introduction to the Social Sciences,* 1913, 1922; *Introduction to Sociology,* 1913, 1927, 1931, 1949; *Essentials of Social Psychology,* 1917, 1923; *A History of Social Thought,*
1922, 1929; *The New Social Research,* 1923, 1927; *Fundamentals of Social
Psychology,* 1924, 1941; *Social Problems and Social Processes,* edited,
1933; *Contemporary Sociology,* 1931; *Leaders and Leadership,* 1934; *Essentials of Americanization,* 1919, 1923; *Immigration and Race Attitudes,*
1928; *The Mexican in the United States,* 1934; *The City Boy and His
Problems,* 1926; *Introduction to Social Research,* 1936; *The Development
of Social Thought,* 1940, 1947. His writings, so the tribute recalled, were
"known for their comprehensiveness and synthetic completeness, the
systematic organization of material, the clear-cut lucid descriptions and
practical applications, the sympathetic understanding of social situations,
and the broad-minded attitude and wholesome spirit which pervade
them all."

In an informal way Professor Bogardus has classified his activities for
us. He says, "My efforts have been given, first, to teaching, in order to
earn a living, in order to have stimulating contacts with young people
with their inquiring minds, in order to keep in touch with youth and

their dynamic outlook on life. Second, there has been a continuous connection with editorial work as editor of sociological monographs, the *Journal of Applied Sociology,* the *Journal of Sociology and Social Research,* and *Research News.* Closely related has been a continuous activity for the past thirty-five years in reviewing sociological books, perhaps two or three dozen a year. Third, research projects have commanded attention. These have dealt with race relations, occupational attitudes, public opinion, the consumer cooperative movement, leadership. Not a little attention has been given to research methods. To assist in teaching, texts and syllabi have been prepared, presenting integrated pictures of various aspects of sociology. Fourth, administrative activities have been carried on for thirty-six years as head of the department of sociology, dean of a school of social work, and now dean of a graduate school. This administrative work has involved in each case a great deal of pioneering, which has required that many obstacles be faced and overcome. Fifth, throughout the years active membership has been maintained on at least from three to five boards of directors of community organizations. These positions have given many first-hand contacts with social problems and offered opportunities for research work."

Bogardus continues, in his special statement for this book, "Perhaps needless to say the five foregoing activities have been carried on both simultaneously and continuously since 1911. Travel has been an outstanding hobby. It has brought first-hand contacts with people in England, France, Germany, Holland, Switzerland, and Italy; in Mexico, Guatemala, El Salvador, Panama, Peru, Chile, Argentina, and Brazil; in Hawaii, Japan, Manchuria, China, and the Philippines."

Bogardus' presidential address printed in the *Publications of the American Sociological Society,* Volume XXVI, 1932, was entitled "Social Process on the Pacific Coast." He thought that invasion and population succession had brought about such changes as to make the Pacific Coast an "experiment station" in human relationships. "Conflict, adjustment, accommodation were incident to the meeting of heterogeneous races and cultures. His assumptions were that the meeting of the East and the West would, through overlapping and interpenetration, bring into existence a new culture." This was in line with his general definition of sociology as "the study of collective and personal behavior in group life" in which the leading sociological data are social groups, personalities, social attitudes, and social processes. More will be presented about Bogardus in Chapters 14, 15, 19, 21, 23.

L. L. Bernard: 1881–1951

A year before Bogardus was getting his Ph.D. degree in 1911 from Chicago's great battery of early sociologists — Small, Henderson, Vincent, Thomas, alongside Mead and others; the same year that Odum was getting his Ph.D. from Columbia; one year before Chapin and two before Ogburn were receiving their doctor's degrees from Giddings, Luther Lee Bernard, the eighth of the sixteen Chicago Ph.D.'s to be presidents of the American Sociological Society, was receiving his Ph.D. in sociology at Chicago and was setting out on an extraordinarily dynamic career of teaching and writing in many fields of sociology as it was to develop from that time on. Perhaps he has had few rivals in the number of specialisms to which he has contributed; in the number of institutions in which he has been professor; in the ever restlessness that made him America's favorite peripatetic professor of sociology; in the range and dynamics of his endeavor; and in the persistence and stubbornness of his devotion to sociology in its many facets; for, in addition to his study, teaching, and writing, it was Bernard, the twenty-second president, who set the incidence for the American Sociological Society's founding of its own official journal, the *American Sociological Review*.

Born in Kentucky in 1881, his academic equipment included the B.S. degree from Missouri's Pierce City Baptist College in 1900, an A.B. from the University of Missouri in 1907, and the Ph.D. degree from Chicago in 1910. Bernard's teaching experience included instructor at Pierce, 1901–3; professor of languages in Lamar College, Missouri, 1903–5; instructor in sociology, Western Reserve, 1910–11; professor of history and social science, University of Florida, 1911–14; professor of sociology, University of Missouri, 1914–17; associate professor and professor, University of Minnesota, 1918–25; professor at Cornell, 1925–26; professor of sociology at Tulane, 1927–28; professor of sociology at the University of North Carolina, 1928–29; professor of sociology at Washington University, 1929–46; and lecturer and visiting professor at Pennsylvania State College, 1947–50. He was visiting professor in the summers at Chicago, North Carolina, the University of Washington, and was research counsel fellow in Argentina.

Bernard's main books include *The Teaching of Sociology in the United States,* 1909; *The Transition to an Objective Standard of Social Control,* 1911; *Instinct,* 1924; *Introduction to Social Psychology,* 1926; *The Development of Methods in Sociology,* 1928; *Sociology and the Study of International Relations,* 1934; *Field and Methods of Sociology,* edited, 1934; *Social Control,* 1939; *Introduction to Sociology,* 1942; *Origins of American Sociology* (with Jessie Bernard), 1943; *War and Its Causes,* 1944. At the time of his death in January, 1951, he was working on a sort of monumental story of American sociology and other books for which many pages of manuscript had already been written.

From his long and wide experience and observation, Bernard wrote, in 1949, "In my opinion, the field of sociology, as of every other science, social or pre-social or anti-social, is wherever it can plant itself and raise a crop, that is to say, produce some valid data about the ways in which men coadapt themselves to the world — physical or social — in which they live. That is to say, sociology in my opinion is the science of human coadaptation, which I would substitute for adaptation. This is the essence of the ecological emphasis and the word itself goes back to a conception which I worked out in my student days, over forty years ago. I might claim to be the original human ecologist, but I do not, since there are so many others who covet that title more than I. But I do believe that I invented the key word in that analogical phase of sociological science.

"Since almost no sociologist reads the contemporaneous writings of other sociologists, perhaps I should make clear just what I set out to accomplish in my systematic classification of the environments. First, I divided the natural environments into the inorganic, including the cosmic, climatic, geographic, and inorganic resource factors which condition man's behavior directly and indirectly (mainly the latter). Secondly, the organic natural environments included the fauna and the flora, which made such a strong direct impact upon the collective behavior of primitive man and which have received so much emphasis from the anthropologists.

"I divided the cultural environments into four types, corresponding to my four-fold classification of culture (which again the anthropologists, remaining content with an old dualistic classification now one hundred years old, have not discovered, perhaps because they, like the sociologists, do not read what others have to say on systematic matters):

(1) the material cultural environment; (2) the bicultural environment, consisting of learned overt behavior patterns, mainly neuro-muscular skills; (3) the psychocultural or symbolic cultural environment, consisting of language forms and their accumulated cultural forms; and (4) the derivative control (chiefly institutional) cultural environments. These four phases of cultural environments include the sum total of man's collective learned achievement and thus serve as his cultural environment when conceived as a unit. Each of the first three forms of the cultural environment is derived from the natural environments by transforming some aspects of these environments as a by-product of man's adjustment to them. The fourth cultural environment is derived from — is a functioning composite of — the other three cultural environments. That is why it is called derivative. The word control is included in its title because it is integrated from the other three phases of cultural environment for the function of conditioning or controlling human cultural coadaptive responses to both the natural and the cultural environments. This integration usually takes the form of institutions.

"Since sociology studies the processes of coadaptive adjustment, it must seek its data wherever they are to be found, and this most often leads the sociologist across the conventional borders of economics, political life, religion (not theology), anthropology, psychology, and biology. He may penetrate into the traditional domains of archaeology, paleontology, chemistry, and physics as well as other preserves."

Bernard wrote that the chief opportunities of sociology lie "in the direction of making a closer and more realistic contact between sociological theory and life. I have no patience with that phase of intellectual timidity sometimes characterized as the 'ivory tower' attitude, nor has the public. Of course, the theoretical conclusions of sociology should not be influenced by the personal equation. Research should be as detached as possible as far as a method is concerned, but it should not shun the responsibility of being directed toward the solution of social problems, where these exist. Just as in political science, the sociologist must consider himself at the service of a public wise enough to make use of his knowledge of public affairs and needs. It was with such a view in mind that I wrote my *War and Its Causes* and my *Social Control*. I am sure that students feel this way about the field of sociology. In the applied field it is already making a valuable contribution, but a little more boldness in projecting needed social policies would, I think, call forth a generous response on the part of thinking people. In the field of sociological theory, sociology would do well to attack some of the pressing problems of our age, such as democracy, war, class and race conflict, international relations, welfare policies. The work of Leonard T. Hobhouse might well serve as a valuable example in this connection."

With reference to his own procedures and methods, some of which remind us of Ward and Sumner, both in reading habits and in the voluminous notes on file, Bernard writes: "In the fifteen years following my first efforts in 1909, I worked as constantly as my teaching duties would permit on the analysis of the literature of biology, neurology, psychology, education, sociology and the other social sciences insofar as they dealt with the subject of instinct. I must have read one thousand volumes in those fifteen years. I collected thousands of pages of notes and aroused a marked interest in my students with reference to the subject, echoes of which I still hear after thirty years. Jokes were sometimes made about my obsession with the subject at annual meetings of the American Sociological Society. In the winter of 1917–18, my first year at the University of Minnesota, I wrote out a first draft of the misuse of the instinct concept in the social sciences. This rather voluminous summary of my documentary material served thereafter as the basis for the reduction of my data to monographic form for publication. Six more years were spent in further collection of material relative to the use of the instinct concept and in reducing it to statistical and critical form. In 1921–22 I was awarded the first Amherst Memorial Fellowship to enable me to complete the work. This freed me from my regular duties at the University of Minnesota for a year and by the end of 1923 I had the book, *Instinct: A Study in Social Psychology,* ready for the press." This book appeared in Odum's "Social Science Series," in 1924.

Bernard, like his colleagues, was called upon to do many things in kindred fields. On request he enumerated some of them. He held many positions on committees and in associations in sociology and social welfare work, the most important of which was the presidency of the American Sociological Society in 1932. He was also treasurer of the Florida Conference of Charities and Corrections and chairman of the Florida Child Labor Committee early in his teaching career. He served for some years as chairman of a St. Louis committee to promote normal conditions for children in the underprivileged sections of the city. He was, from 1933 to 1936, a member of the National Council of the American Association of University Professors and was a member of a group that worked unsuccessfully for certain reforms in that organization. He became early (1911) by invitation, a corresponding member of the Institut Solvay of Brussels and was later elected to membership in the Institut International de Sociologie, also to membership in the Association for Historical Investigations of Argentina, and to a similar position in the Masaryk Sociological Society of Czechoslovakia, which conferred a medal upon him for his work in sociology. At different times he was on the editorial staffs of *Sociologus, Social Forces, The Journal of Educational Sociology, American Sociological Review, Social Science,* and for a time edited his own *American Sociologist.* He was national chairman of Alpha Pi Zeta, a social science fraternity, in 1924 and 1925. For ten years (1937–46) he served as national president of Alpha Kappa Delta, the sociology honor fraternity. When president of the American Sociological Society he appointed the committee that recommended the establishment of an official journal for the society. He pushed the resolution through and named the new official organ the *American Sociological Review,* the story of which is told in Chapter 23.

More about Bernard's work will be found in Chapters 14, 15, 17, 21, 23.

E. B. Reuter: 1881–1946

Edward Byron Reuter continued the succession of leading sociologists who were born in the Middle States and remained there to do most of their work. He was the ninth of the Small disciples to become president of the American Sociological Society as its twenty-third president in 1933. If we add those presidents who were professors at Chicago, namely Small, Vincent, and Park, the resulting twelve constitute a little more than half of the total up to this time, while at least seven more "Chicago men" follow Reuter as presidents of the society.

Mary Schumaker, in an unpublished paper, gives the details of Reuter's early life. He was born in Holden, Missouri, on July 19, 1881, and died at Nashville, Tennessee, on May 28, 1946, at the age of 65 years. Like many other scholars of his day, he acquired his secondary and advanced education over a long period of years — twenty-two, in his case

— interrupted by periods of teaching or other employment. Reuter first entered the University of Missouri in 1906 and immediately began the study of social science. Although his major interest was in sociology, he was greatly influenced during his undergraduate studies by such economists as Davenport and Veblen. He received his A.B. and B.S. degrees there in 1910, and his M.A. from the same university in 1911. He spent the next three years as principal of a high school in Tuolumne, California. Returning to his graduate studies, he entered the University of Chicago in 1914 and remained there until 1917. At Chicago he was under the special influence of Small, Thomas, Park, and Mead. In 1919 he submitted his doctoral dissertation, *The Mulatto in the United States,* and was awarded the Ph.D. degree, *magna cum laude.* According to Clyde W. Hart, in his and Reuter's *Handbook of Sociology,* "At Chicago, under the tutelage of Small, Thomas, Park, and Mead, Reuter discovered a conception of sociology that to his critical mind appeared to be logically defensible and practically useful. To its systematic development, exposition, and application he devoted himself throughout the remainder of his life. . . ."

Reuter's professional career in the field of sociology began in 1918 when he went to the University of Illinois as instructor of sociology. In 1919 he served as professor of sociology at Goucher College. He went to Tulane University in 1920 as professor of sociology and director of the Red Cross School of Social Work. In 1921 he accepted a position as associate professor of sociology at the State University of Iowa; he remained at Iowa for the major portion of his professional life, serving as professor of sociology and chairman of the department of sociology from 1924 to 1944. In the summer of 1944, following his retirement from Iowa, Reuter moved to Fisk University where he replaced the late Robert E. Park as "Professor of Sociology and Consultant in Racial Research." He held this position until his death in 1946.

Reuter also served as visiting professor at the University of Hawaii during the school year 1930–31 and at the University of Puerto Rico during the year 1941–42. He spent the summer of 1928 lecturing at the University of Colorado, the summer of 1930 at Cornell University, the summer of 1939 at the University of Michigan, and the summer of 1941 at Stanford University. He taught at the University of Chicago for one quarter in 1935 and at the University of Minnesota for one quarter in 1940.

Reuter was an active and influential participant in the development of the sociological profession, serving as president of the American Sociological Society in 1933, as secretary-treasurer of the Sociological Research Association from 1936 to 1938 and as president of this group in 1939. He was a fellow of the American Association for the Advancement of Science. From 1928 until a few months before his death in 1946, he was consulting editor of the McGraw-Hill "Publications in Sociology" series. He served approximately ten years as an advisory editor of *The American Journal of Sociology.*

Although Reuter was nearly forty years old when he made his first contribution to the literature of sociology, the volume of his publications has been considerable. He wrote six books: *The Mulatto in the United States,* 1918; *Population Problems,* 1923, revised in 1937; *The American Race Problem,* 1927, revised in 1938; *Race Mixture,* 1931; *Introduction to Sociology,* 1933; with Clyde W. Hart, *Handbook of Sociology,* 1941. He edited two additional volumes; *The Family,* 1931; *Race and Culture Contacts,* 1934. He contributed parts or chapters to Dublin's *Population Problems,* 1926; Young's *Social Attitudes,* 1931; Park's *An Outline of the Principles of Sociology,* 1939; and Thompson's *Race Relations and the Race Problem,* 1939. During the period 1917 to 1946 he published over thirty major articles in the various professional journals and over 115 reviews of contemporary books in the field of sociology.

Reuter's work falls into three definite areas of sociological interest: race and culture, population, and sociological theory. Five of his books, nearly two-thirds of his articles, and more than one-half of his reviews deal with race problems or population theory or consider the nature of the relationship between biological and social phenomena. Nearly all his other works are systematic formulations of general sociological theory or discussions of specific questions within the general realm of theory. He did, however, make several brief excursions into other areas, such as the family, the sociological theory of adolescent behavior, education, social work, birth control, etc.

More about the work of Reuter will be found in Chapters 15, 19, 20.

Ernest W. Burgess: 1886–

Of the senior American sociologists who were born beyond the borders of the United States, four became president of the American Sociological Society. These were all heads or chairmen of departments in American universities: James Q. Dealey at Brown, E. W. Burgess at Chicago, R. M. MacIver at Columbia, and Louis Wirth at Chicago. Other heads of departments at America's largest institutions who were not native included Pitirim Sorokin, chairman at Harvard, Maurice Davie of Yale, and Paul Lazarsfeld of Columbia.

Ernest W. Burgess, the twenty-fourth president of the Society, continued the University of Chicago succession, having received his Ph.D. degree in 1913, twenty-seven years after his birth in Ontario, Canada, in 1886. He came to the University of Chicago by way of Oklahoma, graduating in 1908 from Kingfisher College, and from Ohio where he was instructor in Toledo University in 1912–13. Before coming back to the University of Chicago where "Park and Burgess" became the best-known pair of American sociologists in the textbook world, he was assistant professor of sociology at Kansas from 1913 to 1915, and at Ohio State in 1915–16. He was then assistant professor at Chicago from 1916 to 1921, associate professor from 1921 to 1927 and professor since 1927.

Like his colleagues at Chicago and in other urban universities he was called on to participate in numerous activities in closely related fields of endeavor. He was acting director and director of the Behavior Research Fund of Chicago from 1930 to 1939. He was secretary of the Chicago Area Project, 1934–43; secretary of the National Conference on Family Relations, 1938–41; president in 1942. He was a member of the Chicago Recreation Commission, the Chicago Crime Commission, and the Citizens Association of Chicago. Before being elected president of the American Sociological Society, he was its secretary-treasurer from 1921 to 1930, and he was editor of *The American Journal of Sociology* from 1936 to 1940. He was a member of the American Association for the Advancement of Science, American Statistical Association, the Sociological Research Association (president, 1942), Social Science Research Council (chairman, 1945–46), American Association of Social Workers, the Mental Hygiene Association.

Returning now to an earlier statement in which Park and Burgess were featured, it seems likely that their text *Introduction to the Science of Sociology,* published in 1921, was the most influential sociology text of any that had been written and perhaps of any that has yet been published. This was true in a number of ways. In the first place, the book immediately recaptured the Chicago tradition for its great body of graduates in sociology and became the "Bible of Sociology" for them all. That is, the Park and Burgess book was a major contribution from the workshops of the Chicago sociologists worthy of Small and Vincent and Thomas and carried the science of sociology far beyond their advanced stages. The book was so well organized and so mature and comprehensive that, although it was intended as an introductory text, it was usually required of all graduate students in classes taught by Chicago alumni. It put together the concepts of the social process, relying on the work, not only of Small's beginnings, but of Cooley and Ross. Only Ross has approached the comprehensiveness of its treatment of social interaction and social process. Many years later, and continuously, texts like Kimball Young's continued to develop and to adapt the elements in this text, and many students of race and minority groups drew on its concepts of conflict, accommodation, assimilation, acculturation, amalgamation, even as Park himself, a student of race relations, sought to utilize their concepts.

Burgess also collaborated with Park in *The City* in 1925. This book, while largely a recording of the results of current studies, was also a pioneer in the new field of human ecology being developed at the University of Chicago. This, again, set the Chicago group in a new span of leadership, which was continued for many years in their urban studies. McKenzie at Michigan, Wirth at Chicago, Hollingshead at Indiana and Yale continued the direct succession, while scores of younger sociologists made "ecological studies" which, although often little more than studies of the spatial distribution of phenomena in cities, nevertheless built up the prestige and following of the Chicago group to such an extent that Bernard later was to lead a revolution against its powerful influence.

In many ways it may be said that the strong points of Burgess were to be found in his work as collaborator, in his almost limitless capacity and will to cooperate and in his tireless efforts in the direction of students, in meeting with committees and action groups, in his capacity as editor, and in projecting studies and programs of work. Scarcely less definitive, in that it immediately ranked Burgess at the top of the sociologists utilizing new objective ways of measurement, was his *Predicting Success or Failure in Marriage,* in collaboration with Leonard Cottrell of Cornell who was to become the president of the American Sociological Society in 1950. Other collaborations included *Personality and the Social Group* with Herbert Blumer; *The Belleville Survey* with J. J. Sippy; *The Lawrence Survey* with F. W. Blackmar.

As a product of the 1934 meeting of the American Sociological Society of which he was president that year, Burgess edited and published the proceedings in 1935 under the title, *The Human Side of Planning.* In this volume appeared his presidential address entitled "Social Planning and the Mores," in which he concluded that the mores and backgrounds of America were such that democratic planning could be achieved and that the United States might thus lead the world of nations. This speech was addressed to the New Deal era and was therefore somewhat prophetic of the need for planning in the "one world" order that was to develop after World War II.

In an ex-officio way Burgess has maintained his place in the influence upon American sociology in several ways. He was co-author of the most influential of all general textbooks, he was editor of *The American Journal of Sociology,* following Small and Faris; he was chairman of America's most prolific department of sociology, along with Faris and Ogburn; and he was generous in his services on committees and commissions and in having the good will of professional folk in many fields. His voluntary services as secretary of the American Sociological Society for so many years has not been equaled.

Burgess' contributions might be said to be about equally distributed in a half dozen areas. First, his theory and concept of sociology may be summarized simply in his statement that "from a philosophy of society sociology is emerging into a science of society." Burgess was generally credited with the greater part of the work of completing the Park and Burgess *magnum opus,* while Park was supposed to have set up the main frame of reference and outlines. In a second area, namely in the study of marriage and the family and in his participation in local and national family organization efforts, Burgess' work came to be known as one of the special sources in this field. Approximately a fourth of his published articles were in this field. His third special area was in the field of delinquency in which about a fifth of his articles were published, and in which he did yeoman service in committees, conferences, and organizations. A fourth field was personality study in relation to social adjustment, a field in which, again, about a fifth of his articles were published.

Burgess contributed some ten articles on research and methodology, besides several others relating to methods in social work, criminology, and community study, in addition to the chapter on "Social Research" in *Twentieth Century Sociology,* summarized in Chapter 15 of this book. He wrote no less than six articles dealing with social work interrelations with sociology and contributed a number of biographical sketches, including one on Frank W. Blackmar.

More about Burgess and his work will be found in Chapters 14, 15, 17, 18, 20, 23. See especially Burgess' definitive statements on methodology in chapter 15 and on ecology in chapter 20.

CHAPTER 10

From 1935–1938:
Chapin, Fairchild, Faris, Hankins

The story of American sociology as reflected in the continuing catalogue of presidents of the American Sociological Society from 1935 to
1938 continues with the same general distribution of leaders by regions
and institutions and by varied contributions that may be said to reflect
a sort of sturdy stability of sociology in American education. The trend
away from the predominance of the Middle States began in this third
ten and continues all the way up to 1950. From the East from this point
on are Fairchild of New York University, Hankins of Smith College,
MacIver of Columbia, Sanderson of Cornell, Lundberg of Bennington,
Vance of North Carolina, Kimball Young of Queens college, Carl Taylor of North Carolina State and Washington, D.C., Franklin Frazier of
Howard, Talcott Parsons of Harvard, and Leonard Cottrell of Cornell.
Of those elected from eastern colleges two transferred to the West,
namely Lundberg to the Far West at Washington and Kimball Young
to the Middle States at Northwestern. With the exception of MacIver
whose doctor's degree in philosophy is from the University of Edinburgh, Faris whose degree was in psychology from the University of
Chicago, and Parsons whose degree was from Germany, all of the others
held Ph.D. degrees in sociology from American universities. From Chicago came Sutherland, Queen, Sanderson, Cottrell, Frazier; from Columbia came Chapin and Hankins; Fairchild was from Yale, Young
was from Wisconsin, Taylor from Missouri, Lundberg from Minnesota,
Vance from North Carolina.

F. Stuart Chapin: 1888–

Next to the last of the six "Giddings Men" to become president of the
American Sociological Society, beginning with Lichtenberger and ending with Hankins, was F. Stuart Chapin as the twenty-fifth in 1935, the

others being Gillin, Ogburn, and Odum. Chapin was born in Brooklyn, New York, on February 3, 1888. He received three degrees from Columbia, the B.S. in 1909, the A.M. in 1910, the Ph.D. in 1911, and was University Fellow, 1910–11. He went to Minnesota's department of sociology as professor and chairman in 1922 and director of the School of Social Work and was still in charge in 1950. Like Gillin, Bogardus, Queen, and Odum, he had headed a curriculum of training for social work and had come to Minnesota from the directorship of the Smith College Training School for Social Work. Before that and after receiving his Ph.D. degree from Columbia, Chapin, like Ogburn, had started out as instructor in economics, first, at Wellesley in 1911–12, then in a succession at Smith: instructor in economics and sociology, 1912–14; assistant professor, 1914–15; associate professor, 1915–19; professor and Director of the Training School for Social Work, 1919–22.

Chapin's participation in allied fields was even more varied than that of most of his contemporaries, indicating again the responsible role of the sociologist in American education and community leadership. In the nearer academic field he was editor-in-chief of the *Social Science Abstracts,* 1928–33; he was editor of the Harper "Social Science Series" after 1926; and he has been a member of the editorial board of the *Journal of Child Development* since 1935. He was also cooperating editor of *Sociology and Social Research* and advisory editor of *The American Journal of Sociology,* as well as contributing editor of *Sociometry.* He was fellow of the American Statistical Association and the American Association for the Advancement of Science and was a member of the Sociological Research Association and of the Institut International de Sociologie. In the field of public relations, he was, like Hayes, Weatherly, Gillin, Bogardus, Bernard, Odum, and Taylor, president of a state conference of social work and was a member of the American Public Health Association, National Association of Housing Officials, American Public Welfare Association, American Association of Social Workers. Chapin's main books include *Education and the Mores,* 1911; *Introduction to the Study of Societal Evolution,* 1913; *Field Work and Social Research,* 1920; *Cultural Change,* 1928; *Contemporary American Institutions,* 1935; *Experimental Designs in Sociological Research,* 1947.

Chapin writes something of his matured appraisal of the field and methods of sociology and of his own contributions in a special paper for this book. First, he writes that "Personal experience in the field of sociology since 1909 has led to the conviction that the chief contribution of the sociologist is made in the clarification and description of relational phenomena of human society. It has seemed to me that whenever I have been called upon to participate in some cooperative research program or to advise on some action program of civic interest, the contribution that I may have made has been in seeing and trying to describe relationships among social factors which my training and lifelong interest in sociology have given me. Relational phenomena in human society are first expressed in conceptual forms, these constructs tend to integrate into systems of explanation, then follows the effort at objective description of the component factors, this in turn leads to efforts at social measurement, and in rare instances, the terminal state is an effort to observe under conditions of control, that is, to set up experimental design studies of (a) the effects of social forces, or (b) an appraisal of means-ends schema expressed in social treatment or social reform to achieve desired adjustment situations.

"With this point of view in mind, it seems to me that a so-called 'new' field of sociological effort (really not new, except for a revival of interest and somewhat more realistic and experimental approach) is in 'group dynamics.' Studies are now being made of what the factors are that make for successful committee meetings, successful conferences, group exchanges of information and insight to ameliorate tensions and conflicts often associated with race prejudice, special-interest group prejudices, etc. Another new field is the study of housing in relation to family life and individual adjustment. This field has great possibilities because many of the factors are tangible and also focal in any society. The study of social institutions is related to the two just noted. Here the functional aspects of structure and the factors in change and growth, as well as in deterioration and in disintegration, are being analyzed."

Next, in general, a summary of trends in his own work follows the same consistent pattern. He writes, in 1948, "Insofar as I have tried to develop a conceptual framework to my thinking, this may be stated in terms, first, of the concepts used which seem to have gained acceptance; and second, the concepts which seem to have escaped attention, but which I hope to elaborate more fully in subsequent writing. First, the

concepts that seem to have been accepted: (1) my hypothesis and definition of social institutions as consisting of a nuclear pattern of four
type parts: (a) common reciprocating attitudes and conventionalized
behavior patterns; (b) cultural traits of symbolic value to which human
behavior is highly conditioned; (c) cultural objects possessing utilitarian
value, material objects that satisfy creature wants; and (d) oral or written specifications of the inter-relationship among a, b, and c, — codes!
These concepts were developed in my *Cultural Change* in 1928, and elaborated in greater detail in my *Contemporary American Institutions* in
1935. My theory of the cycle of social growth appeared originally in my
Cultural Change in 1928.

"Second, in groping for further explanations of relational phenomena
in human society on the conceptual plane, I have tried to state, but without adequate examples, two hypotheses which I am still working on,
and which I think have some merit: (1) many social forces consist of
the unplanned consequences of combinations of independently planned
social actions (which appeared in my presidential address before the
American Sociological Society in 1935). Examples are: inflation, a run
on a bank, many wars, etc. Each of these phenomena are resultant forces
that appear out of a combination of separate and independently initiated
means-ends schema; and (2) there exist in society certain natural recuperative social processes which operate without benefit of social reform,
in the group-building process (by way of social participation and social
growth) to effect an equilibrium of adjustment that is in its total effect
essentially unconscious and unplanned. This appeared in the *Review*
in April, 1939. In a sense, these two hypotheses are efforts to state opposing trends in society. In each case I have attempted to measure
them, in references cited and more recently in my *Experimental Designs.*"

Finally, the biggest opportunity of sociology according to Chapin, is
"to ameliorate acute problems of human relationship by the development of (1) a point of view on human relationships which is a tolerant
over-view; (2) to develop the needed tools of social description (more
and more accurate sociometric scales); and (3) to use experimental designs to (a) appraise the social values of social programs seeking adjustment, and (b) to measure the effects of the more impersonal social forces

(see my hypotheses about unplanned consequences and natural recuperative social processes). Since I regard the problems of human relationship as recurrent throughout history, I am convinced that there are no 'solutions' of social problems; only amelioration is possible. The word solution has meaning in chemistry and in mathematics; to use it in the study of human relationships is a mark of semantic disorder."

Other than personal influences, Chapin ascribes his interest in sociology to reading. "I was influenced to go into the field of sociology through my personal discovery of the theory of organic evolution. That is, my first contact with this theory in 1908 had a revolutionary influence upon my thinking, and stimulated me to see if I could describe 'social evolution.' (My book *Introduction to the Study of Social Evolution* in 1913 was an abortive effort and still earlier, in 1911, my Ph.D. thesis *Education and the Mores*.) My original undergraduate major in physics and mathematics stimulated me to try to apply scientific method to the study of society."

Chapin's presidential address was entitled "Social Theory and Social Action" and was published in the new *American Sociological Review,* Volume I, No. 1, February, 1936. In this address he discussed the connections between contemporary social theory and contemporary social action. There are two different but overlapping fields of social action: (1) planned social action directed toward goals; (2) unintended consequences that follow from the interrelationships among their personal social forces. He gives examples of how impersonal social forces may be set in motion by the unplanned combinations of independent individual behaviors. This is increasing as a result of modern technology. Planned and unplanned action work together.

There is in social theory a counterpart to this dichotomy of the field of social action: (1) normative social theory including all utopian ideologies; (2) non-normative social theory concerned with formulating principles of relationships that explain consequences that follow certain social action. Because of the increase in unplanned activity, more widespread study of non-normative social theories is needed. Also, a larger proportion of social concepts should be operationally defined. He discusses the criteria of a good or sound social theory, and how it may be applied as a guide to social action.

More about the work of Chapin will be found in Chapters 15, 18, 22.

Henry Pratt Fairchild: 1880–

As break-away from William Graham Sumner, Henry Pratt Fairchild, Ph.D. from Yale in 1909, was the twenty-sixth president of the American Sociological Society in 1936. Fairchild had continued the pattern of western-born, eastern-trained and eastern-tenured that had so regularly alternated from sociology's beginnings with eastern-born western identification, for he was born in Dundee, Illinois, in 1880, and received his A.B. degree from Doane College, Nebraska, in 1900. Before taking his Ph.D. at Yale in 1909, he had been instructor in the International College at Smyrna, Turkey, and at Doane College; he became professor of economics and sociology at Bowdoin College immediately after receiving his degree. He was, then, assistant professor of economics at Yale from 1910–12, and assistant professor of the science of society from 1912 until 1919. He came to New York University as professor of social economy and director of community service and research from 1919–24, was professor of sociology after 1924 and chairman after 1938 of the Department of Sociology in the graduate school. He was awarded an honorary LL.D. by Doane College in 1930. He was president of the Eastern Sociological Society, 1931–32; of the Population Association of America and of the People's League for Economic Security, 1934–38; American Eugenics Society, 1929–31, and the Film Audiences for Democracy and Town Hall Club. He was fellow of the American Association for the Advancement of Science and of the American Geographical Society. He had been executive secretary, while at Yale, of the Connecticut State Commission on Child Welfare, and later educational director of the University Settlement in New York. He was immigration agent in Europe for the United States Labor Department. In addition to his books, Fairchild has contributed, in a vigorous and militant manner, more than fifty articles in major publications. Of these, more than a third were on immigration, nearly a fourth each on population and economics, with a half dozen on race; and others on family, social work, and world organization.

Fairchild's main books include *Immigration and World Movement and Its American Significance,* 1913; *Outline of Applied Sociology,* 1916; *Elements of Sociology,* 1924; *Foundations of Social Life,* 1927; *Survey of Contemporary Sociology,* 1934; *General Sociology,* 1934;

People: The Quantity and Quality of Population, 1939; *Dictionary of Sociology,* editor, 1944; *Race and Nationality,* 1947.

In answer to requests for estimates of his work for presentation in this book, Fairchild says, "As to my own conception of sociology, in general, I believe that the subject should be thoroughly human, closely tied to the observable behavior of everyday human beings, comprehensible to any intelligent laymen who wants to take the trouble to go into it conscientiously, and of practical significance and value to humanity. This last item I regard as very important. I have never subscribed to the doctrine that 'practical' or 'applied' sociology ranks on a lower level than 'pure' sociology. I believe that the utilization of sociological theory can, and should, be just as scientific and scholarly as the building up of the theory. The sociologist, as a citizen, has the same responsibility as any other citizen — no more and no less — to take an active part to the best of his ability in helping to guide the affairs of his community. As a sociologist, he is better equipped — or should be — than the ordinary citizen to make his participation sound, constructive and effective. I believe that American sociology as a whole is moving into a sounder position on this point than used to be the case.

"I suppose I am what is known as a 'popularizer.' This is consistent with what I have already said. Believing that most of the basic sociological laws and principles are comprehensible to the lay mind if properly presented, and believing also that to the extent that they penetrate the thought and emotion of the average citizen we shall have better political and social action, I have done a great deal of lecturing and have served on innumerable boards, committees, and councils and have been an officer in many organizations. In these ways I may have had some slight influence on the course of social evolution in my own country and elsewhere. Imre Ferenczi once told me that in Europe I was recognized as the 'leader of the restrictionist camp in the United States,' with respect to the great immigration controversy. I probably contributed my small bit in getting birth control as far out of the dark miasmas of prejudice, superstition, ignorance, and fear as it is today.

"It follows logically that I believe there should be a great future for sociology in throwing the pure light of truth on the pathway of deliberate social progress, and I believe that it is actually making headway in that direction. I think the time is not far distant when business and financial concerns will employ sociologists much as they do economists today."

Fairchild tells how he was "led" into sociology. He says: "I got into sociology through an early interest in immigration. I grew up in the little town of Crete, Nebraska, in the midst of a farming region settled largely by Germans and Bohemians. By the time I had made up my mind to go into teaching as a lifework and was about to begin graduate work, I had developed a keen interest in immigration, and regarded it as a problem of the greatest importance. I went to Yale to study immigration, and thereupon discovered that if I wanted really to understand that subject I must know sociology. I had never had an hour of undergraduate education in sociology (for obvious reasons), a fact which has tended to make me lenient — perhaps too lenient — toward my own graduate students who are apologetic for the lack of a broad undergraduate grounding in the subject.

"In some way or other I must also have developed a very early interest in population, for at the tender age of nine or ten I remember asking myself over and over, 'What is going to happen when the world gets full?' It was a natural development that, after having spent years in the study of immigration and in the support of what I believed to be a sound immigration policy in the United States, and having seen my country adopt a really sound and constructive legislative program, my special interests should have turned to the broader field of population."

Concerning his own work, Fairchild writes: "My main contribution to sociological theory I believe to be twofold, first, my insistence that the economic relationships of men in society are a necessary and legitimate part of sociological study, and second, my emphasis on the time element in sociological laws and generalizations."

Fairchild's presidential address was published in Volume II, No. 1, of the *American Sociological Review*. He writes: "My basic position in the former field [economic relations] was set forth in my presidential address before the A.S.S., 'Business as an Institution.' It is interesting, to me at least, that the particular theoretical contribution by which I would most prefer to be remembered, and the one which I regard as of the greatest potential service to humanity, lies in the domain of economic relations. It is the doctrine of the physical and mathematical impossibility of monetary profits on a society-wide scale, which was first publicly announced in my *Harper's* article, 'The Fallacy of Profits,' and later developed in my books, *Profits or Prosperity?* [1932] and *Economics for the Millions* [1940]. This theory is now pretty generally accepted by liberal economists (where you can find them), and its recognition by the general public and influential leaders of thought would have a profound effect on the attempt to perpetuate the capitalistic, or private-price-and-profit, type of economic organization."

Finally, Fairchild elaborates on his second main interest, saying, "My stress on the time element in sociology, summarized in my would-be epigrammatic statement, 'every sociological generalization should be dated, including this one,' stems from my conception of the ultimate particles of sociology as individual human beings, men, women, and children. It is out of the character of these particles that the phenomena of sociology arise. And these particles are constantly changing. Not only do the basic types modify in response to physical and cultural evolution, but the individual is constantly in a state of change.

> 'You never see two alike any one time,
> And you never see one alike twice.'

In other words, human nature, in its practical manifestations, does change continuously. And since human nature changes, the phenomena that arise out of it must change, and the generalizations based on those phenomena must be subject to endless modification. I have no patience with the persistent and vehement effort to prove that sociology is a 'natural science.' This proposition strikes me as either false or meaningless."

More about Fairchild and his work will be found in Chapters 19, 20.

Ellsworth Faris: 1874–

As chairman of the Department of Sociology and Anthropology at the University of Chicago following the great pioneer, Small; then, as chairman of the separate Department of Sociology, and editor of *The American Journal of Sociology,* Ellsworth Faris, twenty-seventh president of the Society in 1937, recapitulated magnificently the frontier method of American sociology in making its way through great difficulties in the rapid growth of American universities. For here was the first great department with its powerful heritage of Small, Vincent, Henderson, and Thomas, closely allied with Mead and Angell in psychology, so completely depleted as to have only the old "Master," incapacitated with time and the weakening of a strong heart, and with one young but promising assistant. The problem there was to rebuild the department which had led all others in both distinguished professors and number of Ph.D. graduates, without the momentum or money of the early university and President Harper under whose auspices Small had worked. Add to this the fact that Faris had not even the direct heritage of the Small mantle but came dichotomously through psychology and anthropology to undertake such a task and was under both personal and financial difficulties and we have a situation and achievement that will rank Faris high up in the final hierarchy of those who achieved most for American sociology.

In a relatively short time through Faris, Chicago had reached dominance perhaps above its former status, with Faris and Park, Burgess, Ogburn, Stouffer, Wirth, and Blumer. Here also was a preview of the new anthropology-sociology, in which the work of Ralph Linton and Edward Sapir, Fay-Cooper Cole and Robert Redfield, set a new pace from its genesis with Faris' first organization efforts. Then add to this the continuing stream of graduate students, their enthusiasm and loyalty to Faris in the light of his stimulating, albeit sharp, and driving direction of many studies and we have almost a fair estimate of Faris' ex officio rating in the catalogue of American sociologists. If he is not recorded as author of many books, neither were such prominent dynamic professors as Adams of Hopkins, Edwin Gay of Harvard, Burgess of Columbia, and others in other fields of academic endeavor. Only the total record of Faris can tell the story.

From his birth in Salem, Tennessee, in 1874, up to 1950, as emeritus professor, his seventy-six years reflect the biography of an era. He was graduated from Texas Christian University in 1894 and received his M.A. there in 1896. Then from 1897 to 1904 he was missionary to the Congo and, being then invalided home, he had to begin life all over again. He took up teaching when the president of Texas Christian University sent him a telegram offering an appointment. He had spent two quarters at the University of Chicago while on furlough from Africa in 1901-2, and so he went again in 1906 for two quarters for "refresher courses" to prepare for his work in Texas. He was professor of philosophy and sacred history for five years until he broke away, feeling the necessity of advanced graduate work. In 1913 he had completed his work for the doctorate in psychology but accepted a one-year appointment in the Department of Philosophy at the State University of Iowa. The next year, 1914–15, he was in Chicago in the Department of Psychology, after which he was called back to Iowa in psychology. When World War I broke out, he became Director of the Iowa Child Welfare Research Station. In 1919 he was called to Chicago as successor to W. I. Thomas in the Department of Sociology on the basis of his interest in the ethnological material which his African experience had intensified and made concrete. His chief interest was in social psychology, and it was the plan of Professor J. R. Angell that he should be a sort of liaison man between the departments of psychology and sociology.

Faris' task in rebuilding the Department of Sociology was a difficult one. Albion W. Small was almost a valetudinarian by that time and had to go softly on account of a heart condition. The department was designated in the catalogue as "Sociology and Anthropology." Frederick Starr was the lone anthropologist, out of favor with the administration and embittered. When he did retire, the president was quite content to let anthropology fade out of the picture but Faris busied himself, securing Ralph Linton, then F. C. Cole, and afterwards Edward Sapir and Robert Redfield. Since there had never been more than one man in anthropology, all these finally became a bit restless with their growth. Consequently, the hive swarmed and a separate department was organized with Cole at the head.

In the meantime, sociology had grown very fast. When Faris came to the department in 1919 there were only two others, Small and Burgess. The others had either left or were in wartime activities. He persuaded Park to return to the campus and in due time Faris succeeded to the chairmanship, first of the combined departments and later of sociology. Stouffer, Wirth, Blumer, and others were added to the staff to take care of the flood of students that came after the war. The securing of Ogburn from Columbia was a triumph and it became a landmark in Chicago's history. Where formerly no one was competent to give a course in statistics, Ogburn and Stouffer both contributed distinguished teaching in the department. Faris points out that "Men of the Park school were scornful of statistics and the statisticians seemed at times to have a superior air because they got the answers in exact figures though whether exactness always corresponded with accuracy was sometimes a question." It was Faris' pleasant duty to try to keep the peace between the strong-minded rivals, prophetic of what would happen again at Chicago, at Columbia, and other places.

At Chicago, Faris devoted his energies chiefly to social psychology giving several undergraduate and also graduate courses in that general field. He also had a lively interest in the origin of social institutions, inheriting the courses of Thomas on social origins. He gave courses in the ethnology of Africa and had several courses on various aspects of what we used to call primitive behavior. Faris succeeded to the editorship of *The American Journal of Sociology* and for ten years carried on there till he persuaded Burgess to take over.

In the meantime, Faris had his routine limitations to production. His salary in 1919 was $4000, the sum which Thomas had been receiving only a year before. And though the amount was raised from time to time yet a large and expensive family and invalidism in it made it necessary for him to supplement the basic amount by outside activities. He taught straight through the year, autumn, winter, spring, and summer, for eleven consecutive years — leaving no leisure to write during a three-month vacation, for there was for him no vacation. In addition he taught in the downtown University College twice a week in the late afternoon or evening and this he did for many years. He managed to publish an article here and there from time to time, often working over a paper assigned to him at some meeting and sending it to a learned journal.

Faris could tell how several books he planned to write got only as far as a few chapters but remained unwritten; and how, spurred by his friends, he finally published some of his contributions in a book called *The Nature of Human Nature,* after twelve years out of print. Faris could also point to a row of books on his shelf in his library which were cooperative volumes, and in which he is represented by one chapter among the others. He also edited some three volumes, each involving much work but not contributing very much to his output of separate titles. But if Faris did not write much he inspired a number of good books, several of which were outstanding contributions that took form as doctoral theses under his direction and involved much work on his part, the sweet reward of which was to feel that he had trained and inspired a promising scholar.

Concerning his matured appraisal of the field and methods of sociology, Faris wrote as of 1950, "I have greater enthusiasm for sociology than ever before. And this is not on account of what has been done but because of my belief in what will be done and the supreme desirability that it may be done. A basic science of human nature we do not have, but our welfare, if not our survival, depends on its discovery or creation. The blunderings of managers of industry, the stupidities of labor leaders, and above all, the colossal mistakes of politicians — these would not be, had we a mature sociology. The 'field' is very hard to define, for an examination of the programs of the American Society reveals that new fields of interest and concentration are constantly appearing. The accepted conventional 'fields' are enough to refer to at the moment. It is difficult and even undesirable to set limits. My own interest is in what is known as Social Psychology and my effort has been to make a contribution to the understanding of the nature of personality and the antecedents of deviant conduct. This has led me into studies of persons, crowds, mobs, religious sects, preliterate magic, and child behavior. But my colleagues have chosen many other aspects of human life for their study and I rejoice at every earnest effort."

On the other hand, the old-time fire, humor, and satire is reflected in his comments on method, "As to the methods of sociology, I think they are lousy — they stink! Not that some of the men do not have sound ways of investigating their problems. I mean that there is no method so well developed and so highly perfected that the tyro in sociology takes it on in humility and modesty, as do our students in physics, chemistry, biology, or astronomy. Our young bucks spend much of their time writing in a horrible jargon to tell what they think is the matter with sociology. They should tarry in Jericho till their beards be grown." This verdict reminds one of Harry Elmer Barnes's mood early in 1950 when he said that when Giddings or Ward or Small said "The cat is in the hat," they said it in so many words and *the cat was in the hat*. But it takes some of the younger boys two or three pages to try to say it in figures, and in the meantime, the hat has tipped over and the cat is out and gone.

In his progressive work with students, Faris propounded a new theory of imitation that brought students all the way from Paris to Chicago to study. He was among the first to attack the McDougall doctrine of instincts, although there was a spontaneous revolt by many scholars at about the same time. And he was fighting in the ranks of the men who opposed the extremes of Watson and the now obsolescence of Freud. Faris regretted that his magnum opus was never written. It would have set forth an account of human nature and personality that would find a place for all the older categories called mental, as growing out of action and conduct. A systematic and consistent theory of human nature, the origin and development of personality as emerging from the activity of the human being in the presence of and in contact with his fellows — this had been his chief concern. Unfortunately, the whole has never been published.

In his presidential address in 1937 Faris discussed "The Promise of Sociology." This speech was printed in the *American Sociological Review*, February, 1938, Volume III, No. 1. He pointed out that sociology has come far in the short time that it has been under study. Social thought has changed from the conception of the Middle Ages that the world was immobile, fixed in all aspects, to the modern idea of change and emphasis on opinion of men as the basis of truth. There is no longer one doctrine accepted as truth.

Comte's three stages may be used as a basis for a new division into five stages: (1) preliterate, or primitive, (2) literate, (3) theological, (4) metaphysical, (5) scientific, which may be divided into two, one of which is getting off to a promising start, and the other of which is well advanced. The scientific attitude was until recent decades limited to the physical world. But today people are as bewildered in the face of the forces of human nature as they once were by physical forces. We assume the laws of human nature can be known, and understood, and accepted, and predicted as natural. The scientific stage with regard to mankind is beginning. It is no longer helpful to erect a hierarchy of sciences; they must be studied as interdependent.

Faris contributed some forty articles to various journals, including approximately half in *The American Journal of Sociology,* and others in *Social Forces, The Journal of Religion, Sociology and Social Research, American Sociological Review*. In his introduction to *The Nature of Human Nature,* Faris presents a baker's dozen of premises: 1. The reality of culture as a body of phenomena with laws of its own. 2. The priority of culture, meaning that the most important aspects of a person are to be traced back to influences existing in the culture into which he comes. 3. The inertia of culture; that is, that it changes slowly and tends to produce itself indefinitely. 4. Culture is a phenomenon of nature, or a result of the activities of man the animal in the pursuit of food, the rearing of children, etc. 5. The actions of men are prior to their thinking, and reasoning is an attempt to overcome the difficulties that impede action. 6. Imagination is a phase of events; a wish is the beginning of an act. 7. A human being is a being which has a self, a characteristic possessed by no other being. 8. Personality is relative to groups. It is a dramatic role played to others and can be understood only in social terms. 9. An organized personality consists of tendencies to modes of action, called attitudes, and is the result of social living. 10. The object of education is the production of approved and useful habits and attitudes. 11. The study of the origin and nature of cultural formulations and cultural changes is the only way to understand, appreciate, and deal with differing cultures. 12. Conflicts between nations, races, classes, and sects must be regarded as problems demanding solution, which an adequate science of human nature is capable of solving. 13. Values are non-rational in origin, but are capable of modification either by reason or by force. An adequate science of human nature would aid in finding world community values without recourse to machine guns.

More about the work of Faris will be found in Chapters 1, 21, 23.

Frank H. Hankins: 1877–

The last of the Giddings' Ph.D.'s to become president of the American Sociological Society was Frank Hamilton Hankins who was the twenty-eighth president in 1938, exactly thirty years after receiving his degree at Columbia in 1908. One of the first things Hankins did in the way of promoting sociology was to reinforce the intention of Howard W. Odum to go on to Columbia University to take his degree under Giddings, for Hankins had gone directly from his doctorate at Columbia to Clark College as an instructor and as lecturer in Clark University where Odum was working for his doctor's degree in psychology under G. Stanley Hall. So well did Hankins teach the Giddings' principles and so critically did he approach his teaching of sociology that any doubt was eliminated that might have lingered in Odum's mind about continuing at Columbia after receiving his degree at Clark.

It was gratifying to note that Hall, who had brought to Johns Hopkins the German patterns of graduate work and had introduced Freud and other noted German scholars to America, had held Giddings in high esteem, and Giddings in turn had admired Hall. The first assignment that Giddings gave Odum, who was Hankins' first student to come on so quickly in 1909 to Columbia, was a critique of Lester F. Ward's *Psychic Factors of Civilization.* Giddings was pleased with Odum's utilizing the new framework of psychology to arraign Ward's book, which Giddings had always thought inadequate. Another interesting coincidence was found in the fact that later in the 1920's Hankins had become editor, with Harry Elmer Barnes, of the book review section of *Social Forces* at the urgent request of Odum who was its editor. It is doubtful if Hankins ever did a better and more vigorous piece of work than in his series of reviewing of books on sex, religion, race, population, and biological aspects of society.

Hankins remained at Clark University from 1908 to 1922, first as instructor and lecturer, and then in a year was promoted to assistant professor of political and social science from 1915 to 1917, and then to full professor from 1917 to 1922, when he went as professor of sociology to Smith College, where he remained until his retirement in 1946. Including Clark, where he formed a partnership with Harry Elmer Barnes, he completed at Smith, again with Barnes, considerably more than a quarter of a century of vigorous teaching and study including a few years of tempestuous criticism by Smith alumnae because of some of their studies of sex. Like Faris at Chicago, Hankins was noted for his keen satire and his lashing out at customs and persons. His reviews and those of Barnes, together with Bernard's articles, resulted in the publication in the 1920's of a brochure "Anti-Christian Sociology as Taught in Social Forces."

Among the years most enjoyed were his two years (1946-48) as visiting professor at the University of Pennsylvania, where he found his graduate seminars unusually satisfying. Among other teaching experiences, he was lecturer at L'École Libre des Sciences Politiques, Paris, France, during the winter of 1921; professor of social science at Amherst College for three years 1923-26 visiting professor at Columbia University during the summers of 1916, 1918, and the spring of 1927; at Cornell during the summer of 1924; at the University of Oregon during the summer of 1926; at the University of California during the summer of 1939; professor at the University of the Army at Biarritz, France, from 1945-46.

Hankins was elected the first president of the Eastern Sociological Society, 1930–31. He was a member of the American Association for the Advancement of Science; the Sociological Research Association; the American Population Association, of which he was president in 1945; the International Population Union; the American Society of Naturalists; the American Eugenics Society; the Association for Research in Human Heredity; the American Association of University Professors; the Euthanasia Society of America; the National Committee for Planned Parenthood; the American Humanist Association; the Institut International de Sociologie. He was a contributing editor of *Social Forces,* first editor of the *American Sociological Review,* 1936–37; member of the editorial board of *Birth Control Review,* and of Alpha Pi Zeta, and Tau Kappa Alpha.

His doctor's dissertation, *Adolphe Quetelet as Statistician,* was his first published work, in 1908. His next book *The Racial Basis of Civilization* in 1926 was translated into French in 1935; his last book to date was a sociology text, entitled *An Introduction to the Study of Society,* 1928; revised edition 1935. In collaboration with others, he contributed to several important works, including the *History and Prospects of the Social Sciences, Introduction to Sociology, Readings in Sociology, Political Theories, Recent Times, Biology in Human Affairs,* and *Contemporary Social Theory.* In addition, he has contributed main articles to a number of reference works, including the *New International Yearbook,* from 1907–19 inclusive, *Nelson Encyclopedia, New International Social Science Encyclopedia, Standard Jewish Encyclopedia, American Yearbook, Dictionary of Sociology,* and *Webster's New International Dictionary.* His articles in various professional journals included two each in *The American Journal of Sociology* and the *American Sociological Review* and eight in *Social Forces.*

Hankins has thought of himself primarily as a teacher rather than a researcher. He says, however, that he has always felt that in order to keep alive "the teacher must have some field of intellectual inquiry in which he was endeavoring to extend the boundaries of knowledge, or clarify basic concepts, etc. I have been gratified by the very considerable number of my students who have gone into academic sociology and are now teaching in institutions all over the country — California at Berkeley, Minnesota, Pennsylvania, Florida, North Carolina."

Hankins points out how the biological aspects of social life have consistently held a central place in his interests since his study of Galton and Pearson over forty years ago. Associated therewith have been his interest in the heredity-environment problem, the inheritance of human traits, race and population questions, and problems of sex and family life. Hankins continues, "I make no claim to special originality in my contributions to any of these fields. My *Racial Basis of Civilization* was the first direct attack on the Nordic doctrine and all its ramifications after World War I, but it was about ten years too early to receive attention outside a limited group. It was translated into French in 1935. On the heredity-environment problem, I consider my most important contribution to be the concept of organic response as over against the concept of organic plasticity, so widely accepted by sociologists. This was set forth in my presidential address as first president of the Eastern Sociological Society and afterwards published in *Social Forces* in modified form."

From his seminars as visiting professor at Pennsylvania in 1948, Hankins wrote that for several recent years he had been trying to make a study of the basic trends of western culture from its backgrounds in the Middle Ages to the present. The purpose was to work out a few tenable ideas regarding the basic factors in social dynamics. In this field, Hankins insisted that there is literally nothing that one could call systematic. This in spite of Sorokin's mysticism, Parsons' obscurities, and on back to Hegelian antitheses. This study was begun by Hankins at Smith and was continued with a graduate seminar at Pennsylvania. The premises are that "Over the long view the economic changes seem to be primary; political theories arise as rationalizations of new class or sectional interests; new religious doctrines grow up as sanctions of new economic modes. Basically, culture change must be seen as the slow changes in the every-day activities of increasing proportions of the populations, these changes in daily routines carrying with them changes in folkways, mores, techniqueways [sic] and stateways, and eventuating in new values and new ideologies."

More about the work of Hankins will be found in Chapters 14, 19, 23.

CHAPTER 11

From 1939–1942:
Sutherland, MacIver, Queen, Sanderson

The next four presidents of the American Sociological Society reflect perhaps the greatest diversity of any four. Although all except MacIver hold doctorates from Chicago, each represents a clearly demarked field different from the others. They are representatives, therefore, of American sociology's specialisms and its over-all principles and applications. Although Sutherland had specialized in criminology, his frame of reference was always that of scientific sociology. MacIver's special focus upon government and the community always ends up with the broader study of society. Queen, although claiming priority in the relation of sociology to social work, nevertheless holds strongly to the premise of sociology and social research. Finally, Sanderson's rural sociology is, like Zimmerman's and Sorokin's, grounded in the assumption that rural sociology, like all sociology, can be studied only in the framework of sound sociological theory and research.

Edwin H. Sutherland: 1883–1950

Sutherland, like many of the leading sociologists, as already noted, came to sociology from another field. Like Odum, he was teaching Latin and Greek in a small college. He had plans to take graduate work in history, but found that a course in sociology was a prerequisite for graduate work in history, and consequently he took a correspondence course in sociology to meet this requirement. From this he decided to select sociology as a minor while keeping history as a major. Following his A.B. at Grand Island College in 1904, Sutherland entered the University of Chicago and took one course in sociology during the summer of 1906. From this he became interested in sociology and decided to make sociology the major rather than the minor. He completed his Ph.D. degree work at the University of Chicago in 1913, at thirty years of age.

Sutherland, the twenty-ninth president of the American Sociological Society in 1939, was born in Nebraska in 1883, thus continuing the succession of sociologists born in the Middle West, received his doctorate from Chicago and continued his lifework over a long period of years in the middle western universities. After receiving his Ph.D. he was professor of sociology, William Jewell College, 1913–19; assistant professor of sociology, University of Illinois, 1919–25; associate professor of sociology, University of Illinois, 1925–26; professor of sociology, University of Minnesota, 1926–29; University of Chicago, 1930–35; head of the Department of Sociology, Indiana University, 1935–49. He was also visiting professor of sociology, University of Kansas, 1918; Northwestern University, 1922; University of Washington, 1942. He was president of Indiana University Institute of Criminal Law and Criminology; of the American Prison Association; of the Chicago Academy of Criminology; of the Sociological Research Association.

In addition to Sutherland's more than fifty contributed articles to journals, he collaborated in *Recent Social Trends,* being author of the chapter on crime; in *Social Attitudes,* by Kimball Young; in *Prisons To-Day and Tomorrow.* His main contributions include *Unemployment and Public Employment Agencies,* 1913; *Criminology,* 1924; *An Ecological Study of Crime and Delinquency in Bloomington,* 1937; *Principles of Criminology,* 1939; *Twenty Thousand Homeless Men* (with Locke), 1936; *The Professional Thief,* 1937; *White Collar Crime,* 1949.

Writing for *American Sociology,* Sutherland makes clear how his primary interest in theory does not conflict with his special field of criminology and how his special interest in criminology is primarily sociological. He says: "The ultimate objective of the sociologist should be to make universal propositions about society. Preliminary to this, of course, is a good deal of specific research on society. By 'society' here, I mean society in the abstract, rather than a particular community, region, nation, or other geographically bounded collection of people. I have selected criminal behavior as the specific area of concentration. My interest in criminal behavior is not in the control of crime, but rather in the light that an intensive study of this behavior may throw on society. In the study of criminal behavior from this point of view, I have been interested primarily in reaching a general or universal proposition that would at the same time be an explanation of criminal behavior and be consistent with and related to universal propositions which would explain other kinds of behavior. Moreover, I have felt that this explanation should be consistent with the statement . . . that the sociologist should attempt to understand society. I should like to be featured as a sociologist who was interested in the general theory of society, and attempted to assist in developing this general theory by concentrated study on criminal behavior."

Sutherland raised some important questions when he said, "I am somewhat discouraged about sociology because of the difficulty of formulating research problems that will be directly and explicitly connected with the general objective I have outlined above. It is relatively easy to state a research problem that is limited so that it is practicable for a master's or doctor's dissertation, but the importance of these research projects is generally questionable. This, I believe, is tending to produce a large number of detached and unintegrated research studies, with the principal justification that they give concrete findings. As an academic discipline, sociology will be more attractive than it is now if it is linked up with vocational training and vocational opportunities. It is questionable, however, whether this will contribute significantly to the development of sociology as a science."

Sutherland's presidential address in 1939 on "White Collar Criminality" was one of the few such addresses that received front-page publicity in the daily newspapers. It was published in the *American Sociological Review* in February, 1940, Volume V, No. 1, and developed later into the volume on *White Collar Crime*. Here Sutherland has analyzed "white collar crime" to augment his hypotheses attributing the causes of crime to social phenomena rather than to "received" biological and emotional characteristics within the criminal. In this address the argument was made that many business and professional men commit crimes which should be brought within the scope of the theories of criminal behavior. Evidence concerning the prevalence of such white collar crime was secured in an analysis of the decisions by courts and commissions against the seventy largest industrial and mercantile corporations in the United States under four types of laws, namely: antitrust, false advertising, National Labor Relations, and infringements of patents, copyrights, and trademarks. This resulted in the finding that 547 adverse decisions were made, branding the behavior in question as illegal, yet only 49 (9 per cent) of the total were made by criminal courts and were *ipso facto* decisions that the behavior was criminal. In his analysis of the remaining 498 adverse decisions, Sutherland concluded by logical exposition that 473 of them involved criminality according to abstract criteria generally regarded by legal scholars as necessary to define crime, namely, legal description of an act as socially injurious, and legal provision of a penalty for the act. This differential implementation of the law in regard to the crimes of corporations in these 473 cases eliminated or at least minimized the stigma of crime. Sutherland says that it may be excellent policy to eliminate the stigma of crime in a large number of cases, but that the question at hand is why the law has a different implementation for white collar criminals than for others.

An estimate of Sutherland's work in relation to sociological theory has been given by Robert K. Merton, in his article on "Sociological Theory" in *The American Journal of Sociology,* Volume L, No. 6, pp. 462–73, 1945. Merton had defined six types of work, often lumped together, which he says have characterized the recent history of sociological theory. They are (1) methodology, (2) general sociological orientations, (3) analysis of sociological concepts, (4) "post factum" sociological interpretations, (5) empirical generalizations in sociology, and (6) sociological theory. He cites Sutherland's studies in white collar crime as an instructive example of conceptual clarification in his demonstration of an equivocation implicit in criminological theories that seek to account for the fact that there is a much higher rate of crime, as "officially measured," in the lower than in the upper social classes. These crime "data" have led to a series of hypotheses that view poverty, slum conditions, feeblemindedness, and other characteristics held to be highly associated with low-class status as the "causes" of criminal behavior. But in the light of Sutherland's clarification of the concept of crime to include white collar criminality among business and professional men (criminal behavior which is less often reflected in official crime statistics than are the misdeeds of the lower classes) the presumptive high association between low social status and crime may no longer obtain. The significance of such conceptual clarification, states Merton, "is that it provides for a reconstruction of data by indicating more precisely just what they include and what they exclude. In doing so, it leads to a liquidation of hypotheses set up to account for spurious data by questioning the assumptions on which the initial statistical data were based. By hanging a question mark on an implicit assumption that violations of the criminal code by members of the several social classes are representatively registered in the official statistics, this conceptual clarification had direct implications for a nucleus of theories."

More about Sutherland will be found in Chapter 16.

Robert Morrison MacIver: 1882–

Like many of those before him, R. M. MacIver, born in Scotland in 1882, and thirtieth president of the American Sociological Society in 1940, came to sociology from another field. His earlier studies were in ancient history, in political science, and in economics, but he had the restless feeling that underneath the matters usually treated in these areas there was a social matrix without the exploration of which these subjects were cut off from their roots. Consequently, he came at last to devote his major energies to sociology itself. From realistic experience and from writing and editing a half dozen volumes on social relationship in defined situations, and trying to apply sound theory to them, MacIver came to ripe maturity. He pointed out, in this connection, that "It is not easy to be a sociologist — it implies too much. Perhaps that is why sociologists so often take refuge in some particular field of techniques and narrow the horizon in order to get their job done. I could wish on the whole that sociologists were less defensive and less engrossed in methodology, more critical, and more conscious of opportunities. Above all, I should like to see them more engaged in attacking the great sociological issues of a rapidly changing world. This would bring them into the center of things, instead of their remaining, with their researches, on the peripheries."

Here observations are easily seen to be logical outgrowths of his background and experience as well as of his current keen interests and participation in intercultural situations and conflict. He received his M.A. degree from Edinburgh University in 1903 and his D.Ph. in 1915 from the same institution, with in between a B.A. from Oxford. He was lecturer in political science at Aberdeen University, 1907, and in sociology in 1911. He then came over to the University of Toronto as professor of political science from 1915 to 1922, when he became head of the department, and remained there until 1927. From Toronto he came to Barnard College as professor of social science in 1927. He was Lieber professor of political philosophy and sociology at Barnard and Columbia from 1929, and chairman of the Department of Sociology, 1940 to 1949.

During World War I, MacIver was vice-chairman of the Dominion of Canada War Labor Board. He has been fellow of the Royal Society of Canada, of the American Academy of Arts and Sciences, the American Philosophical Society, and a member of the Institut International de Sociologie. He had the honorary degree of Litt.D. conferred upon him by Columbia University in 1929 and by Harvard University in 1936. He gave the Louisiana State University Citizenship Lectures in 1938, published as *Leviathan and the People,* and the Weil Lectures in American Citizenship at the University of North Carolina in 1949, published in 1950 as *The Ramparts We Guard.* Since 1946 he has been active in many national conferences on intercultural relations and on world order and has written well and reviewed many books in these fields.

In addition to his books, MacIver has contributed many articles to professional journals and to the metropolitan papers. One of his most critical papers, read at the 1930 meeting of the American Sociological Society, discussed the question of whether sociology is a "Natural Science," in which MacIver deplored the tendency toward objectivity primarily as an end. He has constantly stood out against substituting statistical method for sociology. MacIver's main books include *Community — A Sociological Study,* 1917; *Labor in the Changing World,* 1919; *Elements of Social Science,* 1921; *The Modern State,* 1926; *Relation of Sociology to Social Work,* 1931; *Society — Its Structure and Changes,* 1932; *Economic Reconstruction,* 1934; *Society — A Textbook of Sociology,* 1937; *Leviathan and the People,* 1939; *Social Causation,* 1942; *Toward an Abiding Peace,* 1943; *The Web of Government,* 1947; *The More Perfect Union,* 1948; *Discrimination and National Welfare,* 1949; *The Ramparts We Guard,* 1950.

With reference to his own verdict on current society, Professor MacIver writes, "The more I live in the field, the more I realize that the fundamental problem of sociology is to explore the basis of the relationships between men and, perhaps above all, between groups of men; to investigate the historical determination of these relationships, the sociopsychological responses of which they are the expression, and the various patterns of interdependence between them.

"It seems to me that this fundamental problem calls for a corresponding development of methodology which will be more exacting and less simple than that which is current in much of our research. One reason for this is that the problem involves emphasis on the comparable factors in different types of situations. The investigation of these would make statistical investigation only a starting point and never the goal of inquiry. There is a vast job of exploring the intricate patterns of interdependence in which economic, political, cultural and other elements interact and blend. Take, for example, the question of Negro-white relations, on which so much study has been expended recently. I take it because we have made reasonable progress in that area, but for the most part the studies neglect the interplay between the situational responses of Negroes and whites, and, therefore, are not sufficiently oriented to the vital questions of the directions of change and to the causes of the patterns unfolding in them. It is true a beginning has been made to grapple with these issues, but it needs to be considerably developed."

MacIver began his sociological work with a somewhat broad survey entitled *Community*. This was before he had, in any professional sense, an interest in the sociological field. Thereafter, he "played around with some minor studies of labor organization and of population changes, before coming to the conclusion that for me the most effective way to develop the principles I tried to suggest in my first book were in the field of political sociology. This led to my books *The Modern State, Leviathan and the People,* and . . . *The Web of Government.*"

Concerning the procedures involving interdisciplinary work, MacIver writes, "An interesting question arises in this question concerning the role of sociologists who seek to include areas dedicated to other social sciences. I believe that this extension of sociology is eminently justified and involves no conflicts of jurisdiction, consideration of difference of approach and of emphasis. It is within the field of sociology to explore the social psychology that lies back of all human relationships, and here too there should be a great future for our subject. Social psychology is still too narrowly interpreted but is gradually extending from the exploration of social personality to the exploration of the personality complex of groups."

With reference to his own work, MacIver points out that the studies he has made "involve our getting behind the descriptions of relations to the dynamics. Unless we do this, we are helpless in dealing with the most pressing issues that come before sociologists, those concerning social change and its interpretation." MacIver's presidential address in 1940 was "Some Reflections on Sociology during a Crisis" and was printed in the *American Sociological Review,* February, 1941, Volume VI, No. 1. It was pointed out that, when a crisis challenges our routines, we are forced to think back to the values on which they rest . . . we have lived through a year of cumulative crisis; what are we doing as sociologists? . . . A crisis offers revelations concerning the social nature of man, and gives rise to phenomena that are of profound social significance. What are we doing to investigate them?

One of the neglected tasks, important because it is revealed by crisis, is the study of social images. These images are often dark and distorted and may have caused the present plight of civilization. They are the projection of our social values, of our group and nation, which divide nation from nation. Science must bring social images into closer correspondence with social realities. We must study the ways men divide and the ways they unite.

In MacIver's *The More Perfect Union* may be found an excellent illustration of his realistic sociological approach to our most important problems of human relationships. This is one of the few books that rate a careful reading by every sociologist who seeks to explore the effectiveness of applied social theory in realistic situations as well as by all those who seek amelioration of group conflict and control of intergroup discrimination. This book, together with MacIver's cooperative efforts in intercultural and intergroup relationships in the last few years, along with his *Toward an Abiding Peace* and his editing of other series, reinsure his enduring high place among social scientists.

More about MacIver will be found in Chapters 14, 15, 17, 18, 21.

Stuart A. Queen: 1890–

More than any other president of the American Sociological Society, Stuart A. Queen, the thirty-first president, in 1941, may be said to represent the larger field of social work. This is true both in his record and in his own expressed choice of specialisms. Of the other presidents who

had directed schools or courses in training for social work no one had
had the first-hand professional experience that Queen had gained during
the earlier years of his career, and of those who had written on social
work no one had reflected such predominance of social work emphasis,
nor contributed so many articles on this subject. Odum had headed the
School of Public Welfare at North Carolina and had edited a special
volume of *The Annals* of the American Academy of Political and Social
Science on "Public Welfare in the United States," had written two
minor volumes on social work and public welfare, and had been president of the North Carolina Conference for Social Service; but all this
grew out of his primary function of building a department of sociology,
founding a research institute and the journal, *Social Forces,* from which
emerged a separate school allocated to social work and public welfare.
Nor did Odum keep close to social work in later years except as a member
of the National Conference of Social Work and of its executive committee, and as a member of the American Association of Social Workers.
Much the same was true of Bogardus who, although he remained head
of his graduate school of social work, was more interested in sociology
and social research. So, too, with F. Stuart Chapin who had earlier been
director of the Smith College Training School for Social Work and later
director of the Minnesota training program for social work, and who
collaborated with Queen in the preparation of the Social Science Research
Council's *Research Memorandum on Social Work in the Depression.* Yet
all along Chapin had been much more directly interested in social evolution and in sociology and social research and methodology. Gillin at
Wisconsin, even while he was on leave with the American Red Cross, had
consistently maintained his primary interest in sociology, featuring criminology and pathology as special fields of sociology. Queen, on the other
hand, had consistently estimated that his primary interest and perhaps
his main concern was in the relationship between sociology and social
work. Like Jesse F. Steiner who had gone to the University of North
Carolina in the early 1920's as professor of social technology, Queen had
been associate professor of social technology at Goucher College. Like
Gillin and Steiner, both of whom had been in charge of social work
education programs for the American Red Cross in its national program, Queen had been director of the Potomac Division, even as Odum

had been director of Home Service in Camps and Camp Cities in the Southern Division during World War I.

Queen's social work experience began immediately after he received his A.M. degree at the University of Chicago when he became executive secretary of the California Board of Charities and Corrections from 1913 to 1917. He was then director of the Texas School of Civics and Philanthropy in 1917–18. Then, after receiving his Ph.D. degree from Chicago in 1919, he was director of educational service for the Potomac Division of the American Red Cross, 1919–20 at the same time that he was associate professor of social technology at Goucher College. From Goucher he was made head of the Simmons School of Social Work in Boston where he remained for two years from 1920 to 1922. Kansas-born Queen found his work in Boston in education for social work none too congenial from the first, and after considerable trial and error, he went back to sociology and was professor at the University of Kansas from 1922 to 1930. Once again, however, he was persuaded to break into the social work field and for two years from 1930 to 1932 he went into the practical field as executive in the Detroit Community Fund. Finally then, he returned for good to sociology and has been professor of sociology at Washington University since 1932 where also as dean of the College of Liberal Arts, 1946–49, he might appear to have been a sort of balance wheel between his colleagues, L. L. Bernard and Frank Bruno.

The story of Queen's transfer from another field to sociology is a familiar one, after the manner of many of the earlier sociologists. Like Odum he was majoring in Greek until he came under the influence of a dynamic teacher in the new field. Born in Fredonia, Kansas, in 1890, he received his A.B. degree from Pomona College twenty years later and had gone back to Kansas. About his transfer he writes, "I was a major in Greek at Pomona College and at the University of Nebraska, until, by a happy accident, I took a course in sociology with George Elliott Howard, whose ponderous three volumes on Matrimonial Institutions give no slightest hint of the fascinating personality and challenging teacher that he was in the classroom. This man's personal influence is directly responsible for my change to sociology and for the decision to do graduate work in this field at the University of Chicago."

Continuing the emphasis upon the social work aspects, Queen writes,

"I really do not feel competent to say what of my probably too varied activities is least unimportant, but it is probable that, looking across the years, which are coming to be rather numerous, chief emphasis might properly be laid on my concern about the relationships between sociology and social work. First of all, I have insisted upon their differentiation as two distinct fields of interest and activity. Second, I have pointed out that they have, actually, and potentially, numerous points of contact and possible collaboration. I look upon sociology as one of the foundation stones for the profession of social work, not forgetting that this is only one of many functions which may be performed. Also, for 16 years, I have given a great deal of time to the development of research projects which reach into both fields. It seems to me that this is one of the most important and fruitful areas for exchange of experience and for teamwork."

On the other hand, like Gillin and Sutherland, Queen never loses sight of the sociological foundations and looks forward to definite gains for sociology. He writes: "I think, through the American Sociological Society and our regional societies, as well as in other ways, we are laying, quite properly, great emphasis on research and the development of new knowledge in our field. I am sometimes fearful that we may forget our obligations to pass this knowledge on in a variety of ways, but particularly through effective teaching. It seems to me sometimes that our young sociologists are almost apologetic about devoting time and effort to the teaching job. In this teaching, it seems to me we must develop both general principles and specific applications. We must challenge students to relate their academic course work to the real world about them, but I would not have us confuse our function with that of the clergyman or the politician. I do not believe that it is the privilege or the responsibility of the sociology teacher to issue statements to the effect that 'So and so must be done' or 'Such and such ought to be abolished.' Rather we should help students to assemble reliable information about significant problems; to think clearly about them; analyze situations to see what they are, how they came to be, what are their implications; are there any alternative possibilities; if so, what they are, and at what cost might they be realized."

In addition to his books, Queen has contributed no less than thirty articles of which a dozen were in *Social Forces,* four in the *American*

Sociological Review, three in *Sociology and Social Research,* two in *The American Journal of Sociology,* and five in *The Survey.* Of these a dozen deal primarily with social work, a half dozen with sociology and social work, another half dozen with community and social problems, and three each with teaching and with sociology in crisis. Queen's main books after his doctoral dissertation, *The Passing of the County Jail,* 1920, were *Social Work in the Light of History,* 1922; *Social Pathology* (with Mann), 1925; *American Charities and Social Work* (with Warner and Harper), 1930; *Social Organization and Disorganization* (with Bodenhafer and Harper), 1935; *Research Memorandum on Social Work in the Depression* (with Chapin), 1937; *The City* (with Thomas), 1939; *Social Pathology* (with Gruener), 1942.

Queen's presidential address to the American Sociological Society "Can Sociologists Face Reality?", was published in the *American Sociological Review* for February, 1942, Volume VII, No. 1. In this address and in two other articles in *Social Forces,* Queen recounts the problems brought about by the economic depression, armament races, bureaucracy and centralization, dictatorships, urbanism, family decline, etc. He notes that sociologists are not called upon much to assume administrative responsibility, but they are beginning to be called upon to furnish factual data and some interpretations for certain social phenomena. This means that sociological research is the means by which sociologists play roles in contemporary society, especially with reference to governments. There is need for more information about cultural lags, the social processes involved in revolution, changing values (social security vs. individual thrift, production for use rather than for profits, home ownership, international peace, "the art of living" rather than "making a living," etc.). The sociologist must study origins, processes, trends, in a scientific manner.

More about Queen will be found in Chapters 16 and 18.

Dwight Sanderson: 1878–1944

Born at Olio, Michigan, September 25, 1878, Sanderson was graduated from the Michigan State College at nineteen years of age, and received his B.S. in agriculture at Cornell a year later in 1898. Like many others he came to sociology from another field. In this case, with twenty years of special study, teaching, administration, and publishing in the fields of entomology and zoology, Dwight Sanderson went from a fellowship in sociology at Chicago to Cornell as professor of rural sociology in 1918 to make a complete transfer to the field of sociology. With the exception of an excursion to Chicago for his Ph.D. in 1921, Sanderson continued at Cornell until his retirement and death in 1944. He was the thirty-second president of the American Sociological Society in 1942, and had been president of the Rural Sociological Society and the American Country Life Association. Continuing the succession of those who were born in the Middle West and spent their lives largely in the East, Sanderson pioneered in the field of rural sociology which was later to organize its own society and to found its own journal, *Rural Sociology*. Sanderson was recognized as an American entomologist as well as an American sociologist, having been president of the American Association of Economic Entomologists in 1910 in addition to the presidencies mentioned above.

On the way to his twenty-five years as professor of rural sociology and the head of this department in Cornell University, Sanderson had been successful in research, teaching, and administration in agricultural education in state college and experiment stations. After graduating from Cornell in 1898 he went to Maryland Agricultural College as assistant state entomologist, from which in the fall of 1899 he became entomologist at Delaware Agricultural Experiment Station, where he remained until 1902, when he became entomologist of the State of Texas and professor of entomology in the Texas Agricultural and Mechanical College. Then in 1904 he became professor of zoology at New Hampshire College, now the University of New Hampshire, and later in 1907 he became director of its Agricultural Experiment Station. From New Hampshire in the fall of 1910, Sanderson went to West Virginia to be dean of the College of Agriculture and director of the Agricultural Experiment Station, where he remained until 1915, when he went to Chicago (1916–17) as a fellow in the Department of Sociology, thus bridging the distance between his entomology and sociology.

Sanderson's transfer to sociology came as a logical sequence to his many activities in agricultural colleges. As head of the work of a college of agriculture and its new and expanding experiment station, it did not take him long to move into the field of human relationship and leadership; nor did it take him long to apply the scientific method utilized in zoology to realistic inquiries into the rural community. In his twenty years as entomologist his articles and bulletins in the extension divisions numbered perhaps a hundred. He published at least four volumes, two of which were texts, *School Entomology,* in 1916, and *Elementary Entomology,* 1911. Two others in 1902 and 1911 were on insects and pests injurious to crops and orchards. In addition to his books, his contributions to rural sociology included approximately twenty main articles and as many book reviews. Of the articles, eight were published in *Social Forces,* seven in *Rural Sociology,* three in *The American Journal of Sociology,* one each in the *American Sociological Review, The Survey,* and *The Family.* Of the reviews, eight were in *Rural Sociology,* six in *The American Journal,* three in the *Review.* His reviews covered most of the texts in rural sociology and such books as Mumford's *The Culture of Cities,* Lord's *Behold Our Land.* Sanderson's books included *The Rural Community,* in 1932, *Rural Community Organization,* in 1939, *Leadership for Rural Life,* 1940, and *Rural Sociology and Rural Social Organization,* 1942. In addition to these he was responsible for many bulletins in the extension field.

Sanderson sought in his writing to contribute to rural sociology as such rather than primarily to the study of rural problems. Sociology, as a science of society, is considered as studying groups of human beings and therefore sociology studies group relationships or forms of human association. To describe and classify phenomena is the first step and he has done both in his studies of the rural community as rural society. His main contribution here was to describe the community in terms of structure and function in the realistic patterns of centers and hinterlands.

Sanderson's 1942 presidential address had for its subject, "Sociology— a Means to Democracy"; it was printed in the *American Sociological Review,* February, 1943, Volume 8, No. 1. In this address he pointed out that events have challenged our naïve faith in democracy and forced a new interpretation: democracy is a process toward an ideal relationship that will evolve in the future as it has in the past; it rests primarily upon our attitudes toward others and is fundamentally a faith in a desirable system of human relationships. It is fairly well agreed that political democracy is almost impossible without economic democracy. It involves two principles: the supreme worth of the individual and his responsibility for participating in activities for the common good. Democracy is thus not merely a system, but a moral issue and a religious faith. Democracy has developed as a response to the exigencies of new social situations. Contributions sociology can make to democracy and how it may best function to advance democracy in the future can be discovered through the study of (1) the value of the social self found in group participation; (2) the role of status; (3) the importance of social heritage; (4) the cultural lag; (5) the social order and social control; (6) population factors; (7) race relations. Studies of the above may be applied toward the solution of current problems.

Sociology can do more than analyze society as it exists; it can furnish knowledge of the structure and processes of society, which is necessary if men are to assume responsibility for its intelligent control. Some of the basic problems related to maintenance of a democracy include: (1) centralization of power of government as well as other national groups; (2) discussion and public opinion in a time of crisis; (3) role of the expert; (4) participation and socialization; (5) classes and mobility; (6) group analysis; (7) sociology of business and industry; (8) leadership; and (9) evaluation.

More about Sanderson and his work will be found in Chapters 17 and 21.

CHAPTER 12

From 1943–1946:
Lundberg, Vance, Young, Taylor

In one respect our next four presidents of the American Sociological Society differ from the mode of the forty: no one of them received his degree from either Chicago or Columbia. Lundberg was awarded the Ph.D. degree by the University of Minnesota; Vance, by the University of North Carolina; Young, in psychology by Stanford; and Taylor, by the University of Missouri. This group conforms less to a general pattern of American sociologists than most of the others. Although distinctively representative of American sociology in the range of their interest, in the distinctive nature of their work, and in their institutional representation, they reflect more of the individual quality than of group conformity. Lundberg, with Read Bain and M. C. Elmer earlier, was not afraid to put his efforts into the business of surveying communities, of trying to do concrete research, and of writing articles rather than books. Vance followed no sociological precedent or methodology in initiating his studies in human geography and in the human factors of economic situations, nor in his subsequent studies of population, ecology, demography, and regionalism as strong threads in an enduring fabric of sociological theory. Kimball Young was irrepressible in the enthusiasm and sweep of his work and in the persistence of his efforts. Carl Taylor was the first of the governmental representatives to become president of the Society and would be difficult to hold within the bounds of any routine sociology.

George A. Lundberg: 1895–

From the central Northwest, to the Middle States, to the Northeast and to the Pacific Northwest, then Northeast again and back to the Pacific Northwest, George Lundberg's log, if we could use his objectivity-tropism to measure the degrees of direction, the distance of extent, and the sociological area of his coverage, might well typify the surveying of his plot of American sociology. Sometimes called the gadfly of American sociology, Lundberg can scarcely be "surveyed" in any other way than by giving the boundaries and the directions and degrees of his highly motivated work. He was typical of the regional representation of the presidents of the American Sociological Society of which he was the thirty-third, in 1943. He also came to sociology through "channels." Lundberg estimates that he came into sociology, like many of the others, through the influence of teachers of sociology. In somewhat the same way in which George Howard of Nebraska had started Queen on his way, so Gillette at North Dakota set the incidence for Lundberg's dynamic course in American sociology, while L. L. Bernard spurred him on. Lundberg, however, was a sort of Giddings "variate from type" in that he was one of the few presidents who had not received his Ph.D. from Chicago or Columbia, although he did hold a fellowship at Columbia and devoted a special period to research there.

In answering the question of what factors influenced him to go into the field of sociology, insofar as one is capable of making such an analysis, Lundberg thought his story on this point was a very common one, namely, an interest in how to alleviate the social ills of our time more efficiently than by the methods observed to be current. He writes further that "For all my emphasis upon science, scientific method, and the importance of keeping clearly before us when we are acting in the scientific role and when we are taking the citizen's role, I have never lost sight, I think, of the fact that science is an instrument of man's living on the earth and that in the end our interest in the advancement of science is merely to provide a more efficient tool for the attainment of whatever objectives each generation may cherish as making life worthwhile. As usual, among the factors that determined my choice of field was the contact with teachers of unusual caliber, and in this connection, I must mention the good fortune I had in early coming under the influence of Professor J. M. Gillette of the University of North Dakota. The subsequent tutelage of L. L. Bernard, and others, merely confirmed my course, but also laid foundations that I feel have turned out to be sound."

Born in Fairdale, North Dakota, in 1895, Lundberg took his A.B. degree at home, being graduated from the University of North Dakota in 1920, having had courses with John M. Gillette, himself a pioneer sociologist. He then went on to the University of Wisconsin for his A.M. degree in 1922, and three years later received his Ph.D. degree from the University of Minnesota. Directly from his doctorate in 1925 he went to the University of Washington for two years as assistant professor of sociology and statistics; he returned there in 1945 as Walker Ames professor and head of the department. In between these appointments he had followed a vigorous, continuous, dynamic, and restless search for a more satisfying sociology. Two years at Pittsburgh as director of research and two years more at Columbia and later his position as research supervisor of the Federal Emergency Relief Administration at Washington had given Lundberg the opportunity to continue his exploration of methods of research. Subsequently to 1934, he centered his efforts at Bennington College on the making of his *Foundations of Sociology*, establishing a distinctive reputation as a sort of frontiersman in the quest for "objective" sociology, moving away from the beaten paths with the resolution of a Daniel Boone. In some respects he reflects some of the Bernardian striking out for new territory.

With the exception of his *Foundations of Sociology*, the heart of his contributions and his methods were reflected in his more than fifty articles and brochures, in his militant "advocacy" in the American Sociological Society, and in his persistency and high motivation toward the goals of objectivity as he saw them. And in this area, his sponsorship of and collaboration with Dodd in his *Dimensions of Society* in the earlier period, and later as colleague in an ambitious program of research at Seattle, constituted a special feature of his total part in American sociology.

Lundberg has contributed no less than eight articles to the *American Sociological Review*, six to *Social Forces*, five to *The American Journal of Sociology* and others to the *Philosophy of Science, Harpers*, and *Sociometry*. His books include: *Social Research*, which was a study in the methods of gathering data, originally published in 1929 and revised in 1942. In 1929 he edited the *Trends in American Sociology*, with Read Bain and Nels Anderson. *Leisure: A Suburban Study* appeared in 1934, with collaborators Mirra Komarovsky and Mary Alice McInerny. His magnum opus, *Foundations of Sociology*, was published in 1939, and his *Can Science Save Us?* appeared in 1947.

Lundberg says that he is convinced that the so-called problem of values is a pseudo-problem and that the field of ethics and values does not represent the separate world that it is frequently assumed to be, and that it therefore does not require a different technology and approach from that of other social problems. He says further, "I am now prepared to argue that the whole preoccupation of mankind throughout the centuries with the word 'ought' has been merely another semantic confusion. Such a statement as 'we ought not to steal' *and any other 'ought' statement whatsoever,* can be shown to owe its peculiarity and its apparent difference from any other ordinary scientific statement of fact to certain unspoken premises which are always implied in 'ought' statements. Actually, it amounts to this: If we steal, then we are likely to suffer retribution of some sort. If we don't want to suffer the retribution, then don't steal. When 'ought' statements are thus fully stated they become identical with any other scientific statement, all of which are of the 'if . . . then' type. That is, *they are predictions of what will probably occur under stated conditions,* and in this respect differ not at all from scientific statements except that the probability and conditions of the former have not as yet been so fully worked out, on account of the lack of development of the social sciences."

In his paper, "The Proximate Future of American Sociology: The Growth of Scientific Method" in *The American Journal of Sociology,* May, 1945, Lundberg said sociology was in process of transition from the natural history stage of scientific development (in which men were interested in gathering huge masses of empirical data from all over the world from every traveler to distant countries and in attempting to reduce the whole to some kind of order), to the *atomic stage* where scientists turn their attention increasingly to more and more intensive studies of increasingly small areas on the theory that, as happened in atomic theory in physics, the relationships observed in small microcosms will also throw a flood of light upon the macroscopic universe in its farthest reaches. Lundberg reminds us that he has personally been interested for at least ten years primarily in what he calls micro-sociology and will probably devote himself mainly in the future to the exploration of fundamental human relationships to be observed in very small groups and the attempt to generalize these observations into principles that may hold for human society in its largest reaches.

Lundberg in his appraisals made especially for *American Sociology,* calls attention to the fact that inasmuch as the early part of his career was largely devoted to social surveys, from local communities to studies of national scope, this change in interest, or at least in activity, might be overlooked in some quarters. He says, "It might also seem like a contradiction to some that my defense of quantitative methods, for example (and my views here have been fully vindicated), are perhaps least applicable to the type of work which now is my chief interest. This may be true so far as the statistics of large numbers is concerned. But that does not mean that I think mathematics any less important in the social sciences. I believe, for example, that studies in the social sciences like von Neumann and Morgenstern's book on *The Theory of Games and Economic Behavior* may represent a very important development in the social sciences.

"In any event, I shall probably devote myself in the future mainly to problems in inter-human relationships in very small groups and shall not hesitate to leave entirely the beaten and respectable paths for the luxury of pursuing a long shot that may pay off. I prefer to do what I believe *should* be done because I think it is scientifically important and intellectually challenging, rather than what the world, the foundations, and one's colleagues demand that one do for income and academic preferment. I suppose I have been fortunate in my academic career to be able to do pretty much as I liked, and I have indulged in the luxury of saying what I pleased, when I pleased. I sometimes wonder whether the most important research done in the world is not what people steal time from their regular employment to do, rather than what they are paid and honored for doing."

About his work and how it may be rated, Lundberg recalls that it is true that the situation in sociology "when I came on the scene was such that the normal course of events frequently projected me into the role of a crusader, agitator, and a leader of a faction. To undertake scientific work in a jungle, it may be necessary first to hack out, through other than scientific work, a clearing for a cabin in which scientists can work. It may be necessary occasionally to widen that clearing, and finally take an occasional potshot against the former inhabitants of the area who hang around the periphery disturbing or interfering with one's scientific work. I conceive of my polemic writing as of this nature. Similar forays are occasionally necessary against those who try to make social science a tail to some particular political, economic or sectarian kite. Someone has to do this dirty work in order that scientists, and especially students may have the opportunity to work unhampered by such distractions. I shall continue to make such discursions when I think it desirable.

"This role I regard as important but incidental, and I should certainly prefer to be regarded as a scholar who has made some contribution toward bridging the gap between the natural and the social sciences. If, in the end, my *Foundations of Sociology* will be regarded as some small contribution of a scholarly nature to fundamental sociological theory and especially toward bridging the gap between the sciences, I should regard that as the realization of an ambition of long standing. At the same time, it remains a fact that I have been happiest when working intensively with a small group of students on research for which there was not at the time any similar study to serve as a model, and which was highly uncertain in its outcome. I refer here to such a study as my 'Social Attraction Patterns in a Village,' published in *Sociometry,* in 1938. I should like to return to that kind of work as soon as possible and to pursue it without much regard as to whether my generation will regard it highly or not."

Lundberg continues, "In summary and at the risk of repetition, I should say that my work can be divided into three types which have gone forward simultaneously from the beginning: Trying to clear up theoretical controversies which impeded advancement of sociology and inhibited the students from undertaking the kind of projects which must be undertaken if sociology is to become a science. One of my very first papers illustrates this interest. In September, 1926, I published in *Social Forces* a paper entitled 'Case Work and the Statistical Method,' in which I tried to clear up an issue that persisted for the next fifteen years at least. In 1941 I discovered, through a long exchange of letters with Professor Gordon Allport of Harvard, that a long part of this controversy rested on a semantic difficulty having to do with the meaning of the word 'case' (I send you herewith a copy of that correspondence). Accordingly, I presented a small paper to the Sociological Research Association that year under the title 'Case Studies Versus Statistical Methods: An Issue Based on Misunderstanding,' which was subsequently published in *Sociometry* in November 1941. Nearly all of my writings in defense of the quantitative approach, measurement, scales, etc., belongs in this part of my work, much of it necessarily of a polemic nature because the position it attacked was entirely of that nature — namely, a philosophical argument attempting to show that human social behavior was beyond the reach of the recognized methods of natural science. To break down that barrier has certainly been a major objective of all of my work. For my generation I have always conceived it as the most important contribution that could be made to bring sociology in under the main tent, namely, the domain of natural science, in order to enable us to take advantage of the magnificent results of centuries of development of the techniques of mathematics and logic and the general rules governing empirical procedures which have been developed in the other sciences. My *Foundations* obviously aims to contribute to this, as does my *Can Science Save Us?* I suppose my *Social Research* also belongs here."

Lundberg's 1943 presidential address had for its subject "Sociologists and the Peace." This was printed in the *American Sociological Review,* February, 1944, Volume IX, No. 1. This address is representative of Lundberg in his effort to make realistic application of sociological principles. He saw little reason to believe that the peace settlement after World War II would be much more satisfactory than in 1919. There had not been a sufficient change in the conditions that determine a peace settlement. These conditions are: (1) The social sciences must have advanced to a point where they could reliably specify the requirements of an enduring peace. (2) They must have attained such public respect that their voices would be influential. There is little reason today to believe that their counsels will be heeded in the near future. But there is a tendency in that direction and the social scientists must be prepared. The first problem in that respect is to develop adequate professional criteria. We must develop demonstrably superior knowledge and techniques, and must gain public acceptance of them.

"The past ten years in sociology have brought about achievements toward a scientific approach to sociology. There are three general areas of progress: (1) special success in demography, regionalism, communications and interpersonal relations; (2) invention of new methods and tools; (3) re-examination of the whole sociological vocabulary. If human relations are what they are because they have never been systematically, extensively and scientifically studied so that better techniques of adjustment could be invented, then sociologists may point the way toward world peace."

In one respect only does Lundberg strike a pessimistic note and that is in the need for recruiting more able sociologists and the relative naïveté of some sociologists in predictions of solutions for which there is absolutely no ground whatever. "In the same way, there is an incredible amount of naïveté about what can be done about certain social ills, many of which are inherent in the nature of society itself. Much of the more idealistic agitation regarding minority problems is of this character. It is still possible to secure the support of sociologists for programs which violate all known principles of sociology and which have not the slightest prospect of success. At the same time, I know of no way of correcting this defect except to continue along the lines we are working."

More about Lundberg will appear in Chapters 14, 15, 17, 21.

Rupert B. Vance: 1899–

Like George Lundberg, Rupert Bayless Vance, the youngest of all the presidents of the American Sociological Society, and its thirty-fourth, in 1944, followed no conventional school, set his own pace, and, well-grounded by general sociology, moved into his own special fields. He was one of the few who did not belong to the Small and Giddings successions, although, like Lundberg again, he might be labeled as of the third generation of succession, Lundberg from Small; Vance from Giddings. Born in Plumerville, Arkansas, March 15, 1899, he received his A.B. degree from Henderson-Brown in 1920, A.M. from Vanderbilt University in 1921, and followed the customary course of teaching a few years before going on toward his Ph.D. degree. He went from Vanderbilt to Talikina, Oklahoma, High School as principal for two years, then for two more years as instructor in English in South Georgia College, 1923–25. Following this he was awarded a fellowship at North Carolina and received his Ph.D. in sociology there in 1928. He was awarded the honorary LL.D. by Hendrix College in 1936. Along the way he has done yeoman service in committee assignments and brochure publications for the Social Science Research Council and others. In 1950 he was specialist in population studies for the United Nations.

Vance tells something of the way in which he became interested in sociology and transferred to this field. He writes that he was attracted to sociology by a certain feeling of the mystery of unsolved problems and the breadth of a fresh new science. He continued, "My first teacher certainly lacked any technical approach to the field, but he taught the subject from a broad and philosophic point of view. Frank A. Fetter's two-volume *Economics* and Henry P. Fairchild's *Applied Sociology* were my introduction to these fields. Last year at the Princeton Bi-Centennial I told genial old Dr. Fetter how fascinated I had been by his concept of psychic income. Of course, I have talked with Fairchild about the way his sociology first appealed to me. I read Park and Burgess soon after it came out. After a Master's in economics at Vanderbilt, my decision to come to North Carolina was fixed by reading Howard W. Odum's editorials in *Social Forces*."

Like most of his colleagues, he was called upon to participate in many varied efforts and to teach in universities in several regions of the nation. He cooperated especially and in a number of capacities with the Social Science Research Council, the Population Association of America, the National Resources Committee, the Southern Regional Committee of the Southern Regional Council, the Social Security Board, and the Rosenwald Fund. He was not only president of the American Sociological Society in 1944, but was a member of the executive committee from 1944–46 and was president of the Southern Sociological Society also in 1938. He worked closely with other social sciences, being a member of the American Economic Association, the American Academy of Political and Social Science, the American Statistical Association, the Population Association of America, and the Association for the Advancement of Science. He was research associate in the Institute for Research in Social Science at the University of North Carolina from 1929 to 1937 and has been professor of sociology and research professor in the Institute since 1937. In 1945, he was elected Kenan research professor. He has been invited to teach as visiting professor in summer or special semesters in each of the major regions of the United States, including Columbia University, the University of Texas, the University of Chicago, the University of Washington, and has been special consultant on population for the United States Census and the United Nations.

Although Vance's major interest is in sociology itself as the science of society, his approach to social theory has been in the best tradition of science in the sense that he derives his theory from empirical studies of fundamental aspects of society within the framework of the regional setting of time and spatial relations. His latest contributions to the studies of population and social structure are major contributions to demography, ecology, and regionalism in which structure and function are so interrelated as to form a construct that approximates the ideal type observed in the setting of changing reality. His historical studies of regional culture afford realistic testing grounds for hypotheses and for the continuing application of theory. In addition to his numerous articles, his teaching and direction of research, and his contributing editorship of *Rural Sociology* and *Social Forces,* his main contributions have included *All These People,* 1944; *Research Memorandum on Population Redistribution,* 1938; *Rural Relief and Recovery,* 1939; *Farmers without Land,* 1937; *How the Other Half Is Housed,* 1936; *The South's Place in the Nation,* 1936; *Regional Reconstruction for the South,* 1935; *Human Geography of the South,* 1932; and *Human Factors in Cotton Culture,* 1929. His forthcoming volumes include a major text on *Population* and *The Contemporary South,* the tenth and final volume of the series, *History of the South,* published by the Louisiana State University Press.

Concerning his own work, Vance writes that "Logically, one's ideal of sociology should grow out of a well-considered definition of society. All of us, I am sure, will be inclined to build a definition of sociology that will include the things we have worked on in the way we have worked at them. *Understanding Society* reiterates that society is a number of societies. E. T. Hiller's recent *Social Relations and Structures* has a definition of a society with its appeal. It runs as follows: *A Society is a normally constituted population which has developed as a culturally integrated group. It is organized to promote most if not all the interests of its members; is able to support itself; is by nature self-renewing and thus has continuity and indefinite durability.* In discussing the unity of society, Hiller has made the following addition to his definition: Its members share in a status-prescribed manner of living, cooperate in the chief concerns of life, live in interdependence with one another and think of themselves as belonging together in important respects.

"This leaves unsolved for me the most important problem of the future of *general sociology.* The distinction is sometimes made, more often by European than by American scholars, between sociography and sociology — the former being descriptive of a society; the latter generalizations about the concept *society*." Vance sees sociography as basic to general sociology provided one can go from description to generalization by good empirical methods. He is sure there are sufficient regions and sufficient societies to offer bases for valid generalization, but he also wonders about the time element.

Allowing for the broad coverage of sociology, Vance feels that "its focus should be narrowed or expanded as desired to include the community, the regional society, the national society. At the same time sociology finds it difficult to focus on the blurred and indefinite outlines attributed to the as yet unorganized (and unrealized?) *Great Society*. In this field, however, projective or generalized principles may aid in time in building organizations out of the theory of organization, and thus give sociology a share in developing world unity and integration. . . . Most of our young sociologists, by the way," Vance guesses, "would not recognize this as an action program, if it were offered to them as a life-time project."

On the theme of sociology's promise and development, Vance says, "If one looks at detailed sectors of sociology, such as population, culture, social organization and the social economy, one will find no lack of first-rate achievement. It is when these things are moved outside the field and claimed by other (and often later) specialists that sociologists go into the dithers and rush around trying to carve out new and unheard-of areas on which they can start all over again. Philosophy, mother of all the sciences, was the first to have the dismaying experience of seeing her chicks turn out ducklings and take to the water.

"Undoubtedly, sociology needs a unifying body of principles and a common method of analysis to be used by all its practitioners. This is what *General Sociology* ought to be — not an introductory synthesis and not a history of social theory nor a man-by-man analysis of theories. We must also get away from the factor-by-factor analysis in which one chapter retails what the geographers would say if they were allowed to say it, another what the experts in biology would better, etc.; only to break down when the attempt is made to integrate these things into anything but a hodgepodge." In Chapter 25 we shall emphasize further Vance's feeling that "while social science is many sciences, sociology must achieve the dignity and integrity of one science."

In Vance's more specific comments upon his own work may be found more penetrating appraisals of sociology. He writes further, "Certainly, I cannot harbor the feeling that this perennial problem of sociology is the nearer solution because of any work of mine. The things I studied I often left untouched; the things I left unstudied I sometimes tried to do. I took a difficult minor in psychology and I've never written a word in the field of social psychology. In a way, I have worked around the periphery and thus sometimes managed to get identified with fields other than sociology. I have never had a course in either human geography, population, human ecology, or social structure and yet I would like to think of them as my chosen fields. O. E. Baker nominated me to the Association of American Geographers — a membership I resigned after five years. Carter Goodrich thought I was an economist when he asked me to work with the Study of Population Redistribution. There was a time when work in tenancy led some to classify me with the rural sociologists. The editors of the *History of the South* persuaded me to attempt the last volume for their series. I have sometimes said that it must be fun to be a dilettante, but dilettantes are not supposed to work very hard. All of these things have enabled me to examine one region from different facets, but they have not brought me much closer to the core and essence of sociology. Regionalism focuses many disciplines on the one area under study, and anyone who follows this line takes a calculated risk that leads to trespassing on other people's preserves.

"I have often wondered how we might better relate population to a valid conception of general sociology. The title of the course at Chicago, 'Population and Society,' offers a lead and I have recently gone back to the work of Chicago's brilliant young economist who died all too soon. James A. Field defined population as a human group in the process of change and pointed out that the concept should have the dynamic implications of its verb, the process of peopling, the setting up of a people in a given part of the world. In class lectures he wrote:

" 'In its ultimate sense the term population may be taken to mean the provision and stock of men, and hence the material and stuff out of which human affairs come and by reason of which the problems of the numbers and quality of this human stuff exist. . . . Such a dynamic interpretation is necessary to express the sense of process, going on, growth, significant action, together with the control of this process which . . . gives us the idea of population as a human group in the course of change. Population thus comes to involve all the activities — economic, cultural and social — to which men attach value. . . . The content of population problems at any moment in history is determined by the desires and ideals which men hold to be the principal matters of human concern. . . . These are likely to change rapidly and often in a conflicting manner. In consequence the field of population problems has always been one of heated controversy.'

"To follow one segment of general sociology as far as it can reasonably be carried is a task that would appeal to me greatly. I wonder if I will ever embark on such an undertaking. The higher reaches of population involve more mathematics than I possess; theory is of the past and stems from historical studies rather than contemporary analysis. Ecology and social structure, the relation of spatial and social structure, for the time being, intrigue me most. The future may tell, who knows?"

Vance's 1944 presidential address had for its subject, "Toward Social Dynamics," and was printed in the *American Sociological Review,* April, 1945, Volume X, No. 2. In this address Vance stressed the point that human energies furnish the dynamics of society; dynamics are the changes in society. It is in the social process that individual energies are merged and channeled. Conflict is the ultimate means of registering and consummating social change. There is no valid estimate of how much of social dynamics is lost in deadlock and conflict. Auguste Comte made dynamics a master idea in the theory of human society. He was followed by Spencer and Ward. The basic doctrines that were comprised in social dynamics have been criticized and have suffered diminution in scope and value. Economic theory, however, has retained the category of economic dynamics and has subjected dynamic processes to qualitative analysis. It is with an over-all view of changes in society, its institutions and values that social dynamics should be concerned. The study of social movements offers a most enlightening vista to social dynamics. The essence of dynamics is change, but if dynamics is defined in terms of values, the trend is not toward chaos but toward the development of new forms of order. Any dynamic society must be measured by dynamics rather than by static values. New striving in society finds the impetus to dynamics (1) in crises involving the breakdown of social order, (2) in the development of invention and technology, and (3) in the progressive creation of new values involving the demand for new forms of order.

More about Vance and his work will be found in Chapters 15, 20, 21, 25.

Kimball Young: 1893–

Like the account of his successor, Carl Taylor, whose retelling of the social incidence which brought him into the field of sociology appears in the next section, Kimball Young's story is so realistically representative that it is relevant to the total record of American sociology. Here was an American of the third generation of the great frontiersman, Brigham Young, born in Provo, Utah, in 1893, graduated from Brigham Young University in 1915, taught high school for a year in Arizona, and then entered into a breathtaking trek across new fields "back East." Young spent five quarters at the University of Chicago in sociology, took off from there to Stanford University in California for a Ph.D. in psychology in 1921, was assistant professor in the University of Oregon for two years, then across to New England as assistant professor at Clark University, stamping ground of Hankins, Odum, and Frazier. Then he went back to Oregon as associate professor in 1922 to 1926, thence to the University of Wisconsin as associate professor of sociology from 1926 to 1930 and professor of social psychology for ten years, 1930 to 1940; then again to the Northeast as chairman of the Department of Sociology at Queens College until 1947, and then back again to the Middle States as head of the Department of Sociology at Northwestern University. And in the meantime he had been author of some of the most popular textbooks used widely in all parts of the nation by thousands of students in the rapidly expanding American sociology.

As was the case with most of the presidents of the American Sociological Society, Young, the thirty-fifth president, in 1945, was influenced by his teachers and by his reading of some of the classical source books. He could, he wrote, write a long piece about his coming of age in sociology but instead gives only some highlights to be published in *American Sociology.*

"My father, as you know, was a son of Brigham Young and brought up in the faith of the Mormons. Yet he was a well-read man — only had a third-grade schooling, formally — knew Shakespeare, Sam Johnson, and most of the hard-headed literary lights of English literature. He read Tom Paine, Robert Ingersoll, Darwin, Huxley, and especially Herbert

Spencer. He even tackled Schopenhauer, though I fancy he found him a bit tough going. Politically he was a 'Jacksonian' democrat — and this in the midst of the Reed Smoot type of Republicanism. (Incidentally, he 'knew everybody' worth knowing in Mormondom, and Smoot was a close personal friend. You see, our family were among the élite of the Church, so even though he was looked upon as heterodox, he was liked and respected. This helped in my own adjustment, too.) Now my father and an old friend of his, Doctor Richards — also a son of a prominent Mormon — would spend hours on end arguing politics, economics, religion, and philosophy. I used to hear them while I was at play and though I did not understand much of what they said, I gathered a critical attitude, a questioning frame of mind, from hearing them checkmate each other in their own disputations.

"Added to this was my own reading of some of the simpler items in Ingersoll and Paine, at about the coming of puberty. But with respect to sociological interests and teaching, it was such books as Tylor's *Anthropology,* which I read when 13 years of age, and various histories, that set me on my way.

"In high school (which was the preparatory department of the Brigham Young University, at Provo, Utah) I had excellent teachers, especially in civics, history, and literature. In college it was John C. Swenson, sociologist, Joseph Peterson, psychologist, and William Chamberlain, a philosopher, who gave me the chief shove toward sociology and social psychology. I devoured the first two volumes of Cooley, which were texts in a course in social psychology. I cut my sociological teeth on Small and Vincent, and we even made little community maps and the like, along the lines of those in that long-forgotten but, for its time, invaluable book. But I majored in history, as there was not yet a separate department of sociology.

"After a year of teaching in a high school in Arizona — English and history — I took off to Chicago, under the stimulation of William J. Snow, another teacher at the Brigham Young University who told me about W. I. Thomas and his course in 'Social Origins.' (I had never heard of Thomas till then, and had read nothing of his.) The five quarters at Chicago, where my record was very sound, as a student, 'fixed' me for sociology and social psychology. Within two quarters I had become 'reader' for Thomas and was reading like mad everything I could lay my hands on in sociology and social psychology. G. H. Mead had a great influence on me, but I took work with Small, Park, Burgess, E. S. Ames, G. B. Foster, and others.

"However, I took my doctorate in psychology under Terman at Stanford, and used my work at Chicago to fulfill my requirements for a full or double minor. But though I taught straight psychology for some years after taking the Ph.D. my first love was social psychology and the psychology of personality. With regard to the latter, I must add one more comment. At Oregon, beginning in 1920, I gave what must have been one of the first courses under the title: 'Psychology of Personality.' I used Wells' *Mental Adjustments* as the basic text and had the students read Freud and other dynamic psychologists."

In addition to a large number of articles in the current social science journals, Young's main works include *Mental Differences in Certain Immigrant Groups,* 1922; *Source Book for Social Psychology,* 1927; *Social Psychology,* 1930, 1944; *Social Attitudes* (with others), 1931; *An Introductory Sociology,* 1934, new editions, 1942, 1949; *Source Book for Sociology,* 1935; *Personality and Problems of Adjustment,* 1941. Young was general editor of the "American Sociology Series" for the American Book Company, member of the board of editors of the *Journal of Social Psychology,* and *The American Journal of Sociology.* He combined his broad interest in the social sciences, being a member of the Social Science Research Council, of the American Psychological Association, and of various local and regional organizations. While at Wisconsin he also collaborated in *The Madison Community,* produced with R. D. Lawrence, a bibliography on censorship and propaganda.

His evaluation of sociology's status and trends, as of 1948, as is the case with most authorities, could be expanded beyond this preliminary estimate. He begins by saying, "Sociology is just now — say in the past ten years — beginning to mature. When I began as a student with Thomas, Park and Small, in 1916, the work was still largely oriented along philosophic lines. Thomas and Park were just beginning to stress empirical field studies, but without being able to give the graduate student much in the way of rigid training in method. (I had my first course in statistics, for example, with James A. Field, an economist.) However, under Park I did the first, or one of the first, ecological field studies in Chicago, working the area north of the river along Clark Street to Chicago Avenue. (I am told that later the graduate students literally 'wore out' my M.A. thesis, reading it as a 'bad' example and as a warning 'what not to do.') It was not till the early 1930's that more rigid methods began to take root. Remember, how in the late 1920's we discussed method with such sound and fury, but no one did much empirical research. Gradually the movement started: Chapin, Rice, Burgess, the group at North Carolina, and later Stouffer and his whole generation. Today we are beginning to look a little like a science.

"As one who has produced a tolerably successful textbook, I should say that our students are beginning to reap the benefits of this empirical trend. But as to theory to go along with it, that is another story. We now need a synthesis — say as of 1950 — and we have no Aristotles around, although Parsons, Merton, and Lundberg have acquitted themselves pretty well."

Concerning his own work, he says: "If I have made any special contribution to sociology, it has been in social psychology and with reference to this one matter: I have long maintained (a) that not all learning is cultural learning (that is, the learning in which we are interested); (b) that basic to cultural learning, or conditioning, if you prefer this term, is social learning which is older than culture; (c) that is to say, social learning is found not only in man but in all mammals, especially the primates; (d) as a result of this we find many of the basic features of social order among the prehuman, higher forms, e.g., apes and monkeys, such as familial group, play group, dominance and submission, prototype of in-group vs. out-group, and others; (e) and finally that even in human society we find social learning which is not identical to what we call 'cultural' learning. Those who stress cultural determinism scout this and do not properly recognize the difference. Now, for want of a better term I have called this 'personal-social' learning or conditioning. It is not a happy term but I do think the idea is important. Few people have paid any attention to it, and most of those who do have misconstrued my meaning a bit. Burgess comes near to it in his discussion of the psychogenics of the personality."

More specifically, Young writes: "In any case, this is my one original contribution to social psychological theory, although others also considered the matter in varying ways. Second to this, I believe I have done a tolerable job in bringing together cultural anthropology, sociology, and social psychology. This is seen in my sociology books, and in my *Social Psychology* itself.

"I think of myself as a social psychologist, concerned with both basic phases: (a) collective behavior, e.g., crowds, fashion phenomena, public opinion, and like areas; and (b) personality development and operation. To me we need to tackle really big problems, but those which can be made manageable. We neglect our possible contribution to international affairs. We have not as yet tackled industrial problems as we should. And even in the field of majority-minority groups we have messed around trying to rationalize rather than understand conflict and intolerance. Until other persons than members of minority groups begin to tackle these topics seriously, we won't advance very much. Most people are afraid to go at the problems honestly because they fear the Jews and Negroes won't like what they find out. As to our biggest need, it is still methodological, but we are making advances."

Kimball Young's presidential address was entitled "Society and the State: Some Neglected Areas of Research and Theory," and was published in the *American Sociological Review* in Volume XI, No. 2, pages 137–46, April, 1946.

More about Young and his work will be found in Chapters 14 and 21.

Carl C. Taylor: 1884–

About the same time that Odum was returning south from his sojourn in Philadelphia as research expert in the Bureau of Municipal Research to become professor of educational sociology and rural education at the University of Georgia, L. L. Bernard was giving the first course in rural sociology in the South at the University of Florida. As a result of the success of Bernard's courses there he was invited to the University of Missouri where in three years his classes were enrolling more than one hundred and fifty students in rural sociology. Among these students was Carl Taylor, who was to go to North Carolina State College as professor of rural sociology in the same year in which Odum went to the University of North Carolina to head the new Department of Sociology, where Bernard, a few years later, taught and worked again with Carl Taylor. Each of the three became president of the American Sociological Society, Taylor representing American rural sociology as the thirty-sixth president, in 1946. Taylor points out that this course with Bernard

was the first and only course he ever had in rural sociology but that it
was enough, alongside his appointments and associations, to set the
incidence of a lifetime devoted primarily to sociological endeavor in the
rural field.

Taylor's account of how he came into sociology is so representative of
the story of American sociology and of American rural sociology that it
merits recording in some detail. He features some five steps in his gradual development and training in this field. He writes: "As a boy working on the farm until I was almost 20 years of age, never having seen
inside a high school, I became tremendously appalled with my lack of
intelligence about society and the world. Undoubtedly the things that
developed this state of mind were a father who had done some college
work away back around 1860, a brother 13 years older than I who had
not only completed his undergraduate work but gone into graduate
work, and intelligent persons who visited my father in our home — ministers, Chautauqua speakers, editors of farm journals, etc. I therefore
decided to leave the farm and study for the ministry. I know no other
reason for selecting this profession than that my older brother had pursued it and probably because the majority of the above-normal intelligent persons who visited our home were ministers. In my experience
they were the people who saw beyond and reached beyond the local horizons in their conversations with Dad.

"When I left the farm I entered a preparatory department of college
and spent three years completing high school work. I had not completed
my preparatory work before I became convinced that other fields than
the ministry would lead me much further in the understanding of the
world and society. I took all the courses in sociology that were available
in my undergraduate days but took an even greater number of courses
in philosophy, because more courses in that field were available. It was
during the first year after my undergraduate work, while I was teaching
public speaking at the University of Texas — not too onerous a task —
that I read more widely in the fields of philosophy and sociology and decided to do graduate work in sociology. I went into sociology because it
was more apprehensible, more graspable. The next summer (1912) I
went to the University of Missouri for graduate work and the summer
following to Columbia University. Peculiarly enough, I went to the
University of Missouri primarily because of men who were teaching in

the two fields which I expected to pursue as minors, namely Davenport and Veblen in economics and Max Meyer in psychology.

"I suppose the reason I selected rural sociology, although there literally was no rural sociology when I made the decision, was my own background on the farm. I remember saying to Clarence Yokum, head of the department of psychology and philosophy at the University of Texas, where I took my Master's degree in psychology in 1914, that I was going to be a rural sociologist. He said 'There isn't any such thing as rural sociology is there, and there may never be.' I replied that everything that I had seen from boyhood to that moment convinced me that what I had learned about psychology and sociology needed to be applied to an analysis of rural life. The only rural sociology course I could take at the University of Missouri, or for that matter any place else at that time (1914) was Dr. L. L. Bernard's graduate seminar in which each student followed his separate topic or thesis. I took that course and outlined what I thought were thirty-two lectures in rural sociology. It was the only rural sociology course I ever had except to audit Kenyon Butterfield's course in rural organization at Massachusetts State College of Agriculture while I was teaching economics and sociology at Mt. Holyoke College in the spring of 1916.

Born in rural Shelby County, Iowa, in 1884, Taylor received his A.B. degree from Drake University in 1911, his A.M. from Texas in 1914, and his Ph.D. at the University of Missouri in 1918. He had held fellowships not only at Missouri, but at Texas, at Columbia University, and at Chicago. He was instructor for two years at Texas. He was for two years, also, instructor at Mt. Holyoke in economics and sociology, after which he returned to Missouri as assistant professor of sociology from 1918 to 1920. Then he went to North Carolina State College, where he also became dean of the graduate school for ten years from 1923 to 1933. Taylor's work in research, teaching, and publication naturally gave him such recognition as would make him available for the governmental program being enacted at Washington during the 1930's. First, he was applied sociologist with the Subsistence Homestead Division of the United States Department of the Interior, then from 1934 to 1935 he was regional director of the Land Policy Section of the Agricultural Adjustment Administration, from which position he became assistant administrator of the Resettlement Administration. Since 1936 he has been chief of the Division of Farm Population and Rural Welfare of the Bureau of Agricultural Economics of the United States Department of Agriculture.

In the academic field he has worked closely with the American Country Life Association, the Rural Sociological Society (president, 1939), the Farm Economics Association, and the American Association for the Advancement of Science. He was awarded the honorary degree of D.Sc. by the North Carolina State College. In addition to his numerous articles, his main works include his latest volume on *Rural Life in the United States,* 1949, in which he and his colleagues present American rural problems from the regional and empirical viewpoint; *Rural Sociology,* 1926, revised, 1933; *Human Relations,* 1927; *The People of the Drought States* (with Conrad Taeuber); *Disadvantaged Classes in American Agriculture* (with Wheeler and Kirkpatrick); and in 1947, *Rural Life in Argentina.* In his earlier days he published, in 1919, *The Social Survey — Its History and Method,* and in 1923, *Economic and Social Conditions of North Carolina Farmers.*

In reply to the inquiry about those items in his own work likely to be overlooked, Taylor at first dealt with this part of his story quite briefly. His immediate colleagues, however, on being apprised of this, suggested that they add to what Taylor had said. Taylor therefore listed first what he had recorded and then added what his colleagues wrote. He named, first, a study of the farmers' movement in the United States, a study similar to John R. Commons' study of the labor movement. On this Taylor was reminded that he had spent between twenty and twenty-five years but as yet had published very little. Second, was a statement that, together with a number of colleagues, he had attempted to make a fairly systematic analysis of rural social organizations in the United States. Third, he was continually attempting to make his colleagues in the Bureau of Agricultural Economics, most of whom are economists and not sociologists, understand that the so-called "level of living" of farm families is a relatively fixed cost in the operation of the total agricultural plant of the nation and that more important than an analysis of the competing elements in the level of living is a study of the expenditures for the total level of living as an expenditure competing with those of farm operation and investments. Fourth, he named his continuous attempt to combine the techniques of the cultural anthropologist and the sociologist in actual field work. Fifth was a rather wide experience in administration and public relations in which he had learned a great deal about certain systems of human behavior that could never have been learned in academic circles.

Taylor insists that, although he is thought of as a rural sociologist, as a matter of fact he is a rural sociologist only because rural life, rather than urban life, delinquency, poverty, or some other field of human behavior has been the laboratory in which he has worked. Then he continues, "Whether warranted or not, I would like to be featured as a social or cultural psychologist working in the laboratory of rural life. I probably also am thought of by my colleagues as a person who is interested in the practical application of social knowledge. I think I somewhat resent the notion that this interest compromises me as a professional sociologist. My own conviction is that this interest makes me a realist in the correct use of that term. I know that my experience with practical affairs has driven me to a conviction that men of practical affairs have a lot of social knowledge. I should like, therefore, to be featured as a sociologist who is definitely convinced that social knowledge is validated by folk experience and practical effective behavior in everyday human affairs as well as by so-called scientific procedures. Because this conviction is based, I believe, upon social observations, I am convinced that good sociology must be a combination of science and common sense."

Taylor concludes that the greatest opportunities and needs of sociology are to furnish guidance, or at least intelligence in the fields of social behavior. It is trite to say, he writes, "that sociologists are dealing with live phenomena and therefore automatically dealing with activity and that the science of sociology must therefore be constructed of analyses of the very things and persons which constitute the everyday activities of people all around us. Until sociological knowledge can be gained and expressed in terms which hundreds of thousands of persons can understand and use, sociology will be a body of knowledge compelled to work through extremely remote controls, this notwithstanding the fact that its phenomena are the most important things to all people."

More about Taylor and his work will be found in Chapters 15 and 17.

CHAPTER 13

The Latest Four up to 1950:
Wirth, Frazier, Parsons, Cottrell

The latest four presidents of the American Sociological Society
through 1950 — Franklin Frazier of Howard University, Louis Wirth
of the University of Chicago, Talcott Parsons of Harvard, and Leonard
Cottrell of Cornell — stand in contrast in many ways to the first four —
Ward, Sumner, Giddings, and Small. The times are different, the men
are different, their sociology is different, and in many ways the challenge
of 1950 is different from the challenge of 1900. Yet the story and the
challenge remain the same in that the setting is that of American sociology in a changing world, with increasing complexities and opportunity
for the new science of society. Sociologists in 1950 differ from sociologists
of the early 1900's pretty much as literary leaders of today differ from
early writers, as early educators differ from later ones, as later economists
and historians differ from earlier ones. Leadership and distinction in the
1950's belong to the many rather than to the few, as, in the new world,
transitional society is infinitely more complex.

Louis Wirth: 1897–

In contrast to his distinguished colleague and forerunner, Albion W.
Small, who, as an American, went to Germany for his degree in sociology, Louis Wirth, born in Germany, came to America and two years
after his naturalization in 1924 received his Ph.D. degree in sociology at
the University of Chicago, and a little more than two decades later had
become professor of sociology, associate dean of the graduate school and
thirty-seventh president of the American Sociological Society, in 1947,
consultant and adviser for the Social Science Research Council of the
National Resources Planning Board and the Federal Public Housing Authority, as well as a moving force in, and president of the American Council on Race Relations. Nearer home, he was chairman of the University

Committee on Education, Training, and Research in Race Relations and director of planning for the Illinois postwar planning commission.

Wirth's story is again representative of American sociology in many ways. Graduating from the University of Chicago in 1919, with an M.A. in 1925 and a Ph.D. in 1926, he began as a social worker in 1919, acted as director of the delinquent boys' division of the Bureau of Personal Service, 1919 to 1922, started in the University of Chicago department of sociology as instructor from 1926 to 1928, became assistant professor in 1931, associate professor in 1932, and professor in 1940. His only excursions of any length away from the university were as associate professor in Tulane University, 1928–30, and research fellow in Europe for the Social Science Research Council in 1930–31.

Wirth, like so many others, came into the field of sociology through the influence of teachers. He writes: "I started out as a pre-medical student at the University of Chicago and in the course of my undergraduate work, as part of my optional courses, took some courses in sociology. This brought me in contact with Park, Burgess, Thomas and Small, and once having been exposed to them I soon discovered that there was the field where I wanted to work. I was enthusiastic and radical in those days in a sense that I believed a science of human behavior was not only possible but indispensable. What I read in the course of my studies impressed me as rather disappointing. Through the inspiration and the help of those teachers whom I have mentioned above, I was impelled to go on and do what little I could to make our knowledge in this field perhaps a little less disappointing to others."

Wirth belonged to various organizations including the Institut International de Sociologie and the Masaryk Sociological Society. He was a member of the Sociological Research Association and associate editor of *The American Journal of Sociology*. In addition to many contributed articles to the sociological journals, *The Survey*, and others, his main published work includes *The City*, with Park and others, 1925; *The Ghetto*, 1928; *Our Cities: Their Role in the National Economy*, 1937; *Urban Government*, with others, 1938; *Urban Planning and Land Policies*, with others, 1939. He was also editor of *Contemporary Social Problems*, 1939, and *A Decade of Social Science Research*, 1940.

Wirth's contributions and methodology may be best understood from his own partial estimates. He regards sociology "as the study of what is true of man by virtue of the fact that everywhere and always he lives a group life. Of course, all of the social sciences are concerned with human nature and the social order, but each, on account of its own history as an intellectual discipline, emphasizes some aspects more than others. Thus, the economists are concerned with what is true of man by virtue of the fact that at least some of the things he seeks are scarce and that, hence, he has to 'economize.' The political scientist is interested in what is true of man primarily by virtue of the fact that there are differential power relationships between men and, hence, that there is such a thing as the state and the formal organization of authority, as in government.

"Sociology, then, as I conceive it, is a general social science in the sense that the questions it asks about human nature and the social order are of a kind that cut across different specific contexts and accent the group factor in human behavior which, of course, is also present in the economic and political spheres. In another sense, sociology is a specific discipline in that it focuses on the nature and genesis and forms of the human personality and of attitudes (social psychology); in that it also is concerned with the structuring of group life; formal and informal groups; social stratification; social mobility; castes; classes; status groups; racial and ethnic groups; communities, urban and rural; sects and denominations, races and nationalities; the family and so forth (social organizations)."

Concerning the scientific nature of sociology, Wirth has a great deal to say. "Insofar as we wish to be a science, however, we must seek to establish valid generalizations. Hence, we are concerned with a description of unique instances only insofar as they can be used for the establishment of generalized descriptions and more abstract general propositions. We should try to carry our findings to as precise a point of mensuration as the data and our techniques allow. I do not, however, agree with those who believe that measurement is the only criterion of science. The propositions at which we arrive should have predictive value, but here again quantification is not a necessary element in prediction. There are certain aspects of our subject that lend themselves especially well to quantification, such as population studies where we are dealing with countable units, but as in other fields, I would be content if for the time being we could arrive at an approximate magnitude expressed in such terms as 'more or less' hoping, of course, that sometime we might also be able to say 'by how much.' It is my impression that in a good many mensurative studies the original categories we employ are so rough and the units of measurement so vague that the more refined mathematical statistical procedures are somewhat out of place or at least premature."

Wirth is among those who wish to re-examine the concepts of values as related to sociology. "In my conception of sociology, I should not omit mention of our relationship to values. We are, of course, as scientists or would-be scientists, interested in understanding what is, rather than what ought to be. But it has been my experience that almost everything we do is tied up with the problem of values. Values determine our intellectual interests, the selection of our problems for analysis, our selection and interpretation of the data and, to a large extent, also our generalizations and, of course, our application of these generalizations. Therefore, I believe the sociologist, like other social scientists, must make greater efforts than physical and biological scientists to make explicit the value premises from which he proceeds."

Concerning his own work, Wirth sets down some of the things that he would like to have regarded as more or less representative of what he has done. About theory he writes: "I have, myself, worked a great deal in what is called the fields of Theory and History of Sociology, but most of what I have read of sociological theory had, for the most part, been best left unwritten, and most of what I have read of the history of sociology has been less an analysis of the cumulative growth of knowledge in our field than a piecing together of what so and so has thought about this or that, which seems to me to be a poor substitute for the history of an intellectual discipline. In my work in theory, especially through my years of teaching it to graduate students, I have tried to emphasize that theory is an aspect of everything they do and not a body of knowledge separate from research and practice. By theory I mean the definition of interests of scholars, the assumptions with which they start, the conceptual framework in terms of which they analyze their materials and the types of generalizations which they develop as they are related to other generalizations in the field as a whole or knowledge as a whole.

"Next to being a theorist, I believe I have done something in the field of human ecology and the study of the community, especially the urban community. My interest in this field began largely through the stimulation of Robert E. Park and Ernest W. Burgess. My first publication in this field was a bibliography of the urban community which appeared in Park et al., 'The City,' which I still think has had considerable influence upon the formulation of courses and the writing of textbooks in the field of 'urban sociology.' In my work on 'The Ghetto' I fused two interests, namely my interest in racial and cultural relations. I have done perhaps more in the field of the city than in any other field. My published works, so far, are largely incorporated in the National Resources Planning Board's reports of the committee on urbanism, of which I was a member. In the course of my membership on that committee I did much of the research and writing, particularly on the volume 'Our Cities — Their Role in the National Economy' which I think was something of a pioneer study and became a rare thing among government publications, namely a best seller. The 'Local Community Fact Book' on Chicago was a further development of my interest in the urban community. I think this work, too, established something of a pattern for urban community studies. The one publication in this field for which I have received perhaps more requests for reprints than for anything else I have ever done is the article in 'The American Journal of Sociology' entitled 'Urbanism as a Way of Life' which seeks to set forth a systematic, theoretical framework for the sociological analysis of urban phenomena.

"My second interest is in what is known as the sociology of knowledge. This is a field which is misnamed and with the misnaming of which, unfortunately, I have had something to do. It should rather be called the sociology of intellectual life. You may recall that I translated and wrote a rather extensive introduction to Mannheim's 'Ideology and Utopia' and thus introduced this work to the English-speaking public. I have written very little in this field myself, aside from an article or two, but I have underway a monograph on the sociology of science which I hope will have some value. I have also directed a number of Doctors' theses in this field, such as one on the sociology of art and another one on the sociology of literature which begin to open these fields to empirical inquiry.

"My third, and at the present time, my main love is the field of race relations and minority problems. I have published a number of things in this field including a number of articles in the *Journal,* a little monograph for the Social Science Research Council on 'Problems of Minorities in War Time,' a chapter in Linton's book on 'The Science of Man in the World Crisis' entitled 'The Problem of Minority Groups' which some of my friends think is one of the best things in the field, probably because it attempts to establish a typology of minorities. In this connection I cooperated with the Myrdal projects and published with Herbert Goldhamer a monograph in that series on miscegenation. I think in this field our action has so far outrun our knowledge that we must concentrate our efforts for some time to come on fundamental research concerning the nature and functioning of prejudice and antipathy, on problems of discrimination, on segregation, and on intergroup tensions and conflicts that furnish a more reliable basis for social action.

"I have also had a good deal of interest and experience in the field of housing and planning. Because I believe that planning is one of the roads by which we may preserve a democratic society, I have written and worked a good deal in this field."

"What I think about sociology and its task in the present-day world is perhaps best set forth in my Presidential Address. Although the subject matter of this paper was primarily consensus and mass communication, I believe similar ideas would also be relevant to problems of housing, planning, international relations, race relations, and others. I believe the time is past when we will be educating and training sociologists primarily to go out into the world to educate and train other sociologists. Sociologists will, of course, still be required to keep up the continuity of learning in their field, but more and more of them will be using their sociological knowledge as research workers, as analysts and as policy makers in the various fields of social life, such as government, labor, business, welfare, and education. They will be involved in the field of international relations, in industrial relations, labor relations, administration, race relations, social work, social psychiatry, mass communications, housing, planning, and a variety of other fields. There they will have to win their way by what they can contribute to the understanding and solutions of problems of human social life. I do not think we can win prestige either with academic administrations or with the public merely by asserting that we know something and can find out something. We have to earn the prestige by what we can show we actually do know and by demonstrating the importance of what we have discovered in the course of intellectual competition with other scientific disciplines and with common sense knowledge."

Wirth's presidential address was entitled "Consensus and Mass Communication" and was published in the *American Sociological Review,* for February, 1948, Volume XIII, pages 1–15.

More about the work of Wirth will be found in Chapters 19 and 20.

Franklin Frazier: 1894–

Ten years after Frank H. Hankins had become the twenty-eighth president of the American Sociological Society, the second of his students at Clark University became the thirty-eighth president in 1948. This student was E. Franklin Frazier who studied with Hankins during his last year as professor at Clark, as Howard W. Odum, the twentieth president had done during Hankins' first year as instructor. Frazier, who credits Hankins with influencing him to venture into sociology, went on to the University of Chicago for his Ph.D. instead of Columbia, thus augmenting again the Chicago succession.

Frazier's story is again so realistically representative of the story of American sociology that it helps to illumine the whole picture. For Frazier, after teaching in various institutions in the South, had become president of the Eastern Sociological Society, as his colleague, Charles S. Johnson, under whom he taught at Fisk University, had come from the East to become president of the Southern Sociological Society shortly after Frazier had been elected by the Eastern Society. Johnson went on, however, to head the Fisk University Research Institute and to become president of that university, whereas Frazier continued to specialize in sociology and to become vice-president, member of the executive committee, and president of the American Sociological Society. Frazier was born in Baltimore, moved southward, then north and east, then west and back to Washington's Howard University where he developed a strong sociology department and research program from which then he was elected president of the Society at fifty-four years of age.

Concerning the factors that led him into sociology, Frazier writes somewhat at length. He says: "During my college days at Howard University, when my curiosity to learn everything was at fever heat, my course of study embraced a wide range of courses, including mathematics and physical science, literature, Latin, Greek, French, German, as well as the social sciences with the exception of sociology because I heard that it was not presented in a serious fashion. However, through reading widely, I came across Giddings' *The Principles of Sociology*. While I was fascinated by the subject, especially his manner of presentation, I did not decide to follow sociology as a specialty. While in college I had developed a keen interest in social problems. I was a member of the Intercollegiate Socialist Society and I was president of the Political Science Club.

"After leaving college I continued my interest in socialism. But after accepting my first teaching appointment at Tuskegee Institute, I began to take an intense interest in the Negro problem. I was militant in my opposition to the existing race relations and urged young Negroes to assume a militant attitude toward discrimination and oppression. After a year at Tuskegee I went to teach at Lawrenceville, Virginia. I resented being drafted in a war which, in my opinion, was essentially a conflict between imperialistic powers and in view of the treatment of the Negro in the United States the avowed aim, to make the world safe for democracy, represented hypocrisy on the part of America. During this time I nourished the ambition to take graduate work in sociology because it appealed to me as the social science which most nearly provided an explanation and understanding of race and class conflicts. As I look back now, it appears to me that during this period I was developing an objective outlook on racial and other social problems which was divorced in a sense from my reaction to these problems as a person and as a member of society.

"The opportunity to pursue graduate work in sociology came in 1919 when I received a scholarship to study at Clark University, Worcester, Massachusetts. Under Professor Frank H. Hankins, whose courses were concerned primarily with social theory, I began seriously my career as a sociologist. I have the feeling that the intellectual discipline which I received during my year at Clark University had a marked influence on my development as a sociologist. It provided me with a broad intellectual outlook that was uncontaminated by such matters of expediency as interracial policies in the United States. This does not mean, of course, that I accepted entirely Hankins' position on racial and social problems;

it means that the study and analysis of social problems were pitched upon a high intellectual level.

"Later I spent a year as a research fellow at the New York School of Social Work, where I began to make empirical studies of social problems. For example, I made a study of the Negro longshoremen of New York City which was partly financed by the Russell Sage Foundation and is in the library of that institution. Then I spent a year in Denmark studying the folk high schools. This gave me an opportunity to get a view of the culture of a small nation, especially the culture of its folk. While studying in Denmark, I had an opportunity to spend some time in Germany and France and a few days in England. While in France I attended the Second Pan-African Conference in 1921, where I met the leaders of the colonial peoples. When I went to the University of Chicago, I had this rich background of experience as a basis for my sociological studies in the family and race relations. It was at the University of Chicago that I developed a clearly defined conception of the field of sociology and acquired the technical knowledge and skill to carry on sociological research."

The factual record of Frazier's academic background and progression starts with his graduation from high school in Baltimore, Maryland, in 1912. Then he received the A.M. in sociology from Clark University, Worcester, Massachusetts, in 1920. He was research fellow, New York School of Social Work, 1920–21, and fellow of the American-Scandinavian Foundation to Denmark, 1921–22 where he studied folk high schools. His last degree was the Ph.D. in sociology at the University of Chicago, in 1931.

His teaching experiences included instruction in mathematics, Tuskegee Institute, Alabama, 1916–17; in the summer school at Fort Valley High and Industrial School, Fort Valley, Georgia, 1917; English and history, St. Paul's Normal and Industrial School, Lawrenceville, Virginia, 1917–18; and mathematics, Baltimore High School, Baltimore, 1918–19. He was director of the summer school at Livingstone College, Salisbury, North Carolina, in 1922, and instructor in sociology, Morehouse College, Atlanta, Georgia, 1922–24. He was director of the Atlanta School of Social Work, Atlanta, Georgia, 1922–27; research assistant, University of Chicago, 1927–29; special lecturer, department of sociology, Fisk University, 1929–31; research professor, department of sociology, Fisk University, 1931–34; professor and head of the department of sociology, Howard University, 1934 to the present. He was also regular part-time instructor, New York School of Social Work, Columbia University, visiting professor of sociology, New York University, summer of 1944 and 1947, and visiting professor of sociology, Sarah Lawrence College, spring, 1945.

Like those of most of his contemporary sociologists, his experiences were varied. He received a fellowship from the John Simon Guggenheim Foundation, 1940–41, to study the Negro family in Brazil and the West Indies; he was resident fellow of the Library of Congress, 1942–43; fellow of the Library of Congress since 1943; fellow of the Inter-American Society of Anthropology and Geography; fellow of the American Association for the Advancement of Science; and a founding member of the Institute Internacional de Estudios Afroamericanos. He was president of the Eastern Sociological Society; president, District of Columbia Chapter, the American Sociological Society; and director, Economic and Social Survey of Harlem for Mayor LaGuardia's Commission on Conditions in Harlem, 1935–36. Subsequently, he was a member of the consultant groups for UNESCO in 1950.

In addition to numerous contributions to journals including *The American Journal of Sociology, American Sociological Review, Social Forces, The Nation, The Forum, Current History, The Crisis, Opportunity,* and *Common Sense,* his main work includes *The Negro Family in the United States,* 1939, revised, 1948; *The Negro Family in Chicago,* 1939; *Negro Youth at the Crossways,* 1940; *The Negro in the United States,* 1949; *The Free Negro Family,* 1932; "Traditions and Patterns of Negro Family Life," in E. B. Reuter (ed.) *Race and Culture Contacts,* 1934; "Durham: Capital of the Black Middle Class," in *The New Negro,* edited by Alain Locke, 1925; "La Bourgeoisie Noire," *Anthology of American Negro Literature,* edited by V. F. Calverton, 1929; "A Comparison of Negro-White Relations in Brazil and in the United States," *Transactions of the New York Academy of Sciences,* 1944; "The Negro and Racial Conflicts" in *One America,* edited by Francis J. Brown and Joseph S. Roucek, 1945; and "The Racial Issue" in R. M. MacIver, editor, *Unity and Difference in American Life,* 1947.

From his teaching and research and from "reflection upon theoretical problems as they have been influenced by research," Frazier gives his appraisal of sociology as of 1950, as follows: "Sociology in the broadest sense, as I conceive it, is concerned with the study of human nature which is a product of human association. Human association involves the interaction of human beings and since for human beings social behavior involves meanings there is a subjective element which cannot be ignored. As a result of human interaction personality comes into existence and personality involves subjective elements. The study of this phase of the sociological process falls within the field of social psychology. In addition to the formation of personality, the social process results in the organization of persons in social systems.

"By a social system I mean, of course, a system of human relationships, institutions, etc. A community may be defined as a social system or social organization having a locus in space. These social systems may consist of a family group or of a nation depending upon such factors as spatial relations, the character of communication, and the nature of the contacts existing between human beings. This appears to me to be the special subject matter of sociology. The important factor is the character of the social system because the social system is the frame of reference in which sociological phenomena should be studied. (This concept of sociology is opposed to the atomistic conception of society, although I recognize that ecological studies treat people atomistically in some phases at least.) For example, the polarity which is implied or involved in the distinction between Gemeinschaft and Gesellschaft and sacred and secular societies represents two different types of social systems. (I should hasten to add that our conception of a social system should be based upon empirical studies and our conception of social systems should be tested by empirical studies.)

"The point which I wish to emphasize is the structural nature of social phenomena which are the subject of sociological research. I do not mean the structural aspect of social phenomena in the merely formal sense without content. For example, I feel that the sociologist should study the structure of power because it is an aspect of social reality and an important aspect of social control which all sociologists agree is one of the central problems of their discipline. It seems to me that if we study social phenomena as a part of a social system such concepts as folkways, mores, conflict and assimilation would acquire a new significance as tools for research. Moreover, I should add that I refer to social systems in their dynamic as well as static aspects. The dynamic or changing character of social systems is of major concern today.

"It is my firm conviction that the development of sociology depends upon empirical research. But if empirical research in sociology is to contribute to the development of sociology it must be based upon concepts which are sociologically significant. It is my feeling that much empirical research is not significant because it is not based upon concepts which are basic in sociology. Very often when empirical studies are based upon sociological concepts, they are concerned with minutiae and almost microscopic phases of the social process. This criticism applies to both the statistical and the case study method. Technical perfection in either method is important but the crucial point is that if either method is used in a study, does it provide answers to important questions? In the work which I have done in sociology it has been my aim to find answers to significant sociological questions or to determine the adequacy of certain sociological concepts.

"I feel that my work in sociology falls in two major fields of interest: *Race and Culture Contacts* and *The Family*. This has been owing partly to the fact that I have felt that the most fruitful approach to the study of *Race and Culture Contacts,* especially those aspects as regards acculturation and assimilation, was through the study of the family. At the same time I have an interest in the study of the family which is independent of its relation to *Race and Culture Contacts*. For example, I have been interested in studying such purely sociological problems as the development of the interest of the male in the family, the establishment of masculine authority and discipline in the family life, and the influence of family traditions on the stability of the family and the behavior of its members.

"I consider myself primarily a scholar. I do not consider myself a Negro leader or an interracial leader. I have studiously avoided what has appeared to me to be a pitfall which lies in the path of most educated Negroes, namely, being forced into the role of a Negro leader. Generally, this has not only resulted in the expenditure of energy which might be devoted to intellectual achievement, but it has also resulted in the narrowing of the intellectual outlook of Negroes and sometimes in encouraging intellectual dishonesty. Naturally, as the result of my educational and scholarly attainments I exercise a certain intellectual leadership in college and perhaps more widely in educational circles."

Frazier's presidential address was entitled "Race Contacts and the Social Structure" and was published in the *American Sociological Review,* Volume XIV, February, 1949, pages 1–11.

More about Frazier and his work will be found in Chapters 3, 18, and 19.

Talcott Parsons: 1902–

In a number of ways Talcott Parsons, the thirty-ninth president of the American Sociological Society, in 1949, recapitulates much of the earlier pattern of the sociological succession. That is, he came into the field from economics, and he found the chief incidence and preparation of his sociological work in Europe. At Amherst College where he graduated in 1924 at twenty-two years of age, he concentrated in biology, but through the stimulation of Walton Hamilton, one of the newer institutional economists and later professor in the Yale School of Law, he was influenced to do graduate work in economics. Then, like Small, he took his doctor's degree in Germany, having received his Dr. Phil. at Heidelberg in 1927 on the basis of his thesis on "The Concept of Capitalism in the Theories of Max Weber and Werner Sombart." On the way to Heidelberg, however, Parsons, in 1924–25, had begun his studies in sociology and anthropology at the London School of Economics with L. T. Hobhouse and Morris Ginsberg and with Bronislaw Malinowski. Then, at the end of this year, Parsons was awarded one of the postwar fellowships for study in Germany and was assigned to Heidelberg University where he spent the year 1925–26 learning of the work of Max Weber, whom he then introduced to American sociology, translating his "The Protestant Ethic" and making it a sort of "classic" for young American sociologists. From this point Parsons developed his structure-function theory, first presented in his *The Structure of Social Action,* published in 1937 and later developed in a series of *Essays in Sociological Theory, Pure and Applied,* republished in a volume of that title in 1949.

Yet even then Parsons was still primarily in the field of economics. As told in the biographical sketch by Bernard Barber, in the volume of essays, pages 350–51, Parsons' next period of development was as instructor in the department of economics at Harvard University. "There he was in close contact with a group of distinguished men such as Taussig and Carver who were still essentially adherents of classical economic theory. Stimulated by them Parsons set himself the task of trying to answer his questions by an intensive study of the work of Alfred Marshall, the great classical theorist and co-discoverer of the principle of marginal utility. In Marshall's writings Parsons traced out the implicit set of social values on which the theory of free enterprise rested. This study convinced Parsons that the status of the value element for classical economic theory was logically treated as residual. In his own systematic theory it was to become a positive category. In these years Parsons was also studying the works of the French sociologist Émile Durkheim, who rejected Spencerian individualism and sought to establish the independent theoretical status of what he considered the reality *sui generis* of the social factor. In *The Division of Labor*, Durkheim pointed to the non-contractual element in contract; in *Le Suicide*, to the significance for individual behavior of relative states of integration of the social system; and in *The Elementary Forms of the Religious Life*, to the close relation between the religion of a society and its ultimate values. Parsons' appreciation of these insights was another important step toward the formulation of a more adequate conceptual scheme for social theory.

"At Harvard Parsons also came under the influence of the economic historian, Edwin F. Gay, whose investigations of the antecedents of nineteenth-century industrial capitalism in England traced out the developments leading from mediaeval feudalism to a full-blown market system. His study of the putting-out system is only one of his classic products. But perhaps a more important influence came from another 'chance' encounter, with the distinguished physiologist, L. J. Henderson. He discussed Pareto with Henderson, especially Pareto's attempt to construct a system of social theory on the model used in the natural science of mechanics. From Henderson, also, he obtained a greater sophistication in the nature of scientific theory and methodology.

"All these bodies of thought, then, are the major components that went into *The Structure of Social Action*, published in 1937. In this book Parsons showed the convergence of the theories of Durkheim, Pareto and Weber in a single new body of theory, and their relation to Marshall's type of economic theory. What he had long before started with as simply the non-economic elements were demonstrated to have independent status in this theory. This book also contains, incidentally to this larger purpose, a careful examination of some of the detailed work of these theorists. Since 1937, Parsons has dealt with the theory of social action systematically, rather than historically. His efforts in this direction have been presented in courses at Harvard University and in a still unpublished manuscript. Also since 1937, Parsons has come to be increasingly interested in the significance of another whole body of thought, that of Freud and the diverse trends stemming from him. It is particularly through the motivational categories of Freudian and depth psychology that Parsons believes it is necessary to approach the theoretical problems of the dynamics of social systems."

Parsons' professional work in America has been almost exclusively at Harvard in a university succession from instructorship in economics from 1927 to 1931, instructorship in sociology from 1931 to 1936, assistant professorship in 1936, associate professorship in 1939 to professorship in 1944. In 1946 he became the first chairman of the Harvard Department of Social Relations.

In addition to some three dozen articles, Parsons has published his translation of Max Weber's *The Protestant Ethic and the Spirit of Capitalism*, 1930; *The Structure of Social Action*, 1937; and *Max Weber: The Theory of Social and Economic Organization*, 1947. He contributed chapters to Georges Gurvitch's *Twentieth Century Sociology* and Louis Finkelstein's *Unity and Difference in the Modern World*, 1945; and to the *Encyclopaedia of the Social Sciences*. Of his articles, five were in the *Quarterly Journal of Economics*; four in the *Journal of Political Economy*; three in the *International Journal of Ethics*; five in the *American Sociological Review;* two in *Social Forces,* and two in *The American Journal of Sociology.*

In addition to his books and articles, Parsons' general frame of reference for his sociology may be seen from two other special sources, namely, the courses which he has most recently taught at Harvard and in the summer sessions at Columbia and Chicago, and in his 1949 presidential address before the American Sociological Society. His main courses have included those on the theories of Pareto, Durkheim, Simmel, Tönnies, and Weber; on the special sociologies of religion and of the professions; on social institutions; on economics; and on social structure. In his collaboration with other authors he has been especially interested in intercultural relations and in the culture of the Jewish people.

Parsons' 1949 presidential address brings up to 1950 his special contribution on the role of systematic theory in sociology. The subject of his address was "The Prospects of Sociological Theory" and it was published in the *American Sociological Review,* Volume XV, February, 1950, pages 3–16. The heart of his contribution is a threefold approach. First is the essential and exclusive value of theory in the total frame of reference for sociology and research. Next is his concept that all verifiable empirical knowledge involves theory insofar as it develops cogitable systems. Finally, systematic theory is best illustrated by the Parsons structure-function theory of interrelationships, such as, for instance, the institutions. Inherent in the definition of institutions is the structure-function theory of sociology. Thus institutions are "patterns governing behavior and social relationships which have become interwoven with a system of common moral sentiments which in turn define what one has a right to expect of a person in a certain position."

Parsons recapitulates the pattern of the first presidents of the Society in at least three main ways. In the first place, his work reflects a new wave of sociological importation from Europe in the works of Weber, Pareto, Durkheim, Tönnies, Malinowski, which is similar to that of the period in which Ward, Sumner, Giddings, and Small reflected the works of Comte, Spencer, Ratzenhofer, and Gumplowicz. In the earlier period, European sociology had its impact upon an indigenous American social problem — the social-science movement from which there emerged the American sociological development. In the later Parsonian work the revivification of European sociology finds its impact against the American trend toward the statistical and objective methodology of empirical research. In Parsons also there is the revivification of the earlier pattern for systematic theory in sociology, often declared obsolescent by many of the younger sociologists. Parsons is again reminiscent of the earliest period of sociology in that he came into the field of sociology, as has been pointed out, from economics.

In an article on "The Systematic Sociology of Talcott Parsons," published in *Social Forces,* for May, 1950, Alvin Boskoff, seeking to analyze and appraise the work of Parsons, finds seven areas in which he estimates contributions have been made. These are in the classification of the role of theory in research; the structure-functional method of analysis; certain important concepts and definitions; the analysis of institutions; the outline of systematic theory in sociology; the voluntaristic theory of action; the analysis of specific structures and roles, kinship, occupations, professions; the analysis of certain modern problems of aggression, fascism, anti-semitism; and the analysis of the work of Weber, Durkheim, and Pareto.

More about the work of Parsons will be found in Chapters 3, 15, 18.

Leonard S. Cottrell, Jr.: 1899–

Leonard Cottrell, fortieth president of the American Sociological Society in 1950, was following earlier patterns of combining administration and educational endeavors with sociology. First, in reorganizing the Cornell work in sociology by integrating its rural sociology and agricultural experiment extension studies into an effective sociology curriculum and then combining this with anthropology to develop a department of sociology and anthropology he laid the basis for not only effective teaching and general research but for extended research through special grants for area studies in cultural anthropology. Next, Cottrell's notable work as Chief Sociologist in the Research Branch of Information and Education in O.C.S. of the United States War Department from 1942 to 1945 was in the same general character and resulted not only in distinctive administrative work, with many confidential reports on the morale of American soldiers, but made substantial contributions to the pioneering work, *The American Soldier,* especially *Combat and Its Aftermath, 1949,* the second of four volumes on *Studies in Social Psychology in World War II.* Finally, in 1948 Cottrell became Dean of the College of Arts and Sciences at Cornell.

The reference to earlier patterns is to some of the first presidents of the Society who were elected from administrative positions. Small was dean of Graduate Studies at Chicago as was Blackmar at Kansas. Vincent was president of the University of Minnesota, where Malcolm Willey was later dean and assistant to the president. Bogardus at Southern California and Taylor at North Carolina State were at one time deans of their graduate schools. Queen was dean of the School of Liberal Arts at Washington, while Odum was dean at Emory Unversity.

Cottrell was born at Hampton Roads, Virginia, December 12, 1899, took his B.S. degree at Virginia Polytechnic Institute in 1922, the M.A. at Vanderbilt in 1926, and his Ph.D. at Chicago in 1933. He was instructor at Chicago from 1931 to 1935; assistant professor of sociology at Cornell from 1935 to 1938; professor in 1938–39; professor and chairman of the Department of Sociology and Anthropology from 1939 to 1948; and dean of the College of Arts and Sciences from 1948 to 1951 when he went to the Russell Sage Foundation as Director of Research. He is fellow of the American Association for the Advancement of Science and was a member and vice-president of the directors of the Social Science Research Council.

Perhaps his two most distinctive contributions are his earlier work with Ernest W. Burgess on *Predicting Success or Failure in Marriage* and his latest work in the broader field of social psychology in the war in which as chairman and participator in the research branch of the Army's Information and Education Division, which produced what Gordon W. Allport estimates history will date the birth of a "newly coordinated science of human relations between the years 1940 and 1950." In his "A Review of *The American Soldier*" before the 1949 sessions of the Sociological Research Association, Allport characterized the monographs as "magnificent." Earlier in his career, Cottrell collaborated in a number of publications including *Delinquency Areas*, 1920, *The Development in Social Psychology*, 1941. For the Social Science Research Council's Committee on Social and Economic Aspects of Atomic Energy he wrote *American Public Opinion on World Affairs in the Atomic Age*, in which he made an analysis and interpretation of public reaction to the new role of the United States in world affairs. Cottrell here pointed out the sources of confusion and contradiction in public thinking, as gathered from a study of the combined results of several national surveys. Among his other contributions are: "Roles and Marital Adjustment," *Publications of the American Sociological Society*, Volume XXVII, 1933, pp. 107–15; "The Prediction of Adjustment in Marriage," *American Sociological Review*, Volume I, 1936, pp. 737–51 (with E. W. Burgess); "Part-time Farming in the Southeast," U. S. Printing Office, 1937 (with R. H. Allen *et al.*); "Research in Causes of Variations in Fertility: Social Psychological Aspects," *American Sociological Review*, Volume II, 1937, pp. 678–85; "A Research Note on Differential Fertility with Respect to Birth Order," *Journal of Social Psychology*, Volume 9, 1938, pp. 49–56; "The Case Study Method in Prediction," *Sociometry*, Volume 4, 1941, pp. 358–70; editor, Social Science Research Council memoranda series on *Social Aspects of the War*, issued in mimeographed form by the Social Science Research Council, 1941; "The Adjustment of the Individual to His Age and Sex Roles," *American Sociological Review*, Volume VII, 1942, pp. 617–20; "The Analysis of Situational Fields in Social Psychology," *American Sociological Review*, Volume VII, 1942, pp. 370–82; "The Present Status and Future Orientation of Research on the Family," *American Sociological Review*, Volume XIII, 1948, pp. 123–29.

Cottrell's field is clearly in the special sub-science of social psychology through which he seeks more scientific ways of studying human relations and interpreting them to society effectively enough to make sociology a dynamic science in the modern world. He writes: "Sociology is or can be a science of human relations. It is constantly faced with the risks on the one hand of dealing in broad generalities that have little or no content or meaning and on the other of pursuing atomistic and trivial investigations. Its greatest present needs are an integrating theory of social dynamics and social structure and a methodology appropriate to such a body of theory."

Cottrell tells something of the incidence of his coming to sociology from a prospective specialization in natural science. He writes: "Immediately following World War I, I was studying biology as an undergraduate. Through some of my extracurricular activities I was made aware of many problems in human relations in our society and in the rest of the world. By the time I was a senior I realized that I was more interested in the processes of social life and the problems of the social system than I was in the more conventional preoccupations of a biologist. Moreover, I had arrived at the opinion that the special fields of biology, such as genetics, did not promise the answers I was seeking. Someone suggested that I was probably interested in studying sociology (a word I had rarely encountered), and mentioned Professor Gus Dyer at Vanderbilt. I went to that school and upon registering for courses in sociology I met Professors Ernest T. Krueger and Walter C. Reckless fresh from the University of Chicago. They were enthusiastic teachers and were kind enough to encourage my growing interest in their subject. Upon my completion of the Master's degree with Krueger and Reckless I was recommended by them to the faculty at the University of Chicago for further graduate work. At the University of Chicago I had the advantage of studying under Park, Burgess, Faris, Mead and others in sociology and social psychology. My interests have been consistently focused on the dynamics of human interaction and its products both individual and collective."

Cottrell's presidential address at the 1950 meeting of the American Sociological Society at Denver, entitled "Some Neglected Problems in Social Psychology," was published in the *American Sociological Review,* Volume XV, December, 1950, pages 705–712. In it he stressed three problems, namely, empathic responses, the self, and the situation. Cottrell says that he is prepared "to argue that they are not only neglected but are of basic importance. The empathic processes are crucial in social integration; the self organization is the most important resultant of these processes; the concept of the situational field is fundamental to all modern social psychology. The solutions of these three problems together with a suitably consistent theory of motivation without question will form the core of a matured social psychology able to undertake its obligations and responsibilities as the basic social science." Thus, he continues his interests of long standing in the dynamics of human interaction to the study of which he seeks to effect the cooperation of sociology and social psychology in new attainments of great promise. More about Cottrell is given in Chapters 14 and 25.

PART III

American Sociology as American Sociologists: Authors of Texts

CHAPTER 14

General Sociology: Introductory Texts and "Principles"

Insofar as sociology is primarily a college and university subject, taught in sociology courses in institutions of higher learning, it may be defined in terms of courses taught and of teachers and textbooks in the total field of sociology. In Chapters 4 to 13 inclusive we have sketched out the story of forty teachers who happened to be presidents of the American Sociological Society, while in Chapters 21, 22 and 23 will be found information about others. We now come to the important segment of American sociology as reflected in sociology textbooks. Such texts fall mainly into two categories. The one consists of texts in *general sociology*. These will include elementary introductory texts and "principles," of sociology, introductory texts in social psychology, and texts on the history of social thought, social theory, and methodology. The other consists of texts in *special sociology,* or sub-sciences of sociology, such as social problems and pathology; the community, rural, urban, and industrial sociology; race, ethnic minority groups, folk; population, demography, ecology, regionalism; and others. In many institutions the introductory course may alternate between the "theoretical" and the "social problem" approach, in which case there are a number of "standard" introductory texts on social problems. Sometimes the more advanced "principles" will be taught in connection with the history of social thought and social theory. Also in the field of general sociology, methods of social research may be required of all students who major in sociology, so that increasingly statistics and other methodological approaches belong in the category of general sociology, at the same time that they offer fields for advanced specialization. In somewhat the same way texts in social psychology may be used as special sociology, and may be pursued further as advanced specialization. Anthropology, as introductory theory, reflects its rapid rise as a coordinate subject and as an integrated part of study and research in basic culture. The trend toward integration of social psychology and anthropology will be treated in Chapters 22, 24, and 25.

American Sociology as Sociology Textbooks

In some ways, therefore, the story of American sociology can be told in the textbooks that have been written by the sociologists from the beginning up to now, for, in the earlier days when there were so few texts, every volume contributed was, for all practical purposes, used as a text. The first departments at Chicago and Columbia were set up primarily on the graduate level, and it was true that candidates for graduate degrees were practically required to know every book on sociology in America, alongside reading from European sources.

Later on, texts used for graduate study, such as Giddings' *Principles,* Small's *General Sociology,* Ward's *Pure and Applied Sociology,* as well as the notable Park and Burgess *Introduction to the Science of Sociology,* came to be used as introductory texts, although they were originally "advanced" books.

The old "masters," Giddings, Ward, Small, were proud to record the sale of a few hundred copies of their books as encouraging news in the growth of sociology, as compared with subsequent sales of texts by some of their former students with more *thousands* than there were *hundreds* in the earlier years. Thus, the texts of one of Giddings' students by 1950 had sold more than 250,000 copies, while those of one of Small's, including foreign translations, had sold over a million. On the other hand, the books of E. A. Ross, the senior living sociologist in 1950, had sold an aggregate of nearly a million copies. The first texts were essentially "principles" of sociology, outlining the framework of the fundamentals for the study of society in general. Since there had been undergraduate preparation in very few colleges, practically all graduate students had to begin with the elementary work. Thus, nearly all that was written on sociology in America at that time was incorporated in the books of Ward, Giddings, and Small, with the exception of Sumner's *Folkways,* which became a pillar for the groundwork of later advanced cultural sociology. Ward's *Dynamic Sociology, Outlines of Sociology, Pure Sociology,* and *Applied Sociology* constituted a rather comprehensive course on sociology and they remain to this day impressive contributions to a new field. The first of these was published in 1883 and the last in 1906. Giddings' first three major texts coincided closely with Ward's last three, his *Principles of Sociology* in 1896 and his *Elements of Sociology* in 1898, the same year as Ward's *Outlines,* followed by a second edition of his *Principles* in 1899 and his *Inductive Sociology* in 1901. Small's *General Sociology,* then, came along in 1905.

There were, however, in the meantime, several smaller, elementary textbooks designed primarily to teach undergraduate students rather than to set forth the principles of the new social science. These included Small and Vincent's *Introduction to Sociology* in 1894, both authors from the University of Chicago and both later presidents of the American Sociological Society. Also, from the University of Chicago in 1898 was C. R. Henderson's *Elements of Sociology.* In the same year an Americanized German minister and scholar, J. H. W. Stuckenberg, turned sociologist, came out with his *Introduction to Sociology,* to be followed in 1903 by his two-volume work, *Sociology: The Science of Human Society.*

Then for the first five years of the new century there were five elementary texts of some distinction. In 1901, Fairbanks' *Introduction to Sociology* appeared, followed by Carroll D. Wright's *Outlines of Sociology,* in 1902, which provided for the early use of census materials for the study of American society. Wright had been United States Commissioner of Commerce and Labor and had at one time assigned Florence Kelly to the first major survey of city slums in Chicago. In 1905, three of the early popular texts appeared: namely, Blackmar's *Elements of Sociology,* Ross's *Foundations of Sociology,* and Dealey's *Textbook in Sociology.*

A Rapidly Growing Catalogue

From this point on, the stream of sociology texts was continuous, broadening and deepening until 1950. In comparison with the earlier

source-springs, the flow might be said to be at flood tide, at least nine
new texts appearing since these lines were written in 1949 up to 1951.
Of the texts prepared primarily for introductory courses in general sociology, and exclusive of texts on special aspects of history, theory, social
problems, and specialized sociologies, all of which will be treated in subsequent chapters, no less than a hundred could be catalogued, including
revised editions. Of these, the largest number utilized the title *Introduction*. The next in order were *Principles* or wording like *"The Study"*
or *"The Science of Society."* Then followed the variant, yet uniform
titles *Outlines, Sociology, Elements, Foundations, Fundamentals,* etc.
The catalogue of texts in general chronological order, together with the
identification of author, by institution, affords a recapitulation of much
of the story of American sociology already told. The catalogue of the
most widely used texts, not including all new editions, gives, for tabu-
lation, only the skeleton titles, omitting specific descriptive phrases.

Year	*Title*	*Author*	*Identification*
1883	*Dynamic Sociology*	Ward	Brown
1894	*Introduction to Society*	Small	Chicago
1896	*Principles of Sociology*	Giddings	Columbia
1898	*Outlines of Sociology*	Ward	Brown
—	*Introduction to Sociology*	Stuckenberg	At large
—	*Elements of Sociology*	Giddings	Columbia
—	*Elements of Sociology*	Henderson	Chicago
1899	*Principles of Sociology*	Giddings	Columbia
1901	*Inductive Sociology*	Giddings	Columbia
—	*Introduction to Sociology*	Fairbanks	At large
1902	*Outline of Practical Sociology*	Wright	Clark
1903	*Pure Sociology*	Ward	Brown
—	*Sociology*	Stuckenberg	At large
1905	*Textbook in Sociology*	Ward	Brown
—	*General Sociology*	Small	Chicago
—	*Elements of Sociology*	Blackmar	Kansas
—	*Foundations of Sociology*	Ross	Wisconsin
—	*Textbook of Sociology*	Dealey-Ward	Brown
1906	*Applied Sociology*	Ward	Brown
1909	*Sociology*	Dealey	Brown
1910	*Sociology—Social Problems*	Ellwood	Missouri
1914	*Inductive Sociology*	Giddings	Columbia

Year	Title	Author	Identification
1915	Outlines of Sociology	Blackmar-Gillin	Kansas-Wisconsin
—	Introduction to Sociology	Hayes	Illinois
1916	Outline of Applied Sociology	Fairchild	New York University
1916	Fundamentals of Sociology	Kirkpatrick	Wisconsin
1917	Introduction to Sociology	Bogardus	Southern California
1918	Sociology	Hayes	Illinois
1919	Elements of Sociology	Giddings	Columbia
—	Outline of Applied Sociology	Fairchild	Yale
1920	Principles of Sociology	Giddings	Columbia
—	Principles of Sociology	Ross	Wisconsin
—	Principles of Sociology	Clow	Wisconsin Normal
—	Principles of Sociology	Dow	Baylor
—	Introduction to Sociology	Findlay	Minnesota
—	Sociology	Dealey	Brown
1921	Introduction to the Science of Sociology	Park-Burgess	Chicago
1923	Principles of Sociology	Bushee	Colorado
—	Human Relations	Carver	Harvard
—	Elementary Sociology	Finney	Minnesota
—	Outlines of Sociology	Ross	Wisconsin
1924	Scientific Study of Human Society	Giddings	Columbia
—	Elements of Social Science	Fairchild	New York University
—	Outlines of Sociology	Case	Southern California
1925	Sociology—Social Problems	Beach	Stanford
1926	Human Relations	Taylor-Brown	North Carolina State
1927	Foundations of Social Life	Fairchild	New York University
—	Science of Social Relations	Hart	Duke
—	Science of Society	Sumner-Keller	Yale
—	Introduction to Sociology	Wallis	Minnesota
—	An Introduction to Sociology	Barnes-Davis	Smith-Yale
1928	Principles of Sociology	Binder	New York University

Year	Title	Author	Identification
1928	Principles of Sociology	Lumley	Ohio State
—	Introduction to the Study of Sociology	Hankins	Smith
1929	Introduction to Sociology	Dawson-Gettys	McGill-Texas
—	Introduction to Sociology	Hankins	Smith
1930	Man and Society	Haas	Wisconsin
—	Principles of Sociology	Ross	Wisconsin
1931	Introduction to Sociology	Groves	North Carolina
—	Society	MacIver	Columbia
1932	Civilization and Society	Giddings	Columbia
—	Concepts of Sociology	Eubank	Cincinnati
—	Principles of Sociology	Reinhardt-Davies	Nebraska-Washington State
—	A Survey of Society	E. J. Ross	Trinity College
1933	Outlines of Sociology	Ross	Wisconsin
—	Introductory Sociology	Cooley and others	Michigan
—	Principles of Sociology	Hiller	Illinois
—	Educational Sociology	Snedden	Teachers College
—	Introduction to Sociology	Reuter-Hart	Iowa State-National Opinion Research Center, Chicago
1934	Rudiments of Sociology	E. J. Ross	Trinity College
—	General Sociology	Fairchild	New York University
—	Sociology	Bogardus	Southern California
—	Introductory Sociology	Young	Northwestern
—	Introduction to Educational Sociology	Finney-Zeleny	Minnesota
1935	Dynamic Society	Elliott and others	Penn State College for Women
—	Introductory Sociology	Murray	Notre Dame
—	Introduction to Sociology	Dawson-Gettys	McGill-Texas
1936	Introductory Sociology	Kulp	Teachers College
—	Principles of Sociology	Phelps	Pittsburgh
1937	Introductory Sociology	Sutherland and Woodward	Texas

Year	Title	Author	Identification
—	Practical Sociology	Zeleny	State Teachers, St. Cloud, Minn.
—	Introduction to Sociology and Social Problems	Beach	Stanford
1938	Fundamentals of Sociology	Boettiger	Lawrence
1939	Outline of Principles of Sociology	Park, Reuter and others	Chicago
—	General Sociology	Wright-Elmer	Pittsburgh
—	Fundamental Sociology	E. J. Ross	Trinity
—	Introductory Sociology	Gregory-Bidgood	Alabama
—	Foundations of Sociology	Lundberg	Washington
1940	Introduction to Sociology	Groves-Moore	North Carolina-Texas
—	Sociology	Ogburn-Nimkoff	Chicago-Bucknell
1941	Handbook of Sociology	Reuter	Iowa State
1942	Introduction to Sociology	Bernard	Washington University
—	Introduction to Sociology	Gillin-Gillin	Wisconsin-North Carolina
1946	Sociology	La Piere	Stanford
1947	Sociology: A Synopsis of Principles	Cuber	Ohio State
—	Understanding Society	Odum	North Carolina
1948	Cultural Sociology	Gillin-Gillin	Wisconsin-North Carolina
—	Social Life: Structure and Function	Bennett-Tumin	Ohio State-Princeton
1949	Human Society	K. Davis	Columbia
—	Basic Sociological Principles	M. E. Jones	Wyoming
—	Man in Environment	Paul H. Landis	Washington State
—	Society	MacIver-Page	Columbia-Smith
1950	Sociology	T. C. McCormick	Wisconsin
—	Fundamentals of Sociology	Seba Eldridge and others	Kansas
1951	Elements of Sociology	Martindale-Monachesi	Minnesota
—	Sociology	Rouček-Warren	Bridgeport-Alfred

Lack of Uniformities

An examination of these texts and their adoptions for classroom teaching will confirm the verdict that sociology taught to American students is what American sociologists have published in their texts. Of the forty presidents of the American Sociological Society, no less than twenty-seven were themselves authors of introductory textbooks. Approximately the same number wrote texts in special fields, writing perhaps as many as fifty books. Thus, while the heart of college sociology can almost be identified somewhere in the textbooks written by the presidents whose lives we have sketched, a still larger number of texts have been produced by others. The texts of the later vintage tend to present sociology primarily as a classroom subject rather than as "principles" of the science of society. This comes about for several reasons. In the first place, the large enrollment in sociology calls for not only many texts but for variety. Therefore the publishers offer attractive publishing terms and, in competition, solicit new texts. By the same token sociologists seek not only to meet the need but to excel with something "better." Under these circumstances it would be expected that lack of uniformity and of any standardized content of texts and method would reflect the unevenness and personalized nature of American sociology, as identified in the flow of textbooks. The nature of this diversity will be described subsequently.

In a number of ways, however, there has been consistency and uniformity in the sociology taught to students in the introductory texts. One is the fidelity with which the work of a number of sociologists constitutes items of standard reference. In such elements as processes, interaction, social organization, culture elements, many uniform sources are used. Another is the almost uniformity with which the sociology of most texts is indexed, cross referenced, and documented by citations from other texts in the same fields. This is evidenced in the coincidence that the more than three hundred sociologists who are indexed in a half hundred texts constitute almost the same catalogue as an index of *Who's Who* in contemporary sociology. An example may be found in the work of Charles H. Cooley whose texts were neither best sellers nor were they prepared to please the teacher; nevertheless, they remain today standards of reference. So, too, of all the sociologists, Cooley is quoted more often and consistently in the approximately fifty selected texts most widely used in the last thirty years. Out of 47 texts analyzed, Cooley is indexed and quoted in more than three-fourths. As compared with others, of the more than three hundred authors cited, less than forty were cited in as many as half the texts. So, too, of the eight source books or reference books prepared as texts for class use, Cooley again leads in selected readings and is featured in six of the eight, which is true of only two other authors. It is interesting to note that in the 47 of the most widely used texts, dating from 1949 back, 304 sociologists were quoted or cited in the index. These references vary greatly and reflect the popularity of certain authors as well as the "following" which certain texts had achieved. The two ways of indicating frequency of quotation are, first, in the number of texts in which each author appears, and second, in the total number of times indexed. Cooley appears in 37 texts; Giddings and Thomas in 36 each; Ross and Ward in 35 each; Sumner in 34; Park and Burgess in 28; Keller, Ogburn and Small in 27; Barnes, Bernard, Chapin, and MacIver in 25; Bogardus and Kimball Young in 24; Ellwood, Faris, Gillin, McKenzie, Sorokin, and Znaniecki in 23; Reuter, Odum, Lundberg, Hornell Hart, Groves, and Fairchild in 22; Folsom, Hankins, Lumley, Willey in 21; and North, Queen, Warren Thompson, Todd, Wallis, and Shaw in 20.

Of the 304 sociology authors indexed, 39 were listed more than a hundred times in the 47 texts examined. The sociologists indexed most often included Park and Burgess with 538 and 436 references to each author respectively. Cooley follows with 434 citations; Sumner, 417; Ross, 374; Thomas, 366; Giddings, 304; Ward, 294; Small, 174; all of which indicates that the early leaders were still dynamic in the sociological text field. Of others who were cited more than a hundred times, Barnes, Bernard, Bogardus, Chapin, Ellwood, MacIver, Ogburn, Sorokin, Kimball Young are the top references, with the following in some general order of frequency: Gillin, Groves, Hankins, Lundberg, McKenzie, Odum, Reuter, Warren Thompson, Carle Zimmerman, Malcom Willey, Lumley, Lynd, Hiller, Folsom, Ellsworth Faris.

An Extraordinary Catalogue of Text Content

The range and variety of topical treatment and the nature of the contents of introductory textbooks as reflected in chapter titles also illustrate something of the semantics of the sociological story. From the forty or more texts studied it is possible to catalogue more than a thousand distinctively worded topics and perhaps more than a hundred general fields into which they may be re-grouped for relatively practical purposes. Of the thousand topics, perhaps not more than a hundred overlap so specifically as to preclude listing. This of course is not surprising nor significant except as a rough index of lack of uniformity and perhaps as a basis upon which to seek some such consolidation as would lead to the adoption of certain standard elementary terms. At the present time, 1950, it would appear that the tendency is toward still more heterogeneity rather than uniformities. This is discussed more critically in Chapters 24 and 25.

A number of studies have been made to ascertain the range and nature of sociology courses taught and the texts being utilized. In a symposium published in *Social Forces* for March, 1931, E. B. Woods, R. E. Baber, F. H. Hankins, C. A. Dawson, and M. M. Willey discussed five different approaches. Pertinent to this chapter was Baber's reporting on textbooks, their content and their use. He divided his list of forty or more texts into five groups: *First,* those sociologists who approach sociology through the medium of social problems. The *next* group consists of those who feel that the best approach to sociology is through the vast field of social origins and social evolution. A *third* group would approach sociology through a general orientation course in the whole field of the social sciences. The *fourth* group goes farther than the one just described, for it frankly considers sociology as a synthesis of the other social sciences. Finally, there is a *fifth* group that insists that sociology is a science in its own right. This group believes that the best approach to sociology is through the analysis of social interaction. . . .

Another later symposium, published in *Social Forces* for December, 1934, which represented a much larger number of sociologists, some twenty from all the regions of the nation, arrived at somewhat similar conclusions. These included L. L. Bernard, of Washington University; R. Clyde White, of Indiana; Dwight Sanderson, of Cornell; H. P. Fairchild, of New York; T. D. Eliot, of Northwestern; A. E. Wood, of Michigan; C. A. Ellwood and Howard Jensen, of Duke; J. H. S. Bossard, of Pennsylvania; H. C. Brearley, of Peabody; E. T. Krueger, of Vanderbilt; A. J. Todd, of Northwestern; Wilson Gee, of

Virginia; E. B. Reuter, of Iowa; Stuart Queen, of Washington University; J. J. Rhyne, of Oklahoma; M. M. Willey, of Minnesota; E. S. Bogardus, of Southern California; M. T. Price, of the University of Washington; Stuart Rice, of the United States Bureau of the Census. If we try to summarize this symposium by "groups," it seems likely that four variations, with overlappings, and not all contradictory, emerge. One group sees sociology as a science that focuses upon a continuing and flexible series of "problems" basic to research and analysis. Another conception, on the other hand, sees it as a body of social techniques, of *practical* problems centering around these other theoretical problems, the objectives being a better adjustment and readjustment of people to the natural and cultural environment of life. A third group would assume a specialized sociology that may attempt to formulate laws of personal and social development. A fourth group would expand the interpretive function of sociology to comprehend more rigorous and realistic inquiries into human values and into standards for their measurement and attainment.

Five special articles have been published in the four sociological journals since 1940. Emory Bogardus published one in *Sociology and Social Research,* pages 356–63 of Volume 25, in 1940–41. L. L. Bernard published another in *The American Journal of Sociology*, pages 534–48 in Volume L, 1944–45, in which he summarizes studies of 441 college catalogues after 1940. The other inquiries were made respectively by Raymond and Ruby Jo Kennedy, Robert Kutak, and Judson Landis and were published in the *American Sociological Review,* Volume VII, pages 661–75, 1942; *Social Forces,* Volume 24, pages 56–66, 1942; and the *American Sociological Review,* Volume XII, pages 113–16, 1947.

Social Psychology Texts by American Sociologists

Although social psychology is also a special area of sociology as treated by many sociologists and a special area of psychology as treated by many psychologists, it has been an integral part of American sociology from the earlier work of Giddings and Ward, followed by Ross's *Social Psychology* and Cooley's and Thomas' basic foundations, on through the record of texts by American sociologists catalogued in this chapter. Since the trends toward integration of social psychology and anthropology will be discussed in Chapter 24 we need here give only the general status and catalogue of texts.

In a symposium of papers on the subject matter and methods of social psychology, presented at the annual meeting of the American Psychological Society by eleven psychologists, and published in *Social Forces* in May, 1937, Floyd Allport writes on page 455: ". . . because the contributors were psychologists, it was thought best to limit ourselves to the psychological approach omitting the sociological viewpoint and the controversy over group and individual except where these forced themselves into the discussion. . . ." And again, on page 456: "In the last few years social psychology has been vigorously developing in two somewhat diverging directions. The sociologists have studied and systematized the subject from one point of view and the psychologist from quite another."

In this chapter, as in other specialisms, we have limited our discussions primarily to the work of sociologists rather than attempt to present the entire picture of social psychology, more of whose authors are psychologists than sociologists and whose genesis goes far back into the history of psychology and which has a notable heritage in philosophy and education as well. Accounts of the general and historical field, with psychologists, sociologists, philosophers intermingled, may be found in a number of references, including Barnes, Becker, and Becker's *Contemporary Social Theory,* Chapter 12, by Kimball Young and Douglas Oberdorfer, and Chapter 13, by Alexander Goldenweiser; in Gurvitch and Moore's *Twentieth Century Sociology,* in Chapter IX by James Woodard and pages 554–55 of Chapter XVIII by R. E. L. Faris; as well as in parts of Barnes' *Introduction to the History of Sociology;* House's *The Development of Sociology;* Fay B. Karpf's *American Social Psychology;* Lundberg, Bain, and Anderson's *Trends in American Sociology.*

The main textbooks in social psychology written by sociologists are catalogued by dates, authors, and their institutions:

Year	Title	Author	Identification
1893	*Psychic Factors in Civilization*	L. F. Ward	Brown
1901	*Some Prolegomena to Social Psychology*	C. A. Ellwood	Missouri
1902	*Human Nature and the Social Order*	C. H. Cooley	Michigan

Year	Title	Author	Identification
1908	Social Psychology	E. A. Ross	Wisconsin
1912	Sociology in Its Psychological Aspects	C. A. Ellwood	Missouri
1917	Introduction to Social Psychology	C. A. Ellwood	Missouri
—	Social Psychology	E. S. Bogardus	Southern California
1922	Principles of Social Psychology	J. M. Williams	Hobart
1923	Essentials of Social Psychology, 4th edition	E. S. Bogardus	Southern California
—	Personality and Social Adjustment	E. R. Groves	North Carolina
1924	Instinct	L. L. Bernard	Washington
—	Fundamentals of Social Psychology	E. S. Bogardus	Southern California
1925	"Social Psychology" (in H. E. Barnes: History and Prospects of the Social Sciences)	Kimball Young	Northwestern
1926	Introduction to Social Psychology	L. L. Bernard	Washington
1929	Personality and the Social Group	E. W. Burgess	Chicago
—	"Trends in Social Psychology" (in Lundberg, Bain, and Anderson's Trends in American Sociology)	J. F. Markey	Wheaten
1931	Social Psychology	J. K. Folsom	Vassar
1932	American Social Psychology	Fay B. Karpf	New York
—	Social Psychology	E. T. Krueger and W. C. Reckless	Vanderbilt
1934	"The Sources and Methods of Social Psychology" (in L. L. Bernard's Fields and Methods of Sociology)	Jessie Bernard	Penn State
—	"The Sources and Methods of Social Psychiatry" (in L. L. Bernard's Fields and Methods of Sociology)	J. K. Folsom	Vassar
1936	Social Psychology	R. T. La Piere	Stanford
—	Social Psychology	J. M. Reinhardt	Kansas
1937	The Nature of Human Nature	E. Faris	Chicago

Year	Title	Author	Identification
1937	"Social Psychology" (in E. P. Schmidt's *Man and Society*)	Herbert Blumer	Chicago
1938	*Collective Behavior*	R. T. La Piere	Stanford
1940	"Psychological Studies of Social Processes" (in Barnes and Becker's *Contemporary Social Theory*)	D. W. Oberdorfer	Northwestern
—	*Personality and Problems of Adjustment*	Kimball Young	Northwestern
1941	*Development in Social Psychology, 1930–1940*	L. S. Cottrell and Ruth Gallagher	Cornell
1944	*Social Psychology* (rev. ed.)	Kimball Young	Northwestern
1945	"Social Psychology" (in Gurvitch and Moore's *Twentieth Century Sociology*)	J. W. Woodard	Temple
1950	*Social Psychology*	T. M. Newcomb	Michigan

CHAPTER 15

General Sociology:
History, Theory, Research, and Methods

Like many other concepts, the term "social theory" in American sociology has more often been used in a general and inaccurate way than with specific and authentic definitive meaning. Something has already been said about the dichotomy of "elements" and "principles" as applied to introductory textbooks in sociology. Just as in many of these texts the terms "elements," "principles," "theory," and "foundations" have been loosely used as titles for descriptive systems or units of sociological study, so references to "social theory" in general, and more particularly to courses in the curriculum listed as "social theory," have referred more often to the history of social thought than to realistic social theory. Catalogue courses in "social theory" have almost uniformly carried the connotation of the *history* of social theory and they have utilized most frequently the very limited and standardized, but excellent, bibliographies listed in the earlier historical summaries by L. M. Bristol, J. P. Lichtenberger, E. S. Bogardus, P. A. Sorokin, and F. N. House, and later by C. A. Ellwood, H. E. Barnes, and Howard Becker.

The First Period of Historical Study

In reality there have been several overlapping stages in the teaching and development of what is commonly called social theory. The first was in the earlier days of graduate sociology at Columbia, Chicago, Yale, and the others, in which the core required readings consisted primarily of the "theories" of European scholars. This was the period also when "theory" consisted of "systems" and when each sociologist sought to present an all-embracing systemization of sociological theory with special emphasis upon some basic factor or force in the total social process. Such theories were those of Durkheim, Kropotkin, Gumplowicz, Tarde, Giddings, DeGreef, Fouillée, and Ratzenhofer.

The next stage followed when the cumulative theories catalogued in graduate study were incorporated into texts that were primarily the history of social thought and had become one of the basic requirements for undergraduates. Two of the first texts were products of graduate work; namely, L. M. Bristol's *Social Adaptation* at Harvard and the *Development of Social Theory* by Lichtenberger at Columbia. Likewise, H. E. Barnes' *Sociology and Political Theory* was a product of his Columbia graduate work. The rapid rise of the history of social thought in the curriculum followed closely a similar practice in the history of education and the history of philosophy with the same general beginnings with Plato and the early philosophers.

The first of the texts giving résumés of the history of social thought was that of L. M. Bristol, for many years head of the Department of Sociology at the University of Florida until his retirement in the early 1940's. His *Social Adaptation,* a product of his Harvard work published in 1915, was for some time about the only text of its kind. A similar text was the *Development of Social Theory,* published in 1923, by James P. Lichtenberger of the University of Pennsylvania, which was built around the theorists themselves, as contributors to sociological thinking, rather than around the theories as such. A year earlier than Lichtenberger, Emory S. Bogardus had published his *A History of Social Thought* which had been reprinted a number of times. In his *Contemporary Sociological Theories,* 1928, P. A. Sorokin attempts to deal more with the character and validity of theories than with the authors per se. *The Range of Social Theory,* 1929, by Floyd N. House, includes such areas as science and social policy, human geography, theories of population, race and nationality, the movements of population, natural areas, community study, competition and the division of labor, commerce and the market. A later book was C. A. Ellwood's *History of Social Philosophy* in which he attempts to tell the story of all that man has thought regarding "human relations, their origin and destiny."

The Second Stage of History and Theory

The next stage might be said to begin with Harry Elmer Barnes's series of prodigious works on historical sociology and the Bernards' *Origins of American Sociology.* Although Barnes and his collaborators, the Beckers, undertook to incorporate, along with the history of social theory, as much of the principles of sociology as possible and the interpretation of the societal and biographical settings, the emphasis was still primarily historical. The main Barnes contribution included *The History and Prospects of the Social Sciences, Social Thought from Lore to Science* with Howard Becker, *Contemporary Social Theory* with Howard and Frances Becker, *Introduction to the History of Sociology,* and *Historical Sociology.* These will be examined subsequently in the light of the search for principles and methods in the sociological setting.

Robert Merton protests this inaccurate usage of the term "social theory" in the discussion on Parsons' "The Position of Sociological Theory" reported in the *American Sociological Review* for April, 1948, page 165, when he says that "The attractive confusion of sociological theory with the *history* of sociological thought should long since have been dispelled. This is not to deny the great value of steeping oneself in the history of sociological thought. It is only to deny that the history of theory and currently applicable theory are one and the same." And yet in American social theory, it has been difficult to distinguish between what Merton calls the "selective accumulation of those parts of earlier theory which have survived the test of decades of research" from the "large conceptions which were dissipated when confronted with rigorous tests" as well as from "the false starts, the archaic doctrines, and plain errors of the past."

Difficulties of Defining Theory as Tested Findings

Yet such distinctions as Merton suggests are difficult to make for several reasons. In the first place, relatively few "theories" have been "tested" by either research or rigorous application to reality. For instance, Robert E. Park's students were wont to admire his special theories of race and culture, yet he was forever complaining that few would go out and test them in the light of human contacts. So, too, Franklin H. Giddings almost bitterly complained that sociologists, unlike scholars in medical science, were either reluctant to try out his "theories" of inductive measurement or they did not have the ability to do so. Another reason for this difficulty of definition has been the lack of agreement among sociologists concerning so many of the so-called theories of so many "schools" of thought. This may be illustrated by an examination of such voluminous "histories" of social theory and social thought as those of Harry Elmer Barnes. For instance, in the one-volume Barnes and Becker *Contemporary Social Theory,* of the authors who are indexed with more than ten reference pages, there are twice as many European authorities as American and more anthropologists, psychologists, philosophers, historians, economists, and geographers together heavily indexed than there are sociologists. It is difficult to search out and to identify *sociological* theory from an inventory of *Contemporary Social Theory* in which there are scarcely *more than one hundred* American sociologists indexed out of a total of nearly twenty-five hundred names in the total index, and especially when few sociologists can agree upon what to select. Or again, from the bibliography, "Guide to Sociological Specialities" and special bibliographies, out of some five hundred titles, scarcely more than sixty titles are by American *sociologists,* and less than one hundred from any sociologist.

Of the heavily indexed authors, the list of both European and American sociologists indicates again the fact that for the most part social theory in American sociology has been primarily a history of social thought and a catalogue of a great variety of reported special approaches to social theory. The heavily indexed European "theorists" listed in *Contemporary Social Theory* include Bagehot, Buckle, Comte, Darwin, Durkheim, Freud, Galton, Gumplowicz, Goethe, Hegel, Hobhouse, Huxley, Jung, Lombroso, Malinowski, Malthus, Marx, Montesquieu, Novicow, Pareto, Parsons, Quételet, Ratzel, Ratzenhofer, Ritter, Adam Smith, Sombart, Spencer, Spengler, Simmel, Tarde, Toynbee, Tylor, Westermarck, Wines, Wundt, Znaniecki, Max Weber, Alfred Weber, and von Wiese.

The American sociologists indexed in the same numerical ratio include Barnes, Becker, Bernard, Bogardus, E. W. Burgess, Cooley, Ellwood, Faris, Giddings, Hankins, Lundberg, McKenzie, Ogburn, Park, Parsons, Ross, Small, Kimball Young, Ward, Sorokin, Sumner, and W. I. Thomas. Manifestly, these were cited more because of what they wrote about certain aspects of social theory as classified by the authors of *Contemporary Social Theory* than as major theorists themselves. In fact, this text on *Contemporary Social Theory* may well be the continuing point for our brief story of "Social Theory" as it has been and is a part of American sociology. Its content, alongside the contents of Barnes's other books on historical sociology and of the earlier "histories," will indicate how, for the most part, social theory and sociological theory have been synonymous with each other and with the history of social thought in contrast to the more recent concepts of social theory as being the synthesis of the best results of empirical study in special fields integrated into what might be called some universal conceptual scheme. There is, too, an increasingly accurate definition of *sociological* theory as not being synonymous with *social* theory.

The Setting of the Bernards' Treatises

This period, ushered in by Barnes, continued with the Bernards' *Origins of American Sociology,* in which they have contributed a thorough survey of the beginnings of sociology in the United States, emphasizing its European heritage and American social reform aspects. Perhaps the next stage begins about the time of L. L. Bernard's *The Fields and Methods of Sociology.* Essentially the *Proceedings* of the meeting of the American Sociological Society at the 1932 session when Bernard was president, this volume undertakes to interpret the main divisions and sections under which sociologists are accustomed to working. These fields have been enumerated in Chapter 1. Another volume in this era was *Trends in American Sociology,* edited by George A. Lundberg, Read Bain, and Nels Anderson. These three editors endeavored to set forth the domains and methods of sociology, in the opinion of some younger sociologists of the period. This trend toward the study of sociological theory in terms of contemporary summary rather than historical backgrounds was continued in a collaborator's volume, *Twentieth Century Sociology,* edited by Georges Gurvitch and Wilbert Moore. As indicating an insistent demand for authentic summaries, this book, written in the most tentative and routine fashion, found a very wide use and adoption among American sociologists. As a symposium with fifteen authors not all sociologists, and although hurriedly edited and incomplete and not well balanced in subject matter, it represented the most complete approach to a general summary of the subject of modern social theory up to 1945. A more conservative estimate of status and trends was made by Floyd N. House. Following his *The Range of Social Theory,* in 1929, which has been discussed in earlier pages, House published *The Development of Sociology,* in 1936, in which he attempts to cover the whole field of sociology, ranging from the contributions of social theorists and philosophers to the present division of theory into various specialities.

Finally, one of the most illuminating and comprehensive studies of social thought, both in its historical perspective and in a specialized field, is Melvin J. Williams' *Catholic Social Thought: Its Approach to Contemporary Problems*. In this volume, published in 1950, Williams "attempts to provide a survey of the origin and progress of Roman Catholic social thought, and an analysis of its outlook on present-day society." The book treats the whole field in six parts, namely "Background and Development of Catholic Social Thought," "Catholic Contributions to Social Theory," "Cultural and Historical Aspects of Contemporary Catholic Social Theory," "Sociological Trends in Contemporary Catholic Economic, Political, and Legal Thought," "Some Catholic Applications of Sociological Theory to the Study of Social Groups and Social Problems," and "Conclusion: Retrospect and Prospect." Among the special contributions that Williams offers are notations on individuals who have contributed to general theory, but with the Catholic background, such as LePlay. In general, Catholic sociology follows three categories, namely "theoretical sociology," "pure sociology," and "practical or applied sociology." An indication of the range and scholarship involved in the treatise may be had not only from its fifteen chapters but from its author index, in which more than fifteen hundred authors are cited, and its twenty-page subject index. The book supplements well our brief treatise on Catholic sociology in Chapter 21.

Sociological Theory Basic to Research and Sound Science

There are three other ways in which the status and trends of social theory in American sociology may be appraised. One is the revivification of European theory as reflected in the increasing emphasis upon the work of European sociologists. Another is the tendency of some American sociologists to develop systematized theory either in textbooks or special contributions. The third way is reflected in the current trend toward making sound social theory the essential basis for practical work and to develop such theory from the systematization of results from actual research. It follows from this that the new concept and practice of theory are essentially also a part of the new research and methodology.

As examples of the revivification of European theory the greatly increased interest in and use of a number of works may be cited. Among these are Talcott Parsons' revival of Max Weber; Howard Becker's systematic theory based upon von Wiese; Alfred Weber's *Culture and Civilization*; Mannheim's *Ideology and Utopia* and *Man and Society in an Age of Reconstruction*; Tönnies' sociology of *Gemeinschaft* and *Gesellschaft*. Examples of the tendency toward sytematization in texts or workings might be Talcott Parsons' *Social Structure*, MacIver's *Social Structure*, MacIver's *Social Causation*, Sorokin's *Social and Cultural Dynamics*, Zimmerman's functional theory of the family in *The Family and Civilization*, Odum's folk sociology in *Understanding Society*, Ogburn's technology and cultural lag, in *Social Change*.

Current Sociological Theory

The final trend or stage is that in which contemporary sociology undertakes to define its theory in relation to the reality of social relationships and to integrate it with the best methodological approaches to social research and the systematization of results. An appraisal of this current trend to make sound theory basic to all sociology in order to insure effective research methods may be found in a symposium of sociological theory already quoted and in Robert Merton's "The Bearing of Empirical Research upon the Development of Social Theory" published in the *American Sociological Review* for October, 1948, and recapitulated as Chapter III, page 98, of his *Social Theory and Social Structure*. Merton insists that "The stereotype of the social theorist high in the empyrean of pure ideas uncontaminated by mundane facts is fast becoming no less outmoded than the stereotype of the social researcher equipped with questionnaire and pencil and hot on the chase of the isolated and meaningless statistic. For in building the mansion of sociology during the last decades, theorist and empiricist have learned to work together. What is more, they have learned to talk to one another in the process. At times, this means only that a sociologist has learned to talk to himself since increasingly the same man has taken up both theory and research. Specialization and integration have developed hand in hand. All this has led not only to the realization that theory and empirical research *should* interact but to the result that they *do* interact."

Theory as Essential Methodology

One way of clarifying the relation of theory to research is to note new trends in sociology as they are developing and to relate these to the total story of American sociology. It is customary to inquire of sociology candidates for the Ph.D. degree concerning the status and trends of sociology. Perhaps the general question most frequently asked is something like this: Discuss recent trends in the development of sociology; what are the chief differences between today's sociology and that of earlier days? It is likely that the most commonly reported answer is that the present-day sociology is more objective, devotes itself more rigorously to empirical research, and has relegated the older "systems" of generalizations to the realm of earlier sociological stages, or the history of social thought, or to social philosophy. This, of course, is the teaching of the professors and reflects the verdict of the majority of sociologists. Harry Elmer Barnes, on page x, in his voluminous *An Introduction to the History of Sociology,* insists that "It is not likely that there will be many more attempts to create systems of sociology. . . . In other words, the era of systematic sociology has come approximately to an end." Barnes specifies further that sociology [in 1948] had come to an "era and stage where systematization was gradually but rather completely replaced by specialization in some more restricted field of description and analysis." Still further, he estimates that "Sociological writing from this time onward promises to be mainly specialized forms of social theory."

Although these generalizations, without clearer definition and qualifications, represent a rather dogmatic temporary prediction, and are perhaps in some contrast to some trends in the natural sciences and philosophy, they do offer a very realistic basis upon which to review the expanding developments in research and methodology in sociology. Any such review must begin with the assumption of a great lack of agreement among sociologists concerning methodology and the relative objectivity of scientific methods of sociology. There is, for instance, Cooley's notable statement that Sumner's *Folkways* represents the best in methodology that sociology had produced in contrast to other assumptions that Sumner's work was without the pale. There was Giddings' early direction of such concrete studies as James Mickel Williams' *An American Town* and other inductive studies for which he set the schedules in his *Inductive Sociology*. There was also Giddings' pioneer insistence upon the statistical method and there is the general assumption on the part of many later sociologists that Giddings reflected only an outworn systematization of sociological theory. And there was later MacIver's satirical characterization of the extreme claims for statistics over against Ogburn's insistence that it is not likely that we can scientifically study any phenomena that we cannot measure by statistics.

Cooley on Methodology and Research

Some of these earlier and later discussions reflect the realism of the story of American sociology up to now with its projection into the future. We must not forget that Cooley is more frequently indexed in more texts than any other sociologist. Cooley's statement was made at the annual dinner of the American Sociological Society in 1927 and was published in his later *Sociological Theory and Social Research,* on page 325. He began his discussion by saying, "Like everyone else I have been thinking a good deal of late about research, methodology, and the like, and it has occurred to me that a promising way to approach the matter would be to ask, What is the most successful work of research that American sociology has produced? No doubt opinions would differ about this, but it seems to me, on reflection, that if a vote were taken, bearing in mind that the question refers to factual methods and results as distinguished from more speculative sociology, a plurality of the voters, if not a majority, would probably be found to favor Sumner's *Folkways*.

"What strikes me most strongly when I consider this question is that *Folkways* does not conform to any of the current canons of methodology. It is not *quantitative*; it does not proceed by *statistical method*; it is not made up of *case studies*; it is not *psychoanalytic,* nor yet *behavioristic,* according to the doctrine of the sect that goes by that name, since much of the material it uses is based on sympathetic imagination. Moreover, it is not in any great measure a work of direct observation at all! It is almost all second-hand. And, last and worst, its objectivity is open to question. There is reason to think that Sumner was by no

means an unbiased man, but was, on the contrary, noted for a somewhat dogmatic individualism and pessimism that were not without
influence upon his treatment of the folkways."

The Role of Methodology and Research

Before reviewing further specific works of American sociologists, it
is well to indicate the place and role of research and methodology in
the structure of sociology as it has developed up to now. The statement
of Wesley C. Mitchell, noted economist, that the best methodology is
always essentially the best way to do research in a particular field, must
still be relevant and it conforms to our beginning statement that sociology will utilize all known methods that have been authenticated in
their own fields. We have pointed out in *Understanding Society* that
the field of sociological research lies somewhere between the field of
social problems and the field of responsible social theory. Both the study
and the "solution" of problems manifestly are conditioned by the range
and adequacy of social research which must be basic to the understanding. On the other hand, sound and responsible social theory grows out
of the coordination and systematization of the results of research and
the findings of what are usually called empirical studies. Thus, the
methods of research are not only fundamental in the effort to make
sociology increasingly scientific, but they help us to interpret the nature and the range of practical problems and their interrelationship with
"theoretical" sociology. The newer trend is clearly to make the function
of responsible social theory relate social problems to the increasingly
larger and more varied stores of empirical materials that are being
made available.

It must be clear that the problems and the methods of research are
of the greatest significance in the total profile of sociological theory in
its role of research and of interpretation of sociology. Social research,
therefore, cannot be considered apart from sociology any more than the
socially behaving individual can be studied apart from the society in
which he lives. This newer and more dynamic interpretation of research
both accentuates its importance and prevents it from becoming an unrelated specialization or an intellectual fad.

Robert Merton, in a special comment for this book, sets up five points of the characteristic *interplay* between theory, method, and empirical research in sociology. Two of these are important here. He writes,

"First, I believe that there is more than one road to theoretically oriented sociological knowledge: not only *from* logically connected abstract propositions *to* systematic empirical data, but also *from* empirical observation *to* reformulated and clarified abstract propositions. It seems to me a dangerous simplification (or a disguised moral imperative) to argue that empirical research *must be* confined to 'testing' predesignated hypotheses. That is only one pattern of theoretically pertinent research." He insists that there is more than one pattern through which empirical research *advances* (not merely, tests) social theory.

"Second, I believe that through this two-sided interplay, we achieve some measure of *continuity* in sociological knowledge. Working back and forth between theoretical constructs and sociological data, we are less likely to end up with a series of disconnected studies, bearing little relation each to the others. This effort to arrange our work so that there is a maximum of continuity and cumulation in knowledge seems to me . of the first importance."

Burgess and Elmer on Methodology

Excerpts from the verdicts of contemporary sociologists as presented in Chapters 4 to 13 and written for this book indicate both certain general trends and agreements as well as considerable diversity of opinions. They also indicate a sort of endless area for discussion that needs to be integrated and made more articulate in a comprehensive treatise. Brief evidence in three other considerations, however, may be given here in conclusion. One is a short summary by Ernest W. Burgess and M. C. Elmer of the chief approaches and stages of methodology. Another is reference to sociometry and other very special techniques. A third is the listing of certain areas of sociological theory that still challenge effective methodologies if they are to be well developed.

Burgess' statement in Chapter 2 of Gurvitch and Moore's *Twentieth Century Sociology,* entitled "Research Methods in Sociology," assumes that there are two basic methods of research, statistics and case study, around which exist questions that involve almost every consideration of sociological method. The two developed to meet the dual opportunity of studying the subject matter of sociology in both its internal and external aspects. The separation, however, is arbitrary, existing only in abstraction; therefore, both methods must be used to secure valid and significant information.

The case-study method is associated with a realist view of society, statistics with the nominalist view. Both grew as efforts to apply scientific methods to the study of human behavior. Both are related, though perhaps in opposite ways, to the significance of concepts, while some studies have attempted to bridge the gap between concepts and data-gathering. Thomas and Znaniecki gave the original sociological impetus to the case-study method. The use of ideal types based on case studies has led toward statistical measurement of their extent. Statistics developed in the concern of biology with population data and of psychology and education with mental measurement; sociologists have adopted the techniques but have made little contribution to method. One move to bridge the gap between social analysis and statistics is in sociometry, which attempts to define, analyze, and chart social forms and processes susceptible to measurement. Views on case study range from seeing it as an adjunct to statistics, as an interpretation of statistics, or as complementary to statistics, to its being a scientific method in itself. In the current trends toward both inductive research and conceptual analysis, and interdisciplinary research, continued growth of both statistical and case-study methods is indicated.

Elmer's statement is taken from the September–October, 1949, *Sociology and Social Research*. He points out that "By what men have done, we learn what men can do. This is especially true in the area of social research." Further, "The background for social research might cover a variety of aspects, but for this paper it will be divided into three stages: (1) the long-time development of techniques for objective and mathematical study of mass data, in which the mechanics of statistics has reached an effective level of reliability; (2) the relatively recent emergence of a sociological approach and recognition of the need for application of research methods to social phenomena; (3) the establishing and selecting of definite procedures and fields of research, the attempt to break down causal factors to determine units of measure, and the beginning of the study of more minute and specific aspects of social situations."

Sociometry as Method

The story of the "definite procedures" is a long one and must be told primarily through the examination of those procedures. We have already called attention to the Sociological Research Association, which, however, has done little more than set itself up. Statistical methods constitute a separate specialism, while the operational theories of Dodd's *The Foundations of Society* require concrete expert attention for adequate description. Sociometry is also a specialism outside the realm of general methodology. It was defined in the anniversary volume of *Sociometry* in 1949, page 108, by J. L. Moreno, developer of the Sociometric Institute, as "The Mathematical Study of Psychological Properties of Populations; the Experimental Technique of and the Results Obtained by Application of Quantitative Methods." He says further that this effort to "find an experimental foundation for sociology" has gone and is going through many changes. Other definitions cited by Moreno are "the inquiry into the evolution and organization of groups and the position of individuals within them"; and again as "the science of group organization" attacking "the problem not from the outer structure of the group, the group surface, but from the inner structure."

The story of American sociological theory and method has been and still is one of kaleidoscopic change and of wrestling with semantics. It has often happened that those who insist on empirical research and concrete techniques and specific methodologies bog down on the processes of realistic inquiry or in the generalities of semantics, so that most of the "new" areas of social theory still challenge sociology to apply a dependable methodology.

A Chronological Catalogue of Texts

Of the "standard" texts on the history and development of sociological theory, the following are firsts.

Year	Title	Author	Identification
1915	Social Adaptation	L. M. Bristol	Florida
1922	History of Social Thought	E. S. Bogardus	Southern California
1923	Development of Social Theory	J. P. Lichtenberger	Pennsylvania
1924	Sociology and Political Theory	H. E. Barnes	Smith

Year	Title	Author	Identification
1927	American Masters of Social Science	H. W. Odum (ed.)	North Carolina
1928	Contemporary Sociological Theories	P. A. Sorokin	Minnesota, Harvard
1929	Trends in American Sociology	G. A. Lundberg, Read Bain, Nels Anderson	Washington Miami Chicago
—	Range of Social Theory	F. N. House	Virginia
1936	Development of Sociology	F. N. House	Virginia
1938	Social Thought from Lore to Science	H. E. Barnes, Howard Becker	At large Wisconsin
—	History of Social Philosophy	C. A. Ellwood	Duke
1940	Contemporary Social Theory	H. E. Barnes, H. Becker, F. B. Becker	At large Wisconsin
1943	Origins of American Sociology	L. L. Bernard Jessie Bernard	Washington Pennsylvania State
1945	Twentieth Century Sociology	Georges Gurvitch Wilbert Moore	Paris Princeton
1948	Introduction to History of Sociology	H. E. Barnes	At large
—	Historical Sociology	H. E. Barnes	At large
1949	Essays in Sociological Theory	Talcott Parsons	Harvard
—	Social Theory and Social Structure	R. K. Merton	Columbia
1950	Catholic Social Thought	Melvin J. Williams	Florida State

Among the texts most commonly serving as references for methodology are the following:

Year	Title	Author	Identification
1920	Field Work and Social Research	F. S. Chapin	Minnesota
1924	Scientific Study of Human Society	F. H. Giddings	Columbia
1925	The History and Prospects of the Social Sciences	H. E. Barnes	Smith
—	Principles and Methods of Statistics	R. E. Chaddock	Columbia
1926	The New Social Research	E. S. Bogardus	Southern California

Year	Title	Author	Identification
1927	Technique of Social Surveys (1st edition, 1917)	M. C. Elmer	Pittsburgh
—	The Social Sciences and Their Interrelations	W. F. Ogburn, A. A. Goldenweiser (eds.)	Chicago
1928	Research in the Humanistic and Social Sciences	F. A. Ogg (ed.)	Wisconsin
1929	Social Research	G. A. Lundberg	Washington
—	An Introduction to Social Research	H. W. Odum, Katharine Jocher	North Carolina
—	Research in the Social Sciences	Wilson Gee	Virginia
1930	Methods and Status of Scientific Research	W. E. Spahr, R. J. Swenson	New York University
1931	Methods in Social Science (A Case Book)	S. A. Rice	Pennsylvania
1933	Methods in Sociology	C. A. Ellwood	Duke
1934	The Technique of Social Investigation	Luther Fry	Rochester
—	The Fields and Methods of Sociology	L. L. Bernard (ed.)	Washington University
—	Social Science Research Organization	Wilson Gee	Virginia
—	The Method of Sociology	Florian Znaniecki	Illinois
1935	Criteria for the Life History	John Dollard	Yale
1936	Introduction to Social Research	E. S. Bogardus	California
1938	The Rules of Sociological Method	Émile Durkheim	Paris
1939	Social Research	M. C. Elmer	Pittsburgh
—	Foundations of Sociology	G. A. Lundberg	Washington
—	Scientific Social Surveys and Research	P. V. Young	Southern California
1941	Statistics for Sociologists	M. J. Hagood	North Carolina
—	Elementary Social Statistics	T. C. McCormick	Wisconsin
1942	Social Research	G. A. Lundberg	Washington
1947	Experimental Designs in Sociological Research	F. S. Chapin	Wisconsin
1948	The Recruitment, Selection, and Training of Social Scientists	Elbridge Sibley	Social Science Research Council, New York
1950	Social Science Research Methods	Wilson Gee	Virginia

CHAPTER 16

Special Sociology:
Social Problems and Social Pathology

In the two preceding chapters we have presented something of the record of *general sociology* as it is found in textbooks of five categories. These were introductory texts and principles; the history of social thought; social theory; research and general methodology; and introductory texts in social psychology. We come now to examine the fields of *special sociology*. In Chapter 25 we are cataloguing some of the numerous specialisms that American sociologists have reported as basic to their own research and teaching. In the present chapter we shall tell something of the story of the main concentration of "problems" in relation to the total field of sociology and follow in subsequent chapters with the other major areas including the community, rural, urban, and industrial sociology; the family, marriage and institutions; race, ethnic minorities, folk; population, demography, ecology, regionalism.

Continuing logically, these next five chapters therefore represent both an elaboration and a subdivision of the field of general sociology, for in the first place the majority of introductory textbooks include in their content categories of most of the subsciences or special sociologies, while research into any or all of these specialisms more and more becomes basic to sound social theory and a testing ground for methodology. In contemporary sociology there is not only a certain trend in conceptualization but changes in the nature and number of problems due to changing civilization. We may explore this by comparing the textbooks we have discussed in Chapters 14 and 15 with the more than four hundred specialisms.

First, an analysis of the content of the forty-seven texts utilized by items of subject matter integral enough to constitute a separate chapter shows an extraordinary number and variety of special areas of study. The results of this study coincide closely with analyses of earlier textbooks, but stand in some contrast to the specific specialisms. Thus, in the symposium reported in *Social Forces* for March, 1931, on page 329, Baber finds ten of the twenty-one texts examined devoting at least a third of their space to "social problems" and another nine with one-fifth given over to the problems approach. On page 342 of the same symposium, Malcolm Willey suggests eleven special fields in which material for factual study is available and fields "by general consent, ordinarily regarded as sociology." These fields are the study of crime and the problems of the criminal; the study of the family; the study of population; the study of race relations; the study of recreation; the study of poverty; the study of the humane movement; the study of intercommunication; the study of the newspaper as an institution; the study of housing. General sociology for Willey is envisaged as a separate differentiated social *science* aware of types of problems; but "problems" designated as "fields of research" or "areas within which factual data may be amassed" rather than "situations calling for remedy or reform." In some ways this concept may be said to describe current trends in the study of social problems to which must be added an increasing concentration on such problems as stratification, class, structure, function, group dynamics, small groups, personality, communications technics, and others as noted in Chapters 24 and 25.

Now, turning to our analysis of the forty-seven introductory texts, we note that many of the texts feature social problems in one way or another and so give incidence to the "problem" approach to which we refer again in this chapter. The chapter treatments that connote the problem area and approach are numerous and may be classified from the catalogues toward the end of this chapter. Illustrations would include: marriage and the family, crime and the criminal, race relations, class, caste, conflict, adjustment, control, organization, personality, disorganization, community problems, morality, population, mental disorders. Back again to the "social problems" books, the catalogue of more than four hundred topics as indicated by chapter headings shows the same general lack of uniformity as was noted in Chapter 14 for the general introductory textbooks.

General and Special Sociology

This dichotomy of *general sociology* and *special sociology* has an early American heritage in a number of ways. The exact terms, as far as they have been identified, were first used in sociology by Giddings in his early work, particularly his *Inductive Sociology,* while subsequently in his last published contribution, "An Intensive Sociology," published in *The American Journal of Sociology* in July, 1930, he anticipated something of the role of empirical research in social theory so much emphasized in the 1930's and 1940's. In his *Inductive Sociology,* page 8, he wrote, "Sociology may be divided into General, or Fundamental, Sociology, and Special Sociology. General Sociology is a study of the universal and fundamental phenomena of societies." Special Sociology was applied to those inquiries "dealing minutely with some one phase of social organization, social activity, or social development." In his treatise on "Intensive Sociology" he defined sociology as a comparative study of societies and estimated that "intensive studies in sociology will presumably clarify and define our idea of what sociology itself becomes when we divest it of accretions and admixtures taken up from other sciences." Sociology, Giddings continued on page 14, "cannot profitably continue to rehearse the story of cosmic evolution from the beginning or to project wishful thinking through an endless hereafter."

This distinction between general and special sociology is important in identifying again the field and meaning of sociology itself, as contrasted with what is ordinarily called "applied sociology" or with special applications of sociology to ameliorative situations. We emphasize the fact that specialisms such as social problems, social pathology, crime and penology, marriage and the family, rural and urban sociology, and others *are not primarily applied sociology,* although more often than not they have been so treated. In the strictly sociological sense, as indicated by Ward for instance, applied sociology is not possible until principles have been worked out for application to special situations. This is a fundamental distinction. This does not mean that there are not and will not continue to be ample works in the "special problems" field that are primarily ameliorative; but they are primarily in the social work disciplines rather than sociology as such. What is emphasized here is the importance of the sociologist studying life situations in order both to derive and to perfect his theory and to test it. This is well illustrated in the case of Robert E. Park's sociological theories concerning race and culture contacts as found in his 1950 posthumous *Race and Culture* in which Park is reflected as believing that sociological theory should grow out of the study of human behavior in special areas and situations. This does not mean again that sound theory so derived should not then be applied immediately to the same areas, but it means the scientific processes of studying and of applying are different. Reuter's studies of the Negro had the same sort of focus, so much so that he was often criticized for not being interested in the Negro's welfare.

In many ways, therefore, special sociology, and often more appropriately special *sociologies,* afford the sociologist his best approach to scientific research and realistic sociology. It is here that the sociologist can find a special delimited field and problem to which he may apply the most rigorous scientific methods, and come out with genuinely empirical results with reference to human behavior and societal phenomena. Here the assumption is twofold. First, like all sciences, sociology will seek to discover facts in each specialized area and provide the basic research for sound social theory in an integrated structural analysis of society. In the second place, the premise underlying these special sociologies is sound; namely, that one of the best ways to understand social behavior and to make universal propositions about society is to concentrate on special areas. This is another way of saying that there are subsocial sciences within the larger field of sociology, just as there are in physical science. Illustration: The family may be designated as a subsocial science of sociology, as ecology has been designated a subscience of biology.

Examples of Special Sociology

This approach is well illustrated by the work of two, among others, of the presidents of the American Sociological Society in the specific area of criminology. These are John L. Gillin and Edwin H. Sutherland. Although Gillin has been author of many texts and worked widely in this field of teaching and elementary sociology, he feels that it is in the special field of and researches in criminology that he has made his greatest contribution to sociology. And this is the reason: "In all of these studies," he says, "I considered that criminology was a part of sociology, not something distinct from it. Their [the criminals'] behavior was *social* behavior. It was defiant behavior, but it was a part of the whole social complex. It was the result of social conditions. I tried to find out how it fitted into the social whole, and why it departed from the norms of the group in which these individuals were reared, or in what respect their behavior was a part of the pattern of behavior that was normal to their subgroup."

So, too, Sutherland would classify himself as a "sociologist interested in the general theory of society and attempting to assist in developing this general theory by concentrating on criminal behavior." He "selected criminal behavior as the specific area of concentration." "My interest in criminal behavior," he said, "is not in the control of crime or even knowledge that might contribute to the control of crime, but rather in the light that an intensive study of this behavior may throw on society. In the study of criminal behavior from this point of view, I have been interested primarily in reaching a general or universal proposition that would at the same time be an explanation of criminal behavior and be consistent with and related to a universal proposition that would explain other kinds of behavior. Moreover, I have felt that this explanation should be consistent with the statement that the sociologist should attempt to understand society." Thus the scientific study of criminology by the sociologist becomes the scientific study of society. On this premise he will study not only crime as a pattern of human behavior and relationships but will study the environmental and conditioning factors relevant to the total area or system of society.

A third example may be cited from the Sorokin-Zimmerman *Principles of Rural-Urban Sociology,* pages 8 and 9, in which they approach the study of rural society as a segment of general sociology. "Since Rural Sociology is a special branch of sociology, its tasks in its specific field are practically the same as those of general sociology. Correspondingly, the fundamental task of rural sociology is to describe the relatively constant and universal traits or relations of the rural social world as distinct from the non-rural or urban social universe. In this description, rural sociology, like general sociology, concentrates its attention not at the traits which are peculiar to a given rural aggregate at a given time, but at the traits and relations which are typical for the rural social world generally as distinct from urban social phenomena generally. In other words, rural sociology describes the rural-urban differences which are repeated in time and space and, in this sense, are constant characteristics of the rural in contradistinction from the urban social phenomena."

"Social Problems" as Special Sociology

Perhaps the best way in which this dichotomy of general and special sociology may be illustrated in American sociology is in the study of social problems. Like social theory, the term "social problems" has been used with widely varied meanings and little consistency. Yet the meaning for sociology is quite clear from an examination of the several most common usages. The first major area we have already described as basic to the American social science movement, namely, the attempt to find a new social science through the avenue of the study of social problems. It was as if the challenge of American problems to American scholars to develop a realistic social science for their solution was so logical as to be a "natural." Yet the prospect staked out by the frontiersmen was never developed, largely because of two trends. One was to make problems and their solutions action programs synonymous with sociology; the other was the other extreme of ignoring problems in the too-theoretical philosophical study of society. In retrospect, the question may well be raised of how dynamic and scientific sociology might have become if it had developed its research into realistic problems in the framework of American society alongside the European philosophy of society which became the primary frame of reference. What, for instance, might have emerged in the scientific study of population through an early enrichment of the United States census and an equally enriched cultural analysis of the folk and regions of the expanding American society? Or, if American sociologists, setting up their theoretical systems of societal analysis, had then made "problems" an integral part of their testing grounds and illustrations even as "problems" must supplement normal theorems in the mathematical sciences.

Yet, even so, social problems as a concept and practice has had, and now has, a large place in the total configuration of American sociology. Forgetting for the moment the role of necessity in the ever-widening situations of adjustment, which problems play in challenging study and research, we may note perhaps four main areas in which social problems constitute basic threads in the total fabric of American sociology. First, the elementary course in social problems has constituted one prong of the dichotomy of introductory sociology. That is, it has been held by many that the beginning of sociology should be through the avenue of actual social problems rather than through the realm of abstract theory. On the other hand, many have held that general sound theory is first necessary before the student can comprehend the nature of problems.

The most common compromise has been a combination of the two, either in a single course or in separate courses. One of the most popular of the earlier textbooks was Charles A. Ellwood's *Sociology and Modern Social Problems,* which was reputed to have sold a million copies and was translated into several languages for use in other countries. A second way in which the social problems approach has been an integral part of the sociological curriculum has been on the levels of social pathology and social deviation or disorganization. Many of the texts and courses have consistently made social problems synonymous with social pathology. A third way in which social problems has played an integral part in the total picture of sociology is in utilizing the social problems course, on the one hand, as preprofessional for social work, public health, or other applied fields, or as the total sociology for general liberal arts or citizenship training for students who do not expect to become sociologists.

The Problems Genesis of Sociology

In reality, the "social problem" background may be characterized as basic in a fourth and even more important role. This may be indicated in two main ways. In the first place, the genesis of sociology in general as well as in America is often ascribed to "the need" for sociology in the increasing complexity of modern society from the nineteenth century "progress" toward modern civilization. In the next place, there has been an increasing tendency to recognize the "problem" basis for genuine empirical research in American sociology as sociologists have come into more realistic understandings of dynamic social theory. With reference to the origins of sociology, even the historians of sociology, such as Harry Elmer Barnes, are inclined to identify the problems situation as basic to the rise of sociology. Barnes notes two aspects of this on page 3 of his "Development of Sociology" in *Contemporary Social Theory.* He points out that probably the most important factor "was that general groping for social betterment produced by the misery that came in the wake of the industrial revolution and the factory system." There were three facets to this approach. One was that of the earlier Utopian sociologists who sought the perfect life and happy system. A second was the search for a science of progress as symbolized by Comte and Saint-Simon. The third was the stubborn insistence of sociologists like Spencer, Gumplowicz and Sumner, that the study of sociology and its problems might offer "irrefutable proof of man's inability to improve his social surroundings through any conscious effort at an artificial redirection of the trend of social evolution." In all three cases the *problem basis* was and is fundamental.

This is indicated anew by the increasingly large number of sociologists who seek to interpret sociology and to study scientifically societal phenomena through the medium of social problems as special delimited areas of inquiry. They not only offer their texts for introductory courses in sociology but seek to do research and to apply their findings in and through these fields. More accurately, this area of social problems may be said to follow the dichotomy already described as applying to sociological texts. That is, social problems are of two sorts, each of which may be designated by a coordinate dichotomy.

In *American Social Problems,* Chapter 1, and in *Understanding Society* on pages 496-98, I have pointed out that the social problems which sociology explores, far from constituting only a catalogue of pathological conditions or of essentially concrete problems of maladjustment, are primarily the normal problems of societal growth and development. The sociologist will not neglect these important specific problems in which he is called upon to contribute to amelioration programs in many concrete applications, but he will study them primarily in broader perspective and will find in each of them relationship to the larger problems of society.

Two Types of Social Problems

This dichotomy of special sociology over against applied sociology for the sociologist may be illustrated further by contrasting two types of the same general problem, namely, the *scientific problem* and the *ameliorative problem,* or, in the language of Giddings and Sumner, the *societal* and the *social problem.* The scientific problem, coinciding in general with the *societal,* connotes the long-time universal sociological approach, which seeks to find the answer to certain questions and situations occurring throughout the field of social relationships in whatever periods or areas. The *ameliorative* or *social* problem focuses upon a specific situation here and now in which maladjustment or pathology has occurred, and seeks to improve the situation and to "solve" the problem in the sense of eliminating the objectionable features and providing for adjustments. In reality every major "social" problem, of course, comprehends this twofold nature and in the true sense of applied sociology, the sociologist can contribute little to the ameliorative problem until he has first studied its long-time and generic factors.

This distinction between the scientific and the ameliorative problems, therefore, is fundamental for the understanding of the field of general sociology, which explores the scientific problem and leaves the ameliorative problem to social work or social agencies. This does not mean that sociology and social work do not cooperate closely and that each is not necessary to the other. It means rather that there is a division of labor. Just as the agricultural chemist studies soils and the processes of leaching and erosion in his laboratory, but does not undertake to go out into the field and do the remedial job, leaving that for the farmer, the agronomist, or the soil conservation worker, so the sociologist seeks to discover the truth about problems and to make these truths available for as many people and agencies as may use them.

Classifications of Social Problems

In American sociology as reflected in its textbooks on social problems, this dichotomy between social problems as an introduction to sociology and social problems as applied sociology does not always appear. Like the Sociology I of the general introductory textbooks there is relatively little uniformity in the textbooks on social problems as may be seen from an analysis of the leading texts in this field. Perhaps it is more nearly possible to classify the score or two of "problems" texts into categories than was the case with the more than one hundred introductory texts. One of the 1949 texts, *An Approach to Social Problems,* by Abbott P. Herman, on page 9, undertakes to classify within the field of sociology five different types of inquiries into the nature of social problems. These are the "Social Problems Approach," the "Social-Disorganization Approach," the "Cultural Lag Approach," the "Value-Structure Approach," and the "Community Approach." In all these the frame of reference is assumed to be that of adjustment and the tools for adjustment in social change, which is forever resulting in new social problems or readjustment to old social problems. This classification is cited more for purposes of illustration and analysis than for exact identification, since only a relatively small number of texts was analyzed.

Perhaps the best classification for the purpose of understanding the role of the social problems approach in American sociology is a relatively oversimplified general grouping consisting of four main types. These would be, *first,* social problems as introductory sociology; *second,* social problems as social pathology, social disorganization, or deviation; *third,* social problems as specialisms devoted to a single area such as crime, delinquency; and *fourth,* occasionally social problems as social planning and social process. Here, again, classification and identification can be accurate enough only for general purposes with as much detailed study of the several texts as may be desired for more specific purposes. In general, introductory texts for Sociology I are those by Barnes, Binder, Bossard, Gillin, Landis, North, Odum, and Phelps. Social pathology or deviation is well illustrated in Brown, Bodenhafer, Gillin, Elliott, Ford, Mangold, Mowrer, Mann, and Queen. Criminology and penology are represented by Barnes, Cantor, Gillin, Haynes, Morris, Parmelee, Parsons, Reckless, Sutherland, Taft, and Wood. In the planning and process approach North and Bossard assume the objectives of social direction; Odum has a number of special sections on social planning; while in Bossard's emphasis on social change and Phelps' specifications for reform there are implications of social planning. From our general analysis of the main textbooks on social problems, it appears that they afford the same general diversity that is found in the introductory texts in principles of sociology. Chapter and division headings offer scores of instances approximately the same.

Samplings from Social Pathology

The approach to social problems through what is often termed social pathology again fits into a sort of natural dichotomy. Here it is possible to select even more specialized fields than in the area of general problems. Thus, in special fields such as poverty, dependency, and delinquency, the sociologist can specialize in both research and in practical work. The assumption is that the chief scientific problem here is one of adjustment or adaptation on the one hand and diagnosis of deviation or disorganization on the other. Perhaps Stuart A. Queen's work on *Social Pathology* and John L. Gillin's *Social Pathology* may best illustrate the central rôle of social pathology in the total sociological curriculum. We recall that Queen, a former president of the American Sociological Society, regarded himself as primarily a sociologist contributing to social work. How social pathology may be interwoven with the scientific study of society may be seen from the statement of the objectives of his *Social Pathology,* revised in collaboration with D. M. Mann and Jeanette R. Gruener in 1940. "Our own purpose," wrote the authors in the preface, "is to take certain difficult human situations as they appear on the surface, analyze them into their constituent elements and discuss their significance primarily from the standpoint of sociology. We realize that in so doing we run the risk of producing another 'hodgepodge.' We appreciate the fact that our chapter headings — unemployment, illegitimacy, divorce, etc., — do not constitute a classification of socially pathological conditions. We use them because they represent the point of *contact* with difficult situations. These are the things which appear first. Hence, beginning with them, we seek to point out physical, mental, economic and social factors which may be involved. We undertake to correlate several viewpoints and techniques, but our emphasis throughout is upon the sociological interpretation."

Gillin's *Social Pathology,* probably the most widely used text in the field, likewise emphasizes the special sociological frame of reference. Gillin says, "Social pathology is the study of man's failure to adjust himself and his institutions to the necessities of existence to the end that he may survive and meet fairly well the felt needs of his nature." "As early as 1914, when I was writing my first book in sociology (in collaboration with Professor Blackmar), I felt the importance of considering the pathological aspects of social life in the scheme of things sociological. In the years which have followed I have tried to work out more thoroughly the place of social pathology in sociological theory. I could not be satisfied with the treatment of social maladjustments dissociated from the social organization and processes out of which they grew, or at least with which they were associated. This book is an attempt to unite in theory what are actually joined in life."

Another sociological approach was that of the late James Ford of Harvard in his *Social Deviation*. The angle of approach according to Ford

was the "deviation or inadequacy of the individual, its sources, consequences, and correctives. Physical or mental abnormalities, antisocial
behavior, delinquency, low standards of living and dependency, and the
interrelations of these various maladjustments and of their social treatment and prevention are thus treated together under the caption of social pathology, or the sociology of sub-standard statistical groups." He
defines social pathology as "that branch of applied sociology which is
concerned with the classification (nosology or taxonomy), causation
(etiology), structure (anatomy), conditions or manifestations (symp-
tomatology), and treatment (therapeutics) of handicaps, poverty, delinquency, or other forms of individual and social inadequacies or maladjustment." (Page 6.)

The Source Book Approach

Finally, a quick review of the whole field of social problems may be
had from the 1950 volume *Analyzing Social Problems* edited by John E.
Nordskog, Edward C. McDonagh, and Melvin J. Vincent. In its 805
pages, with discussions and source materials, fourteen major areas are
documented with selections from the writings of more than one hundred authors, the majority of whom are sociologists, and there is a remarkably comprehensive and up-to-date bibliography to complete the
story.

The general frame of reference is that of sociological analysis with
the sound assumptions of accurate definitions. Thus in the half dozen
chapters on "Social Problems Defined" by Case, Hart, Merrill, Fuller,
Bossard, and Ogburn, it is possible to ascertain a relatively complete and
accurate understanding of the status and role of social problems in the
total sociological picture. The main concentrations treated are population problems, ethnic relations, industrial relations, personality disorganization, family disorganization, juvenile delinquency, criminal behavior, educational problems, social-reform movements, social planning
problems, war and peace problems, and world organization. Specifically,
the editors state on page v, the purpose of the volume "has been to
stimulate interest in sociology" and unity is provided for the book in
"the emphasis on the reciprocal relationships of social institutions and
the interrelationship of social problems, as well as the general theme of
social disorganization and amelioration."

Corresponding to the introductory texts in general sociology catalogued in Chapter 14 are the texts on social problems listed below. Many
of these have also served as introductory texts for Sociology I. Here, as
elsewhere, they are catalogued to show the succession of texts from 1900
to 1950.

Year	Title	Author	Identification
1910	Sociology and Modern Social Problems	C. A. Ellwood	Missouri
1920	Major Social Problems	R. M. Binder	New York University
1922	Problems of American Democracy	H. R. Burch	Pennsylvania
1927	Problems of Social Well-Being	J. H. S. Bossard	Pennsylvania
—	Man's Quest for Social Guidance	H. W. Odum	North Carolina
1928	Social Problems	J. L. Gillin	Wisconsin
1932	Social Problems and Social Planning	C. C. North	Cincinnati
—	Contemporary Social Problems	H. A. Phelps	Pittsburgh
—	Social Problems	J. L. Gillin (and others)	Wisconsin
1933	Current Social Problems	J. M. Gillette, J. M. Reinhardt	North Dakota
1934	Social Change and Social Problems	J. H. S. Bossard	Pennsylvania
1938	Problems of Modern Society	P. W. Paustian	Nebraska
1939	Society in Transition	H. E. Barnes	Smith
—	American Social Problems	H. W. Odum	North Carolina
1940	Social Problems	C. M. Rosenquist	Texas
1942	Problems of a Changing Social Order	J. M. Gillette, J. M. Reinhardt	North Dakota, Nebraska
—	The American Way of Life	Barnes, Ruedi, Ferguson	At large
—	American Social Problems	M. E. Walsh	Catholic University
1943	Social Problems	Gillin, Dittmer, Colbert	Wisconsin
1945	American Social Problems	H. W. Odum	North Carolina
1947	Contemporary Social Problems	H. A. Phelps	Pittsburgh

Year	Title	Author	Identification
1948	Problems of American Society	J. F. Cuber, R. A. Harper	Ohio State University
1949	Social Problems in America	A. Mc C. Lee, E. B. Lee	Wayne University
—	An Approach to Social Problems	A. P. Herman	Redlands
1950	Analyzing Social Problems	Nordskog, McDonagh, Vincent	Southern California

Catalogued below are the principal texts on social pathology and the more specialized volumes on criminology and penology written by sociologists. Listed chronologically with them are two early doctor's dissertations at Columbia University.

Year	Title	Author	Identification
1902	Crime in Its Relation to Social Progress	A. C. Hall	Columbia, Ph.D.
1909	Responsibility for Crime	P. A. Parsons	Columbia, Ph.D.
1918	Criminology	Maurice Parmelee	Smith
1924	Principles of Criminology	E. H. Sutherland	Indiana
1925	Social Pathology	S. A. Queen	Washington University
1926	Criminology and Penology	J. L. Gillin	Wisconsin
—	Crime and the Criminal	P. A. Parsons	Oregon
1930	Criminology	F. E. Haynes	New York University
1932	Social Pathology	G. B. Mangold	Southern California
—	Social Disorganization	M. A. Elliott, F. E. Merrill	Pennsylvania College for Women
1933	Social Pathology	J. L. Gillin	Wisconsin
1934	Criminology	A. Morris	New York University
1935	Criminology and Penology	J. L. Gillin	Wisconsin
1938	Crime and the Community	Frank Tannenbaum	New York University

Year	Title	Author	Identification
1939	Crime and Society	N. F. Cantor	University of Buffalo
—	Social Deviation	James Ford	Harvard
—	Principles of Criminology	E. H. Sutherland	Indiana
1935	Social Organization and Disorganization	S. A. Queen, W. B. Bodenhafer,	Washington University
1940	Criminal Behavior	W. C. Reckless	Ohio State
—	Social Pathology	S. A. Queen, J. R. Gruener	Washington University
1941	Crime and Its Treatment	A. E. Wood, J. B. Wait	Michigan
—	Social Disorganization	Elliott, Merrill	Pennsylvania College for Women
1942	Social Pathology	L. G. Brown	Ohio State
—	Disorganization	E. R. Mowrer	Northwestern
—	Criminology	D. R. Taft	Illinois
1943	New Horizons in Criminology	H. E. Barnes, N. K. Teeters	New York University Temple
1947	Principles of Criminology	E. H. Sutherland	Indiana
1948	Social Disorganization	R. E. L. Faris	University of Washington
—	Criminology	R. S. Cavan	Chicago
1949	Crime and Penology	J. L. Gillin	Wisconsin
1950	The Crime Problem	W. C. Reckless	Ohio State

CHAPTER 17

Special Sociology: The Community, Rural, Urban, and Industrial Sociology

Perhaps no areas of special sociology will reflect the realistic develop-ment of American sociology with all its consistencies and contrasts, trends and neglected aspects, more than the four areas of the commu-nity, rural and urban society, and industrial civilization. In three of these there are new trends: in the sociology of community; in rural sociology; and in industrial sociology. All of these special sociologies are peculiarly appropriate for research and theoretical development in the frame of reference of social change, while the sociology of the community or of special societies, long neglected, may well become the structural basis for the new trends in group sociology, in contrast to and yet in harmony with the new world community construct. In all probability, if a single area of societal structure were to be sought out for the measurement of greatest social change, it would be in the realm of community, from the early simple primary relationships of rural, religious, kinship groups to the complex, urban, industrial society toward which advanced state civi-lization tends to move. In the continuum from the early to the later, four areas of special sociology, perhaps, have emerged with relatively clear-cut delineation. These are the community structure, organization, be-havior; rural society with the rapidly developed rural sociology; urban society and the study of urban problems; industrial society and indus-trial sociology. Perhaps a fifth may be emerging in the area of state civili-zation and world society.

One of the main reasons why the sociology of the community has been so often neglected was because *community* and *society* were relatively synonymous in the framework of early societies in the structure and dynamics of societal evolution. Every known people or assemblage liv-ing a life in common, the anthropologists tell us, has some form of or-ganization in association in some areal setting; that *was* society in community form. As late as 1947, in *The World Community,* Louis Wirth's distinction between community and society was questioned and debated at length in a symposium to which Kimball Young, Margaret Mead, Ruth Benedict, Talcott Parsons, and others contributed. In this symposium, page v, it was stated that the "study of the history, origin, composition, structure, characteristics, and functioning of communities and societies, and of the relations among such entities, is one of the tasks of the social sciences." Perhaps another reason for the neglect of the scientific study of the community was the rise of the community organization movement in the late 1920's and the tendency to consider the community as a subject for "practical" sociology or action programs or as the primary base for social problems, to all of which aspects sociologists have contributed substantially.

The Beginnings of Community Study

Having thus emphasized the limitations of community study as special sociology, it remains to be said, however, that the literature of community constitutes an appreciable segment of the total story of American sociology. Especially is this true if we search out special evidences of community study in which communities and societies are interrelated or in which the community is the vehicle for looking at society. Of the earlier sociologists, Giddings and Cooley come nearer to exemplifying the scientific study of the community as special sociology than any others. At least a dozen of Giddings' earlier Ph.D. students made community studies the basis for their doctoral dissertations. In 1904, Thomas Jesse Jones published his *The Sociology of a New York City Block.* Jones later specialized in intercultural relations and was director of the Phelps Stokes Fund in which fellowships were awarded for the study of Negro communities in the South and elsewhere. In 1906, James Mickel Williams published *An American Town,* which then was followed by his special emphasis upon the rural community and social psychology. In 1925, he published *Our Rural Heritage* and in 1920, *The Expansion of Rural Life.* In 1908, Warren H. Wilson published his *Quaker Hill* and, like Williams, later devoted himself primarily to the rural community as head of the division of Church and Country Life for the Board of Home Missions of the Presbyterian Church, U.S.A. He was a pioneer in this field of the rural community in his wide travels in all regions of the United States. In 1912, he published *The Evolution of the Country Community* and was consistently a leader in the Country Life Movement.

In 1909, Howard Woolston published his *Study of the Population of Manhattanville* and subsequently specialized in Neo-Malthusian population theories and in the study of the urban community, publishing at least two major works on the city and on urban sociology. Two other Giddings students published Ph.D. dissertations in related fields, namely, A. A. Tenney, Giddings' long-time associate, on *Social Democracy and the Population* and Michael Davis on *The Psychological Interpretations of Society*. N. L. Sims published his *A Hoosier Village* in 1910.

Returning to the Giddings foundations for the study of the community, three evidences of his priority in this special area of sociology may be cited here. One was his *Inductive Sociology* in which he attempted to set up objective measures for the study of the social population, of situation, of aggregation composition and unity. He also attempted to measure mental and practical resemblances and also social organization in its nature and forms, its composition and constitution, and its character and efficiency. He attempted to study social welfare and social security in terms of the social personality and the interrelations of personality with community. In this volume Giddings presents maps and graphs based on statistical studies showing distribution of various traits. One shows the relation of vitality and mentality classes for country population, village population, suburban and urban populations. In two other ways Giddings attempted to provide basic schedules for the empirical study and analysis of societies. One was his *action patterns, form patterns,* and *factoral patterns,* presented in Chapter 1 of his *Scientific Study of Human Society,* featuring time and space relationships and interrelated factoral situations in such ways as could actually be applied in the study, let us say, of a mill village or rural community. The other attempt at strictly sociological analysis was his rather notable formula for a societal survey. According to Giddings, on page 186 of his *Scientific Study of Human Society,* "A survey that could properly be described as social and societal would discover, record, map, and graph phenomena that are social or societal in a strict instead of in a loose meaning of the words."

Of the Cooley basic foundations for community study, priority goes to his social organization and his primary groups. In the core of the first he estimates that failure to provide adequate organization is the essence of failure to build a moral social order; and with reference to the second it is in the primary group of neighborhood and community of elders that human nature is formed so that the maintenance of this community process is essential to a surviving society.

Of other earlier sociologists working for doctorates and exploring the community as an area of analysis, Gillette was one of the earliest following the Giddings group but working with Small at Chicago, as did Bogardus, Queen, and Wirth, exploring the community through the university settlement medium. Subsequently, a quartette of near-pioneers in specific studies were not afraid to devote themselves to concrete studies of actual groups and to propose objective ways of surveying the community. These were M. C. Elmer, Read Bain, George Lundberg, Luther Fry. The Lynds and their "Middletown" were also pioneers while R. M. MacIver's *The Community: A Sociological Study,* was a sort of classic in the perfection of its text writing. Later examples are Albert Blumenthal's *Small Town Stuff*; John Dollard's *Caste and Class in a Southern Town;* James West's *Plainville, U.S.A.;* and *The Yankee City* series by Warner and others. In the later community organization movement Jesse F. Steiner at North Carolina, later at Tulane and Washington, set the pace with his *Community Organization* and *The American Community in Action.* Some of the volumes on community surveys have already been noted in the previous chapter on methodology, while others are catalogued below in chronological order.

The Meaning of Community

Since the rural sociologists were more inclined to make the community the basis for special sociological study, the further story follows in the rapid rise of rural sociology in the United States. C. H. Galpin's *The Social Anatomy of an Agricultural Community* was a pioneer. Sanderson's early identification of the community as the smallest geographical unit of people performing all the functions of society, and measured variously from center to radiating points, is somewhat different from the community of town planning specifications or from the ecological community. MacIver's index of the community was that all social relationships may be found within it, as pointed out on page 9 of *Society: Its Structure and Change,* which conforms relatively closely to another textbook frame of reference in which Dawson and Gettys inclined to make the community the single unit of sociological study instead of the *socius* which was Giddings' unit; or the *region,* of the North Carolina group. Louis Wirth on page 12 of the symposium *The World Community* says that "when we use the term 'Community' we seek to isolate and to emphasize the physical, spatial, and symbiotic aspects of human group life, whereas by the term 'society' we wish to bring into focus and to stress the psychic, deliberative, rational, normative, and consensual phases of group existence."

In the newer trends identification of the community apparently is within a twofold frame of reference, on the one hand, of the scientific study of social problems in the unified community setting; and on the other of an analysis of community structure and function but also basic to social planning. These two approaches are perhaps best represented by Jessie Bernard of Pennsylvania State College, whose latest volume has already been discussed, and Gordon Blackwell of the University of North Carolina, whose inquiries tend to utilize measures of interrelationships. According to Blackwell, scientific analysis of community in the localized sense must use a number of the basic conceptual tools of sociology. A framework for community analysis would include the following dimensions: (1) geographic base, (2) population vitality, composition, and trends, (3) institutional structure (including formally organized service agencies and special interest groups), (4) systems of beliefs and values, (5) social stratification and vertical mobility, (6) patterns of interpersonal relationships (social contacts, cliques, prestige, leadership), (7) power structure, (8) ecological patterning (extensity of community, as well as internal variation in the preceding dimensions). This framework obviously does not afford mutually exclusive categories but rather a number of perspectives from which the community may be analyzed in terms of structure-function in all the organic interrelatedness of its parts.

An excellent appraisal of the anthropological approach to community studies is given on pages 20–39 of Julian H. Steward's *Area Research,* published by the Social Science Research Council in 1950. He writes on page 21, "The purposes and methods of community studies are extremely varied, but their importance for area research is that they all apply a cultural or ethnographic method to contemporary society. This method was developed by anthropology in the study of primitive peoples, and it is being applied to modern societies by anthropologists and by sociologists who have some knowledge of anthropology. Community studies are still in a pioneering stage, however, and the potential value of the cultural approach to modern society is only incompletely explored. Applied to primitive tribes, this approach has three distinctive methodological aspects. First, it is ethnographic: the culture of a tribe, band, or village is studied in its totality, all forms of behavior being seen as functionally interdependent parts in the context of the whole. Second, it is historical: the culture of each society is traced to its sources in ancestral or antecedent groups or among neighboring peoples. Third, it is comparative: each group is viewed in the perspective of other groups which have different cultures, and problems and methods are used cross-culturally. Two general criticisms may be made of the way in which the ethnographic, historical, and comparative methods are applied to modern communities. First, the methods have not been adapted to modern communities, which differ qualitatively from primitive ones. Second, the historical and comparative methods have been used hardly at all."

His final verdict, on page 51, is that "The community study approach — that of studying all cultural phenomena and their interrelations within the community — has been found useful in connection with many problems. The approach is still defective, however, to the extent that it fails to treat communities within their larger context and to give adequate attention to aspects of culture and society which have national dimensions. That is, the community approach is not yet sufficiently related to that of the various disciplines which study culture in these larger dimensions. It is also strikingly unhistorical in its modern applications. Many problems do not require historical study, but most of those pertaining to culture change and social relations, which are the concern of many community studies, would be illuminated by a historical approach. Finally, community studies are not comparable, for quite unlike purposes underlie their problems, methods, and reporting of data."

The catalog of special volumes on the community written by sociologists does not include many of the very recent researches into studies of *group* life and organization in which there are, nevertheless, many community aspects. Some of these would be George P. Murdock's *Social Structure*, Robert H. Lowie's *Social Organization*, George Homans' *The Human Group*, Baker Brownell's *The Human Community*, David Riesman's *The Lonely Crowd*, Adolf Berle's *Natural Selection of Political Forces*, Laura Thompson's *Culture in Crisis*, Trigant Burrow's *The Neurosis of Man*, Lawrence K. Frank's *Society as the Patient*, and Paul Meadows' *The Culture of Industrial Man*.

A Chronological Catalogue of Books by Sociologists

Year	Title	Author	Identification
1904	*The Sociology of a New York City Block*	T. J. Jones	Phelps Stokes Fund, New York
1906	*An American Town*	J. M. Williams	Hobart
1907	*Quaker Hill*	W. H. Wilson	New York
1909	*The Study of the Population of Manhattanville*	Howard Woolston	Washington
1912	*The Evolution of the Country Community*	W. H. Wilson	New York
1915	*The Rural Community*	C. J. Galpin	Wisconsin
1917	*Community*	R. M. MacIver	Columbia
1920	*Community Organization*	J. K. Hart	Vanderbilt
—	*Locating the Country Community*	D. Sanderson	Cornell
—	*The Rural Community*	N. L. Sims	Oberlin
—	*Community: A Sociological Study*	R. M. MacIver	Columbia
1921	*The Community*	E. C. Lindeman	New York
—	*Rural Community Organization*	A. W. Hayes	Michigan State
1922	*The Farmer and His Community*	D. Sanderson	Cornell
1925	*Community Organization*	J. F. Steiner	North Carolina
—	*Surveying Your Community*	E. de S. Brunner	Columbia
1926	*The Urban Community*	E. W. Burgess	Chicago
1927	*Village Communities*	E. de S. Brunner	Columbia
1928	*The American Community in Action*	J. F. Steiner	North Carolina
1929	*Middletown*	Robert Lynd, Helen Lynd	Columbia
1937	*Middletown in Transition*	Robert Lynd, Helen Lynd	Columbia

Year	Title	Author	Identification
1943	Toward Community Understanding	Gordon Blackwell	North Carolina
1947	The Small Community Looks Ahead	W. J. Hayes	Vanderbilt
1948	Community Recreation	H. D. Meyer and C. K. Brightbill	North Carolina
1949	American Community Behavior	Jessie Bernard	Pennsylvania State
—	Church and Community in the South	G. W. Blackwell, L. M. Brooks, S. H. Hobbs, Jr.	North Carolina North Carolina North Carolina
1950	Community Organization and Planning	Arthur Hillman	Roosevelt College

The Rural Community First

Jesse F. Steiner in his *Community Organization,* page 15, calls attention to the fact that rural sociologists were the first to feature the study of the community. In the present chapter we have already called attention to the work of J. M. Williams, Warren H. Wilson, and others whose first community studies were expanded into rural sociology. Another earlier influence that set the incidence for rural sociology was the work of K. L. Butterfield and the Theodore Roosevelt Country Life Commission, the report of which was widely circulated and then republished in the 1940's. Working with this group on the nearer professional level were C. J. Galpin, Warren Wilson, and others as noted. The third and most accelerating influence upon rural sociology was the series of programs of the Bureau of Agricultural Economics begun by Galpin and continued through the New Deal, together with the work of several allied agencies in the field of rural life and agriculture, which was a part of the lifework of Carl Taylor as presented in Chapter 12. The fourth specific momentum was the organization of the Rural Sociological Society and the setting up of its journal of *Rural Sociology,* both of which are described in other chapters of this book.

Galpin and Branson

There were several pre-rural sociology influences besides Galpin and the Country Life Movement. Galpin himself has told his story well in *My Drift into Rural Sociology,* published in 1938 and republished in a number of issues of *Rural Sociology*. Galpin was born in Hamilton, New York, in 1864. Like others of his contemporaries he prepared for the ministry and served his church for a number of years, after which he went to Wisconsin where his special field was agricultural economics. Then from 1919 to 1934 he was head of the Division of Farm Population and Rural Life in the United States Department of Agriculture.

Somewhat earlier than this, E. C. Branson established his Department of Rural Social Economics at the University of North Carolina of which he was head from 1914 to 1933. In this capacity he was one of the prime movers in developing the new Department of Sociology which was established in 1920. Branson's work was notable in its emphasis upon fact-finding and especially in the study of the county and country life aspects of society. In particular, Professor Branson pioneered in the discovery of the farm tenant and farm tenancy in the United States. This field of inquiry and "problems" became a major field of study for two decades. Branson also published *Farm Life Abroad* following his observations in Denmark and Ireland in the 1920's. S. H. Hobbs, Jr., who succeeded Branson, is in 1950 apparently the "senior" professor of rural sociology in the United States.

The developed field of rural sociology may be said to comprise three main divisions. In addition to the regular courses in rural sociology, there are special facilities for research and the writing of articles and bulletins, of which there is an impressive catalog. The third area is that of rural extension services, alongside the studies and surveys of communities. This rural service, generously supported by federal funds, has been the occasion for increasing appropriations by the states for rural sociology and research, and has developed an extraordinary array of projects and areas of service that constitute a part of the framework for rural sociology in general. In an inquiry made by H. W. Beers for the Rural Sociological Society, eighty-six sub-areas were listed as indicating the possible range of rural sociology extension activities.

The rise of rural sociology recapitulates the course taken by sociology in general in several ways, but differs radically in at least two. That is, there was a sort of pre-rural sociological era with Wilson, Galpin, Gillette, Butterfield, and the Country Life Movement in which rural sociology grew out of the problem approach. Next, rural sociologies were written by "regular" sociologists and rural sociology became a special sociology along with the family, institutions, urban sociology, and the community. Then, with the founding of *Rural Sociology* and the Rural Sociological Society, rural sociology, while continuing close to the mother discipline, broke away in two main ways: first, in establishing its own medium and eventually setting itself up as a separate entity, and second, in the fact that a larger ratio of its members were not members of faculties of colleges or universities than was the case with the American Sociological Society. The first editions of the new journal included such sociologists as Ogburn, Chapin, Park, and Sorokin, but after the journal became the official organ of the new society in 1938, editors and contributors were primarily rural sociologists. C. M. Grigg, in analyzing the list of contributors, found that approximately 30 per cent from 1936 to 1950 were non-academic rural sociologists and in 1943, 48 per cent were connected with government agencies.

Of these special contributors, approximately 90 per cent were from the U. S. Department of Agriculture, which indicates the special support from governmental sources to which we have referred. Of those rural sociologists who come from the academic field, the largest proportion come from Cornell, Louisiana State University, Wisconsin, Iowa State, Michigan State, Oklahoma A. and M., and North Carolina State.

Volumes on Rural Sociology

The range and nature of rural sociological contributions may best be studied through both the contributed articles in *Rural Sociology* and textbooks in the field. Something of *Rural Sociology*'s articles will be presented in Chapter 23. Of the volumes in the general field of rural sociology the following have had priority in one way or another.

Year	Title	Author	Identification
1906	*An American Town*	J. M. Williams	Hobart
—	*The Country Town*	W. L. Anderson	Cornell
1912	*The Evolution of the Country Community*	W. H. Wilson	New York
1913	*Constructive Rural Sociology*	J. M. Gillette	North Dakota
1917	*Introduction to Rural Sociology*	P. L. Vogt	Wisconsin
1918	*Rural Life*	C. J. Galpin	Wisconsin
1922	*Rural Sociology*	J. M. Gillette	North Dakota
1925	*Our Rural Heritage*	J. M. Williams	Hobart

Year	Title	Author	Identification
1926	Sociology of Rural Life	H. B. Hawthorn	Morningside
—	The Expansion of Rural Life	J. M. Williams	Hobart
1928	Elements of Rural Sociology	N. L. Sims	Oberlin
1929	Principles of Rural-Urban Sociology	P. A. Sorokin (with Zimmerman)	Minnesota and Harvard
—	Rural Sociology	A. W. Hayes	Michigan State
1930	Introduction to Rural Sociology	C. R. Hoffer	Michigan State
1931	A Systematic Source Book in Rural Sociology	P. A. Sorokin, Zimmerman, Galpin	Minnesota
1932	Rural Sociology	R. R. Holmes	Michigan
1933	Rural Sociology	C. C. Taylor	Washington, D.C.
1939	A Better Rural Life	E. Schmiedeler	Catholic University
1940	Sociology of Rural Life	T. L. Smith	Florida
—	Rural Life in Progress	P. H. Landis	Michigan
1942	Rural Sociology and Rural Social Organization	D. Sanderson	Cornell
1946	A Study of Rural Society	J. H. Kolb, Edmund de S. Brunner	Wisconsin, Columbia
1949	Rural Life in the United States	C. Taylor and others	Washington, D.C.

Urban Sociology

American sociologists have done much less in the area of urban sociology than of rural sociology. Many of the approaches have been more nearly those of the study of the city or of urban problems than of urban society itself, or they have been launched on the level of human ecology in which little emphasis was placed upon the process of concentration, which is basic to urbanism. One of the reasons why Sorokin was urged to contribute a volume on rural-urban sociology to the "American Social Science Series" was to chart something of the transition from one to the other and to characterize each as basic special areas for sociological study. Sorokin and Zimmerman did this well in a cross section of rural-urban behavior, institutions, and culture in their *Principles of Rural-Urban Sociology* published in 1929, which was also a sort of summary of

their monumental three-volume *Source Book in Rural Sociology,* prepared jointly with Charles J. Galpin, then still at Washington. Among
the special rural-urban analyses are those on the rural and urban family,
rural-urban religious culture, rural-urban arts, rural-urban migration,
together with special studies of political and social attitudes, criminality
and immorality, and the role of the city in innovation.

The Chicago Group and Ecology

Although American sociologists have studied the problems of the
city or the city itself more than urban society, the University of Chicago
group, beginning with Robert E. Park and E. W. Burgess, and continuing on up to 1950 with Louis Wirth, although primarily featuring ecology, nevertheless included something of urbanism and planning among
their specialisms. Park and Burgess set their urban studies in the frame
of reference of human ecology. As a matter of fact, human ecology for
American sociologists had its rise primarily in their work. Their studies
of urban areas in the city of Chicago resulted in a large body of material
dealing with the areal distribution of social phenomena. Other surveys
of concrete social problems, of crime or delinquency or poverty have
resulted, in which the analysis of areal distribution of phenomena is
entitled ecological. It so happens, therefore, that many of the scores of
concrete studies in cities have been cast in the framework of ecological
distribution of phenomena. This led Edward Shils to report on pages
7-15 of his *The Present State of American Sociology* that American sociologists had made great strides with urban sociology. He made community study synonomous with urban sociology and cited the bulk of
his references from small communities.

Yet, these students of the city did seek to find out if the differences
in the phenomena that compose the framework of the rural and urban
worlds exert a direct or indirect influence on the bodies, health, vital
processes, minds, and psychology of the population living within each
of these worlds. The Sorokin-Zimmerman questioning asks: "Are they
correlated with some typical differences in the forms of social institutions, organizations, cultural and social processes given within each of
these worlds? If such correlations exist and are valid, why and how are
they possible?"

Other Volumes on Cities

Another sociological approach was that of Howard Woolston, in his *Metropolis*. He points out on page 5 that "Cities are the focal points of our civilization. In them are concentrated the forces that control modern life. All kinds of men, all sorts of interests, all forms of institutions are here brought together in intense competition. As the cities progressively absorb a larger proportion of the wealth and population of the whole country, it is obvious that the results of urban selection will in greater degree determine the type of national culture. The city is the modern sphinx that destroys those who cannot answer her demands, but which readily succumbs to the Oedipus who solves her riddle — the development of man."

Still a different angle was that of Earl E. Muntz in his *Urban Sociology*. "With the crowding of human beings into a limited space," he wrote on pages v and 3, "a new code of mores and customs [arises] in response to the need of this more highly artificialized environment of which the modern city is the extreme type. The community interest demands — in an unconscious, vague sort of way which might well be described as a restless urge toward better adaptation — that great enterprises in furthering the artificiality of the environment be carried out for the welfare of the group." Furthermore, "In the civilized world of today culture is constantly becoming more and more city-dominated. In such countries as those of western Europe and in the United States the entire social environment partakes predominantly of urban ways."

The Mumford Approach

Lewis Mumford, in his notable *Culture of Cities,* strikes a new note on the dangers of metropolitan culture. What he says might well be in the pattern of the "ideal type." He says on page 278: "the metropolitan regime opposes these domestic and civic functions: it subordinates life to organized destruction, and it must therefore regiment, limit, and constrict every exhibition of real life and culture. Result: the paralysis of all the higher activities of society; truth shorn or defaced to fit the needs of propaganda; the organs of cooperation stiffened into a reflex system of obedience: the order of the drill sergeant and the bureaucrat. Such a regime may reach unheard-of heights in external coordination and discipline, and those who endure it may make superb soldiers and juicy cannon fodder; but it is for the same reason deeply antagonistic to every valuable manifestation of life. Plainly, a civilization that terminates in a cult of barbarism has disintegrated as civilization; and the war-metropolis, as an expression of these institutions, is an anti-civilizing agent. . . ."

Another elemental factor, that of individuation vs. socialization is introduced by Gist and Halbert in their *Urban Society.* "With the advent of urbanism," they say, "has come an increasing individualization of behavior and a corresponding decline in group consciousness and group solidarity. Accelerated mobility, both social and physical, has weakened the ties that once bound so firmly the members of the family and the neighborhood. Social values and social attitudes in a changing urban environment have undergone a transformation. Fundamental changes have occurred in the mores, and with these changes has come a different conception of the roles of the family, the church, the school, even a different conception of the role of the individual in his group life. These trends caused by the operation of powerful forces peculiar to urban life have undermined the established social order. One result of this trend has been the decline of these groups as agents of social control. This unloosening of social controls without the effective substitution of other forms of control better adapted to an urban environment has left its toll in numerous instances of personal disorganization and demoralization." (Page 394)

Sometimes general students of contemporary sociology, more than sociologists, look at the city. Frederick C. Howe was one who wrote on *The Modern City and Its Problems* in contrast, let us say, to Maurice Davie, on *Problems of City Life.* On sample pages 1, 5, 367: "The great epochs of civilization have always coincided with a highly developed city life"; "The city is no longer an incident, it is the controlling force in modern civilization"; "Even today in the rural districts it does not progress beyond the simplest forms." And another borderline sociologist, Carol Aronovici, on page 175 of his *Housing the Masses,* "When the whole of this country becomes entirely urban, we shall have achieved full civilization; for urbanism is essentially a way of life — which brings into play all of the achievements in which human life becomes sacred."

Maurice Davie sets the frame of reference for his *Study of Urban Sociology,* which is also entitled *Problems of City Life,* when, on the first page of Chapter I, he points out that "the most striking character-istics of present-day civilization are industrialization and urbanization." His approach is that of sociological analysis when he follows his study of the modern social environment with inquiries into the courses and consequences of the growth of cities. He anticipated many trends toward zoning and planning and, strangely enough, after pronouncing the water supply system of New York city "one of the marvels of the modern world" anticipated the crisis of 1949–50 when he raised the question of whether the size of New York and the future size of cities everywhere might be limited by the problem of water.

The limited number of volumes by American sociologists on urban sociology stands in contrast to the overwhelming rule of urbanism in American life.

Year	Title	Author	Identification
1899	The Growth of Cities	A. F. Weber	Columbia, Ph.D.
1925	The City	R. E. Park, E. W. Burgess	Chicago
1926	Urban Community	E. W. Burgess	Chicago
1927	Readings in Urban Soci-ology	Scott Bedford	Chicago
1929	Principles of Rural-Urban Sociology	P. Sorokin, C. C. Zimmerman	Harvard Harvard
1930	Urban Sociology	N. Anderson, E. C. Lindeman	Chicago ·New School
1931	Sociology of City Life	N. Carpenter	Buffalo
1932	Problems of City Life	M. Davie	Yale
1933	Urban Society	N. P. Gist, L. A. Halbert	Missouri
—	Metropolitan Community	R. D. McKenzie	Michigan
1938	Metropolis	H. Woolston	Washington
—	Urban Sociology	E. Muntz	New York U.
—	The Culture of Cities	L. Mumford	New York City
1939	The City	S. A. Queen, L. F. Thomas	Washington University
1948	The Structure of the Met-ropolitan Community	D. J. Bogue	Miami University

The Rise of Industrial Sociology

Although perhaps sociologists almost universally recognize the industrial revolution as the incidence of modern society and its tensions and problems, very few earlier American sociologists sensed the place of industrial sociology in the total complex of society. Yet American sociologists expressed a great deal of pride when in 1919 Arthur J. Todd blazed a new trail, becoming Director of Industrial Relations for B. Kuppenheimer and Company. It is a long way from that to the 1940's when Herbert Blumer was Labor Consultant for more than one of the larger corporations. Todd, born in California in 1878, had received his Ph.D. degree at Yale in 1911, had taught at Illinois, and had been professor and head of the Department of Sociology at Pittsburgh and Minnesota and then at Northwestern University from 1921 to 1943. When he came back into the university field of sociology from his leaves at Kuppenheimer's, Todd was persuaded to write a volume for Odum's "American Social Science Series" under the title, *Industry and Society*. The frame of reference here was that industry constituted one of the six major American societal institutions along with the home and family, school and education, church and religion, state and government, community and association, and, therefore, was a major field of special sociology. If sociology was a study of the science of human relations, then *Industry and Society* was a special area for such study. Todd's book, which was well received in 1933, was, therefore, the first of the contributions of American sociologists to what later in the 1940's marks a trend toward industrial sociology. Todd included in his treatment the relationship of other institutions, education, government, the family, the community, and religion as well as the backgrounds of the industrial order. He anticipated something of the special emphasis upon human factors as well as the interpersonal relationships in industry and social security. The lack of a bibiliography at that time stamped Todd's book as a pioneer, somewhat as the comparison of his treatment with 1950 texts indicates the extraordinary changes that have taken place and are evident twenty years after Todd's book.

In this special area of industrial sociology, the sociologists have had to rely primarily on the economists and on special students of labor and industry as those who have studied the field from the vantage point of more than one social science. The earliest of the major sources of this sort might be featured as the sociological contribution of John R. Commons who taught sociology at Indiana and Oberlin before going to Wisconsin as professor of economics. His earlier special work on good will and administration foreshadowed this new management-labor strategy for both study and adjustment. A later example is the work of Bakke at Yale in a special focus on labor and management studies. There have been a number of special studies of labor in social relations by research students and specialists. Studies of changing structures of industrial New England communities at Yale, such as the one by Ellsworth, and studies of Southern mill villages by the North Carolina group, such as those by Herring and Rhyne, are examples of early empirical studies that might well have been followed up. The Social Science Research Council made several exploratory efforts through bibliographies, special conferences and leads by such industrialists as Filene, but produced no definitive work.

For the next era of 1950 it still remains true, however, that the bulk of source materials will be found in periodical literature from several areas and from many beginnings in many institutions, indicating more specialization in the field of industrial sociology. Among the sociologists and borderline sociologists who have produced books in the field are those listed below.

Year	Title	Author	Identification
1913	*Labor and Administration*	J. R. Commons	Wisconsin
1918	*History of Labor in the United States*	J. R. Commons, Associates	Wisconsin
—	*Readings in Industrial Society*	L. C. Marshall	Chicago
1919	*Industrial Goodwill*	J. R. Commons	Wisconsin
—	*Labor in the Changing World*	R. M. MacIver	Columbia
1929	*Human Factors in Cotton Culture*	R. B. Vance	North Carolina
—	*Welfare Work in Mill Villages*	Harriet Herring	North Carolina
1930	*Some Southern Cotton Mill Workers and Their Villages*	J. J. Rhyne	North Carolina
1933	*Industry and Society*	A. J. Todd	Northwestern

Year	Title	Author	Identification
1938	*The Industrial Worker*	T. N. Whitehead	Harvard
1940	*The Unemployed Worker*	E. W. Bakke	Yale
—	*Citizens without Work*	E. W. Bakke	Yale
1941	*Southern Industry and Regional Development*	Harriet Herring	North Carolina
—	*Life, Liberty and Property*	A. W. Jones	At large
1942	*The Future of Industrial Man*	P. Drucker	Harvard
—	*Millhands and Preachers*	L. Pope	Yale
1943	*Social Aspects of Industry*	S. H. Patterson	Pennsylvania
1945	*Human Leadership in Industry*	S. A. Lewisohn	At large
—	*The Social Problems of an Industrial Civilization*	Elton Mayo	Harvard
1946	*Industrial Relations and the Social Order*	W. E. Moore	Princeton
1949	*The Passing of the Mill Village*	Harriet Herring	North Carolina
—	*Workers Wanted*	E. W. Noland, E. W. Bakke	North Carolina, Yale

CHAPTER 18

Special Sociology: The Family, Marriage, Institutions

Perhaps no two fields of special sociology, representing the subscience approach to general sociology, will reflect so great a change from earlier American sociology to 1950 as those of the family and marriage, treated as one unit in this chapter, and race, ethnic groups, and intercultural relations discussed in Chapter 19. Both were considered by early sociologists primarily as units in the evolution and structure of society with certain relatively fixed assumptions concerning the organic nature of each. In each the changes are primarily of two sorts. One is in the change of status and role and the other is in the changing content of courses and texts in sociology courses in these fields. The family and marriage combination also serves as introductory to the study of social institutions, even as the early study of the rural community anticipated a sociology of the community as a basic institutional approach to the study of the total society.

Ernest R. Groves, writing about the marriage-family system and changes in the university and college curriculum, pointed out, in the preface of the second edition of his pioneer book of 1933, *Marriage,* published just ten years after the first edition, that ". . . at that time only one American university was giving credit courses in preparation for marriage. Now, such instruction is rapidly becoming a conventional part of the program of American colleges. It is doubtful whether there has ever been a more rapid development of a new type of instruction in our institutions of higher learning or, in its social meaning and prophecy, a more significant shift in academic attitude. . . . The present great interest in marriage courses in the colleges has largely resulted from the demand coming from young men and women that they be given, in the spirit of science, worthwhile instruction as a preparation for a life experience which they recognize as supremely important. This request from youth is, I believe, something unique in American academic history, and this fact is itself both a revelation of a fundamental change of social attitude and a promise of a more intelligent and responsible social policy toward marriage and parenthood."

In somewhat the same way with reference to *Social Problems of the Family,* Groves pointed out on page viii of *The American Family,* his second volume replacing the first: "The widespread and serious interest in problems of the American family in recent years is reflected in the instruction offered in colleges and universities by departments of sociology and home economics. The family as a social institution has been lifted out of emotional controversy and has become for serious men and women a subject deserving scientific interpretation and objective study in college courses. The development of instruction in the family and its allied problems has been extraordinarily rapid. So much has happened since the first text [on the family] was published, in 1927, that it is difficult to realize that the former book, when it first appeared, was a pioneer in presenting the family and its problems as a major subject for college instruction in sociology. Now a similar development appears to be taking place in courses dealing with marriage problems, as distinct from those of the family, and what has been perhaps the most emotional of all the topics of discussion within the field of social experience is passing over to the scientist for investigation and to the college instructor for systematic and practical exposition."

The Family as a Subscience of Sociology

With reference to the family, in which marriage and family relationships constitute an integral part, Carle Zimmerman appears to feel that much more change is still needed. For, he points out on page 810 of his *Family and Civilization,* published in 1948, "There is greater disparity between . . . the truth and theories taught in family sociology courses than exists in any other scientific field." Zimmerman's appeal is for the study of the family to become increasingly realistic in its sociological framework. This is in line with our assumptions of the role of special sociology in relation to sociological theory and its application to social problems. The family in this respect is one of the best areas for sociological study, although perhaps the majority of courses in colleges and universities have related more nearly to practical problems, and perhaps half of the source materials in books and periodical literature will be found in allied social science and "practical" sociology as described subsequently in Chapter 22. F. B. Turner of the Arizona State College has summarized an unpublished study of the "Contents of College Courses on the Family and Their Relation to Sociological Theory and Practical Problems," the results of which compare interestingly with Judson T. Landis' "The Teaching of Family and Marriage Courses by Sociologists and Home Economists," in *Social Forces* for March, 1946. Turner found that "forty-six or 28 per cent of the 165 courses studied in departments of sociology were classified as sociological; forty-three or 26 per cent were classified as combination courses; and eleven or 6 per cent were classified as hodge-podge." Turner concludes that the preference for sociological materials by the majority of sociologists may indicate preference for a sociological approach in courses more related to family experience as well as in courses more related to sociological theory. He sees in the dichotomy perhaps an index of promising cooperation between sociologists and social workers insofar as "practical" courses tend to move toward combination courses. This is indicated also by the tendency of sociologists to utilize the techniques of counseling and case work.

Three Main Periods of Writing

Reuben Hill has analyzed the writings on the family in three periods beginning about the same time that American sociology was growing up at Columbia and Chicago. Quoting from Hill's prepared outlines in 1950, the three periods are from 1895 to 1914; from 1915 to 1926; and from 1927 to 1950. Beginning with the twenty-year period of 1895–1914 sociological writings on the family clustered around three principal interests: (a) the origin and evolution of the family and its forms in primitive and historic society; (b) appraisal of the institutional changes in the family since the industrial revolution; (c) contemporary social problems and their control.

During the next decade, 1915–26, the interest of researchers shifted appreciably to the problems of the contemporary family; away from the question of the historical origins of the family. The mores of the family were first questioned seriously during this decade: (a) Quantitative studies of divorce, birth rates, family size showed increased appreciation of statistical methods; (b) The woman's problem and sex came into prominence with books, articles, and monographs appearing frequently on these topics; (c) The interactional approach was launched but really flourished only in the next twenty years.

During the last period, 1927–50, the basic orientation of family research has been toward explaining family disorganization, stressing difficulties in obtaining happiness in marriage, tensions in parent-child relations, and inadequacy in the performance of other family functions; with some noticeable shift in the last ten years to the question of success in marriage, to explain what holds marriage together.

With reference to the contrast in the range of treatment as well as the extraordinary body of literature dealing with so many aspects of the family, it is a long way from George Howard's day, when an article in *Cosmopolitan* damned him for the absurdities of advocating the teaching of anything about sex and marriage, to the present when all major departments of sociology offer courses on some aspects of the subject. This contrast may be vividly noted from the current range of courses offered by two samplings of present-day instruction, namely, Panunzio and Hill who represent the newer trend toward making the study of the family primarily sociological. Hill sets a wide range of subjects for adequate treatment, both in classroom teaching and in bibliographies on marriage and family relations. Among the major fields around which instruction and bibliographies may be built are child study, the care and hygiene of children, the management of children, consumption problems of the family, courtship, divorce, the family itself, the nature of family life, education for family life, heredity, marriage as a special study, marriage counseling, parent and child relationships, planned parenthood, pregnancy, sex, sex instruction, sexual ethics, women.

As an example of a university course planned as "basically scientific" and making an "institutional approach to the study of the marriage-family system in the western world," Contantine Panunzio sets up a twenty-point analysis indicating the essential range of content of the subject in its institutional frame of reference. These points include the pivotal position of the marriage-family system in the institutional order; the origin of marriage, premarital provisions and practices; the sources of mates; the number of spouses; other premarital provisions and practices; the marriage organization; the rights, duties, functions of marriage; the family organization; the procedures, rights, duties, and functions of the family. In the area of institutional and social processes there are hypotheses concerning origin; the development and recurrence of main types; the development of concepts concerning bond, function, telesis; the main association processes; the principal dissociative processes. Concerning the contemporary scene Panunzio treats factors affecting the modern marriage-family system: family size and structure in our time; personality and social problems of atomism, demographic effect, and attempted control; the future of the marriage-family institution; and theories concerning the relation of the marriage-family system to civilization.

Comparative Literature in the Marriage-Family System

From the annual bibliographies prepared by Ernest R. Groves and published in *Social Forces* in December, 1940, March, 1942, October, 1943, May, 1946, it is possible to catalogue several hundred volumes, under major headings that reflect the extraordinary range and variety of materials from all sources, including a majority by non-sociologists, which are still essential materials for the sociologists as they are in great contrast, on the one hand, to the earlier days in which there was relatively little literature in the field and, on the other, to the special limited catalogue of books *by sociologists* listed at the end of this chapter. One way of appraising the dynamics of this field of the family, marriage, parenthood education, and other vital aspects is to examine the flow of books that currently seek to meet the still-growing demand for knowledge and counseling. This literature is of great variety, ranging from the large number of new texts to the very detailed treatment of the specialized fields of marriage, sex, children, in contrast to the earlier periods. The other is the excellent illustration of interdisciplinary cooperation as discussed subsequently in Chapters 22, 24, and 25. A classification of books alone will illustrate vividly the general range and nature of treatment, and the interdependence of several disciplines. Classified into ten groups, the first and largest would include the general study of marriage and the family. Then follow the relatively specialized study of woman; the varied aspects of sex and love life; education and counseling; children and childhood with special reference to the family; special psychological aspects; divorce; parents and parenthood; happiness in marriage; economic aspects.

LEADING SOCIOLOGY AUTHORS AND TEXTS ON MARRIAGE AND THE FAMILY

Year	Title	Author	Identification
1904	A History of Matrimonial Institutions, 3 vols.	G. E. Howard	Nebraska
1906	The Family	Elsie Parsons	Barnard
1912	The Family in Its Sociological Aspects	J. Q. Dealey	Brown
1913	The Primitive Family	A. J. Todd	Northwestern
1914	Family and Society	J. M. Gillette	North Dakota
1917	Social History of the American Family, 3 vols.	A. W. Calhoun	Sterling
1923	The Family and Its Members	A. G. Spencer	Teachers College, Columbia
1926	Sex Freedom and Social Control	C. W. Margold	Michigan
1927	Family Disorganization	E. R. Mowrer	Chicago
—	Social Problems of the Family	E. R. Groves	North Carolina
1928	American Marriage and Family Relations	E. R. Groves, W. F. Ogburn	North Carolina, Chicago
1929	Modern Family	Ruth Reed	Mount Holyoke
1930	Introductory Study of the Family	Edgar Schmiedeler	St. Benedict's
1931	The Family	E. B. Reuter, J. R. Runner	Iowa
1932	Family and Its Relationships	E. R. Groves and others	North Carolina
—	Family Adjustment and Social Change	M. C. Elmer	Pittsburgh
1933	Marriage	E. R. Groves	North Carolina
1934	The Family	J. K. Folsom	Vassar
—	American Family	E. R. Groves	North Carolina
—	Readings in Marriage and the Family	E. R. Groves (with L. M. Brooks)	North Carolina
—	The Family	M. F. Nimkoff	Bucknell
1935	Personality and the Family	Hornell Hart, E. B. Hart	Duke
1936	Family Encounters the Depression	R. C. Angell	Michigan
1938	The Family	Willard Waller	Barnard
1939	Negro Family in the United States	E. F. Frazier	Howard

Year	Title	Author	Identification
—	*Marriage and the Family*	R. E. Baber	Pomona
—	*Predicting Success or Failure in Marriage*	E. W. Burgess (with Cottrell)	Chicago, Cornell
1940	*Family and Its Social Functions*	E. R. Groves	North Carolina
—	*Marriage and the Child*	J. H. S. Bossard	Pennsylvania
—	*Your Marriage*	N. E. Himes	Colgate
1942	*Marriage and the Family*	Howard Becker, Reuben Hill	Wisconsin North Carolina
—	*American Family Behavior*	Jessie Bernard	Penn State
—	*The Family*	Ruth S. Cavan	Rockford
1943	*The Family and Democratic Society*	J. K. Folsom	Vassar
1945	*Sociology of the Family*	M. C. Elmer	Pittsburgh
—	*The Family from Institution to Companionship*	E. W. Burgess, Harvey Locke	Chicago, Southern California
1946	*Your Marriage and Family Living*	P. H. Landis	Washington State
—	*Marriage and the Family*	Edgar Schmiedeler	St. Benedict's
—	*When You Marry*	E. M. Duvall,	National Conference,
		Reuben Hill	North Carolina
1947	*Successful Marriage*	Morris Fishbein (with Burgess)	New York, Chicago
—	*Marriage and the Family*	M. F. Nimkoff	Bucknell
—	*Family in American Culture*	F. E. Merrill (with A. G. Truxal)	Dartmouth
—	*Family and Civilization*	C. C. Zimmerman	Harvard
—	*Contemporary American Family*	E. R. Groves (with Gladys H. Groves)	North Carolina
1949	*Families under Stress*	Reuben Hill	North Carolina
1951	*The Family: A Dynamic Interpretation*	Reuben Hill	North Carolina

Sociology and Social Institutions

The family, universally considered as the basic social institution, may well serve as introductory to the study of other institutions, some of which are often treated in industrial sociology and in the sociology of religion. Although a number of sociologists who have written on the family have assumed the institutional frame of reference, the primary emphasis has been upon this particular special institution of the family-marriage arrangement rather than on the basic theory of institutions. In general, sociologists have not contributed in a large way to the study of institutions. Yet a considerable body of literature devoted to the history and concept of social institutions and their role in total societal behavior has gradually emerged from many studies. In the first place, many of the earlier sociologists in their texts devoted some special attention to institutions. Among the earlier sociologists whose "theory" comprehended institutional behavior were Giddings in his *Principles,* Ward in *Pure Sociology,* Small in *General Sociology,* Park and Burgess in *Introduction to the Science of Sociology,* Henderson in *Social Elements and Institutions,* Sumner in *Folkways,* Sumner-Keller-Davie in *Science of Society,* Cooley in *Social Organization,* Ellwood in *Psychology of Human Society.* Subsequently, American sociologists produced a number of volumes on *institutions.*

Florian Znaniecki in Chapter 8 of Gurvitch and Moore's *Twentieth Century Sociology* concludes that there is little apparent agreement in sociology on either terms or theories regarding social organization or institutions. There are survivals of Spencer's progressively invalidated theory of sociology as a science of societies as organized systems having specialized parts or institutions. There were a number of typologies that distinguished earlier societies with a solidarity of uniformity and later societies organized according to structural and functional differentiation. Institutional research expanded, although much was a philosophical rather than a scientific search for a unifying principle of human society. The French sociological school tended to follow realism; the American school, nominalism. Representative of the latter, first stressing biopsychological theories of institutions, were Small, Ward, and Sumner. Since these disintegrated, constructive analysis has gone forward by classifying institutions as systems or types of order as does Panunzio.

Concepts and Definitions of Institutions

I have pointed out on pages 241–42 of *Understanding Society* that if we seek a single system of or cluster of group organizations in human society that include more of the elements that go into the making of culture than any other, most students will immediately agree that what we call human institutions will come nearer to approximating such a measure than anything else. Institutions reflect the maturing ways of group behavior. So, too, if we search for a set of societal arrangements that more nearly reflect the sum total of cultural order in advanced society, we shall probably agree upon these same institutions. Since the major institutions, more nearly than anything else, represent the universal societal arrangements for order and control and are more nearly than anything else the buffer between the folk culture of the people and civilization, on the one hand, and between the individual and technology and change, on the other, the understanding of these institutions is basic to any final appraisal of culture and any understanding of society.

F. Stuart Chapin, on page 412 of his *Contemporary American Institutions,* reprinted in 1950, defines the term institution "to include economic, educational and political institutions as well as those of the church and the family that are more often identified with sociological study. Approached in this way, the term social institution emphasizes the basic factors common to social institutions of all sorts, and puts the stress on the organization or structure of the thing, rather than upon its specialized function. *A social institution is an organized pattern of the attitudes and behaviors of the members of a group that stands out as a configuration against the field of culture. It consists of segments of individuals' behaviors organized into a system, and not of whole individuals or groups. It consists chiefly of customs and traditions, but in some cases material culture traits are tied into the configuration through the process of conditioning."*

Panunzio's *Major Social Institutions* is itself a fair "introduction" to sociology in the sense that it seeks to describe the well-integrated clusters or systems of human activities that may be called major institutions. He enumerates eight such clusters of activities as the marital, familial, economic, educational, recreational, religious, scientific, and governmental. On page 27 he defines social institutions as "those systems of concepts, usages, associations, and instruments which, arising from the experiences of mankind, order and regulate the activities of human beings which are necessary to the satisfaction of basic needs. They are the basic systems of human activities having considerable permanence, universality, and interpenetrative independence."

Hertzler and His Social Institutions

Among the pioneer works by sociologists on institutions was J. O. Hertzler's *Social Institutions,* published in 1929 and republished again with revisions in 1946. Hertzler's trilogy consisting of *The History of Utopian Thought,* 1923; *Social Progress,* 1928; and *Social Institutions,* 1929, constituted one of the most valued contributions of the 1920's and remains one of the standard works in social theory. Hertzler was born in Jordan, Minnesota, in 1895, did graduate work at Harvard, 1915–17, and received his M.A. and Ph.D. degrees from the University of Wisconsin in 1919 and 1920, respectively. Following his assistant professorship at Wisconsin in 1923, he became professor of sociology at the University of Nebraska and since 1928 has been chairman of the department. Hertzler has been chairman of the executive committee and chairman of the committee on institutions and vice-president of the American Sociological Society and president of the Mid-West Regional Sociological Society. He has taught in summer sessions in a number of regions, including the Northeast, Far West, Southwest, and Middle States. In addition to the trilogy mentioned above Hertzler wrote *Social Thought of the Ancient Civilizations* and collaborated in a number of works including *Race and Culture Contacts* and *Man and Society.*

Hertzler's work on institutions is an excellent illustration of what we have termed "special sociology" as a subscience of general sociology. Thus he emphasizes the fact that his *Social Institutions* is in a sense an introduction to social theory as well as a detailed analytical treatment of social institutions. On pages 1–2, he reminds us that "we run into institutions in whatever approach we make to the task of societal analysis, whether it be by way of social structure, of social operation and function, of culture, of individual behavior, of processes and change, of control, of ecology, of values and norms, or even of social problems and pathology. Every feature of human society which comprehends the action of individuals in their contacts with their fellows represents or involves an institution. Their study may be said to focus one of the primary objectives of sociology as a science, which is the acquisition of a knowledge of the means of living and working together in groups.

Hence, one of the most important tasks of further conceptualization, classification and generalization in the field of theoretical sociology relates to social institutions."

Other Texts on Institutions

L. V. Ballard, in his *Social Institutions* published in 1936, devotes six chapters to the family; five to education; eight to the state; four to the community; five to the church and religion. Ballard omits "industry and work," pointing out, in his preface, that Todd in his *Industry and Society* has shown so well what the sociologist may contribute to that "basic social institution" that "restatement seemed unwise and unnecessary." Ballard's concept of the "species" of social institutions is set forth on page 3 of his *Social Institutions.* "Social institutions," he writes, "are sets of organized human relationships purposively established by the common will. As such, they may be regarded as the end-products of social processes, since it is their specific function to channelize the conduct of the group in action. Group behavior is thus not only charted and compassed but also held within the limits of what the group believes to be consistent with its well-being. Social institutions are forms of social organization, for the relationships they comprehend have been definitely systematized and approved. They are unique, however, in that they have been specifically designated as organizations which perform a group function so vital as to necessitate social sanction and social control."

Of the more recent treatises, Barnes' *Social Institutions* again conforms to his general mode of historical treatment in relation to social changes. Still later, in their *Sociological Analysis,* under the editorship of Robert Merton, and published in 1949, Wilson and Kolb devote Part Five to the institutional and associational structure of community and nation. The theoretical frame of reference is found in the institution as the organized core of values in the culture system. It is "this total system of ultimate values, hierarchically arranged goals, and normative rules of conduct which create social order and make it possible for the society to function as a unit and the individual to achieve his purpose." Continuing on pages 513–14, the term *institution* is used to designate the rules of society that define "social statuses and determine which members of the society will play the roles associated with the statuses. In addition, they organize the statuses and roles in relation to one another so that in general the purposes of the group and the individual can be realized simultaneously."

Social Theory and Special Books on Institutions

The institutions constitute the base for Talcott Parsons' structure-function sociological theory of social relationships. Institutions are characterized on page 276 of his *Essays in Sociological Theory* as "patterns governing behavior and social relationships which have become interwoven with a system of common moral sentiments which in turn define what one has a 'right to expect' of a person in a certain position." These sentiments apply to the definition of the statuses and roles of persons in the social system. Consequently, "The institutional structure of a social system then 'is the totality of morally sanctioned statuses and roles which regulate the relations of persons to one another through locating them in the structure and defining legitimate expectations of their attitude and behavior.'"

Finally, the further record of what sociologists have contributed to institutional theory, other than general theory and the special study of the family, community, and industry, may be explained as trends toward political sociology, educational sociology, and the sociology of religion, all of which appear to be assuming greater roles in the total picture, suggesting perhaps a return to the emphasis placed upon them by earlier sociologists and somewhat neglected by American sociologists in recent years.

The sequence of published books on institutions written primarily by sociologists might well be supplemented by a catalogue of a half-dozen others besides the family, as already given, to give representation to the special institutions: the church, the state, the school, the community, and industry.

SPECIAL VOLUMES BY SOCIOLOGISTS ON INSTITUTIONS

Year	Title	Author	Identification
1898	Social Elements and Institutions	C. R. Henderson	Chicago
1904	Matrimonial Institutions	G. E. Howard	Nebraska
1917	Community	R. M. MacIver	Columbia

Year	Title	Author	Identification
1924	Sociology and Political Theory	H. E. Barnes	Smith
—	Social Life and Institutions	J. K. Hart	Vanderbilt
1926	The Psychology of Social Institutions	C. H. Judd	Chicago
—	The Modern State	R. M. MacIver	Columbia
1927	Man's Quest for Social Guidance	H. W. Odum	North Carolina
1929	Social Institutions	J. O. Hertzler	Nebraska
1930	The U.S. Looks at Its Churches	Luther Fry	Rochester
1933	Research in Rural Institutions	John Black, ed.	Harvard
—	Industry and Society	A. J. Todd	Northwestern
—	Institutional Behavior	F. H. Allport	Syracuse
1935	Contemporary American Institutions	F. S. Chapin	Minnesota
1936	Social Institutions	L. V. Ballard	Beloit
1937	Structure of Social Action	T. Parsons	Harvard
1939	Major Social Institutions	C. Panunzio	U.C.L.A.
1941	The Integration of American Society	R. C. Angell	Michigan
1942	Social Institutions	H. E. Barnes	At large
1949	Sociological Analysis	Logan Wilson, W. L. Kolb	Tulane

CHAPTER 19

Special Sociology:
Race, Ethnic Groups, Folk

In the preceding chapter we associated race and ethnic groups with marriage and the family as areas in which there appear to be greater contrast between earlier and later American sociology than in almost any other area. And yet there is a big difference in the nature of the change in the two fields. In the case of the family and marriage, sociologists have not only published an increasingly larger number of volumes that have been widely distributed but have undertaken substantial research through which sociological theory has been formulated and in which marriage and the family have constituted a subsocial science within the larger field of sociology. More specifically, sociologists have multiplied many times the number of courses being taught in colleges and universities and have gone a long way toward directing the trends in this field, as described in the preceding chapter. All of this is reflected in contrast to the earlier contributions which featured primarily historical studies and the evolution of the family in cultural development.

In the case of race, ethnic minority groups, and intercultural relations, the changes have come about more nearly because of societal pressures in a changed world order. Numerous and notable volumes have been interested primarily in the setting of attitudes and moral imperatives in a democratic order, with special emphasis upon intercultural and international relations, and with still more specialized focus on the American Negro and minority ethnic groups. The majority of contributions have been made by non-sociologists in a sweeping tide of dynamic books, characterized by Louis Wirth in his introduction to E. Franklin Frazier's notable *The Negro in the United States,* as a "long list which includes many distinguished volumes since the publication of Myrdal's *An American Dilemma.*"

There has been practically no original empirical research in the field by American sociologists in the United States in the same way in which sociologists have explored other special areas of sociology. This does not mean that notable frontier work has not been done, especially by Charles S. Johnson and E. Franklin Frazier, among the sociologists, or by Herskovits, Dollard, Warner, Powdermaker, Meade, Benedict, and others of the cultural anthropologists in general writing and experimenting in methodology. Nor does this general appraisal overlook the distinct advances in the two newest, notable texts of 1948 and 1949, namely, *The Negro in the United States* by E. Franklin Frazier and *Negroes in American Society* by Maurice Davie. Nor does it overlook such contributions of sociologists to the field of intercultural relations as R. M. MacIver's *The More Perfect Union,* or Louis Wirth's efforts on behalf of the National Council of Race Relations and Guy B. Johnson's work with the Southern Regional Council, successor to the Commission on Interracial Cooperation, founded and directed by Will W. Alexander. Nor, again, does it underestimate the primary participation in the Myrdal study by Frazier, Stouffer, Wirth, Guy B. Johnson, alongside Myrdal, Sterner, Klineberg, and others. Nor still again does it forget the earlier distinctive work of Robert E. Park and E. B. Reuter alongside the multiple efforts of Charles S. Johnson and others.

World Societal Pressure and the Situation

What does seem evident, as may be seen from the abundant samplings of books listed below, is that the sweep of contemporary "sociological" literature in the field of race, ethnic minority groups, and especially the American Negro, is set within the framework of the larger societal situation with moral directives and political perspective, more than within the framework of sociological theory and social research. The contrast is carried much farther between the assumptions of the earlier sociologists, with their European backgrounds, that race was a relatively fixed and stable biological heritage, with sub-assumptions of superior and inferior capabilities, and those of contemporary intellectuals almost in complete contrast. The contemporary societal pressure in the new directives is in evidence from almost universal trends as indicated, let us say, by the special efforts of the United Nations and leading American scholars. Thus Louis Wirth commending Frazier's *The Negro in the United States* as an example of the study of the Negro in "a broad sociological perspective" in the process of interaction with the larger American society, stresses the fact that "The new position of the United

States in the World calls upon this Nation to exercise an unprecedented role of leadership. This fact gives to our own minority problems and to our method of dealing with them a world-wide symbolic significance. What we do here to build a democratic society will influence the faith in the democratic ideal throughout the world."

Another side of the picture is reflected in such memoranda from the United Nations as *The Main Types and Causes of Discrimination,* published in 1949 and distributed in early 1950. Thus, in contrast to earlier teachings, "contemporary science does not admit the concept of race as meaning a division of mankind into different parts, each of them characterized by a complex of special traits, both physical and mental. Anthropology has failed clearly to establish such a concept. There are, of course, differential characteristics of colour, of skin, form of head, nature and colour of hair, stature, etc. However, experience shows that such characteristics are not constantly correlated; on the contrary they are frequently intermingled. If all white men were dolichocephalic, blonde and tall, with blue eyes, wavy hair, and medium-sized noses; and all Negroes were brachicephalic and small, with black eyes and woolly hair; and all Indians were mesocephalic, medium-sized, with straight hair, hooked noses, etc., then it could be said that mankind, from a physical standpoint, is divided into distinct physical sectors. Indeed the contrary appears to be true; namely, that there is no necessary correlation among the various differential characteristics. As a matter of fact, the most extreme dolichocephalic and brachicephalic types are found among black-skinned men; among white people there are many with blue eyes, but still more with dark eyes; many have wavy hair but a great number have straight hair; dark-skinned people are among the tallest and the smallest human beings; and noses of all types appear in all colours of skin. Therefore, it is not possible to speak of races as distinct human groups, but only of differential characteristics as to the enumerated traits."

Even more definitive and recent is the declaration, prepared for UNESCO by a group characterized as "the world's most noted scientists, in the fields of biology, genetics, psychology, sociology, and anthropology," and reprinted in the July–August, 1950, *Courier,* and published in 1951 as *Statement of Race* by Ashley Montague. United States representatives, in addition to Robert C. Angell, who was acting head of

the Department of Social Sciences of UNESCO, under whose auspices
the report was made, were E. Franklin Frazier and Ashley Montague,
with criticisms by E. G. Conklin, Otto Klineberg, and others. The
Courier document is titled "Fallacies of Racism Exposed" and is offered
"as a weapon — and a practical weapon — to all men and women of
good will who are engaged in the good fight for human brotherhood."
The declaration, unanimously arrived at, confirms current ideologies
that, from "the known facts about human race, . . . scientists have
reached general agreement that mankind is one." The document has
been severely criticized by many population specialists on the ground
that no top scientists contributed to its contents.

It is possible to illustrate both the nature of work being done by
American sociologists and the great change in emphasis by citing here,
as elsewhere, cases of sociologists. For instance, at least a fourth of the
presidents of the American Sociological Society have featured *race* as a
major interest and, with the exception of Park, the fifteenth president,
all were in recent years. And of the ten who were active in this field,
only Hankins was not primarily interested in race relations. Wirth
headed the National Council on Race Relations; MacIver wrote on
intergroup relations; Frazier's main emphasis was on Negro dynamics;
Odum was head of the Southern Regional Council and member of the
Washington Committee on Segregation. Others were Park, Reuter,
Bogardus, Fairchild, Hankins, Parsons. Further illustrations may be
found in such academic groups as The American Association of University Women and Phi Beta Kappa. In 1948 the A.A.U.W. reported forty-
six programs from twenty-one states dealing with minority problems,
while Phi Beta Kappa made the civil rights program a cardinal emphasis.

Changing Concepts

Our main point here, however, is that in the total story of American
sociology this changed viewpoint and accelerated moral motivation
make this particular area rate a continuous review, for, if we seek to
analyze the whole field into its parts, it seems likely that in no aspect
of society has the sociological approach changed more than in that of
race, region, folk, and *intercultural relations.* In the writings of the
earlier sociologists each of these represented a sort of fixed value in the

total evolutionary structure of society. Race was an elemental and relatively unchangeable heritage. Regions were isolated areas of provincial cultures. The folk connoted primitive culture or simple unlettered peoples. Intercultural relations were bottomed in class, caste, nations, international levels, empire, on the one hand; or in academic appraisal of status and philanthropic intervention, on the other. These assumptions no longer predominate, not primarily because of what sociologists have done, but because of the sweep of social change. Here again, sociology, even as education and economics, follows the trend, seeking to effect adjustment more than it creates movements or directs evolution.

It is in the area of race and intercultural relations that sociology now approaches the study of society from a more radical, different viewpoint than it has ever done before. To the sociologist, race is no longer thought of primarily as an isolated biological phenomenon; rather, race is interpreted as a complex of societal conditioning in which culture is considered to be a more dominant factor than biology. I have pointed out in Chapter 7 of *Understanding Society,* on pages 137–38, that, although the "natural" and biological factors are inherent in and basic to the total situation, the major emphasis is on the societal fact of culture, not on the ethnological fact of "race." For this and other reasons that will appear, sociology may well consider substituting the term "folk" for "race" wherever the latter is used loosely in referring to ethnic groups. I have pointed out further that this sociological concept of race is of the utmost importance in understanding all the factors which constitute society as a whole. It is important in primitive societies and in the evolution of all cultures; but it is equally important in the many aspects of social conflict the world over. For the ratio of race-culture problems and folk conflict to all the problems of civilization is a large one; so large that there are many students who feel that, if satisfactory adjustment of racial-cultural conflict could be attained, world peace would be attainable and the great society would become a reality.

Insofar as sociology can present realistic conclusions based on all the evidence available, it explains race as a phenomenon that has been a constant factor in societal evolution. On page 138 will be found a verdict that *"race is the cumulative product of societal and physical forces working together over long periods of time."* Race and ethnic groups with their respective folk cultures reflect powerfully the universal question of why and how so many peoples in so many places, seeking to solve the same needs in similar environments, still differ in many aspects of culture; and why so many people under different environmental conditionings resemble each other. In order to understand the chasm of distance between the early and late concepts, it is necessary only to *look at* our current definition again. Instead of being inherently and organically different from each other, *races are assumed to be group products of the same universal human beings going through the same processes* and, therefore, reflecting both the processes and products of the physical, cultural, and folk-regional conditioning. This does not mean that sociology ignores the common meaning of the term "race" in popular situations in community life, in census enumerations, and in a thousand practical situations. It must necessarily diagnose and adapt to the situation. It means, rather, that back of these practical meanings and uses are certain fundamental scientific facts, rooted in society's folk-regional origin, which, when understood, help both to understand race and all society, and to point the way to the wiser direction of the future.

Earlier and Later Sociologists

We might follow up this story of great change by contrasting the nature of the treatment of race and minority groups as a subject in the scholarly work of America's early sociologists with that of later ones. Perhaps, of the earlier American sociologists, Lester F. Ward came nearer to the contemporary approach than any other. Felton Freeman, in an unpublished doctoral dissertation, has cited a number of earlier sociologists as quoted in the next few pages. He quotes Ward, on page 238 of his *Pure Sociology,* as taking the position that any apparent superiority of one race over another was a cultural product, through superiority of transmission and inheritance of achievement. Said Ward, on page 161 of his *Applied Sociology,* "A mass of evidence seems to be accumulating everywhere to show that social efficiency does not depend to any considerable degree upon race differences, certainly not when only civilized races are compared, and that it does depend almost entirely upon differences in their equipment."

Franklin H. Giddings' contribution to the theory of race was indirect. First, he stressed ethnic and kinship groups as basic to societal evolution. Next, as a sort of corollary of his concept of the consciousness of kind, he explained political groupings, classes, racial exclusiveness by pointing out, on page 18 of his *Principles,* that "within racial lines, the consciousness of kind underlies the more definite ethnical and political groupings, it is the basis of class distinctions, of innumerable forms of alliance, of rules of intercourse, and of peculiarities of policy. Our conduct toward those whom we feel to be most like ourselves is instinctively and rationally different from our conduct toward others, whom we believe to be less like ourselves." And again, on page 191 of his *Civilization and Society,* he held that race prejudice develops out of the racial struggle for existence and is originally an expression of fear, which is in line with the modern viewpoint. On the other hand, Giddings characterized the white supremacy cult as "Nordic foolishness."

William Graham Sumner, like Giddings, interpreted race indirectly. His sociological theory of race relations was through his concepts of the folkways and mores, which are fundamental to a large body of the literature of race. The chasm between races, he thought, is largely explainable by the character of the mores. He made little specific application of his theory to the analysis of race relations in the United States, but he points out that the results of federal coercion of the South "is not at all what the humanitarians hope and expected. The two races are separating more than ever before. The strongest point in the new code seems to be that any white man is boycotted and despised if he 'associates with Negroes.' Some are anxious and try to control. They take their stand on ethical views of what is going on. It is evidently impossible for anyone to interfere. We are like spectators at a great natural convulsion. The results will be such as the facts and the forces call for. We cannot foresee them. They do not depend on ethical views any more than the volcanic eruption on Martinique contained an ethical element. All the faiths, hopes, energies, and sacrifices of both whites and blacks are components in the new construction of folkways by which the two races will learn how to live together."

E. A. Ross, in his early works, followed the assumptions of racial differences of intellectual ability and held that the intellectually superior white race was obligated, in the interest of preserving and advancing civilization, to secure itself from submergence in an overwhelming flood of colored peoples. Exploitation, however, was nowhere justified. In his *Principles of Sociology,* page 66, Ross insisted that "However amiable the dogma that at bottom one race is as good as another, it is not only unscientific, but positively mischievous. . . . On the other hand, recognition of the unequal value of races is fraught with great danger. The conclusion of the whole matter is that what we know about the comparative value of races gives no people room for oppressing, dispossessing or exterminating any portion of mankind." His most explicit early statements on the American race problem will probably be found on page 384 of his *Foundations of Sociology*. Said he, "It is true that our average energy and character is lowered by the presence in the south of several millions of an inferior race." In *Seventy Years of It,* Ross modified his early views considerably, and minimized his emphasis on race differences. On page 126 he wrote, "My observations in the Far East, coming on top of a year of study, altered my sociological outlook in several ways: (1) I lost my faith in race as a key of social interpretation. I envisage a future when race differences will figure far less in men's minds than they do now." So, too, Ross in the preface to *Roads to Social Peace* proposed nothing for eliminating race conflict, because he was sure that he did not know the answers.

Cooley and Thomas on Racial Differences

Charles H. Cooley tended to feel that mental differences accompanied biological differences among races and that a biracial society tended to become a caste society, no matter how equal the social system might otherwise be. He analyzed southern race relations in caste terms. Cooley wrote, on page 279 of *Social Process,* that "in order to have a true race problem the races must mingle in considerable numbers in the same political system. And in that case the ruling factor is not the precise amount of strictly racial difference, as distinct from social, but the actual attitude of the groups toward each other. If this is such as to keep them separate and perhaps hostile, it matters little, as regards the social situation, whether it is based on sound ethnology or not." . . . "Permanent race groups in the same social system constitute race caste. It seems to me that this is beyond comparison the most urgent race question with which we have to deal; not only as regards its present aspects, but because it is likely to have a rapid growth." Cooley was prophetic in raising some questions. "It is doubtful how far it may be possible to reconcile race caste with the democracy and solidarity which are coming to be the ideals of modern nations. In the Southern United States the caste feeling is not diminishing, and while we hope that it is taking on forms more favorable to the cooperation of the races on a plane of fair play and mutual respect, the issue is somewhat in doubt. Certainly the present condition is not in harmony with democratic ideals, and its defenders can hardly claim more for it than that it makes the best of a difficult situation." To Cooley, race was no unitary phenomenon and could not be dealt with in isolation, but only in combination with social and historical conditions; as a gestalt comprehending much more than color, physiognomy, objective differences. The practical question here is not that of abolishing castes but of securing just and kindly relations between them, of reconciling the fact of caste with ideals of freedom and right. This is difficult but not evidently impossible, and a right spirit, together with a government firmly repressive of the lower passions of both races, should go far to achieve it.

In his "The Psychology of Race Prejudice," in *The American Journal of Sociology,* Vol. IX, page 611, W. I. Thomas posited a theory of race relations through an analysis of prejudice. Race prejudice, he thought, was organic, instinctive, a reaction to strange elements of the environment. And in his *Source Book of Social Origins,* page 156, he stated that "in race prejudice we see the . . . tendency to exalt the self and the group at the expense of outsiders." And again race prejudice is defined thus: "The instinct to belittle outsiders is perhaps at the bottom of our delusion that the white race has one order of mind and the black and yellow races have another." Thomas held that race relations in the South were caste relations, and the cultural backwardness of the Negro was due to social and mental isolation. On page 158, "If we . . . make due allowance for our instinctive tendency as a white group to disparage outsiders, and, on the other hand, for our tendency to confuse progress in culture and general intelligence with biological modification of the brain, we shall have to reduce very much our usual estimate of the difference in mental capacity between ourselves and the lower races, if we do not eliminate it altogether. . . ." Thomas concluded that, although organic in basis, race prejudice could be dissipated through the development of sympathetic relationships in human association.

Ellwood and Weatherly before Hankins

Charles A. Ellwood wrote about many of the current stereotypes of "racial temperament" — Negro shiftlessness and sensuality, Negro lack of adaptability to white cultural standards — and credited the advancement that the Negro had attained to the infiltration of white blood. To Ellwood the problem was "how a relatively large mass of people, inferior in culture and perhaps also inferior in nature, can be adjusted relatively to the civilization of a people much their superior in culture; how the industrially inefficient nature man can be made over into the industrially efficient civilized man." On page 217 of his *Sociology and Social Problems,* he followed the older pattern, saying that "It must be stated here that, as Booker Washington has urged, the Negro problem is largely of an industrial nature. It is the unsatisfactoriness of the Negro as a worker, as a producing agent, that gives rise largely to the friction between the two races. . . . When the Negro becomes an efficient producer and a property owner the Negro problem will be practically solved." And he followed the prevailing sentiment that those Negroes who did not agree with this solution of the problem by industrial education were "misled by unwise leaders." But Ellwood also recognized what was later to transcend the narrower view, that is, "while the Negro problem is . . . primarily a question of industrial training and adjustment of the Negro, from another point of view it is a moral question which can never be solved until the superior race comes to take a right attitude toward the inferior race, namely, the attitude of service."

Ulysses G. Weatherly was chiefly concerned with race mixture and wrote about "race and marriage" in *The American Journal of Sociology,* Vol. XV. He held that there was a natural organic aversion, in the mental processes, to intermarriage, and that this aversion existed to preserve race purity as a necessary condition of social development. Further, on page 449, he concluded that the result of such free crossing as has taken place in Latin America is unfortunate, for the hybrid populations are lacking in the stability and social capacity of Europeans and natives alike. With regard to ways and means of dealing with race problems, Weatherly said that the discussion of race has been beclouded by the assumption that accommodation necessarily involves physical amalgamation. It is true that miscegenation is the final step in social integration, but short of that there are other modes of social peace which may, as rough and provisional working arrangements, tide over the acute periods of ethnic antagonism. Race autonomy within a given political unit is one. Another is the 'group economy' plan which has been proposed and partially developed in the southern American states.

The Hankins Book the First

Frank H. Hankins, in the *Racial Basis of Civilization,* was the first to contribute a special volume to this special area. Felton Freeman, in the dissertation referred to previously, quotes Hankins as writing of race as "an ensemble of physical traits, each more or less variable, all inherited as an ensemble within their limits of variation, and sufficiently distinctive when taken together to mark off their possessors from other members of the human species. . . . One cannot . . . explain the general backwardness of the Negro by the lack of social opportunity. Had he been sufficiently gifted he would have made his opportunity somewhere in the midst of the existing cultural milieu. The cause is deeper and must be sought in differences of body and brain structure."

In some ways, a part of Hankins' diagnosis is similar to Park's making race prejudice synonomous with the *folkways* and *mores.* "The assumption of racial superiority is a natural expression of group consciousness; it is a characteristic expression of that solidarity which springs from man's innate gregariousness; and it serves the magnificent purposes of elevating the ego and of sharpening to a fighting edge attitudes of heroic devotion. It has played and will continue to play a leading part in the group struggle for existence and power, and however fallacious be its foundations some form of it seems essential for group survival."

Social Distance and Race

Emory S. Bogardus was one of the most prolific of the earlier sociologists by way of scores of articles in *Sociology and Social Research* in which he approached his many studies of race through social distance. Yet perhaps Bogardus' viewpoint on race is probably best represented by his *Immigration and Race Attitudes* in which, on page 219, he writes that "Racial problems are personality problems. They originate in personal experiences, either direct or derivative. They begin and end in social situations with persons the main actors. They involve changes in the racial attitudes of persons, reversals in these attitudes, development of new or augmentations of old attitudes. Adjustments of racial problems imply changes in personal attitudes. The reduction of these problems depends upon an intensive understanding of the disturbing centers of all human attitudes: namely, personality clashes."

Edward B. Reuter was the next after Hankins to produce a text, and even more than Hankins, was one of the few American sociologists to make race study something of a specialty. Reuter saw the American race problem as a practical problem of the social order, but his main interest was scientific rather than ameliorative. In the United States, he estimated that the dilemma was "the problem of maintaining some sort of harmonious and mutually satisfactory working relations between the two racial groups in the population." He wrote on page 18 of *The American Race Problem,* "But the student of social life is little concerned with the problem in the form in which it interests the reformer and the administrator except as this form of the problem throws light upon the facts and processes of the human social order which he is concerned to understand. His interest is the scientific and only ultimately practical one: the effort to discover the mechanisms, the causal relations, in social phenomena and so provide a basis for social and administrative technique."

Park's Sociology of Race

Like Reuter, Robert E. Park, after his retirement, became visiting professor at Fisk and, as it were, retraced his course in which his main interest sometimes appeared to be that of the Negro. In his earlier *Introduction to the Science of Sociology,* Park dealt at some length with the nature of race prejudice and its understanding as fundamental to future progress in creating a mutual *modus vivendi* of race relations. In 1950, *Race and Culture* was published as a means of featuring all of Park's periodical contributions in this field. In the former, page 620, Park wrote: "It has been assumed that the prejudice which blinds the people of one race to the virtues of another and leads them to exaggerate the other's faults is in the nature of a misunderstanding which further knowledge will dispel. This is so far from true that it would be more exact to say that our racial misunderstandings are merely the expression of our racial antipathies. Behind these antipathies are deep-seated, vital, and instinctive impulses. Racial antipathies represent the collision of invisible forces, the clash of interests, dimly felt but not clearly perceived. They are present in every situation where the fundamental interests of races and peoples are not yet regulated by some law, custom, or any other *modus vivendi* which commands the assent and the mutual support of both parties. We hate people because we fear them, because our interests, as we understand them at any rate, run counter to theirs." That this is true may well be proved by observing the increase in race conflict and prejudice in the wake of new world communications. Nor did Park believe that race prejudice was morally motivated. He wrote, "Race prejudice may be regarded as a spontaneous, more or less instinctive, defense reaction, the practical effect of which is to restrict free competition between races. Its importance as a social function is due to the fact that free competition, particularly between people with different standards of living, seems to be, if not the original source, at least the stimulus to which race prejudice is the response." But also, "Race prejudice is due to, or is in some sense dependent upon, race competition. . . ."

Textbooks on Race and the Negro

Another volume used as text and written by an American sociologist was Donald Young's *American Minority Peoples,* first published in 1932 and subsequently revised. As indicated in the introduction, Young's purpose was "to give new perspective to academic discussions of American race relations as well as to summarize and interpret the outstanding facts in the history and present condition of our minority peoples. . . . The view here presented is that the problems and principles of race relations are remarkably similar, regardless of what groups are involved; and that only by an integrated study of all minority peoples in the United States can a real understanding and sociological analysis of the involved social phenomena be achieved."

The two early books most commonly used as texts in American sociology classes on race relations were Charles S. Johnson's *The Negro in American Civilization,* published in 1930, and *Race Relations* by Charles S. Johnson and W. D. Weatherford, published in 1934. Johnson also wrote many other books and articles, including *The Negro in Chi-*

cago, 1922, co-author; *The Collapse of Cotton Tenancy*, 1935, co-author; *Economic Status of the Negro*, 1933; *Shadow of the Plantation*, 1934; *Preface to Racial Understanding*, 1936; *The Negro College Graduate*, 1936; *Growing up in the Black Belt*, 1941; *Patterns of Negro Segregation*, 1943; *To Stem This Tide*, 1943; *Education, the Cultural Process*, 1944; *Into the Main Stream*, 1948.

Changes in Views and Methods

There are several ways of indicating the radical changes in the sociologists' study and teaching concerning race in the United States. First might be the fact that even to suggest the use of the earlier textbooks in contemporary teaching appears absurd. Another is to note how changing approaches came about and to contrast them with the earlier ones. Still another is to note the present literature and trends as well as to examine the two new notable texts of Frazier and Davie. Olive Stone, writing from the North Carolina group workshops as early as the late 1930's but now on the faculty of the University of California at Los Angeles, thought that the conclusion seems justified that only recently has sociology been able to make either a distinctive or a creditable contribution to the study of race, and this is still in a very limited way. Some of the reasons for this belated performance in a field so definitely sociological are to be found in limitations within sociology itself and in limitations outside of its control. Both types of handicaps seem to have stemmed from fallacies or to have been the consequence of incomplete development. Dr. Stone calls attention to the fact that sociology naturally built the earlier foundation of its approaches and methods of race study upon data and procedures in biology, psychology, and anthropology. Among the fallacious views of these disciplines that she enumerates as later taken over by sociology were: (a) the acceptance of "race" as a scientific term in the zoological sense, (b) the belief in polygenesis and its implications for racial ranking, (c) the tenet that cultural divisions of mankind grew out of physical and mental differences, (d) the concept of racial superiority and its correlation with so-called progress or civilization, (e) the confusion of native intelligence with knowledge, (f) confidence in the instinctual basis of behavior, and (g) the ethnocentric view of individual differences.

Contemporary sociology of 1950, of course, faces the same danger of

building upon fallacies. For here, as in the case of the other social sciences, as well as may be true in philosophy and literature, fallacies may
arise from unwillingness or inability to secure adequate factual data and
to arrive inductively at conclusions from the data, or to face the facts in
the light of the complexity of situations and the sensitivity of peoples. In
the past, prejudices, provincialisms, cultural compulsion, including economic self-interest and tradition, were responsible for much of the unwillingness to examine the question of race objectively and realistically.
The inability to do so was partly attributable to the inaccuracy and inadequacy of tools for measurement and interpretation and to lack of
skill. Such scientific techniques as biometrics, anthropometry, stratig-
raphy, psychoanalysis, mental measurement, linguistics, statistics, etc.,
were either unborn or imperfectly developed. After techniques became
refined, however, skill in the use of them was lacking. For xample,
anthropometric findings were employed illustratively rather than inductively. Philology was harnessed to Aryanism. Intelligence tests, in
the hands of amateurs, became endowed with a potency and finality
never attributed to them by their inventors. Tests, language and non-
language, were taken over bodily from one culture and population and
applied without benefit of rapport between examiner and examined to
an utterly unlike milieu and demotic group.

The Changing Approach of Sociologists

In the first part of this chapter we suggested that the extraordinary
contrast between the earlier sociological approaches and the contemporary society of 1950 was due more to the societal pressures stemming
from the sweep of change and technology than to the creative work
and initiative of the sociologists themselves. This is undoubtedly true
in the same way that the great changes in regional social structure in
race relations will come about more quickly and more surely because
of the powerful world changes than because of regional initiative. Yet
in both cases much of the change and much of the new theoretical framework have grown out of "the day's work." One example of this is in
the case of Robert E. Park. E. Franklin Frazier writes about the Park
evolution in a recent issue of the *American Sociological Review*. In
the June, 1947, issue, writing on "Sociological Theory and Race Relations," Frazier traces Park's changing approach from the state to the

dynamic. On page 270, he writes that "Park's sociological theory was originally a static theory of race relations. His theory not only contained the fatalism inherent in Sumner's concept of the mores. His theory was originally based upon the assumption that the races could not mix or mingle freely. This is apparent even in his concept of the biracial organization. But as Park saw the changes which were occurring in the United States and other parts of the world, he modified his theory to take into account these changes. His latest theory of race relations in the modern world took into account the dynamic elements in the situation."

Three Approaches

It remains now to record something of three other sources of studies in the field of race and ethnic minority groups. Although these will not comprehend the many isolated studies of special culture groups among America's more than fifty national kinship groupings, they will have to suffice for this part of our story at this time. The three sources are from the groups that study race and ethnic groups as *folk*; those that feature the intercultural approach; and the vast popular literature on race, civil liberties, minorities, and especially Negro-white relationships. In general there are two groups within each of the three classifications.

The first group that may be said to study the folk culture aspects may be said to be the cultural anthropologists such as Redfield, Mead, Benedict, Malinowski. Redfield's *Folk Culture of Yucatan*, Murdock's *Social Structure*, and Kroeber's *Social Organization* are notable examples. Another considerable source is that of special studies of the Jewish culture as folk culture. In addition to the North Carolina group, which studies the Jewish culture as *Folk Society within the State Society*, there is a rapidly growing literature on the history and nature of Jewish culture, of which samplings include Samuel S. Cotton's *Judaism: A Way of Life*, 1948; A. I. Gordon's *Jews in Transition*, 1949; Trude Weiss-Rosmarin's *Jewish Survival*, 1950; Solomon Grayzel's *A History of the Jews*, 1947; Louis Finkelstein's *The Jews: Their History, Culture, and Religion*, 1950.

Samplings of the group undertaking to study race as folk at North Carolina during the last three decades will include Milton Metfessel's *Phonophotography in Folk Music*, Guy B. Johnson's *Folk Culture on*

St. Helena Island, Newbell N. Puckett's *Folk Beliefs of the Southern Negro*, T. J. Woofter's *Black Yeomanry: Life on St. Helena Island*; Guion Griffis Johnson's *Social History of the Sea Islands*; Guy B. Johnson's *John Henry: Tracking Down a Negro Legend*; Howard W. Odum's trilogy, *Rainbow Round My Shoulder*, *Wings on My Feet*, *Cold Blue Moon*; Howard W. Odum and Guy B. Johnson's *The Negro and His Songs* and *Negro Workaday Songs*.

One of the most important trends in this field is that of intergroup and intercultural relations. This in turn has two main segments. One may be said to be represented by MacIver's recent work on intergroup activities, such as *The More Perfect Union, Segregation in National Affairs*, and *The Ramparts We Guard*, and Kurt Lewin's *Resolving Social Conflicts*, as representative of many workshops and conferences on human relations. Also there would be classified Bogardus' *Cultural Pluralism and Acculturation* as found in his studies of social distance and epitomized on pages 126–28 of *Sociology and Social Research* for November–December, 1949. The other segment of intergroup relations study is that of intercultural education, which is a separate study of its own. This is typified perhaps best in Ronald Lippett's 1949 *Training in Community Relations*, which is a complete description of the workshop as *a research exploration toward new group skills*, an outgrowth of the research center for group dynamics as founded by Kurt Lewin. The workshops are sponsored by various groups including the American Jewish Congress and many interracial groups, with increasing cooperation by sociologists in colleges and universities.

Non-sociological Works

As in our chapters treating other special areas of sociology, we are, for the purposes of this book, primarily recording the work of American sociologists. Yet in many fields, as we have pointed out in Chapters 2, 15, and 22, much of sociology's most valuable materials must be found in the work of non-sociologists. How large this segment is in American sociology will appear from a study of Chapter 22. In the fieild of race and race relations and of ethnic minority groups these materials are mainly of two sorts. One source is the workshops of the allied social sciences, such as psychology, cultural anthropology, economics, political science, education. The other source is the workshops of intercultural education, international relations, and human relations, as well as that large segment that comes from popular action agencies, special ethnic groups, and many study groups and publishers of literature in this field. And one of the largest segments of all in the popular field is that of fiction. The aggregate of all these, of course, constitutes a powerful segment of the literature of the subject.

We present, therefore, a sort of running sample of an extraordinary bibliography to include Raymond Logan's *What the Negro Wants*; Gunnar Myrdal's *An American Dilemma*; Clayton Powell's *Marching Blacks* and *Riots and Ruins*; Melville Herskovits' *The Myth of the Negro Past*; Hortense Powdermaker's *After Freedom*; Richard Sterner's *The Negro's Share*; Booker T. Washington's *The Story of the Negro* and *Up from Slavery*; Carter Woodson's *Historical Studies*; Brawley's *The Negro Genius;* Otto Klineberg's *Race Differences and Characteristics of the American Negro;* Alain Locke's *The New Negro*; Davis and Dollard's *Children of Bondage*; Charles Wesley's *Negro Labor in the United States*; Robert Weaver's *Negro Labor*; Margaret Halsey's *Color Blind*; Buel Gallagher's *Color and Conscience*; John La Farge's *The Race Question and the Negro;* Carey McWilliams' *Brothers under the Skin;* Mary White Ovington's *The Walls of Jericho Came Tumbling Down*; Lillian Smith's *Killers of the Dream*; the Roses' *America Divided*; James Weldon Johnson's *Along This Way* and *The Autobiography of an Ex-colored Man*; Spencer Logan's *A Negro's Faith in America*; Robert Moton's *What the Negro Thinks*; Roi Ottley's *New World A-Coming*; Richard Wright's *Black Boy*; Edwin Embree's *Brown Americans* and *Thirteen against the Gods*; Walter White's *Lost Boundaries* and *A Man Called White;* Sumner Dahlberg's *Race, Reason, and Rubbish*; Redding Saunders' *No Day of Triumph*; Anna Bontemp's *The Story of the Negro*; Franz Boas' *The Mind of Primitive Man; Race, Language and Culture; Race and Democratic Society;* Ashley Montague's *Statement on Race;* and others listed in Chapter 22 and elsewhere.

Finally, as in other chapters will be listed the principal volumes by American sociologists arranged in chronological order.

Year	Title	Author	Identification
1896	*The Supression of the African Slave Trade*	W. E. B. DuBois	Atlanta

Year	Title	Author	Identification
1896	Mortality among Negroes in Cities	W. E. B. DuBois	Atlanta
1899	The Philadelphia Negro	W. E. B. DuBois	Atlanta
—	The Negro in Business	W. E. B. DuBois	Atlanta
—	The Negro in the Black Belt	W. E. B. DuBois	Atlanta
1901	The Negro Common School	W. E. B. DuBois	Atlanta
1902	The Negro Artisan	W. E. B. DuBois	Atlanta
1903	The Negro Problem	W. E. B. DuBois	Atlanta
—	The Negro Church	W. E. B. DuBois	Atlanta
—	The Souls of Black Folk	W. E. B. DuBois	Atlanta
1907	Economic Cooperation among Negro Americans	W. E. B. DuBois	Atlanta
1908	The Negro American Family	W. E. B. DuBois	Atlanta
—	Race Adjustment	Kelly Miller	Howard
1909	Religious Folk Songs and Poetry of the Southern Negroes	H. W. Odum	Clark, Ph.D.
1910	Social and Mental Traits of the Negro	H. W. Odum	Columbia, Ph.D.
—	Negro Life in the South	W. D. Weatherford	Vanderbilt
1912	The Negro at Work in New York City	G. E. Haynes	New York
1914	Race Orthodoxy in the South	T. P. Bailey	Mississippi
1918	The Mulatto in the United States	E. B. Reuter	Iowa
1920	Negro Migration	T. J. Woofter, Jr.	Columbia, Ph.D.
—	Dark Water	W. E. B. DuBois	Atlanta
1922	The Negro in Chicago	C. S. Johnson, and Others	Chicago Commission
1924	The Negro from Africa to America	W. D. Weatherford	Vanderbilt
—	Races, Nations and Classes	H. A. Miller	Ohio
1925	The Negro and His Songs	H. W. Odum, G. B. Johnson	North Carolina
1926	Folk Beliefs of the Southern Negro	N. N. Puckett	Western Reserve

Year	Title	Author	Identification
—	The Negro in American Life	Jerome Dowd	Oklahoma
—	Negro Workaday Songs	H. W. Odum, G. B. Johnson	North Carolina
—	Racial Basis of Civilization	F. H. Hankins	Smith
1927	The American Race Problem	E. B. Reuter	Iowa
1928	Rainbow Round My Shoulder	H. W. Odum	North Carolina
—	Negro Problems in Cities	T. J. Woofter, Jr.	North Carolina
—	The American Negro	M. J. Herskovits	Northwestern
1929	John Henry	G. B. Johnson	North Carolina
—	Wings on My Feet	H. W. Odum	North Carolina
1930	The Negro Church in Rural Virginia	C. H. Hamilton	North Carolina State
—	Folk Culture on St. Helena Island	G. B. Johnson	North Carolina
—	Black Yeomanry	T. J. Woofter, Jr.	North Carolina
1931	Race Mixture	E. B. Reuter	Iowa
—	The Black Worker	S. D. Spero, A. L. Harris	Columbia
—	Cold Blue Moon	H. W. Odum	North Carolina
1932	Sea Island to City	C. V. Kiser	Columbia, Ph.D.
—	American Minority Peoples	Donald Young	University of Pennsylvania
—	The Negro Family in Chicago	E. F. Frazier	Howard
1933	Races and Ethnic Groups in American Life	T. J. Woofter, Jr.	North Carolina
—	Negro Child Welfare in North Carolina	W. B. Sanders	North Carolina
—	The Tragedy of Lynching	A. F. Raper	North Carolina
1934	The Education of the Negro in the American Social Order	H. M. Bond	Chicago
—	Race Relations	C. S. Johnson, W. D. Weatherford	Fisk Vanderbilt
—	The Shadow of the Plantation	C. S. Johnson	Fisk
1935	The Negro Community of Baltimore	I. de A. Reid	Atlanta

Year	Title	Author	Identification
1935	Black Reconstruction	W. E. B. DuBois	Atlanta
1936	Preface to Peasantry	A. F. Raper	North Carolina
—	Landlord and Tenant	T. J. Woofter, Jr.	Washington, D.C.
—	A Preface to Racial Understanding	C. S. Johnson	Fisk
1937	Caste and Class in a Southern Town	John Dollard	Yale
—	The Etiquette of Race Relations in the South	B. W. Doyle	Chicago
1938	The Negro College Graduate	C. S. Johnson	Fisk
—	The American Race Problem	E. B. Reuter	Iowa
1939	The Negro Family in the United States	E. F. Frazier	Howard
—	Race Relations and the Race Problem	E. T. Thompson, ed.	Duke
—	The Negro Immigrant	I. de A. Reid	Atlanta
1940	Dusk of Dawn	W. E. B. DuBois	Atlanta
1941	Growing Up in the Black Belt	C. S. Johnson	Fisk
—	The Myth of the Negro Past	M. J. Herskovits	Northwestern
—	Sharecroppers All	A. F. Raper, I. de A. Reid	North Carolina, Atlanta
1942	Color, Class and Personality	R. L. Sutherland	Texas
1943	Patterns of Segregation	C. S. Johnson	Fisk
—	Race and Rumors of Race	H. W. Odum	North Carolina
—	To Stem This Tide	C. S. Johnson	Fisk
—	Race Riot	A. M. Lee, N. D. Humphrey	Wayne
1945	Black Metropolis	St. C. Drake, and H. R. Cayton	Chicago
—	Color and Democracy	W. E. B. DuBois	Atlanta
—	One America	F. J. Brown, J. S. Rouček	New York, Hofstra
1946	Negro Labor	R. C. Weaver	New York
—	Into the Main Stream	C. S. Johnson	Fisk
1947	Race and Nationality	H. P. Fairchild	New York
—	The Reduction of Intergroup Tensions	R. M. Williams, Jr.	Cornell

Year	*Title*	*Author*	*Identification*
1948	*Caste, Class, and Race*	O. C. Cox	Tuskegee
—	*The Negro Ghetto*	R. C. Weaver	New York
—	*The Negro Family in the United States*	E. F. Frazier	Howard
—	*The More Perfect Union*	R. M. MacIver	Columbia
1949	*Race and Region*	E. T. Thompson	Duke
—	*Negroes in American Society*	M. R. Davie	Yale
1950	*Race and Culture*	R. E. Park	Fisk and Chicago

CHAPTER 20

Special Sociology: Population, Demography, Ecology, Regionalism

This chapter may well illustrate two of the aspects of sociology to which reference has often been made, namely, its nature and development as influenced by the American setting and the interdisciplinary nature of both methods and content. This is treated conceptually in Chapters 24 and 25 in reference to American and European sociology and the sociology of knowledge. The scientific study of population and the consequent advance of demography can be fully explained only in the light of American developments; while both ecology and regionalism had their genesis in American settings. So, too, each of the three specialisms finds its most definitive results in the interdisciplinary cooperation of more than one of the social sciences. Yet, in each of the fields there may be identified two special credit lines for sociology more than for any other social science, namely, considerable new work has been done adequate enough to account for definition and recording; and sociologists have done more than others in both the amount and definitiveness of contributions. In one way, therefore, our task is a relatively simple one of mere reference to what has been done, leaving further study to the exploration of the interdisciplinary fields. In another way, however, the task is more difficult and important, in that these areas of special sociology offer excellent examples again for the description and definition of American sociology in terms of what sociologists do. And finally, it may be in these three areas that, in the immediate future, much will be done by American sociologists as the next fifty years open up unprecedented opportunities.

First, there is the study of population. We have already called attention, in Chapter 12, to Rupert Vance's challenge concerning the possibilities that population, as a specialty, might hold as a segment of general sociology, adequately related to a valid conception of a sociology more matured in general and more concretely scientific. Vance has specified the field of population as one segment of general sociology to be followed, as far as it could reasonably be carried, as something that would appeal to him greatly. What has developed, however, has been the growth of demography as it has been "taught in an appreciable and increasing proportion of the colleges and universities, but usually as only one or two courses in a sociology, or economics, or a biology department," as estimated in "Population Studies in the United States," pages 254–56 of the *Population Index* for October, 1946. It is assumed that the central core of demography "is the study of population size, distribution, migration, and rates of growth." This is in some contrast to the Vance sociological specialization that would concentrate on the population as a human group in the process of change which furnishes the basic material out of which the whole of human affairs is fabricated. In such a subscience of sociology, population would be at the core of studies of urbanism, with the process of concentration and aggregation; of rural society and its changing structures; of migration and mobility; of race and ethnic groups; of world community, and international problems; as well as at the center of the more concrete situations in family, community, personality, and the larger areas of ecology and regionalism.

Turning again to the story of demography as the study of population, it may be noted that the relatively rapid and unique rise of demography has been due to two important changes, namely, the changing structure of American society and the rapid developments in methods of research and, in particular, of governmental support. This American background has been clearly described on pages 254–56 of the October, 1946, *Population Index,* as cited above. "The passing of free land," it is pointed out, together with "the First World War, and the urgency of the immigration problem had quickened interest in population by the beginning of the 'twenties. At the same time governmental functioning at the national, state, and local levels required ever more comprehensive and accurate data on the size and composition of the population, its spatial distribution, and its balance of births and deaths. This increasing availability of census and vital statistics data occurred during a period of rapid advance in statistical techniques and methods. The practical cessation of immigration, rapid urbanization, the downward trend of the birth rate, and the demographic problems of the great depression would have stimulated a prolific literature on population under any circumstances. With improved data, new techniques, and the precise measurement of the demographic transition that was occurring, demography tended to become science rather than literature."

Two special situations involved have been the interdisciplinary approach and the unique support of government agencies. Concerning the first, the *Population Index* continues on page 255, "The fact that demography cuts across the boundaries of so many of the defined fields of knowledge and of academic concentration has had a deep influence on the patterns of its organization as research field and as academic discipline. Population is related to all the social sciences, to psychology, to biology, and to geography, and yet the field as a whole cannot be encompassed within any one of these subject-matter disciplines."

The cumulative backlog of governmental promotion of the study of population is impressive. As described on page 225, as above, "The population research of the last twenty-five years has been unique among the social sciences in the extent to which it has been a function of government, research foundations, and institutions. The Bureau of the Census with its responsibilities for the decennial census, vital statistics, current surveys, and population estimates is the primary source of demographic data. Many other agencies of the Federal government, notably the Public Health Service, the Bureau of Agricultural Economics, the Social Security Board, and the Bureau of Labor Statistics, contribute statistical series, special surveys, and research studies essential to the analysis and interpretation of demographic data or problems. The National Resources Committee during the period of its existence served to some extent to integrate these prolific national data. In the states population research is carried on by universities, Agricultural Experiment Stations, Planning Boards, Bureaus of Business Research, Public Health Departments, and Welfare Departments. Many county and city organizations either carry on demographic studies or make national data available locally."

Finally, the story of "Population Studies in the United States" is told in the setting of "the cooperative activity of a group of students," itemized as follows on pages 255–56. ". . . The Metropolitan Life Insurance

Company has not only sponsored the research of Louis I. Dublin, Alfred J. Lotka, and their co-workers but through its *Statistical Bulletin* has contributed to the dissemination of knowledge in the population field. The Scripps Foundation for Research in Population Problems of Miami University, under the direction of Warren S. Thompson and P. K. Whelpton, has continued in the vanguard of population research from the early twenties to the present. The School of Hygiene and Public Health of Johns Hopkins University is the locus of a long series of bio-metric contributions by Raymond Pearl, Lowell J. Reed, and their students. *Human Biology*, established in 1929, devoted an appreciable pro-portion of its space to reports on demographic research. The Milbank Memorial Fund's contributions to population research under the direc-tion of Edgar Sydenstricker, Frank W. Notestein, and Clyde V. Kiser included a series of pioneering studies of fertility, made either directly by the Fund or in cooperation with other institutions. Reports of these and other demographic studies were carried in *The Milbank Memorial Fund Quarterly*. Regional demography was developed by Howard W. Odum, T. J. Woofter, Jr., and Rupert B. Vance at the Institute for Re-search in Social Science of the University of North Carolina. The Ameri-can Geographical Society under the leadership of Isaiah Bowman sponsored a series of studies of pioneer settlement in the world's re-maining frontier area. The Office of Population Research of Princeton University, established in 1936, edited *Population Index,* the official journal of the Population Association of America, while developing a comprehensive research program oriented primarily toward interna-tional demography. . . ."

American sociologists have, however, made substantial contributions to the study of population as measured by integral books or brochures devoted specifically to this subject. Of the early American sociologists, Giddings appears to have been the first to make "the population" the central core of his societal structure. This he did in two ways; first, as an integral part of his social theory, and second, as a unit in the study of American society, in terms of regional and cultural characteristics. In his "Elements and Structure" as Book II of his *Elements,* Giddings makes situation, aggregation, demotic composition and demotic unity the framework of what he calls "the social population." In his *Inductive Sociology* and *Principles* he centers his analysis of social structure in the

"social composition" and the "social constitution." His societal development providing for zoogenic, anthropogenic, ethnogenic, and demo-
genic association also contributes to an integral framework in which
the social population is the core of social theory. At least two of the
Columbia Ph.D. candidates, writing their doctoral dissertations under
Giddings' direction, wrote on population. As early as 1915 Warren S.
Thompson published his *Population: A Study in Malthusianism*; while
in 1920 T. J. Woofter, Jr., wrote his *Negro Migration,* a statistical study.

Of the earlier American sociologists, the first to produce an integral
volume on population was E. A. Ross in *Standing Room Only?* published in 1927. Although Ross was not a population specialist, his book
was representative of many works that appeared during the 1920's stressing the belief in an overpopulated world. Ross, up to 1950, was still concerned very much with immigration and the quality of the population.
He was inclined to accuse sociologists of neglect of the important factor
of selection. Since the death rate is being controlled more and more,
birth control is necessary to maintain a balanced population. There is
also need in the United States for immigration restrictions. Ross feels
that sociologists have neglected an important opportunity by not stressing the genetics aspect of population more.

Of the American sociologists in colleges or universities — exclusive
of those who have studied urban and rural population and race — who
have written special treatises on some aspects of population as an inte-
gral subject in itself, the most prolific have been Warren S. Thompson,
Rupert B. Vance, Donald R. Taft, H. P. Fairchild, P. H. Landis, T.
Lynn Smith, E. B. Reuter, M. R. Davie. Others have written mono-
graphs, including Dorothy Thomas, P. K. Whelpton, Clyde Kiser,
Kingsley Davis. Of the major authors, the leading specialist has been
Warren S. Thompson whose main works include *Population Problems,
Plenty of People, Population and Peace in the Pacific, Population
Trends.* His *Population Problems,* originally published in 1930, went
into its third edition as early as 1942. Thompson, collaborating with
P. K. Whelpton, wrote *Population Trends in the United States,* in
which statistical studies were made of the national origins of the population; the geographic distribution of native and foreign-born groups;
the age and sex distribution of the population, including age trends by
race, nativity group, and urban-rural differences; the consequences of

this age trend, such as the possibility of a lower percentage of children and a higher percentage of old people; future population trends, including population projections; and a discussion of population policy matters.

The Whelpton volume, in 1938, was a specialized monograph on *Needed Population Research* indicating how to utilize the large amount of data that is now available on population problems and theory from such disciplines as sociology, economics, biology, education, statistics, public health, and indicating some of the blank spots in official population statistics, fertility studies, mortality studies, migration, and optimum size and composition of population.

Three of the presidents of the American Sociological Society contributed volumes, namely, Reuter, Fairchild, and Vance. Reuter's *Population Problems,* 1923, is perhaps the first to insist that the study of population is properly a sociological study in that the number of people in an area affects the social structure and types of mutual relationships and the type and degree of cultural possibility. Henry Pratt Fairchild's, *People: The Quantity and Quality of Population,* 1939, is in contrast a sort of semipopular exposition on population, insisting that the problem of population is the most important problem in the world. *All These People, the Nation's Human Resources in the South,* by Vance, is the first comprehensive sociological study of population in the regional frame of reference. This large statistical work presents a study of the southern population in relation to the national and regional picture, its agrarian and industrial economy, its health and educational resources, plus a section on an effective population policy for the South and the nation for the future. On the same methodological level, Vance also did for the Social Science Research Council a *Research Memorandum on Population Redistribution within the United States.* The purpose of this memorandum was to give what is already known about internal migration and to suggest what additional information is needed for research. Vance's next volume, to be completed soon, is a major text on population, which will exemplify his sociological approach. The major units include the composition, increase, birth rate, declining and differential birth rates, death rate, declining and differential death rates, of populations, also the aging population, internal and selective migration, relocation of population, population trends and education, biology, eugenics and genetics, culture and ethnic factors, future population prospect, and population policies.

The contributions of other sociologists may be noted from the special catalogue of books at the end of this discussion. As was noted in the beginning of this chapter, the contributions of non-sociologists in colleges and universities have been substantial, outranking in time priority and early perspective those of the sociologists. The main volumes in this category are therefore cited in chronological order along with the special treatises by sociologists. They include works by Frank Lorimer, Frederick Osborn, Carter Goodrich, Raymond Pearl, Frank Notestein, Edward M. East, Louis I. Dublin, A. J. Lotka, A. W. Carr-Saunders. Here again, as in other special cataloguings of contributions, the list is, first of all, a catalogue of books and not of periodical literature, which would constitute a long and impressive catalogue of distinctive articles by a much larger number of sociologists.

Year	Title	Author	Identification
1915	Population: A Study in Malthusianism	W. S. Thompson	Columbia, Ph.D.
1920	Negro Migration	T. J. Woofter, Jr.	Columbia, Ph.D.
1923	Mankind at the Crossroads	E. M. East	Hopkins
1925	The Biology of Population Growth	Raymond Pearl	Hopkins
1927	Social Mobility	P. A. Sorokin	Harvard
—	Standing Room Only?	E. A. Ross	Wisconsin
1934	Dynamics of Population	F. Lorimer, F. Osborn	Washington, D.C.
—	Fields and Methods of Sociology	L. L. Bernard	Washington University
1935	Population Problems	W. S. Thompson	Miami
—	Migration and Planes of Living	Carter Goodrich and others	Pennsylvania
1936	Migration and Economic Opportunity	Carter Goodrich	Pennsylvania
—	Human Migration	D. R. Taft	Illinois
—	The American People: Studies in Population	L. I. Dublin, ed.	New York
—	World Immigration	M. R. Davie	Yale
1937	Research Memorandum on Internal Migration in the Depression	W. S. Thompson	Miami

Year	Title	Author	Identification
1938	Needed Population Research	P. K. Whelpton	Miami
—	Research Memorandum on Migration Differentials	Dorothy Thomas	California
—	Research Memorandum on Population Redistribution within the United States	R. B. Vance	North Carolina
1939	The Natural History of Population	Raymond Pearl	Hopkins
—	People: The Quantity and Quality of Population	H. P. Fairchild	New York University
1940	Foundations of American Population Policy	F. Lorimer, E. Winston, L. K. Kiser	Washington, D.C.
1943	Population Problems	P. H. Landis	Washington State
1944	Plenty of People	W. S. Thompson	Miami
1945	World Population in Transition	Kingsley Davis	Columbia
—	All These People	R. B. Vance	North Carolina
1947	Refugees in America	Maurice Davie	Yale
1948	Population Analysis	T. Lynn Smith	Florida

Social and Human Ecology

As is the case in many of our specialisms or subsciences of sociology, human ecology is essentially a subject much interrelated with other special areas, not only of sociology but of biology and zoology as well. Here, as elsewhere in this book, however, our task is to tell something of the story of what American sociologists have done in the field rather than to report on the somewhat voluminous literature in other fields. As relates to the special sociologies already treated in this book, ecology is most clearly interrelated, as developed in American sociology, with the study of the city and with the essential construct of the community. Edward Shils in his *The Present State of American Sociology,* pages 7–10, goes so far as to estimate that in urban sociology, flourishing in the 1920's, was found the genesis of major developments in American sociology. As a matter of record, his references apply to special studies of aspects of urban communities, which came to be designated as human ecology, rather than to any matured theory or framework of urban sociology. The special "subfields" developed included the successions of populations, the interrelations between ethnic groups, the differences among areas concerning crime, delinquency, family traits, the change in status, and such other items as the location of business, centers of activity, specialisms in community life. Manifestly, these valuable studies were not primarily urban sociology as the study of urbanization, which is first of all a process of population concentration and the resulting pattern of modern civilization.

So, too, James A. Quinn's comprehensive "The Development of Human Ecology in Sociology," in the Barnes-Becker *Contemporary Social Theory,* pages 213–44, gives the genesis of human ecology in American sociology in the studies of communities pretty much as we have enumerated their beginnings in Chapter 17. In addition to his citation of non-sociological sources the greater part of his story centers around the community, which is, of course, the central core of plant and animal ecology. Quinn's volume on *Human Ecology,* appearing in 1950, elaborates more fully. Similar references to the origins and development of human ecology may be found in *Urban Sociology* by Nels Anderson and E. C. Lindeman, and other volumes on urban sociology, by Niles Carpenter, N. P. Gist and L. A. Halbert. From Bernard's *Fields and Methods of Sociology,* House's *Range of Social Theory* and *The Development of Sociology,* Odum's *Understanding Society,* together with a score of excellent periodical contributions, as cited by Quinn, it is possible to get an adequate idea of the development of ecology in American sociology. A. H. Hawley's *Human Ecology,* also appearing in 1950, rounds out the story and revivifies the ecological concept.

The Ernest W. Burgess Appraisal

Quinn stated, on page 241 of *Contemporary Social Theory* that "No general systematic treatment of the field has yet been published by a sociologist. The concepts of the field remain in an almost chaotic condition." Since then, both his own new book and Hawley's have appeared, in 1950. Nevertheless, what seems likely is that perhaps most of the scores of "ecological" studies have been primarily catalogues of social phenomena arranged by spatial distribution in urban areas, since the factors of long-time and symbiotic elements have not been adequately incorporated. Ernest W. Burgess' statement, prepared in 1950 for this book, gives a sociological perspective adequate to indicate the field and opportunity for sociologists for the next period of development, for, according to Burgess, "The field of sociology is the study of the ecological, cultural, and social processes in their effect upon human behavior. The sociologist, at the same time, recognizes that human ecology, strictly speaking, falls outside of sociology and that the cultural process belongs primarily to cultural anthropology. His primary concern, therefore, is with the social process. From the standpoint of the ecological process, sociologists study the ecological (or the demographic) community as an aggregate of individuals distributed over a given area. The relations between the individuals of the ecological community are considered in their symbiotic aspects. Competition, or struggle, without self-consciousness being involved, is posited as the central factor in the ecological process. Communication, culture, and institutions in the ecological process are considered only as they affect the symbiotic relations of individuals.

"In *human* ecology, particularly in the modern world, the factor of technology becomes one of major importance. The ecological environment of human beings is man-made. Urbanization, from the standpoint of ecology, may be viewed as the adaptation of people to each other in view of the physical framework of streets, means of rapid transportation, public utilities, skyscraper apartment buildings, the new media of communication, etc. Human ecology, logically, is a separate discipline from sociology. Like population studies, it has become attached to sociology because it provides the substructure for the study of social factors in human behavior. Theoretically, it should supply a similar foundation for anthropology, economics, and political science."

Regionalism in American Sociology

We have noted that Llewellyn and Hawthorn concluded that "for practical purposes, ecology should contribute to regional practices and control." It may be noted also that in his "The Development of Human Ecology," already cited, Quinn footnotes a half page of "examples of the increased emphasis upon regions." Lundberg, referring to regionalism as world ecology on page 132 of *Regionalism in Transition,* a symposium on regionalism published in *Social Forces,* in 1942–43, writes that regionalism "refers, it seems to me, to any study of social behavior in which the emphasis is on the *relation* between the geographic area and the behavior in question. So understood, regionalism is a sort of world ecology, in that its interests extend to the functional, organic relationships *between regions* as well as between parts of each region. In this sense, any behavior whatever (social, physical, biological, etc.) can be studied from the regional point of view, because we think of all behavior as taking place in space. By 'space' in this connection is usually meant geographic space. Elsewhere I have gone farther and pointed out that this is an unnecessary and unwarranted limitation inasmuch as human thinking on any subject tends to structure itself in spatial terms, and that expressions such as 'social space' have precisely the same justification and 'reality' as physical or geographic space. I think this is of importance from certain theoretical and methodological points of view, but need not be elaborated upon in the present connection.

"The use of *region* and *regionalism* as indicated above has given rise to some tortuous discussion as to whether these subjects are properly within the field of sociology, whether regionalism does not infringe upon the domain of geography, political science, public administration, etc. If, as stated above, we mean by regionalism the study of segments of social behavior with special reference to the geographic frame within which it occurs, then it is clearly sociology, and I would not worry about possible overlapping with certain other social sciences in either their pure or applied aspects. . . ."

Lundberg continues: "Regionalism as a sociological theory aims definitely, it seems to me, at a higher integration of sociological theory with scientific theory in general. If so, regionalism cannot avoid (and indeed has not avoided) the problems of a common language with which to designate a whole world of new phenomena as being merely special cases of the general principles of natural science."

In addition to Lundberg's article as quoted above, a number of other contributions complete the symposium of articles published in *Social Forces*. They indicate something of the range of sociological approach. In addition to titles on regionalism and planning, the list includes "A Sociological Approach to the Study and Practice of American Regionalism," "Regionalism and Sectionalism," and "Notes on the Study of Regional and Folk Society," by Howard W. Odum; "Regionalism and Plans for Post-War Reconstruction: The First Three Years," by James T. Watkins; "World Reconstruction and European Regionalism," by

Nicholas Doman; "Regionalism as Illustrated by the Western Hemisphere: Solidarity of the Americas," by Charles E. Martin; "Theoretical Aspects of Regionalism," by Svend Riemer; "Regionalism: Some Critical Observations," by Rudolf Heberle; "Statistical Methods for Delineation of Regions Applied to Data on Agriculture and Population," by Margaret Jarman Hagood; "Some Sociological Aspects of American Regionalism" and "Some Notes on the Social Psychology of Regionalism," by J. O. Hertzler; "The Concept of the Region," by Rupert B. Vance; "The Implications of Regionalism to Folk Sociology," by Hope Tisdale.

One of the more recent trends in regionalism in American sociology has been the integration of regionalism with folk sociology, primarily by the North Carolina group, to provide a realistic and dynamic framework for the analysis of societal structure to construct sound theory of process and of measured social change, to set the incidence for social planning, and to meet the need for a better understanding and direction of contemporary global intercultural relations. Although relatively new and not widely accepted in 1950, both folk sociology and regionalism may be said to have a relatively distinguished heritage in both European and American sociology. This heritage consists of two main branches. The one may be traced as a thread in the fabric of general theory and the other stems from the many special approaches to the study of geographic and environmental factors in society, including much of the later developments in human ecology and cultural conditioning. In addition to its traceable heritage in general sociology, folk sociology draws heavily on cultural anthropology and literary portraiture of folk behavior, while regionalism has its backgrounds deeply rooted in human geography more recently reinforced by the revival of emphasis upon area studies as an integrated field of the social sciences.

Although folk sociology and regionalism each constitutes an integral approach to the study of the structure and function of society, they are inseparable in the larger processes of societal interaction. Thus Patrick Geddes' development of the Le Play regionalism becomes the construct of place, folk, and work, with its many combinations and permutations of folk, place, work; work, place, folk. This implies the folk-regional society as the basis of folk sociology. So, too, Giddings' sustentation areas, together with his interaction of circumstantial pressure with societal pressure, working through the component structure and the constituent civil societies constitute the basis for the genuine folk sociology in the universal regional setting. Also Giddings' dichotomy of the dynamics of a people's development stems first from the regional foundations and second from the folk interactions. The same is true to a great extent in Tönnies' *Gemeinschaft und Gesellschaft* as is also partly the case in Redfield's folk society as symbol of development from the folk to civilization and from the sacred to the secular. More elaborate is Howard Becker's "Sacred and Secular Societies," in the May, 1950, *Social Forces*.

Two observations need to be emphasized here. One is that regionalism, even as demography, stems from several disciplines and the other is that the folk-regional approach has not had any wide acceptance by American sociologists. Concerning the first, something of the range and depth of folk sociology's heritage may be seen by a glance at some of the sources from which authentication of the concept may be sought. In 1949 the University of Wisconsin held a week's symposium on American regionalism, with historians, geographers, anthropologists, sociologists participating. Three sociologists have chapters in the volume being published in 1951 under the title *Regionalism in the United States:* Rupert B. Vance, on "Regionalism as a Tool for Research"; Louis Wirth on "The Limitations of Regionalism"; and Howard W. Odum on "The Promise of Regionalism." The richest source of materials outside of the social sciences is that of literary regionalism with a half dozen series of books on folk and regional culture.

Concerning the second observation, namely, that regionalism as a sociological construct has been little understood or accepted, the first point of emphasis is that, as yet, no adequate treatment has been presented, and that there is generally a misconception of the main core of regionalism. It was pointed out in Odum's "The American Blend: Regional Diversity and National Unity," in *The Saturday Review of Literature* for August 6, 1949, how in contemporaneous society, where area-culture relationships and group intercultural situations constitute the central problem, the conceptualization of regionalism as a structural-functional reference for the analysis of specific cultures, and their relation to each other and to the totality of area-culture situation, becomes increasingly important. Equally important is the definition of the role of regionalism in the reconstruction and balance of conflicting cultures and the clearing up of certain misconceptions about regionalism itself.

In his references to regionalism looking toward the definition of culture, T. S. Eliot complains that "the usual regionalist is concerned solely with the interests of his own region, and thereby suggests to his neighbor across the border what is of interest to one must be to the disadvantage of the other." At the same time he corrects this common misconception of regionalism by pointing out that "the absolute value is that each area should have its characteristic culture which should also harmonize with, and enrich, the cultures of the neighboring areas." This means we must distinguish between what concerns the area primarily and what relates to it, or between an area's place and/or its role in some total structure. In the United States today, both historically and functionally, this is a matter of distinguishing between the old sectionalism that features homogeneity in isolation and separatism, and the new regionalism that features differentiation and integration in an ever-flexible, complex, and conflicting changing social structure. This is what Justice Brandeis foresaw in 1936, when he wrote about a necessary "first step in grappling with our most serious problem!" namely, sectional conflict in the United States.

The literary regionalists, however, are not the only ones who promulgate the fallacy that identifies regionalism with localism or with areal homogeneities due primarily to isolation, either in space through lack of communication and extra-regional relationships, or in time as in the case of primitive peoples. Two American sociologists may be cited specifically. In *Twentieth Century Sociology,* published as recently as 1944 and widely used by sociologists, R. E. L. Faris writes on pages 556-57: "The mobility and fluidity of the United States population, the diffusions and standardization of culture, and other influences of the sort, are having the effect of reducing the regional basis of differences in American culture. If this trend continues, as it appears likely to do, the interest in regionalism may become a historical subject! . . ."

The other example is that of Louis Wirth of the University of Chicago in his paper before the Wisconsin Symposium on American Regionalism in April, 1949. Three of his characterizations of regionalism appear in contradiction to the widely accepted tenets of the new regionalism. One identified it with the long outmoded geographic determinism. Another identified it as a *cult*. A third identified it with a "one-factor theory" in contrast to its multiple approach through the integration of all the social sciences, literature, and other tools of study and planning. Regionalism, he wrote, "must be recognized for what it is, namely, a one-factor theory, which taken alone will furnish only a one-sided, and hence distorted picture of social reality." And again, "it would be naïve to believe that such simplistic interpretations of the complexities of social life have not obscured other equally significant elements and have not led to distorted versions." This is clearly a confusion of regionalism with some of the special concepts of geographic factors in society or with some limited literary picture.

Perhaps we should not be surprised at the limitations of those who have not had time or occasion to sense the structural-functional meanings, for it is easy to follow the old fallacy that regionalism is essentially divisive, or is synonymous with separation, is opposed to centralization, and connotes a doctrine opposed to universalism. Here it must be emphasized that it is not regionalism *or*, but regionalism *and*, since the multiplication of divergent groups and interests in the modern world and their discovery through communication render their integration through regional group units an absolute "must" in any construct of "One World" or "One Nation." It is not regionalism *vs.* universalism, regions *vs.* nation, but regionalism *and* universalism, regions *and* nation in such a construct as the United Nations, or the more limited construct of the unity of "The Americas," or even of "One America" envisaged by so many recent writings.

With reference to the structural-functional definitions of regionalism, it is necessary to re-emphasize the fact that the primary objectives of regionalism are found in the end product of the integration of regions more than in the mere study and development of regions themselves. The regions are studied and planned to the end that they may be more adequate in all aspects of resources and culture; yet regionalism itself is primarily interested in the total integration and balance of these regions.

The third verdict of a sociologist is one of urging an adequate definition of the construct of regionalism. Rudolf Heberle, writing in *Regionalism in Transition,* on page 280 of Volume 21 of *Social Forces,* says that "The very concept of 'regionalism' needs unraveling; the various connotations should be defined and their connections determined; the epistemological and methodological problems of regional studies should be clear in the minds of scholars engaging in such work; the role of sociology in regional studies should be rigidly circumscribed in order to relate these studies to general sociological theory. While thus insisting on a careful theoretical foundation I would nevertheless state emphatically that in this field, as in any important field of scholarship, the success depends primarily on a firm and forceful grasp for things significant, and on the art of combination and synthesis."

Julian H. Steward in his *Area Research: Theory and Practice,* published by the Social Science Research Council in 1950, on pages 54–71 compares two regional studies as being relevant to the present trends toward integration and disciplinary cooperation. These are the Tarascan area studies and the Southeastern United States regional studies. Beginning on page 66, he writes, "Whereas the Tarascan area is distinctive partly because of its heritage from aboriginal times, when it was an independent sociocultural unit, and even more because Colonial Spanish culture has survived there, the Southeastern United States has long been part of a larger whole; and whereas the Tarascan program was developed by anthropologists, the Southeastern United States studies were developed by sociologists. These facts explain at least some of the differences in the two programs. The Southeastern program is noteworthy because of the conceptualization of the regional unit and the methodology for establishing such a unit, and because it calls for a focus upon a particular problem and for interdisciplinary collaboration."

On the "Concept of Region," as utilized by the North Carolina group, Steward writes, " 'The region for purpose of scientific delineation and practical planning, is a major, composite, multiple-purpose, group-of-states societal division of the nation [concept of the larger whole], delineated and characterized by the greatest possible degree of homogeneity [culture area concept], measured by the largest practical number of indices available for the largest practical number of purposes and agencies [quantitative method for establishing a region, see pp. 134–137 infra], and affording the least possible number of contradictions, conflicts, and overlapping.' And further, 'The larger frame of reference for the conceptualization of regionalism is to be found in the construct of the structural-functional reference of total society or "the whole," somewhat after the manner of Talcott Parsons' structural functional theory of relations between the parts and the total in the total system of society.'

"A region is delineated in terms of culture, structure, geography, political organization, and historical trends. The method for delineating a region is quantitative: 'adequate statistical methods applied to a reasonable number of major indices . . . for determining areas of maximum homogeneity . . . The methods proposed for maximizing the homogeneity of states within regions will involve the application at several levels of the factor analysis or principal component techniques for combination of series of single indices into composite indices.'

"This statistical survey technique has to deal initially with a limited number of features. An interesting difference between this procedure and anthropological procedure is illustrated here. The Puerto Rico project and the Central Andean study used questionnaires to ascertain the limits of cultural regions and to discover the principal dynamic, functional features that were to be studied more intensively by qualitative method. The initial surveys were made for preliminary orientation. The sociologists who have participated in the Southeastern studies are more interested in quantification as a basic method. In these studies they make a series of statistical surveys, finally achieving complex correlations. The anthropological procedure leads to qualitative studies of communities as samples of regions. The sociological procedure used here leads to an ultimate correlation of correlations.

"Odum's criteria of area appear to include features of folk culture and to exclude certain features of national culture. That is, regional culture consists of folk culture as it stems from the past and is readapted to national influences. But local manifestations of national technology and political controls — national institutions — represent 'sectionalism,' not regionalism: 'The region . . . is at once an extension and a subdivision of the folk society, characterized by the joint indices of geography and culture and deriving its definitive traits through action and behavior processes rather than through technological functions or areas.'" There is an excellent bibliography of several hundred titles samplings of which may be found in the Wisconsin symposium; *Southern Regions of the United States,* 1936, by Howard W. Odum; *American Regionalism,* 1938, by Howard W. Odum and Harry E. Moore; and *In Search of the Regional Balance of America,* 1945, edited by Howard W. Odum and Katharine Jocher.

PART IV

American Sociology on Other Levels

CHAPTER 21

Regional, Rural, and Other Special Groupings

In addition to the American Sociological Society, the founding of which has been made the key date, and the presidents of which have constituted the first main chroniclers in our story of American sociology, there are other groupings that by 1950 constituted important parts in the total sociological structure. Among the definitely organized groups are the regional sociological societies, the Rural Sociological Society, the American Catholic Sociological Society. Of the many individuals, automatically ranking as important facets of the whole of American sociology, but not always coinciding with the officials of the national, regional, or special groups, are the heads of departments of sociology in major institutions in two main categories, namely, the state universities and others commonly designated as private and denominational colleges and universities. These reflect the continuity of American sociology as identified primarily with colleges and universities and as a product of American higher education as a sort of sociology of knowledge in the sense of being the product of intellectuals at work in American institutions.

The Regional Societies

The first of these groupings are the regional sociological societies affiliated with the parent American Sociological Society. These special groups reflect the increasing tendency to take into consideration the regional structure of American society as well as the more pragmatic consideration of developing the total field of sociology through the recruiting of more sociologists and giving them opportunity for growth, development and participation in the activities of American sociologists. In the twenty years since the election of the president of the first regional sociological society, up to 1950, the six main regional societies have named more than a hundred presidents, have held more than a hundred annual meetings, and have enrolled membership from all the states and all educational institutions where sociology is taught.

Interestingly enough, the number of presidents of the regional sociological societies is greater than the number of presidents of the American Sociological Society, although they are not quite half as old as the parent group. In addition to the six regional societies, there is the District of Columbia branch of the American Sociological Society founded in 1931. Before this, the Ohio Valley Sociological Society had been founded in 1925 and was followed by the Pacific and the Eastern in 1930–31; the Southern in 1936; the Midwestern in 1937; and the Southwestern in 1938. More than one hundred sociologists have served as presidents of the several regional societies and they have represented no less than thirty-one states and twice as many institutions. Among the institutions that have contributed more than one regional president, are Columbia University, Smith College, University of Pennsylvania, Yale University, Vanderbilt University, University of North Carolina, Louisiana State University, Ohio State University, Miami University (Ohio), University of Cincinnati, Ohio Wesleyan, University of Nebraska, University of Missouri, University of Southern California, University of Washington, and University of Oregon. Four institutions provided as many as three presidents, including University of North Carolina, Ohio State University, University of Southern California, and University of Washington. M. C. Elmer was president of two regional societies, namely the Eastern and the Ohio Valley. Eight presidents of the American Sociological Society were also presidents of a regional society, namely F. H. Hankins, H. P. Fairchild, R. M. MacIver, Talcott Parsons, E. Franklin Frazier, Rupert B. Vance, E. H. Sutherland, E. S. Bogardus. As reflecting the composite representation of American sociologists, the Southern Sociological Society had Katharine Jocher for its president in 1943 and 1944 and Charles Johnson as president in 1946. The Eastern Sociological Society had Gladys Bryson for president in 1947 and Franklin Frazier in 1946.

The regional societies may be said to represent an integral part of American sociology for several reasons. They were organized with several purposes in mind and as a logical development of American regionalism. Their functions were primarily threefold. First, they might serve as recruiting means for the American Sociological Society; they were all subsequently affiliated with the national society. Second, they were envisaged, essentially, as means for giving greater opportunity to larger numbers of sociologists, especially the younger members, to participate in conferences and in research efforts. In the third place they would offer a medium for more fellowship and especially for those who often could not attend the annual meetings of the American Sociological Society. This would be especially true of the Far West where the distance element involved more time and expense than most sociologists could afford in attending the national meetings in the East or Central West. On the other hand, perhaps many observers have thought the annual meetings have greatly enriched the conference programs and have increased the production output of American sociologists. It has sometimes been said that the Eastern Sociological Society's meetings have been the most successful in providing programs sometimes estimated to be as good as those of the annual meetings of the parent society.

H. Warren Dunham, president of the Ohio Valley Sociological Society for 1949, writes in the *Ohio Valley Sociologist* for January, 1950: "It is becoming increasingly clear that the regional society is an important factor in our organized professional strength. This has come about because the regional society is large enough to display an effective voice if necessary with respect to professional matters, and is small enough so that each individual member feels that he can be effective if he so desires. Comment is frequently heard to the effect that at the regional meetings persons actually attend the section meetings and exchange ideas. If this view has a general validity, it would point to the regional society as providing a greater intellectual satisfaction to its members than is perhaps possible on the national level." He continues, "The regional society, it would seem to me, has another very important function to perform. It should in the future have a greater influence with respect to organizational problems as they appear on the national level. The regional society provides the opportunity for discussing all issues before they are considered at the national level and for initiating matters of concern to all sociologists which may eventually be considered at the national level. In this manner, the regional society would perform a very important and necessary function and really represent the grass roots for the interests of professional sociologists."

Certainly those sociologists from the East, South, and Midwest have found the meetings of the Far West Pacific groups of extraordinary interest and reflecting a high degree of excellence in the variety and quality of papers presented, in the number and representation of sociologists and in the enthusiasm and fellowship manifested. Judged on these bases, American sociology has gained much by this sort of increment to its total contributions.

James T. Long of Kent University concluded his article, "The Folkways of Regional Sociological Societies," pages 911–19, of the July–August, 1948, number of *Sociology and Social Research,* by saying, "The conclusion seems inescapable that regional societies are playing a significant role in the development of sociology in America today." As relating to the problem of publication of papers in increasing numbers he points out some of the problems involved and reports progress in the several societies. He suggests further progress might be made from the present procedures, which he reports on page 915: "The Southern Society gives to each member an annual subscription to *Social Forces.* The Southwestern Society, which functions as an arm of the Southwestern Social Science Association, has for its publication the *Southwestern Social Science Quarterly* and has one of the editors on its staff with annual dues to include a subscription to the *Quarterly.* The *Ohio Valley Sociologist* and the *Midwest Sociologist* are mimeographed, and news items of various departments of sociology in their respective areas constitute an important part of each. One of the most ambitious publications is that of the Pacific Sociological Society. An official *Proceedings,* which contains the papers and is 50 to 80 pages in length, is published annually by Washington State College as a part of its research studies."

The total number and range of regional personnel may be seen from the roster by years, place of birth, and institutions from which each president was elected.

Eastern Sociological Society

Date	Name	Native State	Institution Represented
1931	F. H. Hankins	Ohio	Smith College
1932	H. P. Fairchild	Illinois	New York University
1933	M. C. Elmer	Wisconsin	University of Pittsburgh
1934	R. MacIver	Scotland	Columbia University
1935	James Bossard	Pennsylvania	University of Pennsylvania
1936	James Woodard	Wisconsin	Temple University
1937	Jerome Davis	Japan	Yale University
1939	J. K. Folsom	New York	Vassar College
1941	Maurice Davie	Canada	Yale University
1942	Talcott Parsons	Ohio	Harvard University
1944	Robert Lynd	Indiana	Columbia University
1946	E. F. Frazier	Maryland	Howard University
1947	Gladys Bryson	Kentucky	Smith College
1948	Donald Young	Pennsylvania	Russell Sage Foundation
1949	Thorsten Sellin	Sweden	University of Pennsylvania
1949	M. F. Nimkoff	New York	Bucknell University
1950	N. L. Whetten	Mexico	Connecticut

Southern Sociological Society

Date	Name	Native State	Institution Represented
1936	E. T. Krueger	Illinois	Vanderbilt University
1937	Wilson Gee	South Carolina	University of Virginia
1938	R. B. Vance	Arkansas	University of North Carolina
1939	E. W. Gregory, Jr.	Virginia	University of Alabama
1940	Fred Frey	Louisiana	Louisiana State University
1941	B. O. Williams	South Carolina	University of Georgia
1942	William E. Cole	Tennessee	University of Tennessee
1943	Katharine Jocher	Pennsylvania	University of North Carolina
1944	Katharine Jocher	Pennsylvania	University of North Carolina
1945	Howard W. Beers	New York	University of Kentucky
1946	Charles S. Johnson	Virginia	Fisk University
1947	T. Lynn Smith	Colorado	Louisiana State University
1948	Coyle E. Moore	South Carolina	Florida State University
1949	Wayland J. Hayes	West Virginia	Vanderbilt University
1950	Lee M. Brooks	Massachusetts	University of North Carolina

Midwest Sociological Society

Date	Name	Native State	Institution Represented
1937	L. Guy Brown	Illinois	University of Missouri
1937	J. O. Hertzler	Minnesota	University of Nebraska
1938	Noel P. Gist	Missouri	University of Missouri
1939	L. D. Zeleny	Minnesota	Colorado State College of Education
1940	C. W. Hart	Illinois	National Opinion Research Center, Chicago, Illinois
1941	Carroll D. Clark	Kansas	University of Kansas
1942	James M. Reinhardt	Georgia	University of Nebraska
1943	James M. Reinhardt	Georgia	University of Nebraska
1944	David E. Lindstrom	Nebraska	University of Illinois
1945	Ernest Manheim	Hungary	Kansas City University
1946	Howard Becker	New York	University of Wisconsin
1946	T. Earl Sullenger	Kentucky	University of Omaha
1947	Lloyd V. Ballard	Wisconsin	Beloit College
1948	Ray E. Wakeley	Pennsylvania	Iowa State University
1949	George B. Vold	South Dakota	University of Minnesota
1950	T. D. Eliot	Oregon	Northwestern

Pacific Sociological Society

Date	Name	Native State	Institution Represented
1930	Emory S. Bogardus	Illinois	University of Southern California
1931	William Kirk	Maryland	Pomona College
1932	Clarence M. Case	Indiana	University of Southern California
1933	George M. Day	Utah	Occidental College
1934	Constantine Panunzio	Italy	University of California at Los Angeles
1935	Howard B. Woolston	Pennsylvania	University of Washington
1936	Charles N. Reynolds	Kansas	Stanford University
1937	George B. Mangold	Iowa	University of Southern California
1938	Samuel Haig Jameson	Armenia	University of Oregon
1939	Glenn E. Hoover	Kansas	Mills College
1940	Martin H. Neumeyer	Missouri	University of Southern California
1941	Jesse F. Steiner	Ohio	University of Washington
1942	Elon H. Moore	Michigan	University of Oregon
1943	Glen E. Carlson	Pennsylvania	University of Redlands

Date	Name	Native State	Institution Represented
1944	William C. Smith	Minnesota	Linfield College
1945	Ray E. Baber	Kansas	Pomona College
1946	Calvin F. Schmid	Ohio	University of Washington
1947	Richard La Piere	Wisconsin	Stanford University
1948	Harvey J. Locke	Minnesota	University of Southern California
1949	George A. Lundberg	North Dakota	University of Washington
1950	Leonard Broom	Massachusetts	University of California at Los Angeles

Southwest Sociological Society

Date	Name	Native State	Institution Represented
1937–38	Carroll D. Clark	Kansas	University of Kansas
1938–39	Warner E. Gettys	Ohio	University of Texas
1939–40	Alvin Good	Ohio	Louisiana State Normal, Natchitoches
1940–41	O. E. Baker	Ohio	Hardin Simmons University
1941–42	W. H. Sewell	Michigan	Oklahoma A. and M.
1942–46	Joe K. Johnson		East Texas State Teachers College
1946–47	J. L. DuFlot		West Texas State Teachers College
1947–48	A. L. Porterfield	Arkansas	Texas Christian University
1948–49	Mattie Lloyd Wooten	Texas	Texas State College for Women
1949–50	Harry E. Moore	Louisiana	University of Texas

Ohio Valley Sociological Society

Date	Name	Native State	Institution Represented
1925	N. L. Sims	Indiana	Oberlin College
1926	E. E. Eubank	Missouri	University of Cincinnati
1927	C. J. Bushnell	Iowa	Toledo University
1928	F. G. Detweiler	Kentucky	Denison College
1929	I. E. Ash		Ohio University
1930	C. C. North	Iowa	Ohio State University
1931	C. W. Coulter	Canada	Ohio Wesleyan University
1932	H. A. Miller	New Hampshire	Ohio State University
1933	Read Bain	Oregon	Miami University
1934	J. E. Hagerty	Indiana	Ohio State University
1935	J. A. Quinn	Iowa	University of Cincinnati
1936	A. A. Johnston	Pennsylvania	College of Wooster

Date	Name	Native State	Institution Represented
1937	F. E. Lumley	Canada	Ohio State University
1938	J. E. Cutler	Illinois	Western Reserve University
1939	M. C. Elmer	Wisconsin	University of Pittsburgh
1940	C. R. Hoffer	Indiana	Michigan State College
1941	E. H. Sutherland	Nebraska	Indiana University
1942	G. W. Sarvis		Ohio Wesleyan University
1943	G. W. Sarvis		Ohio Wesleyan University
1944	L. A. Cook	Indiana	Ohio State University
1945	L. A. Cook	Indiana	Ohio State University
1946	L. A. Cook	Indiana	Ohio State University
1947	P. P. Denune	Ohio	Ohio State University
1948	W. F. Cottrell	Virginia	Miami University
1949	H. Warren Dunham	Nebraska	Wayne University
1951	John Milton Yinger	Michigan	Oberlin

District of Columbia Chapter of the American Sociological Society

A grouping of American sociologists, neither primarily identified with teaching and research in educational institutions, nor with any regional constituency, is the District of Columbia Chapter of the American Sociological Society. This organized group is symbolic and representative of a distinctive segment of American sociology as found in the relatively limited number of sociologists officially employed by the United States government. The chapter's roster of approximately one hundred members includes, however, quite a few members of the faculties of local colleges and universities, as, for instance, the Rev. Paul H. Furfey, head of the Department of Sociology at the Catholic University of America, and E. Franklin Frazier, head of the Department of Sociology at Howard University, H. C. Hoffsommer of Maryland, and H. L. Geisert of George Washington University. In the group, too, are some who have transferred from universities, including Carl Taylor from North Carolina State, Margaret J. Hagood and T. J. Woofter, Jr., former professors of statistics at North Carolina; and Stuart Rice, formerly from Pennsylvania. Among those who work closely with students of population are Philip Hauser, acting director of the Census, Conrad and Irene Taeuber, Frank Lorimer. The presidents of the District Chapter include:

1935	Stuart Rice	1943	Carl Wells
1936	D. L. Willard	1944	E. Franklin Frazier
1937	Frank Lorimer	1945	Elbridge Sibley
1938	Carl C. Taylor	1946	Clyde Hart
1939	T. J. Woofter, Jr.	1947	Margaret Jarman Hagood
1940	Irene Taeuber	1948	Peter Lejins
1941	C. P. Loomis	1949	Raymond Bowers
1942	B. L. Melvin	1950	Austin Van Der Slice

American Catholic Sociological Society

One of the special groupings of American sociologists is that represented by the American Catholic Sociological Society, founded in 1938. In the published *Who's Who among Catholic Sociologists* are catalogued approximately two hundred sociologists representing nearly all Catholic institutions. The Society has also sponsored the *American Catholic Sociological Review,* the first issue of which appeared in 1940. The specialisms, as listed in *Who's Who among Catholic Sociologists,* reprinted from the *American Catholic Sociological Review,* October, 1946, feature historical sociology, social theory and philosophy, European sociology, crime and penology, labor relations, race relations, legislation, religion, the family, group work, social work, anthropology, social problems, social psychology, Christian social thought, social institutions, Latin American relations, pathology, juvenile delinquency. Representative sociologists in this group, and the range and nature of their work, may be studied thoroughly through Melvin J. Williams' *Catholic Social Thought; Its Approach to Contemporary Problems,* 1950. The presidents of the American Catholic Sociological Society as listed by the secretary, Ralph A. Gallager, S.J., include the following:

Date	Name	Native State	Institution Represented
1938	Reverend Ralph A. Gallagher, S.J.	Ohio	Loyola, Chicago
1939	Reverend Raymond W. Murray, C.S.C.	Connecticut	University of Notre Dame
1940	Paul J. Mundie	Pennsylvania	Marquette University
1941	Reverend Francis J. Friedel, S.M.	Ohio	Trinity College, Iowa
1942	Walter Willigan		St. John University
1943	Eva J. Ross	North Ireland	Trinity College, Washington, D.C.

Date	Name	Native State	Institution Represented
1944	Reverend Paul Hanly Furfey	Massachusetts	Catholic University of America
1945	Brother Gerald J. Schnepp, S.M.	Illinois	William Cullen McBride H.S., St. Louis, Missouri
1946	Alphonse H. Clemens	Missouri	Catholic University, Washington, D.C.
1947	Reverend Leo Robinson, S.J.	Oregon	Provincial Oregon Province of Society of Jesus, Portland, Oregon
1948	Franz Mueller	Germany	College of St. Thomas, St. Paul, Minnesota
1949	Right Reverend Monsignor Robert B. Navin	Ohio	Sisters College of Cleveland, Ohio
1950	Clement S. Mihanovich	Missouri	St. Louis University

Rural Sociological Society

The Rural Sociological Society was founded in 1937, growing out of the section on rural sociology that had long been a part of the annual program of the American Sociological Society. C. Horace Hamilton writes that the Society was organized at the Claridge Hotel, Atlantic City, New Jersey, in December, 1937. Approximately seventy-five rural sociologists, in attendance at the annual meeting of the national society, participated in the organization. The organization committee consisted of Dwight Sanderson, chairman, O. D. Duncan, John H. Kolb, Carl C. Taylor, and B. O. Williams. The first officers of the Society consisted of: president, Dwight Sanderson, Cornell University; vice-president, John H. Kolb, University of Wisconsin; secretary-treasurer, T. Lynn Smith, Louisiana State University; Executive Committee members, C. W. Lively and Carl C. Taylor; chairman of the Committee on Research, C. Horace Hamilton; chairman of the Committee on Teaching, Wilson Gee; chairman of the Committee on Extension, J. B. Smith. There was also a committee for rural sociological monographs with T. Lynn Smith as editor, Paul Landis, advisory editor, and Conrad Taeuber, advisory editor.

The presidents of the Rural Sociological Society classified by state of birth and institution from which elected are:

Date	Name	Native State	Institution Represented
1938	Dwight Sanderson	Michigan	Cornell
1939	Carl C. Taylor	Iowa	B.A.E. Washington
1940	J. H. Kolb	Wisconsin	Wisconsin
1941	T. Lynn Smith	Colorado	Louisiana State
1942	C. E. Lively	West Virginia	Ohio State
1943	C. E. Lively	West Virginia	Ohio State
1944	Lowry Nelson	Utah	Minnesota
1945	E. de S. Brunner	Pennsylvania	Teachers College, Columbia
1946	Paul H. Landis	Illinois	Washington State
1947	W. A. Anderson	Missouri	Cornell
1948	C. P. Loomis	Colorado	B.A.E. Washington
1949	C. C. Zimmerman	Missouri	Harvard
1950	C. Horace Hamilton	Texas	North Carolina State

Key Sociologists in State Universities

In our account of the beginnings of American sociology as a college and university discipline, and in Chapter 3, tracing some of the institutional developments, we emphasized the role of the heads of the new departments of sociology in their function of developing and expanding this new social science in American education. It was pointed out, for instance, how Albion W. Small was perhaps sociology's greatest advocate; then later, in giving relatively high ranking to the succession of Blackmar, Weatherly, Howard, Hayes, it was pointed out that their building of departments at Kansas, Indiana, Nebraska, and Illinois in contrast to Commons, Ely, and others who transferred to economics, constituted a contribution that was important to the growth of sociology and that this function was a logical substitute for larger contributions in research and publication. In addition to this they symbolized good teaching and the teacher-student relationship. Much the same situation has been apparent in the continuing expansion of sociology in American colleges. In sociology, as in other standard subjects, too much credit cannot be given the teacher who has carried the burden of teaching his subject and of recruiting students for graduate work as well. As was the case with the earlier pioneers, so with the later sociologists whose lot it has been to develop the new field, they have performed valuable functions in the university administration, in the state programs of public service, and in the making of many addresses requested in communities and in the promotion of the general programs of education and public welfare. From this period in the development of American sociology and education this "ex-officio" function of the professor of sociology and of the younger instructors has been an integral and valuable part of sociology's task.

The first and most logical group of sociologists who are to be recorded in this capacity will be the heads of departments of sociology in the state university. Already these have been featured as also presidents of the American Sociological Society in the state universities of Wisconsin, Minnesota, Illinois, Indiana, Kansas, Nebraska, North Dakota, Michigan, North Carolina, and Missouri. Others have been featured as authors of sociology texts or of books in special fields. It remains at this point to catalogue them in the perspective of their departmental relationships, the places of their birth, and certain routine factors. Here as is the case in most categories, many sociologists qualify for more than one class, thus contributing in several ways to the total story of American sociology. That is, the head of a department may be one of the younger sociologists, he may be a member of the Sociological Research Association, a president of a regional society, the author of one or more books or of several articles, or he may be a liberal cooperator in social organizations. His total story, therefore, is told in the several interactions and interrelationships that make up the fabric of sociology in his particular setting.

Below is the roster of heads or chairmen of departments of sociology in state universities as they were reported at the beginning of 1950. Other early heads of the departments are catalogued in instances where reports could be had.

School	Present Head	Native State	Other Heads
Alabama	S. T. Kimball	Kansas	E. W. Gregory, Jr.
Arizona	F. A. Conrad	Ohio	
Arkansas	Stephen Stephan	Virginia	Vernon Davies
California	R. A. Nisbet	California	
Colorado	G. H. Barker	Illinois	Frederick Bushee
Connecticut	J. L. Hypes	West Virginia	
Delaware	F. B. Parker	New York	
Florida	John Maclachlan	Mississippi	L. M. Bristol
			N. L. Sims
Florida State	M. F. Nimcoff	New York	R. F. Bellamy

School	Present Head	Native State	Other Heads
Georgia	B. O. Williams	South Carolina	T. J. Woofter
Idaho	Harry Harmsworth	Missouri	
Illinois	J. W. Albig	Pennsylvania	E. T. Hiller
			E. C. Hayes
Indiana	Edwin H. Sutherland	Nebraska	Ulysses G. Weatherly
			John R. Commons
Iowa	H. W. Saunders	Iowa	C. A. Phillips
Kansas	Carroll D. Clark	Minnesota	Seba Eldridge
			S. A. Queen
			F. W. Blackmar
Kentucky	Irwin T. Sanders	Kentucky	Logan Wilson
Louisiana	Homer L. Hitt	Texas	T. Lynn Smith
Maine	H. B. Kirshen	England	John H. Ashworth
Maryland	Harold Hoffsommer	Kansas	E. W. Gregory
Massachusetts	J. Henry Korson	Pennsylvania	F. M. Cutler
Michigan	Robert C. Angell	Michigan	R. D. McKenzie
			C. H. Cooley
Minnesota	F. Stuart Chapin	New York	
Mississippi	Morton B. King, Jr.	Tennessee	Paul B. Foreman
			N. B. Bond
Missouri	C. T. Pihlblad	Kansas	Howard Jensen
			Charles A. Ellwood
Montana	Gordon Browder	Virginia	
Nebraska	J. O. Hertzler	Minnesota	G. E. Howard
Nevada	M. J. Webster	Nebraska	
New Hampshire	Charles W. Coulter	Canada	E. R. Groves
New Jersey (Rutgers)	John W. Riley, Jr.	Maine	
New Mexico	Paul Walter, Jr.	New Mexico	
New York (Cornell)	Leonard S. Cottrell	Virginia	Dwight Sanderson
North Carolina	Howard W. Odum	Georgia	
North Dakota	A. L. Lincoln		
Ohio State	Perry P. Denune	Ohio	
Oklahoma	Wyatt Marrs	Texas	J. J. Rhyne
Oregon	E. H. Moore	Michigan	Philip Parsons
Rhode Island (State)	L. Guy Brown	Illinois	
South Carolina	H. H. Turney-High		Croft Williams

School	Present Head	Native State	Other Heads
South Dakota	Forrest L. Weller	Ohio	
Tennessee	William E. Cole	Tennessee	W. B. Jones, Jr.
Texas	W. E. Gettys	Ohio	
Utah	Arthur L. Beeley	England	G. Q. Corey
Vermont	George Dykhuizen	Indiana	
Virginia	Floyd N. House	Michigan	
Washington	George A. Lundberg	North Dakota	J. F. Steiner
			H. B. Woolston
West Virginia	Harold Allan Gibbard	Canada	
Wisconsin	T. C. McCormick	Alabama	John L. Gillin
			E. A. Ross
Wyoming	Ralph E. Conwell	Iowa	

In Private and Denominational Institutions

Something of the development of a number of departments of sociology in institutions other than state colleges or universities has been presented either in relation to some of the presidents of the American Sociological Society in Chapters 4–13, or as examples of the growth of sociology as a college or university subject in Chapter 3. Among these were Southern California, Harvard, Yale, Chicago, Brown. But there are other universities in which the development of sociology has been advanced by sociologists who have served to head the work of sociology and so have contributed important threads in the fabric of American sociology.

Jesse F. Steiner

Among the American sociologists whose contributions have been decisive in more than one university is Jesse F. Steiner. As moving spirit and head of the department at Tulane University, he set a high standard for both research and teaching. Louis Wirth, a later president of the Society was associate professor with him for a number of years as was also L. L. Bernard, from 1927 to 1928. As head of the Department of Sociology at the University of Washington at Seattle from 1931 to 1945, he was again successful, not only building a strong department in a new regional setting but being prominent in the total university program as well. Before his retirement he was instrumental in bringing George Lundberg to head the department and had been elected president of the Pacific Sociological Society. Before Tulane and Washington, Steiner had had a coordinate part in building the Department of Sociology and editing *Social Forces* at the University of North Carolina where he was professor of social technology from 1921 to 1927. Earlier, he had been assistant professor of sociology at the University of Cincinnati. Steiner's background and recruiting to the field of sociology followed the pattern of John L. Gillin. Born in St. Paris, Ohio, in 1880, he came to sociology through the twofold approach of the ministry and social work. In the ministry, after his graduation from Heidelberg Theological Seminary in 1905 and after his ordination in the same year, he had gone as missionary and professor to Japan from 1905 to 1912. In social work he had been assistant superintendent of the United Charities of Chicago, 1915–16, assistant director, Council of Social Agencies, Cincinnati, 1917–18; and National Director of Home Service, American Red Cross, 1918–19, when he was succeeded by J. L. Gillin. As a result of his experience and leadership in A.R.C., he published his *Education for Social Work* in 1921, and became professor at the University of North Carolina where he pioneered in community organization and in research in penology.

Steiner came to sociology through the Department of Sociology at the University of Chicago where Small and Henderson exerted great influence upon him. He received his Ph.D. degree at Chicago in 1915, after having taken an A.M. at Harvard in 1913. He was lecturer at Chicago in 1915–16. At the University of North Carolina, in addition to his pioneering work and teaching, he wrote *Community Organization,* 1925, and *The American Community in Action,* published in 1928; and *The North Carolina Chain Gang,* with Roy M. Brown, in 1928. As a part of his work as a member of the staff of the President's Committee on Social Trends, he wrote *Americans at Play* in 1933 and contributed the chapter on recreation agencies in *Recent Social Trends.* In 1937 he did a monograph for the Social Science Research Council on recreation in the depression. He also published *Recreation and Morale* in 1942. From his earlier studies in Japan he published *The Japanese Invasion* in 1917 and, keeping in close contact with the Japanese situation while at the University of Washington and as visiting professor at the University of Hawaii, he published in 1943 his *Behind the Japanese Mask.* Although Steiner's special field was the community his work in intergroup and intercultural relations was outstanding in the four regional centers in which he worked, namely in the Southeast at North Carolina, in the Deep South at New Orleans, in the Pacific Northwest at Seattle, and in the Orient in Japan and Hawaii. At the mid-century Steiner is again at work in Hawaii and in 1951 is resuming his observations in the "new" Japan.

Pitirim A. Sorokin

First awarded a fellowship and sponsored by E. A. Ross at Wisconsin, P. A. Sorokin came to the top ranks in American sociology when he was appointed head of the Department of Sociology at Harvard in 1930. Previously, he had been professor of sociology at the University of Minnesota from 1924 to 1930 where he had published *Leaves from a Russian Diary,* 1924; *Sociology of Revolution,* 1925; *Social Mobility,* 1927; *Contemporary Sociological Theories,* 1928; *Principles of Rural-Urban Sociology,* 1929. After going to Harvard, in addition to his monumental four-volume *Social and Cultural Dynamics,* 1937–44, Sorokin published with Zimmerman and Galpin a three-volume *Source Book in Rural Sociology,* 1930–31; *Time Budgets of Human Behavior,* 1939; *Crisis of This Age,* 1941; *Man and Society in Calamity,* 1942; *Socio-Cultural Causality, Time, Space,* 1943; *Russia and the United States,* 1944; *Society, Culture and Personality,* 1947; *The Reconstruction of Humanity,* 1948; *Altruistic Love,* 1950; *Social Philosophies of an Age of Crisis,* 1950. In his earlier career before coming to the United States he had published a number of works in Russian, including *Crime and Punishment,* 1914; *Leo Tolstoy as a Philosopher,* 1915; *Elements of Sociology,* 1919; *Systems of Sociology,* 1920–21; *General Theory of Law,* 1920.

Sorokin is one of a number of distinguished sociologists who, although born outside the United States, have achieved their maturity in American institutions. Born in Russia, January 21, 1889, Sorokin came to America in 1923 and was naturalized in 1930. Before coming to the United States he had received the degree of Dr. of Sociology from the University of St. Petersburg in 1922, where he was also professor of sociology for two years. There, he had been a member of various organizations and societies, including All-Russian Peasant Soviet, 1917; Council of Russian Republic, 1917; Russian Constitutional Assembly, 1918.

Since coming to the United States he has been president of the International Congress of Sociology, 1937, and a member of a half dozen European societies.

Sorokin went to Harvard carrying with him a pattern of European scholarship and erudition that was expected to be worthy of the Harvard tradition. His published works are sufficiently monumental to justify this expectation and it is primarily upon these that his place in American sociology will be fixed. Each of his two major works comprehends four volumes, namely, his *Rural-Urban Sociology* together with his *Source Book on Rural Sociology*; and his *Social and Cultural Dynamics*. His total published works might well be grouped into five main divisions. The first would be his contributions that grew out of the Russian Revolution and his experiences during it. In this group would be a half dozen books. The next grouping would consist of his books on the history and theory of sociology, the foundations of which were, in some cases, begun before coming to America, since some of his sources are from Russian sociologists of the earlier period. The third group would be his works on rural sociology, with Zimmerman and Galpin, a sort of monumental reference series that will not have to be duplicated. The fourth division is his notable four-volume *Social and Cultural Dynamics* with his cyclical concept of sensate ideational culture. The fifth division reflects Sorokin's application of his sensate culture constructs to the problems of contemporary society, including his newer ventures into the field of research and the study of certain principles of altruism. Jacques J. Maquet devotes Part II of his 1951 *Sociology of Knowledge* to Pitirim A. Sorokin, Part I being devoted to Karl Mannheim.

Albert G. Keller

Among the most dynamic of all the earlier sociologists and very much after the pattern of Sumner was his successor at Yale, A. G. Keller. Keller's tenure at Yale, continuing the Sumner tradition and bridging the distance between the Sumner sociology and the strong department developed by Maurice Davie, gave him a permanent strategic place in American sociology. Yet Keller would never align himself with the American Sociological Society, would never permit the term "sociology" to be applied to his department at Yale, and in general proceeded his vigorous way outside the fraternity. His writings were numerous, his style excellent, not only in his books but in many plausible articles in the *Yale Review* and other journals in his later years. He protested the manner by which the American Sociological Society was founded and staunchly remained aloof except as he completed Sumner's masterpiece, *Science of Society,* in four volumes and kept the Sumner workshop intact in fine museum fashion at his home in New Haven. He continued the Sumner tradition at Yale but wrote vigorously on his own after the completion of the four volumes. Among his books were *Homeric Society,* 1902; *Queries in Ethnology,* 1903; *Colonization,* 1908; *Physical and Commercial Geography,* 1910; *Societal Evolution,* 1915; *Through War to Peace,* 1918; *Evolution of Man,* 1922; *Starting Points in Social Science,* 1923; *Science of Society,* 1927; *Man's Rough Road,* 1932; *Brass Tacks,* 1938. He was editor of many of Sumner's essays and wrote *Reminiscences of William Graham Sumner,* 1933. Keller was born in Springfield, Ohio, August 10, 1874, and in 1950 was still vigorously writing, his seventy-six years qualifying him with his contemporaries for the long span of life so characteristic of the early American pioneers in sociology. His A.B. and Ph.D. were from Yale and he moved up from instructor in 1900 through assistant professor in 1902 to professor from 1907 to 1942. Like Cooley, at Michigan, Keller scarcely left his campus except for being away from New Haven while a captain in the Morale Staff in the United States Army in 1918.

W. E. B. Du Bois

Two other sociologists rate special priorities both for their contributions to realistic sociology and for their important roles in sociology as a college and university discipline. They are W. E. B. Du Bois and Charles S. Johnson. Du Bois, born in Great Barrington, Massachusetts, Feb. 23, 1868 began very early and completed rather late his notable work at Atlanta University. As identifying him outside the academic record, in between his earlier and later work, he contributed powerfully to what we have characterized elsewhere in this book as "practical sociology" and sociological writings. First, as originator and editor of the pioneering *Atlanta Sociological Studies* from 1897 to 1910, he was among the earliest to apply sociology to empirical inquiries, producing more than a dozen studies, some of which are listed in Chapter 19. He sojourned in New York from 1910 to 1932, as director of publications of the National Association for the Advancement of Colored People and editor of *The Crisis,* and thence went back as head of the Department of Sociology at Atlanta University in 1932 where he remained active until his seventy-sixth year, in 1944. He was conducting a region-wide conference in social research as recently as the late 1940's, with collaborators from the Universities of Chicago, North Carolina, Iowa State University, Fisk University, and many others in which he appeared more keenly aware of his problems and methods than did his distinguished visitors.

Few sociologists have had wider recognition than Du Bois in terms of honorary degrees and few have contributed to more widely read sociological literature. Resting solidly upon his earned academic A.B., A.M., and Ph.D. degrees at Harvard University, he received the LL.D. from Howard University in 1930; from Atlanta University in 1938; the Litt. D. from Fisk University in 1938; and the L.H.D. from Wilberforce in 1940. He was Fellow in the A.A.A.S. and a founder of the Pan-American Congress, and projector of the plan for "The Negro Encyclopedia." He is the author of *The Suppression of the Slave Trade,* 1896; *The Philadelphia Negro,* 1899; *The Souls of Black Folk,* 1903; *John Brown,* 1909; *Quest of the Silver Fleece,* 1911; *The Negro,* 1915; *Dark Water,* 1920; *The Life of Black Folk,* 1921; *Dark Princess,* 1928; *Black Reconstruction,* 1935; *Black Folk, Then and Now,* 1939; *Dusk of Dawn,* 1940; editor of *Phylon,* 1940–44.

Keeping in mind that Du Bois began his Atlanta studies in the 1890's just about the same time that sociology departments were being developed at Columbia University, the University of Chicago, and other pioneering institutions, the succession of his followers constitutes an important segment of American sociology. We have described the work of E. Franklin Frazier, head of the department at Howard University in Chapters 13 and 19. Others who followed at Atlanta were Ira Reid, later professor at Haverford; Mozell Hill currently head of the department at Atlanta; and Forrester Washington, head of the Atlanta School of Social Work.

Charles S. Johnson and Fisk University

Charles S. Johnson, before his election to his current position as president of Fisk University, had been president of the Southern Sociological Society and had developed a notable center for sociological research and teaching at Fisk University. Among those whom he had added to his faculty was E. Franklin Frazier, later to be head of the sociology department of Howard University and president of the American Sociological Society in 1948. Johnson's major published works include a collaboration in the notable *The Negro in Chicago*, 1922; *Race Relations*, 1924; *The Collapse of Cotton Tenancy*, 1935; and he is the author of *The Negro in American Civilization*, 1930; *Economic Status of the Negro*, 1933; *Shadow of the Plantation*, 1934; *Preface to Racial Understanding*, 1936; *The Negro College Graduate*, 1936; *Growing Up in the Black Belt*, 1941; *Patterns of Segregation*, 1946. Few American sociologists have exercised a wider range of influence or participated in such varied academic and public service activities. Born in Bristol, Virginia, July 24, 1893, he was graduated from Union University in 1917 and from the University of Chicago in 1918 and later received the Litt. D. from Union in 1928, and the L.H.D. from Howard in 1941. He was director of research in the Urban League and editor of *Opportunity*, 1923–29; director of social science, Fisk University, 1928–48. He was awarded the Anisfield Award for his *Negro College Graduate* and the Harmon Award for distinguished achievement in science in 1930. He has served in various appointments in the League of Nations, and was a member of UNESCO for the United Nations. He has been on various boards and committees of the Social Science Research Council, the President's Commission on Farm Tenancy, the President's Committee on Civil Liberties, the Julius Rosenwald Fund, the Tennessee Valley Authority, and a score of local and regional organizations. He has been chairman of the Executive Committee of the Southern Regional Council, of the Southern Policy Committee, and a member of the National Council on Race Relations.

Significant has been the influence of Atlanta University and Fisk. Following at Fisk were Preston Valien and Alvin Rose; at Tuskegee and Lincoln was Oliver Cox. Gordon Hancock at Virginia University was a prime mover in the Southern Regional Council. Valien was able to catalogue more than a hundred teachers of sociology in nearly as many institutions in the South alone. Among members of faculties outside the South, Ira Reid had been visiting professor of sociology at New York University and head of the department at Haverford College in 1947. The significance of the catalogue of teachers in Southern Negro colleges was twofold. Besides the quality of work done by many, it was significant that sociology had earned so prominent a place in Southern institutions and that so many instructors had studied sociology in so many universities.

Sociological Research Association

A group that represents an elected personnel of sociologists chosen as qualifying as major sociologists, as measured by the actual achievements of research and publication, is the Sociological Research Association with some seventy-four members, with the top limit of one hundred members not yet filled at the mid-century point. While this list should not be appraised too highly, it does give some measure of what sociology is in terms of sociologists that were voted as top representatives by a limited number of leading sociologists. Except that the association features research as the basis for election, and except that it has often had a program of its own at the annual meetings of the American Sociological Society, it has been little more than a catalogue of self-elected members. Some sociologists have declined membership. The membership for 1950 classified by state of birth and institution follows.

Name	Native State	Institution Represented
Robert C. Angell	Michigan	Michigan
Read Bain	Oregon	Miami (Ohio)
Howard Becker	New York	Wisconsin
Robert Bierstedt	Iowa	Illinois
Herbert Blumer	Missouri	Chicago
Raymond V. Bowers	British Columbia	Air University (Alabama)
Edmund de S. Brunner	Pennsylvania	Teachers College, Columbia
Ernest W. Burgess	Canada	Chicago
F. Stuart Chapin	New York	Minnesota
Harold T. Christensen	Idaho	Purdue

Name	Native State	Institution Represented
John A. Clausen	New York	National Institute of Mental Health (Maryland)
Marshall B. Clinard	Massachusetts	Wisconsin
Leonard S. Cottrell	Virginia	Cornell
Kingsley Davis	Texas	Columbia
Stuart C. Dodd	Turkey	Washington
Ellsworth Faris	Tennessee	Chicago
Robert E. L. Faris	Texas	Washington
Joseph K. Folsom	New York	Vassar College
E. Franklin Frazier	Maryland	Howard
Charles E. Gehlke	Ohio	Western Reserve
John L. Gillin	Iowa	Wisconsin
Louis Guttman	New York	Hebrew
Margaret Jarman Hagood	Georgia	U. S. Department of Agriculture
Paul K. Hatt	Canada	Northwestern
Philip M. Hauser	Illinois	Chicago
Amos H. Hawley	Missouri	Michigan
Reuben L. Hill	Utah	North Carolina
Homer L. Hitt	Texas	Louisiana State
A. B. Hollingshead	Wyoming	Yale
Floyd N. House	Michigan	Virginia
Charles S. Johnson	Virginia	Fisk
Clifford Kirkpatrick	Massachusetts	Indiana
John H. Kolb	Wisconsin	Wisconsin
Richard T. La Piere	Wisconsin	Stanford
Paul F. Lazarsfeld	Austria	Columbia
Alexander H. Leighton	Pennsylvania	Cornell
Olen E. Leonard	Texas	Vanderbilt
George A. Lundberg	North Dakota	Washington
Robert S. Lynd	Indiana	Columbia
Robert M. MacIver	Scotland	Columbia
Thomas C. McCormick	Alabama	Wisconsin
Robert K. Merton	Pennsylvania	Columbia
Delbert C. Miller	Ohio	Washington
Elio D. Monachesi	Italy	Minnesota
Ernest R. Mowrer	Kansas	Northwestern
John H. Mueller	Missouri	Indiana
Lowry Nelson	Utah	Minnesota
Theodore M. Newcomb	Ohio	Michigan
Howard W. Odum	Georgia	North Carolina

Name	*Native State*	*Institution Represented*
William F. Ogburn	Georgia	Chicago
Talcott Parsons	Colorado	Harvard
Stuart A. Queen	Kansas	Washington University
Walter C. Reckless	Pennsylvania	Ohio State
Robert Redfield	Illinois	Chicago
Stuart A. Rice	Minnesota	U. S. Bureau of Census
Frank A. Ross	Illinois	Columbia
Calvin F. Schmid	Ohio	Washington
Thorsten Sellin	Sweden	Pennsylvania
William H. Sewell	Michigan	Wisconsin
Clifford R. Shaw		Chicago Institute Juvenile Research
Henry S. Shryock	Maryland	U. S. Bureau of Census
Raymond F. Sletto	Minnesota	Ohio State
T. Lynn Smith	Colorado	Florida
Jesse F. Steiner	Ohio	Washington
Frederick F. Stephan	Illinois	Princeton
Samuel A. Stouffer	Iowa	Harvard
Edward A. Suchman		Cornell
Edwin H. Sutherland	Nebraska	Indiana
Conrad Taeuber	South Dakota	U. S. Bureau of Census
Irene B. Taeuber	Missouri	Princeton
Paul W. Tappan	Connecticut	New York
Carl C. Taylor	Iowa	Bureau of Agricultural Economics, Washington
Dorothy S. Thomas	Maryland	Pennsylvania
Warren S. Thompson	Nebraska	Miami (Ohio)
Clark Tibbitts	Illinois	U. S. Division of Public Health Methods
John Useem	New York	Michigan
George B. Vold	South Dakota	Minnesota
W. Lloyd Warner	California	Chicago
H. Ashley Weeks	Massachusetts	New York
P. K. Whelpton	New York	Miami (Ohio)
R. Clyde White	Texas	Western Reserve
Malcolm M. Willey	Maine	Minnesota
Robin M. Williams, Jr.	North Carolina	Cornell
Robert F. Winch	Ohio	Northwestern
Louis Wirth	Germany	Chicago
Donald Young	Pennsylvania	Russell Sage Foundation
Kimball Young	Utah	Northwestern
C. C. Zimmerman	Missouri	Harvard

CHAPTER 22

Applied Social Science, Interdisciplinary Efforts, "Practical" Sociology

In contrast to sociology as science and as primarily a college and university subject comprehending the teaching, research, and writing of sociologists on the faculties of American institutions is that other relatively large segment of American sociology that may well be designated as "practical" sociology, allied or interdisciplinary social science, and "sociological" literature, so designated by the public and publishers' classifications. This sociological writing constitutes a very substantial bulk in the total literature of social concern, social interpretation, social relations and dilemmas, and in nearly all of the histories and summaries of social thought. There is also a large "non-sociological" (in the above sense) segment in American sociology that consists primarily in rich source materials utilized by sociologists from allied social sciences and often from intersocial science cooperative efforts. Although all these do not conform to the more accurate definition of sociology as the scientific study of human society in which authentic methods of study by sociologists are utilized, nevertheless they reflect a popular sociology comprehending the teachings, writings, philosophies, and action programs that connote social inquiry, social interpretation, social reform, social welfare, social work, and other applied social work disciplines. They also represent a vast body of facts and knowledge that the sociologist must glean from whatever sources. All of these combined, in contrast to American sociology as an integral special social science primarily in colleges and universities, may be somewhat analogous to much of the earlier European sociology where there were few sociology professors and where there was perhaps general resistance to sociology's becoming a separate integral social science designated as sociology. Sociology in this sense is not only a backlog of what has gone before but continues to challenge American sociologists to accept a broader field of opportunity in the future than they may have done in the very recent past.

Public Expectations for Sociology

In our analysis of the nature and range of sociology in the United States we have already called attention to the considerable expectation of the public that sociology should contribute much to practical situations and to the amelioration of problems that grow out of social change and the tensions of adaptation and adjustment. More and more, as society becomes more complex and dilemmas multiply, there are increasingly reasonable expectations, not only of the general public but of the natural scientists and scholars in the humanities, that if sociology is really the scientific study of society it should be capable of exploring all aspects of contemporary society and from its findings it should be able to provide the basis for both understanding and for ameliorative effort and societal direction. It has sometimes been suggested that, if sociologists will not come to grips with the living society of the contemporary world, others will undertake to give it public articulation, even as literary authors took over biography from the document-ridden historians.

This hope for sociology to become more dynamic in its ameliorative and popular interpretative aspects is especially strong in the increasing number of younger college students who wish to take sociology for special purposes, in a multitude of adults recently graduated in the fields of literature, public affairs, moral and social reform, and in editorial writers and magazine makers and publishers, amongst whom there are many bold adventurers. Thousands of students flock toward sociology with the definite objective of entering "social service," of "helping humanity," of "being worth something to society," of "doing good," and of "solving problems." This is especially true in the fields of race relations, international relations, labor problems, personnel work, alongside the general purpose of doing preprofessional work, preparing for social work, public affairs, journalism, and writing.

To some extent the expectations of the public have been justified in the long and distinguished record of many who have so associated themselves in the study of society and have attempted both to interpret situations and to recommend solutions. In the catalogue of many such notable names may be found a distinguished company whose contributions have been large. And while it is not possible to give an adequate roll of such contributors or always to identify them within a single field, it is possible to approximate such classification both for the purpose of defining their own work and for interpreting these aspects of American sociology.

Five Groupings of "Non-Sociological" Contributions

Chronologically, perhaps the special segments of general source materials and "non-sociological" literature that are nevertheless organic parts of American sociology might be classified into five groupings. *First* would be "American life" sources, since American society is after all the setting for American sociology, on the one hand, as it set the incidence for the "new world," powerfully influenced by but breaking away from the "old world," and, on the other hand, powerfully influencing the later new world culture. Sources here are primarily from general history, literary history, and the economic and political development of the nation. American sociology in the making had to be partly American life, yet in the contemporary era of 1950 and on, many more universities and social scientists are renewing their sources on American civilization. The *second* category is one of presociology vintage in America and consists of the work of many Americans in the field of social problems, practical sociology, applied sociology, social work, and social service in the framework of the National Conference of Charities and Correction, the American Prison Association, and other special ameliorative fields. This notable group, already featured in our chapter on the American background of American sociology, constitutes a catalogue of perhaps a hundred of America's best leaders as described below. The *third* group of "non-sociological" sources would naturally follow, namely, the backlogs of European philosophy, economics, and political science, along with the geographers and others whose works were basic to presociology in America. Some of these have been discussed in our chapter on social theory and the history of social thought. The *fourth* group, then, would be the American scholars and workers who have contributed powerfully to sociology from other fields: anthropology, social work, psychology, history, economics, or those who have contributed through more than one social science or through cooperative research and writing. These are, in some instances, inseparable from many of the European sources. Here again, the movement toward integration of the social sciences and especially the closer working together of sociology with cultural anthropology and social psychology indicates the dynamics of the present as well as the record of the past. The *fifth* and final group, then, would be what may be called general "sociological" literature, as classified by *Publishers' Weekly,* as reflected in series of public affairs publications, and general works in popular economics, sociology, anthropology, and literature, with special reference to drama and fiction with sociomoral theme plots.

Intersocial Science and Allied Fields

Groups three and four, however, are the more logical two from which to begin to review the total field. And we may begin with examples of cooperative intersocial science works and subsequently refer to examples of cooperative research instituted in the 1920's. A first pioneer here was Harry Elmer Barnes' *History and Prospects of the Social Sciences,* which was widely used by sociologists. Published in 1925, it was followed closely by *The Interrelations of the Social Sciences* by Ogburn and Goldenweiser in 1927. Both of these are featured in the chapter on theory and methodology but need to be mentioned here primarily as a part of the record of what was new at the time. They were in line with a considerable movement toward cooperative research and the integration of the social sciences led primarily by Beardsley Ruml and Sydnor Walker of the Laura Spelman Rockefeller Memorial in the 1920's. From funds granted by this and other foundations, more than a dozen university institutes and committees were stimulated and aided in cooperative social research and promotion. Of the younger sociologists, a number have achieved special rating through interdisciplinary work or through their administration of research agencies or other closely allied fields. Donald Young, now director of the Russell Sage Foundation, did notable work with the Social Science Research Council, first as fellowship secretary and later as executive director and especially when the headquarters were in Washington during the World War II. Guy B. Johnson of North Carolina was prime director of sociology studies in the Myrdal *American Dilemma* investigation and was collaborator in Klineberg's *Characteristics of the American Negro.* More than this, he was executive director of the Southern Regional Council in its first difficult years of transition from the old Commission on Interracial Cooperation. Samuel Stouffer, who was a contributor to *Recent Social Trends,* moved into a strategic position as director of research in Harvard's new Department of Social Relations and he did signal work in the study of the American soldier. Gordon W. Blackwell is director of the Institute for Research in Social Science at the University of North Carolina. Robert Merton was director of Columbia University's Bureau of Applied Social Research where he both directed its research and gave momentum to its program at the same time that he continued his theoretical contributions.

Examples of cooperative research and the promotion of interdisciplinary cooperation constitute a part of the history of this phase of allied social science. During the 1920's the Social Science Research Council set up committees for exploring methodology. A major volume was published in 1927 as a result of this work and was entitled *Methods in Social Science: A Case Book*; it was edited by Stuart Rice. Examples of cooperative research as published in major volumes would include *Recent Social Trends,* with more than two score cooperating social scientists, the directors of research being W. F. Ogburn and Howard W. Odum; *The Study of War,* with two volumes, edited and arranged by Quincy Wright; *An American Dilemma,* by Gunnar Myrdal.

Examples of Interdisciplinary Approach to Sociology

A notable example of the interrelations of the social sciences in the history of American sociology is that of sociology at Harvard University in the past and as recently projected into the future. When P. A. Sorokin organized the new department after transferring from Minnesota, his faculty, as announced, included professors of economics, history, philosophy, psychology, and social ethics. The reorganization of the work in 1947 with Talcott Parsons as chairman set up a new department of social relations including sociology, cultural anthropology, and clinical psychology. So, too, as representing a trend in this direction is the widely prevalent practice in many universities of combining sociology and anthropology into a single department.

Cited, too, might be the multi-disciplinary faculty seminar at the University of North Carolina, under the direction of John P. Gillin, engaged in the preparation of a statement of a theory of human behavior upon which a number of fields could agree. Represented were anthropology, philosophy, psychology, sociology, statistics.

Returning now to more specific references to the mixed or borderline sociologists, a good place to start is again with historian Harry Elmer Barnes, himself representative of the intersocial science advocate who cites numerous allied social scientists. Barnes, who has published the most comprehensive works on the history and structure of sociology and the other social sciences, exemplifies, in a very special way, the area of interdisciplinary American sociology. He does this in two ways. In the first place, he classifies himself primarily as belonging to the historical study group and has contributed more to the total social sciences and their specialisms than to sociology itself. In the second place, he states boldly on pages 741–42 of his *Introduction to the History of Sociology* that "probably the largest group of sociologists are what are usually called 'social economists' or 'practical sociologists.' " He lists, among others, E. T. Devine, Samuel McCune Lindsay, Jane Addams, Graham Taylor, Edith Abbott, Mary van Kleeck, Mary E. Richmond, Jessica Peixotto, Robert Woods, James Ford, Porter Lee, R. M. MacIver, J. L. Gillin, Paul U. Kellogg, Philip Klein, R. W. Kelso, S. A. Queen, J. S. Burgess, P. A. Parsons, D. M. Schneider, and Sanford Bates. Of these, MacIver, Gillin, and Queen were presidents of the American Sociological Society.

Also, Barnes lists a great variety of others as sociologists who are ordinarily nowhere so classified as to their primary interests. Thus Everett Dean Martin, the popular extension psychologist, is listed alongside Floyd Allport, L. L. Bernard, E. R. Groves, C. A. Ellwood. Franz Boas is listed alongside Frank Hankins as a student of race, while social biologists are listed as C. B. Davenport, Raymond Pearl, E. G. Conklin, H. H. Goddard, E. A. Hooton, E. M. East; population students are designated as biological sociologists catalogued, again along with Hankins, as W. F. Willcox, J. A. Field, besides W. S. Thompson, F. W. Notestein, H. P. Fairchild, and the other population specialists. James A. Quinn, Nels Anderson, Clifford Shaw, and Milla Alihan are listed as anthropogeographers alongside R. E. Park and Ernest W. Burgess, the ecologists. So too, Shotwell, Turner, and Beard, the great historians are catalogued in the field of "historical sociology."

In somewhat the same way he catalogues English scholars and authors whose works have been widely used as source materials but who are not primarily sociologists. Barnes refers to them as "grist for the sociological mill." Among the more than forty listed are Hobson, the Webbs, Tawney, Cole, Toynbee, Slater, Marvin, Wallas, Marett, Rivers, Duckworth, Carr-Saunders. Of all the English scholars, Barnes, page 605, could "ignore all British writers except Hobhouse in a book formally dedicated to Systematic Sociologists."

Other examples of how great the "non-sociological" literature is in the history and background of American sociology are found in other reference books by Barnes, who has been American sociology's chief historian. For instance, in the preface to *Contemporary Social Theory,* done in collaboration with the Beckers in 1940, permission is acknowledged to quote from the books of eighteen publishers. Of these, only books by Giddings, W. I. and Dorothy Thomas, and Sumner represented sociologists proper. The majority of the authors quoted included Paul Radin's *Crashing Thunder, Primitive Man as Philosopher, The Method and Theory of Ethnology and Social Anthropology*; Reinhold Niebuhr's *The Contribution of Religion to Social Work, Moral Man and Immoral Society,* and *Reflections on the End of an Era*; others were F. H. Allport's *Handbook of Psychology,* W. M. Kranefeldt's *Secret Ways of the Mind,* T. N. Carver's *Religion Worth Having,* Otto Rank's *Modern Education,* James Baikie's *The Life of the Ancient East,* Harry Ward's *The New Social Order,* W. H. R. Rivers' *Instinct and the Unconscious,* L. T. Hobhouse's *Development and Purpose,* S. Freud's *Totem and Taboo,* J. H. Robinson's *The New History.*

As further illustration of the very great number of "allied sociologists" whose works are widely used by American sociologists, the index of names and citations by Barnes and Becker in *Contemporary Social Theory* may be studied. In the general index of authors and references, comprehending considerably more than two thousand names, *scarcely more than one hundred* are sociologists in the more specific sense of being members of the American Sociological Society and of faculties of colleges and universities devoting themselves primarily to teaching and research in sociology. Or again, to take another example, there are some five hundred titles of books listed in the "Guide to Sociological Specialties" of which no more than one-fifth of the authors can be entitled sociologists by any liberal range of definition, except that of contributing to special social problems and general sociological literature. Finally, to take another example from Barnes, his chapter in *Modern Theories of Criminology and Penology,* with more than sixty pages treating nine main headings, devotes less than a half dozen pages to what American sociologists have contributed to the various fields.

Examples of Interdisciplinary Scholars

As in our discussion of social theory there is no disposition to make invidious comparisons between the history of social thought and realistic sociological theory, the purpose being to indicate forcefully that they are not one and the same, so here our purpose is simply to distinguish between the sociologists and the other social scientists or general scholars. This could well be illustrated in no less distinguished an example than Giddings who credits Adam Smith with the genesis of his consciousness of kind. So, too, even as Adam Smith was an economist so was Max Weber a political philosopher, Darwin, a distinguished natural scientist, Westermarck, a notable anthropologist, just as most of the European "sociologists" were primarily philosophers. It comes to pass naturally, therefore, that the distinguishing line of identification is not so clear or simply delineated in the great array of historical cataloguing as is true in *Contemporary American Sociology.*

One way of continuing our story of special contributors to sociology from other fields is to illustrate with examples. An excellent beginning is that of the "Middletowns" by the Lynds, for *Middletown,* one of the most popular and universally known texts used by sociologists, came to sociology through the series of social and religious surveys directed by Luther Fry and Edmund de S. Brunner. Neither of the Lynds was a sociologist or had primary training in sociology. Robert Lynd had been associated with the Commonwealth Fund and was apparently as far from a chair in sociology at Columbia as was imaginable. *Middletown* in manuscript was a report of a survey and it was questioned whether it could be published and how and for what use. Then it was suggested that Clark Wissler write an introduction setting the survey in the framework of the anthropological method of studying the community and its culture. This was done successfully and the book became a best seller. Thus Clark Wissler, the anthropologist, who had already become a standard reference for sociologists for his *universal culture traits* and his *culture area,* contributed again powerfully to sociology while Lynd became a "sociologist" of the first order.

Another excellent illustration of the intersocial science contributions is the work of Melville J. Herskovits of Northwestern University whose researches and writings have been such as to get fellowship support and supporting grants from all three of the learned societies representing the sciences, humanities, and social sciences. Thus Herskovits had done special research under the auspices of the Social Science Research Council, the National Research Council, and the American Council of Learned Societies, besides being awarded a Guggenheim Memorial Fellowship for writing. Herskovits' work becomes a "must" for students of race and ethnic groups.

Popular Borderline Fundamentals

Something of the same sort of necessity befell sociologists who wished to make the study of culture more nearly a frame of reference for sociological study. The studies of Lowie and Kroeber on primitive societies and social organization and the continuity of the cultural process are primary needs. Robert Redfield's *Studies of Folk Society* is basic. Ralph Linton's *The Study of Man* is a first-rate text on sociology. Malinowski, with his functional anthropology and his case studies of sex, alongside Ruth Benedict's *The Patterns of Culture* and Margaret Mead's books on primitive growing up quickly became valuable reference books for sociologists. In later years the Benedict and Mead treatises on race and intercultural relations were widely utilized, as was Mead's *Male and Female.* In the same general field the new techniques of Dollard, Powdermaker, and Warner, through which the anthropological approach to the concrete study of communities, with special emphasis upon behavior, came to be so widely used as to constitute basic sociological source materials, as did the other new types of community studies, exemplified in the "Yankee City Series," and others symbolizing the new empirical research. Something of the same process of moving into the sociological field was true of P. F. Lazarsfeld, head of the Department of Sociology at Columbia University in 1950. Following his coming to the United States in 1933, from the fields of psychology and mathematics, traveling on a Rockefeller Fellowship, he did distinguished work at Princeton in the new field of communications as director of radio research, 1937–40, and was then made professor of sociology at Columbia. He was, with Robert Merton, also director of the Bureau of Applied Social Research. Subsequently, he became head of the Department of Sociology and his associate at Princeton, Kingsley Davis, became director of the Bureau in his stead. Lazarsfeld has traveled and lectured widely devoting himself little to the university itself, having made studies in social psychology for governmental agencies and business concerns up to 1937 when he went to Princeton.

Sociometry and Sociodrama as Sociology

Another notable example of a new specialism coming rapidly into the field of sociology and having wide influence and adoption is the work of J. L. Moreno, founder of *Sociometry* and the Sociometric Institute. Born in Rumania in 1892, trained in philosophy and medicine, he was naturalized in the United States in 1935. In New York he has been inventor, a practicing physician, a practicing psychiatrist, a founder of a sanatorium, of an impromptu theater, of a therapeutic theater. He is the author of *Who Shall Survive?*, 1934; *The Words of the Father*, 1941; *Sociometry and the Cultural Order*, 1943; *The Concept of Sociodrama*, 1943. As indicative of his standing with American sociologists in 1949, in addition to having Ernest W. Burgess on his editorial board for *Sociometry*, an even baker's dozen of major sociologists have constituted the majority of his contributing editors. These are Howard Becker of Wisconsin, Stuart Chapin of Minnesota, Leonard Cottrell of Cornell, Stuart Dodd and George Lundberg of the University of Washington, Joseph Folsom of Vassar, Paul Lazarsfeld of Columbia, E. C. Lindeman of the New York School of Social Work, Charles P. Loomis of Michigan State, Robert Lynd of Columbia, Irwin T. Sanders of Kentucky, Samuel Stouffer of Harvard, and L. D. Zeleney of Colorado State College of Education.

Among the many-sided social scientists contributing to sociology's science materials and backgrounds are the social economists. Cooley himself was very influential in conditioning some of these. John R. Commons and Richard Ely who started out teaching sociology were powerful contributors to the backgrounds of industrial sociology. Walton Hamilton was part product of Cooley, as was Thorstein Veblen who was almost as much sociologist as social economist. Alvin Johnson, starting as an orthodox economist, broke away to become a brilliant author and non-orthodox social scientist, and the director of the New School for Social Research, bridging New York to the old world's refugee scholars.

The psychologists and social psychologists who contributed so abundantly to American sociology are treated in a limited way in a subsequent chapter. But there are more psychologists who write social psychologies than there are sociologists writing in that field. In no way, other than recognition of their many-sided contributions, can the work of the Allports, of Warner and Dollard, of Klineberg and others be given due place or reference. The same is true to some extent of the later psychologists who are authors of a considerable catalogue of social psychologies, too many and too specialized to find common use among many sociologists. Something of the same might be said of the educational sociologists, Snedden, Rugg, and Counts, as well as of Stuart Chase, the popular, unpopular popularizer of economics and a facile interpreter in *The Proper Study of Mankind,* a sort of all things to a part of all men.

Another extensive and important comparative special field of research and study is what has constituted increasingly an entity that may be characterized as Jewish sociology. From *Jewish Social Studies* and samplings of recent books, something of the nature and range of main contributions may be observed. More specifically, the field is discussed by Arieh Tartakower in "New Trends in Jewish Sociology," in *Jewish Social Studies,* April, 1950; by Alvin Johnson in *Social Research* for December, 1947; by Nathan Glazer in "What Sociology Knows about American Jews," in *Commentary,* December, 1949; by Howard W. Odum in "Toward the Dynamic Study of Jewish Culture," in *Social Forces,* May, 1951; and in the *Yivo Annual of Jewish Social Science.*

Source Books for Sociology

In further explanation of the large body of "non-sociological" literature in American sociology several considerations are relevant to the logical situation as it is. In the first place the definitions of sociology necessarily varied widely in the developing stages and continue to vary. Thus far, those who considered sociology a general over-all synthesis of all the social sciences, the utilization of the works of other social sciences, would constitute a necessary marshaling of source materials and methods for the study of general society. W. T. Wiley has tabulated and analyzed the selections published in eight source books utilized by sociologists, ranging from Park and Burgess, Davis and Barnes, Case and Kimball Young, of the earlier ones, to Wilson and Kolb as late as 1948. Of the 680 authors, selections from whose work are listed, approximately only seventy would qualify as sociologists and certainly not more than a hundred could be so classified by the widest possible definition of sociologists. The total categories included more than thirty special areas ranging from geographic exploration to literary criticism. Represented were social work, history, education, philosophy, psychology, psychiatry, social psychology, child study, organized labor, city planning, rural and urban work, economics and commerce, anthropology and ethnology, biology and genetics, political science and public administration, the work of columnists and publicists, jurisprudence, literature and folklore, medicine and public health, race and intercultural relations, and others.

Harry Elmer Barnes

Before turning to the large and distinguished group of practical sociologists, a single notable example of the allied social scientists may well be discussed again here in special perspective. This is Harry Elmer Barnes whose works we have already featured as contributing powerfully to social segments of American sociology. As one of a very few sociologist members of PEN, Barnes might very well be classified as primarily author and writer with his own identification with history as his major field. Born at Auburn, New York, June 18, 1889, he was graduated from Syracuse University in 1913, where he also took his M.A. degree, in 1914. Studies at Columbia in 1915–16 were followed by a year at Harvard. Returning to Columbia as a fellow in history, 1917–18, he took his Ph.D degree there in 1918. He was professor of history at Clark University, 1919–23, professor of history, economics, sociology at Smith College, 1923–30. In addition, he taught at Amherst, the New School for Social Research, and was professor of history in summer sessions at the universities of Montana, Oregon, California, Wisconsin, Cornell.

He probably wrote more books of greater range and variety than any

other author whose books were used liberally by sociologists and probably came nearer to symbolizing the integration of the social sciences
than any other American author. He held membership in the social
science learned societies for sociology, economics, political science, history,
anthropology, ethnology, geography, labor legislation, criminal law. He
also held membership in a half dozen foreign learned societies and was
fellow in the American Ethnological Society, the American Geographical
Society and the American Association for the Advancement of Science,
besides being a member of a half dozen scholarship fraternities. Of his
forty books a half dozen were in the field of penology; about the same
number were devoted to the general, historical aspects of sociology and
social science; about as many to social problems; a dozen to history and
historical treatises on World War II and the meaning of history. His
main books include *Sociology before Comte*, 1917; *History of the Penal
Reformatory and Correctional Institutions of New Jersey*, 1918; *Social
History of the Western World*, 1921; *Progress of American Penology*,
1922; *Sociology and Political Theory*, 1923; *The New History and the
Social Studies*, 1925; *History and Social Intelligence*, 1926; *The Genesis
of the World War*, 1926; *The Repression of Crime*, 1926; *The Evolution
of Penology in Pennsylvania*, 1927; Part I in Davis and Barnes' *Introduction to Sociology*, 1927; *An Economic and Social History of Europe*,
1927; *Living in the Twentieth Century*, 1928; *In Quest of Truth and
Justice*, 1928; *L'Angleterre et la Guerre Mondiale*, 1928; *The Making
of a Nation*, 1929; *World Politics in Modern Civilization*, 1929; *The
Twilight of Christianity*, 1929; *The Story of Punishment*, 1930; *Battling
the Crime Wave*, 1931; *Can Man Be Civilized?*, 1932; *Prohibition versus Civilization*, 1932; *The Money Changers versus the New Deal*, 1934;
History of Western Civilization, 2 volumes, 1935; *An Economic History
of the Western World*, 1937; *Intellectual and Cultural History of the
Western World*, 1937 (new and enlarged edition, 1941); *A History of
Historical Writing*, 1937; *Social Thought from Lore to Science*, 2 volumes, 1938; *Society in Transition*, 1939; *Contemporary Social Theory*,
1940; *The American Way of Life*, 1942; *Social Institutions*, 1942; *New
Horizons in Criminology*, 1943; *Prisons in Wartime*, 1944; *Pennsylvania Penology*, 1944; *Introduction to History of Sociology*, 1947; *Historical Sociology*, 1948.

Barnes was also editor of *A History of Political Theories; Recent Times,* 1924; *The History and Prospects of the Social Sciences,* 1925; *Ploetz's Manual of Universal History,* new edition, 1925; *An Introduction to Sociology,* 1927; *Readings in Sociology,* 1927; *The Illustrated World History,* 1935; *Universal History of the World,* 1937; and others of lesser note.

Pioneers before and with Sociology

America produced few, if any, more distinguished individuals than many of those practical sociologists whose work, for the most part, was contemporary with the earlier sociological professors who inaugurated formal sociology into American universities. As a matter of fact, the group might well be headed by Charles R. Henderson of the Chicago Department of Sociology who was also president of the National Conference of Charities and Correction. He literally bridged the distance between sociology and social work. As illustrating this important segment of applied sociology, as commonly understood, three centers — Chicago, New York, and Boston — afford excellent examples. In Chicago just about the time Albion W. Small was founding his Department of Sociology at the university, Florence Kelley in 1891 was joining Jane Addams at Hull House and Graham Taylor was president of the old Chicago School of Civics and Philanthropy. Charles R. Henderson, professor of sociology at the University of Chicago, was the university representative of this group, which then, reinforced, became the new School of Social Service Administration, a part of the university system, with Edith Abbott and Sophonisba Breckinridge, long-time colleagues in social work education and public administration research, as dean and professor, respectively. The social settlement movement with Jane Addams and later on Lillian Wald in a new setting, with its work with youth, women, labor, child welfare, served as training grounds for some Ph.D. sociologists such as Jesse F. Steiner, Emory S. Bogardus, Stuart A. Queen, and many others.

In New York, the Russell Sage Foundation, the New York School of Social Work and the *Survey* were centers of powerful contributions and over-all services to the applied field of sociology. Shelby Harrison himself was a pioneer, starting with the notable *Pittsburgh Survey* and ending up as director of the Russell Sage Foundation, succeeding the Glenns, both of whom were presidents of the National Conference of Charities and Correction, later the National Conference of Social Work. On his staff at the Russell Sage Foundation was a notable galaxy of social science specialists. Joanna Colcord was director of the charity organization department. Hastings H. Hart was director of the penology department. Mary Van Kleeck was director of industrial relations studies. Then again, Mary Richmond was director of charity organization at the time she produced her notable book *Social Diagnosis*. In this group would be C. C. Carstens of the Child Welfare League of America, whose work was done firsthand in every state of the Union. Porter Lee, long-time director of the New York School, and president of the National Conference of Social Work would be listed also alongside Paul Kellogg, editor of the *Survey* and *Survey Graphic,* often utilized in sociology classes in many institutions.

In Boston, not only the later work of Richard Cabot and Joanna Colcord, already referred to, but the notable contributions of William Healy of the Judge Baker Foundation set new standards of case study of youth and delinquents and became essential teaching materials for all students of crime and penology. So, too, the Gluecks, Eleanor and Sheldon, followed with similar studies of children, women, and delinquents, basing their observations on hundreds of cases.

Again, it is not possible adequately to catalogue and appraise all of that group of authors and workers worthy of the background of coordinate services in American sociology. It is possible, however, to call a long roll of many earlier and later authors who will serve to illustrate our general definitions of their distinguished contributions to the sociological backlog of source materials.

A Roll Call of Allied Workers

Edith Abbott, born in Grand Island, Nebraska, September 26, 1876, sometime dean of the School of Social Service Administration at the University of Chicago, and author of *Women in Industry* and *Social Welfare and Education.*

Grace Abbott, born in Grand Island, Nebraska, November 7, 1878, sometime head of the Children's Bureau of the U. S. Government and author of many brochures on children and immigrants.

Jane Addams, born in Cedarville, Illinois, September 6, 1860, long-time head of famed Hull House and author of *The Spirit of Youth and the City Streets* and of a half dozen other distinguished volumes.

Will W. Alexander, born in Morrisville, Missouri, July 15, 1884, pioneer in race relations, founder of the Commission on Interracial Cooperation, vice-president of the Julius Rosenwald Fund.

Carol Aronovici, born in Rumania, September 18, 1881, noted community and city planner, author of *Housing the Masses* and *Americanization*.

O. E. Baker, born in Tiffin, Ohio, September 10, 1883, the sociological geographer and population planner at Washington, author of *Agriculture in Modern Life* and scores of brochures.

Sophonisba Breckinridge, born in Lexington, Kentucky, April 1, 1866, University of Chicago, long-time team worker with Edith Abbott and author of *Public Welfare Administration*.

Frank Bruno, born in Florence, Italy, June 1, 1874, professor of applied sociology and social work, Washington University, specialist in social administration, and author of *Theory of Social Work*.

V. F. Calverton, born in Baltimore, Maryland, June 25, 1900, sociologist and writer, free-lance writer in economics and sociology, author of *Bankruptcy of Marriage* and *The Making of Society*.

C. C. Carstens, born in Bredstead, Germany, April 2, 1865, notable child-welfare specialist, social worker, Ph.D., University of Pennsylvania, and author of many brochures on child welfare.

Joanna Colcord, born at sea, March 18, 1882, social worker, director of the Charity Organization Department, Russell Sage Foundation, child specialist from Boston, and author of *Broken Homes*.

John R. Commons, born in Hollandsberg, Ohio, October 13, 1862, early professor of sociology at Oberlin College and the universities of Indiana and Syracuse, pioneer in social aspects of labor and author of many books, including *History of Labor in the United States*.

George S. Counts, born in Baldwin City, Kansas, December 9, 1889, dynamic professor of education at Teachers College, Columbia, and author of *The American Road to Culture, The Social Foundations of Education, The Prospects of American Democracy*.

Fred Croxton, born in Huntsville, Illinois, May 3, 1871, member of the Social Security Board, Washington, statistical and Red Cross economist, author of *Industrial Relations*.

Neva R. Deardorff, born in Hagerstown, Indiana, February 11, 1887, Ph.D., University of Pennsylvania, member of the Research Bureau of the Welfare Council, New York, New York social worker.

E. T. Devine, born in Union, Iowa, May 6, 1867, sometime professor of social economy, Columbia University, secretary of the Charity Organization Society, New York, director of the New York School of Philanthropy, author of many books, including *Principles of Relief*.

Edwin R. Embree, born in Osceola, Nebraska, July 31, 1883, militant cultural diagnostician, director of the Julius Rosenwald Fund, author of *The Indians of American* and *Brown America*.

Lawrence K. Frank, born in Cincinnati, Ohio, December 6, 1890, child-welfare specialist and foundation executive, creative thinker and writer on children and culture, author of *Society as the Patient*.

Shelby M. Harrison, born in Leaf River, Illinois, February 15, 1881, distinguished director of the Russell Sage Foundation, author of *Social Conditions in an American City*.

Hastings H. Hart, born in Brookfield, Ohio, December 14, 1851, distinguished expert on prisons, director of penology, Russell Sage Foundation, author of *Restoration of the Criminal*.

George E. Haynes, born in Pine Bluff, Arkansas, May 11, 1880, applied sociologist, secretary of the Commission on Race Relations, Federal Council of Churches of Christ in America, Columbia doctorate in distinguished Y.M.C.A. work, and Phelps Stokes Service, author of *The Trend of the Races*.

Charles R. Henderson, born in Covington, Indiana, December 17, 1848, dean of the early social science professors, professor of sociology, University of Chicago, author of *The Social Spirit in America*.

Alvin Johnson, born in Homer, Nebraska, December 18, 1874, militant social economist beginning with a doctor's degree on trend in orthodox economic theory and ending with directorship of the New School, brilliant author of story and essay, of uncounted comments on social process and reform, and militant guide to youth and refugees in an unorthodox world.

Paul Kellogg, born in Kalamazoo, Michigan, September 30, 1879, distinguished editor of *The Survey*, editor-author of *Pittsburgh Survey*.

R. W. Kelso, born in Washington, Illinois, August 27, 1880, professor of social service, University of Michigan, expert in public welfare, author of *Science of Public Welfare*.

Philip Klein, born in Hungary, May 18, 1889, social worker, director of Research, New York School of Social Work, Red Cross pioneer in social work, author of *Social Case Work*.

Porter Lee, born in Buffalo, New York, December 21, 1879, long-time head the New York School of Social Work, author of *Social Case Work*.

Eduard C. Lindeman, born in St. Clair, Michigan, May 9, 1885, philosopher of community and democracy, New York School of Social Work, Columbia University, author and sociologist, author of *Social Discovery* and *Urban Sociology*.

Samuel McCune Lindsay, born in Pittsburgh, Pennsylvania, May 10, 1869, social economist at Columbia, and author of many legislative programs.

Walter Lippmann, born in New York City, September 23, 1889, columnist of the good society, whose books have been widely used, author of *The Good Society*.

Owen R. Lovejoy, born in Jamestown, Michigan, September 10, 1866, president of the National Conference of Social Work and the American Association of Social Workers, secretary of the National Child Labor Committee, director of the National Youth Committee.

George B. Mangold, born at Waupeton, Iowa, July 7, 1878, California's child-study specialist, professor of sociology at the University of Southern California.

L. C. Marshall, born in Zanesville, Ohio, March 15, 1879, dynamic apostle of "The Story of Human Progress," dean of both the School of Commerce and the Social Service Administration at University of Chicago, author of more than twenty-four volumes and adviser to governmental and social science agencies.

George Herbert Mead, born in South Hadley, Massachusetts, February 27, 1863, dynamic social philosopher influencing the succession of Chicago Ph.D. students more by teaching than by books.

Lewis Mumford, born in Flushing, New York, October 10, 1895, architect of culture and regionalism, and author of the notable *Culture of Cities* and *Technics and Civilization*.

Maurice Parmelee, born in Constantinople, Turkey, October 20, 1882, adventurer in many fields and author of more than a dozen books.

Raymond Pearl, born in Farmington, New Hampshire, June 3, 1879, student of human biology and statistician at Johns Hopkins, author of many treatises on genetics and biology of population growth.

Mary Richmond, born in Belleville, Illinois, August 5, 1861, pioneer in social diagnosis, director of the Charity Organization Department, Russell Sage Foundation, and author of the classic *Social Diagnosis.*

Harold Rugg, born in Fitchburg, Massachusetts, June 17, 1886, long-time professor of education at Teachers College, Columbia, prolific world lecturer on culture and civilization and author of *Introduction to American Civilization, Introduction to Problems of American Culture, History of American Civilization, The Great Technology, Changing Civilizations in a Modern World.*

Upton Sinclair, born in Baltimore, Maryland, September 20, 1878, prolific satirist of social evils, founder of the American Civil Liberties Union, many times candidate for various offices, including governorship and senatorship, author of voluminous literature beginning with *The Jungle.*

Lincoln Steffens, born in San Francisco, California, April 6, 1866, reform frontiersman and militant editor and author of *The Shame of the Cities.*

Graham Taylor, born in Schenectady, New York, May 2, 1851, dean of social science philosophers, minister, professor and president of the old Chicago School of Civics and Philanthropy, author of *Pioneering on Frontiers* (of social action).

Norman Thomas, born in Marion, Ohio, November 20, 1884, perennial socialist candidate for presidency of the United States, minister and preacher of social justice, author of *America's Way Out* and other volumes.

Mary Van Kleeck, born in Glenham, New York, June 26, 1883, director of industrial relations studies, Russell Sage Foundation, vigorous champion for labor, and author of numerous reports.

Harry F. Ward, born in London, England, October 15, 1873, militant preacher and professor of social ethics at Union Theological Seminary and author of *Our Economic Morality, In Place of Profit, Democracy and Social Change.*

CHAPTER 23

Sociological Journals

American sociology reflects three eras or periods as represented by its sociological journals. The first was from the founding of *The American Journal of Sociology* in 1895 at the University of Chicago and extending up to the early 1920's in which the *Journal* occupied the whole field and was the outstanding publication of its kind anywhere in the world. The next period began in 1921 and 1922 with the founding of two new journals to be sponsored and published by university sociology faculties. These were the *Journal of Applied Sociology* at Southern California in 1921 and the *Journal of Social Forces* at North Carolina in 1922. The former subsequently changed to *Sociology and Social Research* and the latter to *Social Forces*. The third period came in with the establishment of two *official* journals in 1936, sponsored and published by the *societies* as official organs as opposed to earlier journals published by universities. These were the *American Sociological Review*, in 1936, as the official organ of the American Sociological Society; and *Rural Sociology*, also in 1936, which came to be the official organ of the Rural Sociological Society when it was organized in 1938. Two other journals entered the field in different capacities, the *Journal of Educational Sociology* in 1927 and the *American Catholic Sociological Review* in 1939.

The American Journal of Sociology

The story of *The American Journal of Sociology* has been distinctive in the annals of sociology anywhere. For many years, from 1895 to 1921 and 1922 with the founding of the *Journal of Applied Sociology* and the *Journal of Social Forces* it stood alone in its field. It was the official organ of the American Sociological Society until the early 1930's when membership in the Society became optional as between the *Journal, Social Forces, Sociology and Social Research*, and the *Journal of Educational Sociology*. After 1936 and the founding of the *American Sociolog-*

ical Review, the *American Journal* had no official connection with the Society. The roster of names in the contributor's index of the *Journal* sometimes reads like a roll call of America's leading sociologists. For instance, in Volumes XIII and XVIII alone, the following *seventeen* presidents and presidents-to-be of the American Sociological Society appear in the contents: Ellwood, Hayes, Bogardus, Fairchild, Weatherly, Giddings, Cooley, Dealey, Ross, Small, Gillin, Thomas, Howard, Chapin, Ward, Blackmar, Bernard. Among the notable leaders in social work and public welfare who appeared in its earlier issues were Jane Addams, A. G. Warner, C. R. Henderson, Hastings H. Hart, Florence Kelley, Walter Rauschenbusch, R. C. Bates, S. P. Breckinridge, Arthur MacDonald, M. B. Hunt, Frances Fenton, Edith Abbott, Julia Lathrop, James Boyd, A. P. Comstock, S. H. Bishop, F. G. Peabody, E. T. Devine, R. A. Woods, Henry Curtis, A. M. Trawick. Among other earlier contributors were Jeremiah Jenks, John R. Commons, Josiah Strong, Shailer Mathews, Carroll D. Wright, James H. Tufts, Paul Monroe, W. F. Willcox, C. R. Woodruff, Roscoe Pound, G. Stanley Hall, Carl Becker, C. E. Merriam, Simon N. Patten.

Ethel Shanas wrote about the *Journal* in Volume L, No. 6, May, 1945, pages 522–33, under the title *"The American Journal of Sociology through Fifty Years."* From C. M. Grigg's abstract it is possible to check the genesis and trends of the *Journal,* which was ten years older than the American Sociological Society itself. The first issue of *The American Journal of Sociology* appeared in July, 1895, with Albion W. Small, chairman of the Department of Sociology, University of Chicago, as its editor. The editorial group consisted of the sociology faculty of the University of Chicago with such men as Charles R. Henderson, Frederick Starr, George E. Vincent, Marion Talbot, Charles Zueblin, and W. I. Thomas. The purposes of the *Journal* as outlined by Small were: (1) to build up a fund of social theory, (2) to make sociology a living discipline, (3) to promote the general welfare, and (4) to serve as a restraining influence on "premature" logical opinion. The doubts about the success of this new undertaking were expressed by Small some twenty years later when he wrote in his notable "Fifty Years of Sociology in the United States, 1865–1915," in the May, 1916, issue of the *Journal:* "When the announcement was made shortly after that the *University Extension World* was to become *The American Journal of Sociology,* the editors had not even promises of material enough to fill the first number. More than that, some of the men whom we tried to interest as contributors advised us to reconsider our purpose, as there could not possibly be in the near future enough sociological writing to fill such a journal. Nevertheless, we issued the first number in July, 1895, while it was still uncertain whether material for a second number the following September could be obtained. Without the prompt and hearty cooperation of Lester F. Ward, followed closely by Professor Ross, the enterprise would scarcely have survived its first year." But in glancing over the leading articles in the first edition, one would scarcely realize the trepidation that the editors felt as the issue contained such articles as "The Place of Sociology among the Sciences," by Lester F. Ward, and papers on democracy by Henry Pratt Judson, on anthropology and history by George E. Fellows, on the Chicago Civic Federation by Albion Small, and two papers on Christian sociology by Paul Monroe and Shailer Mathews. With the second issue in September, 1895, the *Journal* added to its editorial staff a group of "advising editors," which included seven foreign sociologists and three Americans. These were De Greef, Durkheim, Fiamingo, Mackenzie, Schaeffle, Mandello, Simmel, Ross, Sumner, and Ward. Beginning with its first number and through the issue of November, 1944, No. 3 of Volume L, *The American Journal of Sociology* had published 2373 articles in addition to the space given to reviews of current books and to the transmittal of general information of sociological interest.

In 1906 the *Journal* became the organ of the newly organized American Sociological Society. The officers of the Society became the American advisory editors of the *Journal*. In 1908 their names appeared on the masthead along with those of De Greef, Durkheim, Fiamingo, Mandello, Simmel, and Tönnies. This arrangement between the Society and the *Journal* continued until 1936 when the Society founded its own *American Sociological Review,* which was to have its editors elected by the Society. Since that time, the *American Journal*'s official advisory editors were succeeded by a representative group of invited American sociologists. It was estimated that "about the only effect this new arrangement had on the *Journal*'s contents was an accelerated decrease in articles which were primarily sociological 'shop-talk.'" Although the *Journal* has been in operation for fifty-five years, there have been only four editors, Albion Small, Ellsworth Faris, Ernest Burgess, and Herbert Blumer.

Of these, Albion W. Small, Ellsworth Faris, and Ernest W. Burgess have been presented in Chapters 4, 9, and 10 as presidents of the American Sociological Society. Burgess in addition to being president of the Society was also its secretary from 1921 to 1930. So generous was he in these two services as editor and secretary, it was thought the Society was about to overlook him as presidential material.

Herbert Blumer, currently editor, was secretary of the Society from 1931 to 1936. Born in St. Louis, March 7, 1900, he received the A.B. and A.M. degrees from the University of Missouri in 1921 and 1922, and the Ph.D. degree at Chicago in 1927. He was instructor at Missouri and Chicago before becoming associate professor of sociology at Chicago in 1931 and professor at Michigan in 1936–37, after which he returned as associate professor at Chicago in 1937, and has been professor since 1947. He was visiting professor at Hawaii in 1939. He was editor of the publications of the American Sociological Society from 1931 to 1936 and has been editor of the Prentice-Hall Sociological Series since 1934. He was a member of the research staff, Motion Picture Research Council, 1929–31. He served with the War Labor Board as public panel chairman and as liaison officer between the Office of War Information and the Board of Economic Warfare, 1943–44. He was permanent arbitrator for Armour and Company, 1944–45, and chairman of the Board of Arbitration, American Steel Corporation, 1945. He is author of *Movies and Conduct,* 1933; *Movies, Delinquency, and Crime,* 1933; *Appraisals of Social Research,* 1939. In 1935 he edited the publications of the society, with Burgess, *The Human Side of Planning.*

Sociology and Social Research

The second era of American sociological journals began in the early 1920's with the founding of the *Journal of Applied Sociology* at Southern California by Emory S. Bogardus and the *Journal of Social Forces* at North Carolina by Howard W. Odum. According to the records of Emory S. Bogardus, the *Journal of Applied Sociology* had its beginning in the *Sociological Monographs* No. 1, published in September, 1916, by the Department of Sociology at the University of Southern California. The Department of Sociology, which had been established a year earlier in 1915, wished to encourage graduate students in their research work, and so had inaugurated the *Sociological Monographs,* published quarterly for five years, with E. S. Bogardus as "editor of publications." These contained the results of studies by graduate students in sociology on such subjects as: causes of truancy among girls, causes of fatal accidents on highways, teaching of sociology in high schools, causes of truancy among boys, the Russians in Los Angeles, causes of delinquency among fifty Negro boys, community organization, Mexican housing problem in Los Angeles, and relation of wages to cost of living in Los Angeles, 1915 to 1920.

The number of graduate students in sociology increased steadily at the University of Southern California and the products of their research called for more publication space than the *Monographs* could provide. Hence the quarterly *Monographs* became in 1921 a bi-monthly periodical, first of thirty-two pages, then of eighty pages, and, on special occasions, of ninety-six pages. The title became *Journal of Applied Sociology* and the editorial masthead announced Emory S. Bogardus, as editor, with the following sociology faculty members as associate editors: Clarence E. Rainwater, William C. Smith, and Melvin J. Vincent.

Inasmuch as it was desired to stress the research emphasis in sociology the *Journal of Applied Sociology* became *Sociology and Social Research* in 1927. The work of Bogardus is presented in Chapter 9. The editorial body included all faculty members of the Department of Sociology at Southern California. From the first issue of the *Sociological Monographs* to the 1950 issues of *Sociology and Social Research,* a total of 1390 articles have been published in these two periodicals.

Social Forces

The *Journal of Social Forces,* founded in 1922, and becoming *Social Forces* in 1925, might very well be said to have been the product of the Departments of Sociology at the University of North Carolina and Columbia University, for its founding in November, 1922, was strongly seconded by Franklin Henry Giddings, professor of sociology at Columbia University and dean of living American sociologists at that time, and it was Professor Giddings' enthusiasm for the *Journal* to be set up as a national medium of sociology and his preparation of a series of leading articles on the scientific study of human society that were the deciding factors in the establishment of the new sociological journal. For two years Professor Giddings contributed leading articles, which were subsequently published by the University of North Carolina Press under the title, *The Scientific Study of Human Society,* and which in some ways was Professor Giddings' favorite book.

Although *Social Forces* has published more than twice as many articles by authors outside the southern regions as in the South, it early adopted the policy of featuring regional research and planning as one medium of its social study and interpretation. As indicative of the regional-national character of *Social Forces* may be cited its official relation to the national and southern sociological societies and the number and range of its contributions. For the years just preceding the establishment of the *American Sociological Review* as the official organ of the American Sociological Society, *Social Forces* was one of the official journals of the Society. It has been also the official journal of the Southern Sociological Society since the Society's organization in 1936.

Social Forces has published in its first twenty-eight volumes more than two thousand articles and five thousand book reviews and notes, representing some fourteen hundred authors from all the states and regions of the United States, as well as from Canada, the South American republics, Europe, and the Orient. Analysis of the articles and authors shows a wide distribution, including the leading American sociologists, many scholars from the other social sciences, many distinguished publicists and educators. Among the presidents of the American Sociological Society were Franklin H. Giddings and R. M. MacIver of Columbia University; W. F. Ogburn, Ellsworth Faris, Ernest W. Burgess, and Robert E. Park of the University of Chicago; Howard W. Odum and Rupert B. Vance of the University of North Carolina; Edward Alsworth Ross and John Lewis Gillin of the University of Wisconsin. Others, one each from other universities, were L. L. Bernard, Washington University; Emory S. Bogardus, University of Southern California; F. Stuart Chapin, University of Minnesota; Charles A. Ellwood, Duke University; Henry Pratt Fairchild, New York University; John M. Gillette, University of North Dakota; Edward Carey Hayes, University of Illinois; George A. Lundberg, Bennington College; E. H. Sutherland, University of Indiana; Dwight Sanderson, Cornell University; Kimball Young, Queens College; Carl C. Taylor, U.S. Department of Agriculture, Washington, D.C.; Louis Wirth, Chicago; Franklin Frazier, Howard; Talcott Parsons, Harvard.

Among the authors from the other social sciences were Charles A. Beard, Wesley C. Mitchell, John Dewey, Charles H. Judd, Frank Lorimer, Walton Hale Hamilton, Clark Wissler, Robert Redfield, Leonard White, William E. Dodd, Roscoe Pound, Avery Craven, Thomas Nixon Carver, Shelby Harrison, Grace Abbott, Sophonisba Breckinridge, Floyd Allport, E. A. Hooten, Ellsworth Huntington, W. Carson Ryan, Frank H. Knight, William H. Kilpatrick. Among the distinguished editors, publicists, and educators at large were Woodrow Wilson, Edwin A. Alderman, Charles A. Beard, Walter Lippmann, Edwin R. Embree, Jackson Davis, Gerald W. Johnson, Henry Noble MacCracken, Harry Woodburn Chase, A. E. Morgan, Rexford Tugwell, William Allen White.

The editorial board of *Social Forces* for 1950 included Howard W. Odum and Katharine Jocher, editors, together with faculty members of the Departments of Sociology and Anthropology of the University of North Carolina as advisory editors. Odum's work has been discussed in Chapter 8. Katharine Jocher is professor and assistant director of the Institute for Research in Social Science, and is special editor also for research publications. She holds the A.B. degree from Goucher College; the M.A. from University of Pennsylvania; and the Ph.D from North Carolina. She has been visiting professor in summer sessions at Washington State and the University of Virginia and has collaborated on special assignments in the President's Research Committee on Social Trends. She has been especially active in the American Sociological Society, being a member of the executive committee, second vice-president, and chairman of several major committees. She was president of the Southern Sociological Society from 1942 to 1944. In addition to belonging to the sociological societies, she has been a member of the American Academy of Political and Social Science, the American Economic Association, the American Association of University Women, the American Association of University Professors, the American Association of Social Workers, the National Conference of Social Work, the American Public Welfare Association, and the Southern Regional Council. She has been a member of the board of directors of the North Carolina Conference for Social Service and has been national vice-president of Alpha Kappa Delta. She is author (with Howard W. Odum) of *An Introduction to Social Research* and *In Search of the Regional Balance of America*. She has contributed many book reviews and notes as well as being editor of Institute manuscripts and publications.

American Sociological Review

The third era of American sociological journals began with the publication of Volume I of the *American Sociological Review* in 1936, as the exclusive official organ of the American Sociological Society. In its fifteen years up to 1950 the *Review* has published no less than eight hundred major articles. The establishment of the new journal came after relatively long and careful committee consideration. When L. L. Bernard was president of the Society in 1932, he appointed a committee to work on the problem of founding an official organ of the Society. Before that, and throughout the years in which the problem was being studied, Bernard was active in protest against the policy of having *The American Journal of Sociology* as the official journal of the Society, and, at the same time, worked for the establishment of a new journal. About his protest against the policies of certain members of the Society who, Bernard felt, were trying to dominate the Society, he wrote, in 1948, for the record: "I wrote the constitution which was presented in opposition by a committee I had been authorized to appoint and which was adopted by the Society. I also appointed the committee which recommended the substitution of the *American Sociological Review* for *The American Journal of Sociology* as the official organ of the Society and pushed the resolution through to adoption. I named the new organ. I took these steps because the department of sociology at the University of Chicago, under its leader at that time, had become arrogant and was suspected of making the interests of the American Sociological Society subsidiary to those of the Chicago department. As might be supposed, I made a host of enemies out of the persons whose designs I had opposed, but I have never regretted the action I took in these cases. Some of these persons still work against me, but I think my services to the Society will vindicate me."

The story of Bernard's protest movement and those individuals who joined in it is a separate item, which is in itself representative of the growing pains of a rapidly growing discipline. In a separate place the story may well be presented on its own representation. That Bernard was not entirely satisfied with the *Review* might be evidenced by his subsequent occasional publication, on his own, of *The American Sociologist,* in which, however, he often featured primarily South American sociology.

From 1936 to 1950 the *American Sociological Review* had five editors elected by the Society to serve without pay. The first of these was Frank H. Hankins of Smith College, who was editor for 1936–37. Read Bain followed as editor for 1937–41; Joseph K. Folsom for 1942–45; Robert Angell for 1946–48; and Maurice Davie since 1948.

Read Bain

The work of Frank H. Hankins, the first editor, has been described in Chapter 10, as president of the American Sociological Society. Read Bain, the second editor, was born in Woods, Oregon, October 20, 1892; received his A.B. from Willamette in 1916, his M.A. at the University of Oregon in 1921 and his Ph.D. degree at Michigan in 1926. He was awarded the honorary LL.D. by Willamette in 1941, and returned to the Far West as visiting professor at Reed College in 1948–49. He also taught in summer schools at Southern California, Texas, Brigham Young, and Minnesota, and was visiting professor at Harvard in 1937–38. His main work, however, has been at Ohio's Miami University where he went as associate professor in 1927 and where, since 1929, he has been professor of sociology. Bain has been a dynamic force in the American Sociological Society taking prominent part in its meetings, being first vice-president in 1944 and chairman of various committees. He was president of the Ohio Valley Sociological Society in 1934. He has also been secretary-treasurer of the Sociological Research Association. He was author of many articles and was among the earlier sociologists who advocated the same general methods for sociology as those utilized for the natural sciences. He is author and collaborator in *Trends in American Sociology,* 1929; *Social Progress and Social Process,* 1933; *Fields and Methods of Sociology,* 1934; and *Critiques of Research in Social Science,* 1939–40.

Joseph K. Folsom

The third editor of the new *Journal* had been a member of the White House Conference on Children; vice-president of the New York Conference on Marriage and the Family; chairman of the National Council on Parent Education; president of the Eastern Sociological Society; member of the board of directors of the American Eugenics Society and of the executive committee of the American Sociological Society. Born in Poundridge, New York, September 30, 1893, Joseph K. Folsom moved rapidly to complete three degrees: the B.S. from Rutgers, in 1913; the A.M. from Clark in 1915, the Ph.D. from Columbia in 1917. He started his work in teaching at St. Lawrence University in 1914 and followed his Ph.D. in World War I as first lieutenant in the U. S. Army Psychological Service. He came back then as assistant professor of sociology at the University of Pittsburgh, 1919–20. He then moved abroad as director of educational and social services of the Y.M.C.A. in Czechoslovakia in 1920–21. Then he went to Dartmouth as assistant professor of economics from 1922 to 1924; thence to Sweet Briar College as head of the Department of Economics and Sociology, 1924–31. From Sweet Briar he went to Vassar as professor of economics and sociology where he has remained since 1931. Like most of his fellow sociologists he has taught in the summer sessions of a number of institutions, including Columbia, Boston, New Hampshire, George Washington, Virginia, Harvard. He is author of *Culture and Social Progress,* 1928; *Social Psychology,* 1931; *The Family,* 1934; *Youth, Family, and Education,* 1941; and was editor of *Plan for Marriage* in 1938.

Robert Cooley Angell

Robert Cooley Angell, the fourth editor of the *Review,* 1946–48, is currently, in 1950, director of the project on tensions affecting international understanding of UNESCO, and acting head of the social sciences department. Angell was second vice-president in 1947 and first vice-president in 1948 of the American Sociological Society. Like his uncle, C. H. Cooley, he stayed close to the University of Michigan for his degrees and his work; the A.B. in 1921, the A.M. in 1922, and the Ph.D. in 1924. He was then instructor, assistant professor, associate and full professor respectively in 1922, 1926, 1930, and 1935. He served in several capacities in World War I and World War II, being a lieutenant colonel in the Air Corps in 1944, and giving fifteen months' service in the European theater of operations, 1943–45. He is a member of the Sociological Research Association, the Michigan Academy of Arts and Sciences, and Alpha Kappa Delta. He is author of *Sociological Theory and Research* (editor for C. H. Cooley), 1930; *The Campus,* 1928; *Research in Family Law,* 1930; *Introductory Sociology,* with Carr and Cooley, 1933; *The Family Encounters the Depression,* 1936; *The Integration of American Society,* 1941. He has currently completed the manuscript on "The Moral Integration of American Cities." Angell becomes the forty-first president of the American Sociological Society for 1951.

Maurice Davie

Like William Graham Sumner, professor of sociology at Yale University, Maurice Davie, currently in 1950 editor of the *Review,* not only continues the foundation work of Sumner and Keller but has established the Yale department as one of sociology rather than the science of society. Davie was president of the Eastern Sociological Society in 1940–41 and was elected editor by the American Sociological Society of the *American Sociological Review* in 1947. His most recent books include *Negroes in American Life,* 1949, and *Refugees in America,* 1947. Earlier volumes were *World Immigration,* 1936; *Problems of City Life,* 1932; *The Evolution of War,* 1929; *Social Aspects of Mental Hygiene,* 1925; *A Constructive Immigration Policy,* 1923; and *Directory of Community Activities,* 1921. He collaborated on a number of volumes including *Sumner Today,* 1940; *Selected Essays of William Graham Sumner,* 1924; *Essays of William Graham Sumner,* two volumes, 1934; *A Study in Professional Education,* 1930.

Like most of his contemporaries, Davie was called upon to participate in a wide range of allied activities. Although he came into sociology directly through the Yale tutorage with Sumner and Keller, his work included many phases of community and public welfare services. Born in Toronto, Canada, January 22, 1893, he was graduated from Yale College in 1915, took his M.A. in 1917, and received his Ph.D. in 1918. After two years as instructor in Western Reserve University, he returned to Yale as assistant professor of the science of society from 1921 to 1927; associate professor, 1927 to 1932; professor, director of graduate studies in sociology, and chairman of the department in 1932; and William Graham Sumner professor and head of the Department of Sociology since 1944. He was president of the Connecticut Child Welfare Association, 1932–40; State Commissioner on Child Welfare, 1931–33; member of the State Planning Board, 1935–37; of the State Welfare Council, 1936–48; of the board of directors of the Institute for Propaganda Analysis, of the National Institute on Immigration Welfare, of the National Council on Naturalization and Citizenship, of the National Council on Housing Emergency, as well as of various local organizations. He was delegate to the International Sociology Conference in 1937.

Rural Sociology

In the early 1930's a certain specific group, because of their particular interests and facilities for research in a new specialism, organized and met with the American Sociological Society. This grew out of a section on rural sociology from which was organized in 1938 the Rural Sociological Society. *Rural Sociology* became the official organ of the new society two years after its founding in 1936. Since that time this journal has had four editors-in-chief, each being elected for a five-year period. These were Lowry Nelson, 1936–40; Carle C. Zimmerman, 1941–42, with C. P. Loomis completing Zimmerman's term due to his absence in Europe, then being re-elected for the five-year period from 1943 to 1947. Howard Beers was elected in 1948.

Before *Rural Sociology* became the official organ of the newly established Rural Sociological Society, it was issued as a quarterly publication, starting in March, 1936, with the Louisiana State University as its guarantor, and was published by the Rural Sociology Section of the American Sociological Society. At that time there was a board of editors of which Lowry Nelson of Utah State College was chairman. Other members of the board of editors were: J. H. Kolb, University of Wisconsin; C. E. Lively, Ohio State University; Dwight Sanderson, Cornell University; and C. C. Zimmerman, Harvard University. The contributing editors included such men as W. F. Ogburn, University of Chicago; F. S. Chapin, University of Minnesota; W. W. Alexander, Resettlement Administration; Corrado Gini, University of Rome; Robert E. Park, University of Chicago; and P. A. Sorokin, Harvard University. In

1941, the sponsorship of the journal changed to North Carolina State College of the University of North Carolina and is still currently under this sponsorship.

Of the nearly four hundred articles published up to 1950 approximately a third were contributed by workers in some branch of the U. S. Agricultural Service, in or out of the state colleges and universities. Among the institutions represented most frequently were Harvard, Cornell, Ohio State, Louisiana State University, Wisconsin, North Carolina State. Others included practically every state university or land grant college in the United States. The list of authors is practically a roll call of the leading rural sociologists in the United States. Among the contributions were installments of C. J. Galpin's noted "My Drift into Rural Sociology."

The Editors of Rural Sociology

The first editor, Lowry Nelson, was born in Utah in 1893, was graduated from the Utah State College in 1916, and went on to Wisconsin for his M.A. and Ph.D. degrees in 1924 and 1929. He was county agent, editor of *Utah Farmer,* director of extension work and dean at Brigham Young University, besides being regional advisor of Federal Emergency Relief, before going as director of the rural resettlement division of the Resettlement Administration at Washington, 1935–36, and before going to Minnesota in 1937 as professor of sociology. He was director of the Utah Experiment Station, 1936–37. He was president of the Rural Sociological Society, 1943–44. He was author of several monographs on Utah village society and of a textbook, *Rural Sociology,* in 1947. Nelson was a member of the President's Commission on Farm Tenancy and has been a member of the permanent agricultural committee of the International Labor Office since 1937.

The second editor of *Rural Sociology,* Carle C. Zimmerman, went from North Carolina State to Minnesota to Harvard in 1921, 1923, 1931, respectively, where, in each instance, he was in charge of rural sociology. He is author of *Source Book of Rural Sociology* (with Sorokin), *Consumption and Standards of Living, The Family, The Family and Civilization, The Family of Tomorrow.* Zimmerman was born in Missouri in 1897, was graduated from the University of Missouri in 1920, received his M.S. from North Carolina State in 1922, and his Ph.D. from the University of Minnesota in 1925. He was awarded the honorary Sc.D. at North Carolina State in 1942.

Charles P. Loomis, the third editor, was born in Bloomfield, Colorado, in 1905, received his A.B. from New Mexico in 1928, his M.S. from North Carolina State in 1929, his Ph.D. from Harvard in 1932. He has been professor and head of the Department of Anthropology and Sociology at Michigan State College since 1944 and director of the Research Service since 1946. Before that he had had a wide range of service in his field, as senior social scientist, U.S. Department of Agriculture, 1938–42; assistant chief, Division of Training, Office of Foreign Agricultural Relations, 1943–44. He was head of a mission for the Inter-Governmental Committee on Refugees to Andean Countries, 1947. He is translator of *Fundamental Concepts of Sociology* by Tönnies, 1940; *Studies of Rural Social Organization in the United States, Latin America and Germany,* 1945.

The fourth editor, Howard W. Beers, born in Gouverneur, New York, in 1905, took his three degrees at Cornell: B.S. in 1929, A.M. in 1930, Ph.D. in 1935, and has been professor of rural sociology at the University of Kentucky since 1939, and head of the department since 1948. Previously, he had been assistant professor of rural sociology at Washington State, associate professor at Wisconsin and Rutgers University, principal research supervisor of the W.P.A. at Washington. He has been a member of the executive committee of the American Sociological Society and was president of the Southern Sociological Society in 1945. He was visiting professor of rural sociology in the Superior School of Agriculture, Athens, Greece, 1949–50.

T. Lynn Smith, former managing editor of *Rural Sociology,* was born in Sanford, Colorado, in 1903, took his B.S. at Brigham Young University in 1928, his M.A. and Ph.D. at Minnesota in 1929 and 1932. At Louisiana State University he went from assistant professor in 1931–33 to associate professor in 1933–36, to professor and head of the department from 1936 to 1947. From 1947 to 1949 he was professor and head of the Department of Sociology and Anthropology at Vanderbilt University and since 1949 he has been professor of sociology at the University of Florida. Taking a leave of absence from the Louisiana State University in 1942–43, he went to Brazil for the U.S. Department of State, as senior agricultural analyst. He was president of the Rural Sociological Society in 1941–42 and of the Southern Sociological Society in 1947.

C. Horace Hamilton, currently managing editor of *Rural Sociology* in 1950, was born in Texas in 1901 and received his A.B. at Southern Methodist University in 1924, his M.A. at Texas Agricultural and Mechanical College in 1925, and his Ph.D. degree from North Carolina in 1932. He has been head of the department of rural sociology at North Carolina State since 1940. Before that he had been assistant rural sociologist at Virginia Polytechnic Institute, North Carolina State, and rural economist at the Texas Agricultural Experiment Station. He was senior social scientist for the U. S. Bureau of Agricultural Economics in 1939–40. He was consultant, Division of National Institute, American Public Health Association, 1946–49, and chairman of the publications committee of the North Carolina Governor's Health Commission. He was president of the Rural Sociological Society in 1950.

Journal of Educational Sociology

In the early 1930's in the transitional years between the second and third periods of the development of American sociological journals, three journals, other than *The American Journal of Sociology,* were voted by the American Sociological Society as optional choices for members of the Society. Two have been featured, namely, *Sociology and Social Research* and *Social Forces* founded in 1921 and 1922, respectively. The third was the *Journal of Educational Sociology* founded and edited by E. George Payne of New York University in 1927 and transferred in 1936 — the same years as the founding of *Rural Sociology* and the *American Sociological Review* — to Phi Delta Kappa, a national professional fraternity for men in education. In the September, 1939, issue, devoted to "The Development of Educational Sociology: Contributions of E. George Payne," W. F. Ogburn writes of Payne's "Contributions to Sociological Research" and L. L. Bernard of his "Contributions to Sociology" while Henry L. Pritchett writes of "The Place of the *Journal of Educational Sociology* in Sociology and Education." On page 45, Pritchett writes: "The *Journal of Educational Sociology* occupies a place unique in sociological and educational periodical literature. To a certain extent it is a liaison medium between sociology and education, but it has an established place of its own as a journal dedicated to the development of scientific educational sociology. Early in its history it found a welcome place among the approved national journals of the American Sociological Society and of various national educational associations. Throughout the years they have continued to give it high rank among professional periodicals because of the scientific character of its work." A special feature of the *Journal* has been its special issues devoted to some specialism and edited by an authority in the field. For instance, F. Stuart Chapin edited a symposium on social planning; E. R. Groves edited one on education and the family; J. V. Hart edited another on the implication of the Tennessee Valley Authority.

E. George Payne, the first and continuing editor of the *Journal of Educational Sociology* was born in rural Kentucky, worked on the farm and, like Lester F. Ward, worked his way slowly up to a formal college education, first, in the senior college of Chicago where he studied under Small, Thomas, Zueblin, Graham Taylor, and later, in Europe, where he spent nearly three years at the universities of Bonn and Berlin, the Sorbonne, and the Collège de France. He returned to the United States with his doctor of philosophy degree. Before that Payne had served a strenuous apprenticeship in the public schools and teachers college work before coming to New York University and subsequently becoming dean of its School of Education. Payne was editor of more than fifty publications, contributed more than sixty articles to various journals, and was the author of more than twenty-four books. Among the books on educational sociology were *Principles of Educational Sociology,* 1925; *An Outline of Educational Sociology,* 1928; and *Readings in Educational Sociology,* 1935. W. F. Ogburn, writing on pages 31–32 of the September, 1939, *Journal,* characterized Payne as in his research advancing "definitely beyond the emphasis of other educational sociologists in his insistence that any adequate program designed to test the results of educational effort must involve sociological research."

American Catholic Sociological Review

The *American Catholic Sociological Review* was founded in 1939. The *Review* is the official publication of the American Catholic Sociological Society which has been discussed in Chapter 21.

Russell Bartu writes: "The first issue of the *Review* appeared in March, 1940. It is a quarterly and has appeared four times each year, in

March, June, October and December since that time. In all this time it has had only one editor, Reverend Ralph A. Gallagher, S.J., who is and has been the Executive Secretary of the American Catholic Sociological Society since its inception in 1938. Father Gallagher is Chairman of the Department of Sociology at Loyola University, Chicago, and Director of the Institute of Social Administration which grants graduate degrees to students concentrating in industrial relations, personnel and public administration and sociology. The *Review* has averaged about four or five articles each issue. It has a book section in which about twenty books are reviewed each issue. It also contains a periodical review section where articles of interest to our members are summarized. Most of the authors are Catholics, usually teachers of sociology in colleges and universities."

Ralph A. Gallagher, editor of the *Review* was born in Cleveland in 1896, took his B.A. degree in Gonzaga University, Spokane, Washington, in 1920, his M.A. in 1921; second M.A. at St. Louis University in 1930, and his Ph.D. in 1932. He was instructor in St. Xavier High School in Cincinnati, 1923–25; professor and dean, John Carroll University, 1933–36; professor and chairman, Department of Sociology, Loyola, Chicago, since 1936. He is a member of the American Sociological Society and of Alpha Kappa Delta, the sociological scholarship fraternity.

PART V

Toward Inventory

CHAPTER 24

Mid-Century Sociology: Looking Both Ways, Heritage and Trends

The history and development and the trends and status of American sociology at mid-century are much more complex than is indicated by many of the prevailing oversimplified appraisals, which have often been made without adequate review of the total picture or the maturity of historical study. Contemporary American sociology, with its hundredfold measures of change, can no more be considered on the same level with sociology at the beginning of the century than can modern mechanized agriculture or atomic science be compared with simple farming and college laboratories of the earlier period. Nor can this story of American sociology be isolated from the earlier stages or from the intellectual and cultural development of the United States or the intercultural relations of an entirely new era in human society. And yet, tested in the crucible of the succession of years, it reflects a substantial consistency and faces a new civilization-weighted world with cumulative reserve built upon an unbroken heritage. If the earlier sociology may have been an "arm chair science," it reflected a powerful transitional give and take, exercise and struggle to find the best answers within the framework of the European-American frontier, building upon traditional but substantial foundations of a relatively stable philosophy and scientific method. If early sociology was ameliorative and practical and non-sophisticated in general, it still reflected the powerful struggle of the intellectuals of a new society with growing pains trying to evolve a social science that would help solve its problems.

If sociology at the turn of the century featured the study of general society and the "system" pattern of social theory, it reflected not only the almost universal philosophical approach but also the consistency of the best minds in interaction with European philosophy and American higher education, for, between 1850 and 1900 America had discovered Europe, and this discovery became the twin conditioner with the discovery of the western frontiers. And European sociology continued persistently to feature systematic sociology closely knit to philosophy. It is inconceivable that one could write the history of changing society in the new world without the story of the titanic struggle for a new philosophy and a new strategy reflected in the heroic effects of Spencer, Comte, Sumner, Ward, and Giddings, and the counter-effects of multiple interaction processes in the rapidly developing new world.

More than this, however, American sociology in 1950 was still struggling heroically, as were also the physical sciences and the venerable American Philosophical Society, for more realistic and comprehensive integration of the different sciences and of science, philosophy, and the humanities. In the case of sociology, as we shall soon see, the trend was not so much away from "systematic," "theoretical" sociology as it was toward more theory as it might be related to research and the scientific method. Here, as in other aspects of sociology, something more is expected, rather than something less. Once again, however, the situation is a complex one including conflicting views, new and immature methodologies, a new sweep of both semantics and statistics, and, as in American literature, "the divided forces . . . find themselves not clearly and simply divided, but complexly and inextricably involved in their purposes." This quality of appraisal is made vivid on page 1360 of the 1948 Spiller-Thorp-Johnson-Canby *Literary History of the United States* in which it is pointed out that what is demanded is not so much a clear-cut differentiation as a consolidation of beliefs and arguments on all sides. Something of this sort is especially appropriate in the changing and rapidly developing sociology of 1950 and on into the new era.

But in any case, the first essential to a continuing appraisal of American sociology is something of recapitulation and description, set in the framework of some sort of comparative standards of appraisal. Although the record of American sociology is so extensive and rich that there is no substitute for the full story, it is nevertheless possible to summarize the main situation as the setting for appraising status and trends. In summary, such a description would include: (1) the American quality of a sociology with its genesis primarily in Europe, with its parentage partly of continental philosophy and partly of British "social science"; (2) the role of sociology in the development of the social sciences in the United States; (3) the rise of sociology as a college and university subject; (4) the changing content and methods of American sociology; (5) its status in terms of personnel and of departmental organization in institutions of higher learning; (6) its status in terms of courses taught, literature produced, fields of research and teaching; and (7) special trends and developments. Standards of appraisal will include: (1) comparative measures of progress from meager beginnings to greater achievements; (2) comparisons with earlier and later sociology; (3) comparisons of American sociology with European; (4) comparisons with other social science disciplines and with social work and other applied disciplines; (5) approximation of sociological methods to scientific methods of research; and (6) the degree to which sociology's body of materials may be characterized as adequate for a science of society.

In Chapters 1 to 3 we have characterized the earlier sociologists as American pioneers and traced the American and European influences upon the development of sociology in the United States and noted the interplay of the American "problem" factor with general philosophy and special Utopian concepts. We have cited Parrington's *Main Currents in American Thought*; the American historians, Beard, Adams, Schlesinger, Wechter, and others; and the *Literary History of the United States* and other sources, to indicate something of the influence of sociology upon American life and letters. Yet it now seems clear that sociology has had a greater influence upon American history and character than has been commonly assumed. Perhaps it would be more accurate to say that for the most part the influence has been overlooked by both sociologists and the public. Something of this influence has been recorded in Henry Steele Commager's *The American Mind,* 1950, both in his general description of American character and especially in his Chapter 10 where he points out something of the incidence of sociology's first big four — Sumner, Ward, Small, and Giddings — in the setting of comparative cultural history in which what is characteristically American evolved from a great heritage of English and European thought. The historical period selected by Commager is the same one we have selected for the story of American sociology, namely, as pointed out on page viii by Commager, "from the mid-eighties to the present because it seems to me the mid-eighties and nineties constituted something of a watershed in American history and thought and that the period since that time has a certain unity."

How earlier American sociology was influencing America's whole political and economic development is illustrated by Commager on page 216 when he writes, "The issues raised by William Graham Sumner and Lester Ward, shorn of their scholarly trimmings and simplified into such rallying cries as free silver or sound money, private enterprise or socialism, regimentation or planned economy, rugged individualism or social security, filled half a century of history with an increasing clamor. They were hotly debated in remote schoolhouses on the prairies or in cotton fields, in Grange halls and labor temples, on Chautauqua platforms, in gaudy party conventions, in turbulent legislative chambers, and in dignified courtrooms. They were fought out under strange banners and often with murderous weapons in the battles between the Pullman Company and the railway workers, the packers and the cattlemen, the railroads and the farmers, the coal operators and the United Mine Workers, the insurance companies and the state governments, the timber thieves and the Department of the Interior. They were the basic issues of the Populist crusade, the Progressive movement, the New Freedom, and most heatedly of all, the New Deal and the Fair Deal. Their champions were, in the end, not so much the scholars who had formulated them as the businessmen and labor leaders, farmers and bankers, muckrakers and editors, statesmen and judges, who came to see that ideas were weapons. Bryan and Mark Hanna, Theodore Roosevelt and Nelson Aldrich, Wilson and Lodge, Franklin Roosevelt and Hoover, translated the arguments of the social scientists into the vernacular and, when given the opportunity, into public policy."

If sociology has exercised a more powerful influence upon American life than has often been assumed, sociology also has itself been even more powerfully conditioned by American life than has been commonly recognized. This influence of American culture upon sociology not only gave it its American character, in contrast to its European background, but established it as both a well-integrated separate social science, serving both as a cultural subject and a medium for problem and policy exploration. It was not just that a large part of sociology's genesis in the United States was in the social problem approach as we have pointed out, but that, to quote Henry Steele Commager again, on page 54 of his *The American Mind,* "The great issues of the nineties still commanded popular attention half a century later; the seminal minds of that decade still directed popular thought. Problems of isolation and internationalism, of laissez faire and government planning, of the causes and cures of panics, the contrasts of progress and poverty, the humanizing of urban life, the control of business and the rights of labor, the place of the Negro and the immigrant in society, the improvement of agriculture and the conservation of natural resources, the actualization of democracy into social security — all these things which had monopolized public interest in the nineties, seemed no less urgent in the 1930's and 1940's. . . . Fifty years after their formulation the American was still exploring the economic ideas of Veblen, developing the sociological doctrines of Lester Ward, elaborating on the historical theories of Henry Adams and the historical interpretations of Frederick Jackson Turner."

Even more decisive evidence that America has made sociology in its own image and installed itself as leader in the sociological world is the technical measure of sociology's dominance. How surely the new science ultimately became "American" may be seen from all the evidence to be found in the history of sociology and the other social sciences. How "American" contemporary sociology is may be seen further from the striking contrasts between sociology as a social science in the United States and abroad. In the whole territory of the German Federal Republic in 1950 there was just one chair of sociology, that of Leopold von Wiese at the University of Cologne, once offered to Howard Becker but now filled by the Swiss scholar René König. Anthropology was not only unrelated to sociology but was still a biological science as contrasted with its status in the United States where many major colleges and universities had united anthropology with sociology in perhaps the newest trend in the concentration of social science.

On page 3 of *The Social Sciences in Western Germany* (1950), Dr. Dolf Sternberger says, "Although anthropology has man as its subject and accordingly in the United States is joined to the fields of research which devote themselves to human society, it has hardly sought nor found contact with sociology in German universities; the reason for that is evidently that, considering man as a part of nature, German scholars classify anthropology under categories and methods fundamentally different from those of a social science." Sternberger also points out on page 29, Division V, on "Sociology," that of the twenty-seven contributions to the symposium in honor of Alfred Weber's eightieth birthday, six were written in English and six others were by authors writing in German but living in the United States or elsewhere outside Germany; and that Howard Becker contributed a main article in the symposium on Alfred Vierkandt. The status of sociology in Germany is described by Alois Dempf, page 32, when he says that "sociology exists in Germany only with and through individuals, and that it is pragmatically a forbidden science." And finally, on page 35, it is pointed out that it is not surprising that in Germany it was "in particular American suggestions and contributions that led again to a start" of empirical studies.

Or again, the American quality of sociology in the United States may be vividly portrayed by the simple means of characterizing the American sociologists who found the chief incidence of their sociology abroad. What is meant here is not a provincial quality of Americanism but the essential character of American Society which came to be a central power in the new incredible world society. If Albion W. Small was an enthusiastic devotee of German sociology and advised as many as possible of his students to get their learning abroad, there was no more ardent American preacher and promoter of the moral mission of sociology in America. If Thomas and Znaniecki found the basis of much of their inquiry in the peasant world abroad, they also set the fashion for a new American methodology in the United States. If Parsons and Sorokin, with the origins of their sociology deep in the German and Russian hinterlands, translated and transferred much from Europe to America, they proved to be essentially Americans adapting their methods to the leadership of an American Harvard sociology. And MacIver at Columbia, richly endowed with British heritage, became perhaps the most American of these sociologists who applied sociology to the essential study of intercultural relations on the new sociological level of the 1950's, unless it was Louis Wirth, German-born and theoretically nurtured, who excelled in the American way of organization. A Lazarsfeld, grounded in European psychology, teamed up with Robert Merton and launched in the American communications network, sets the incidence again for what is newly American in studies vividly in contrast to the European vintage. A Howard Becker at Wisconsin and a Robert Cooley Angell from Michigan, sojourning in Europe and translating German sociology into American channels, reflect an increasingly American doctrine as do a hundred younger scholars moving upstream and downstream on the flood tide of American area studies and cooperative efforts in UNESCO or in specific assignments in Palestine or Indonesia. Thus, the ways in which the professors in the United States took a European philosophy and welded it into an American fabric of sociology may be clearly seen in the current status of sociology in other parts of the world.

From all of this and much more it might be deduced that American sociologists have yet to explore the rich field of a more realistic sociology of knowledge in new reviews and understanding of American sociology as primarily the product of American intellectuals in interaction with American culture cross-fertilized with European backgrounds, for, apparently contrary to Merton's brilliant treatises on the sociology of knowledge in his introduction to Part XII of his *Social Theory and Social Structure* and especially in his Chapter VIII, on "The Sociology of Knowledge," American sociologists appear in many ways still to follow the European pattern. Insofar as they envisage a sociology of knowledge, much of it appears as a primary methodology or a conceptual scheme, newly discovered and being followed as a lead rather than constituting a major field in itself, rich in realistic opportunities for the study of contemporary society. That is, the sociology of knowledge sometimes appears as a special *ad hoc* theory, primarily concerned with "the intellectual products of experts." The central foci often appear to be upon the methodology of obtaining information about what relatively isolated intellectuals *think* is knowledge and set in the frame of reference of a certain exotic and subjective classification of opinions of knowledge. Such a sociology, then, may be the reflection of mass opinion but more nearly the expression of what the intellectuals think and what they believe the mass thinks. On these assumptions the "empirical" sociologist may not report at all on what *is* but on what *he sees*. Even if accurately recorded within his own limited frame of reference, his report might eventuate in incessant chattering about the relationships and relevancies of the crucial points of interaction between and among his own subjective categories of conceptualizations.

Nevertheless, Merton's keen analysis of certain differences between the American and the European variants of the sociology of knowledge gives profound evidence of the American quality of sociology. Samplings are adequate for illustrations and for their relevance to the new "take off" of sociology in 1950. On pages 201–2 Merton points out that, "If the American version is primarily concerned with public opinion, with mass beliefs, with what has come to be called 'popular culture,' the European version centers on more esoteric doctrines, on those complex systems of knowledge which become reshaped and often distorted in their subsequent passage into popular culture.

"These differences in focus carry with them further differences: the European variant, being concerned with knowledge, comes to deal with the intellectual elite; the American variant, concerned with widely held opinion, deals with the masses. The one centers on the esoteric doctrines of the few, the other on the esoteric beliefs of the many. This divergence of interest has immediate bearing on every phase of research techniques, as we shall see; it is clear, for example, that a research interview designed to yield information from a scientist or man of literature will differ materially from a research interview intended for a cross-section of the population at large."

A somewhat different appraisal is that of Jacques J. Maquet in his *The Sociology of Knowledge,* translated by John F. Locke, and published in the United States in 1951 with a Preface by F. S. C. Northrop. For this volume is "a critical analysis of the systems of Karl Mannheim and Pitirim A. Sorokin," with the American author having the major portion of the treatise in an appraisal which rates Sorokin more effective in the integration of the several disciplines in their relation to the philosophy of knowledge. Yet the "burden" of Marquet's new volume reflects the almost chaotic and indefinite status of the sociology of knowledge and by the same token presents a challenge for sociologists of the new era to do something about it.

Returning to the priority of American Sociology the very fact that Howard Becker was offered von Wiese's chair of sociology at Cologne and that von Wiese acknowledges his indebtedness to and his condi-

tioning by American sociology would be another evidence of the
dominance of American sociology. A point of emphasis that needs to
be repeated is that reference to contemporary American sociology, so
far from connoting provincialism, reflects the opposite. That is, the
younger sociologists no longer need to be provincial, on the one hand,
by assuming that European sociology must remain more mature and
sophisticated, or by apologizing for or pleading the merits of American
sociology.

Von Wiese, as on page 657 of the 1950 Wiese-Becker *Systematic Sociology,* writes of the tragic fate of mankind as if it were some sort of
treadmill getting nowhere and symbolizing futility. American sociology
assumes the great folk continuum of social process — so what of it? It
was so in the phenomenal development of frontier America; it is so in
an unbelievable 1950 new world frontier. It is the process of interaction
and growth, of change and development that constitutes the field-area
of a broader sociological sweep that can pick out as many concrete fields
as may be possible. The prospect of an American professor of sociology
occupying a German chair may be perhaps no more nor less than the
past pattern of German sociologists in interaction with American culture. In the long road of the rise and development of sociology a single
successful scholar, rising from the total process, may be worth the tra-
vail of all that has gone before; or a similar failure may be an equal
part in the processive structure of American sociology.

Max Weber describes a powerful protestant ethic and naïvely, perhaps, marvels at the immaturity and crudeness of an American environment from which he gathers his observations. Myrdal describes a mighty,
moral conflict and finds frustration in his observation of a classless
race structure. Weber never understood America. No more did Myrdal.
American sociology assumes all this as a basic foundation of the heart of
American capitalism and biracial structure and its fusion of folk and
civilization, of rationalization and achievement. This has nothing to do
with right or wrong but with the analysis of American culture. Or,
again, the Amherst College "American Studies of Problems in American Citizenship" look at, let us say, *Puritanism in American Life* and
*The Turner Thesis concerning the Role of the Frontier in American
History.* Of course puritanism is "positive" and of course it is "negative"; of course it is "good" and of course it is "bad." But for sociology it

is American culture, and the values are more like those of the total role that, for instance, colors play in a painting, rather than the exact moral or aesthetic value that a particular moral doctrine might have in varied settings. Of course the frontier had its great influence on American civilization; but also of course there were other factors playing powerful roles in the Euro-American capitalistic frontier domain of the new nation. The sociologist finds in this field of sociology rare opportunity for the study of American society and its place in whatever continuum may serve as a frame of reference.

If the role of sociology has been powerful in the total American development, and if, on the other hand, the growth of American culture has powerfully conditioned American sociology, such that it has transcended the earlier European dominance, it is true also that sociology in the United States has made its major contribution to the over-all development of the social sciences. Sociology was a charter member of the Social Science Research Council, the genesis of which was in the motivation and ideas of the political scientist, Charles E. Merriam. Long before that, however, another distinguished Chicago professor, Albion W. Small, was the most effective pleader for the cooperation and integration of the social sciences. Subsequently, the Social Science Research Council's *Case Book on Methods* was edited by Stuart Rice; the Council's first critique of special examples of scientific studies, that of Thomas and Znaniecki's *The Polish Peasant,* was done by Herbert Blumer. Ogburn was both chairman of the Problem and Policy Committee and president of the Council. Ogburn and Odum were directors of the Council's major project in cooperative research, namely, the President's Research Committee on Social Trends, resulting in *Recent Social Trends* in two main volumes and thirteen monographs. Other sociologists who took strategic part in the Social Science Research Council's earlier work included Robert Lynd, W. I. Thomas, Stuart Chapin, Malcolm Wiley, Louis Wirth, Ernest W. Burgess, R. M. MacIver; and later Donald Young as executive, and others of the younger group, such as Rupert Vance, Samuel Stouffer, Gordon Blackwell, Leonard Cottrell.

In Chapters 1 and 3 we traced something of the rapid growth of sociology in the colleges and universities of the United States. The full measure of this growth is reflected in the curricula and faculties of the

1810 institutions catalogued by the United States Office of Education. In its development and expansion, sociology has followed the patterns of regional distribution that have characterized the national culture's historical development. First were the beginnings in the Northeast, followed quicky by larger developments in the Middle States and then in the Southeast and the Far West and then back again to the Southwest and the Central Northwest. The several "Wests," then, have proved to be a fruitful seedbed for sociologists later to emigrate to the Northeast and the Southeast.

The 1950 concentrations of members of the American Sociological Society were in the order of the Northeast, the Middle States, the Southeast, the Far West, the Southwest, and the Central Northwest. This same general ratio is found in the American Economic Association with its 6631, 1949–50, members being especially concentrated in the Northeast and Middle States, and the American Political Science Association with the Northeast, 829, Middle States, 799, Northwest, 240, Southeast, 225, Far West, 142, and Southwest, 97, in that order. As indicating the American regional pattern, the total membership of the American Sociological Society shows consistent uniformities. Thus, of the 2364 members for which information was available, 979 or 41 per cent were registered from the Northeast; 676 or 28.6 per cent from the Middle States; 248 or 10.4 per cent from the Southeast; 236 or 10 per cent from the Far West; and 91 and 71 or 3.8 and 3 per cent from the Northwest and Southwest respectively. Sixty-three or less than 3 per cent were classified as "foreign." In a catalogue of "Who's Who" of American sociology, foreign percentage was somewhat higher, with 11.7, but the general regional distribution followed the same relative ratio. Of the total 480 who had achieved such uniform distinction as to be catalogued, 161 or 33.5 per cent were registered from the Northeast; 117 or 25 per cent from the Middle States; 72 or 15 per cent were from the Southeast, with the Far West, Northwest, and Southwest in order with 7.3, 5, and 3.1 per cent respectively. The foreign group, the Southeast, and the Northwest had somewhat higher percentages of the "Who's Who" than of the total membership. The Southeast's and the Northwest's gains were primarily due to the ex-officio representation indicated by heads of departments in relatively large numbers of institutions where sociology has been prominently featured. As is the case in *Who's Who in America* there are more ex-officio individuals with less achievement than in the urban intellectual centers.

There are, however, some relatively significant variations in the contrasts between the ratios of those born in the several regions and the places where they are located in their professional work in 1950: of the total, 161 are located in the Northeast while only 95 were born there. On the other hand, 145 were born in the Middle States with only 117 working there, indicating the old "Middle West" to be the main seedbed of American sociologists. Likewise only 67 were born in the Southeast although 72 were located there. That is, the origins of American sociologists in 1950 appeared to follow the same pattern as was reflected in the classification of the earliest presidents of the American Sociological Society. The same general ratio of distribution appears in the enrollment and departments of sociology in the several regions.

In its regional and national development sociology in the United States has contributed substantially to a number of special objectives. It has set the incidence for a valid concept of what is "sociological" in America, both in the academic and in the popular world. This concept, as basic to the science of sociology, has arisen, as all sciences have, through the gradual evolution of knowledge and experience. Yet, because all this is difficult to identify at a given point of origin, the process and structure of the new science often seem vague or even non-existent. It is as if, as once pointed out by Harry Woodburn Chase, if we did not have sociology, we should have to hurry on to establishing something that would be the *same* as sociology, in order to meet the expectations and the relevant needs of all those who seek to find the meaning and the answer to sociological questions and problems. Sociology has made this concept elemental and comprehensive in the structure of American education, American literature, American thought, and American action. Yet, as Gerald Johnson has said, the average American regards sociology somewhat as he does penicillin: "It is obviously a necessity in the modern world. It has worked some marvelous cures and promises to work more, but it is tricky. Unintelligently handled, its toxicity can be terrific and the greatest experts don't know any too much about the after effects."

A second objective mentioned here is that sociology has also contributed powerfully to the integration of American thought and scholarship throughout the regions of the nation as well as to unifying the nation's efforts and ideologies in the major aspects of social thought and social processes. Sociologists have complained that there is not yet a standard requirement for "Sociology I" in the same way that content and methods can be made uniform in the case of physics or mathematics or perhaps economics and history. Yet in two ways sociology has achieved a common language in the major areas of social thought and on the main levels of social processes.

In the first place, insofar as sociology is practically a required subject in colleges and universities in all regions of the nation, it has set the incidence for a common language and a common ground for wholesome and scientific inquiry. This applies to liberal arts colleges, teacher training schools, junior and community colleges, and private and denominational colleges, as well as to the teaching and research programs of all larger universities. The addition of sociology to the programs of Princeton and the University of California, with provisions for the Ph.D. degree on the 1950 frontier, might be said to constitute final evidence of sociology's coming of age with a certain academic maturity. On another level, sociology has contributed perhaps more than any other discipline to the common language and concepts of many aspects of human relationships in the specialisms involved in such areas as community relationships; family and marriage, including research, teaching, education, and counseling; intercultural relations; population, migration, and demography; regional factors in structural and functional relations to analysis and planning; in race relations and especially the Negro in the United States; in many areas relating to social security and public welfare; in many aspects of labor relations and industrial sociology; and in general theory and methodology where there is increasing homogeneity and agreement on main points.

Yet these achievements have brought greatly increased responsibilities in a number of ways. In the first place, the demand for mature scholars with the capacity to direct research, teaching, and community relationships and to make sociology effective, far exceeds the capacity of all of the universities in 1950 to turn out younger candidates and to mature older ones for just what is needed. This proves a very real problem for college and university administrators, both from the viewpoint of their well-balanced curricula and from the viewpoint of insuring strong departments of sociology. The problem also proves a dilemma for the larger departments of sociology offering the Ph.D. degree, in that they may have to re-examine the needs and demands placed upon them if sociology is to hold its own and advance in accordance with its opportunities.

There is another side to the obligations that sociology, by its extraordinary expansion and its efforts toward realistic maturity, has brought upon itself. This is the increasing tendency to make values and interpretations fundamental in sociological theory in the revivification of the frame of reference basis for research problems and projects. But more than this, the very fact of sociology's widening range of specialisms, involving more and more of human relationship and the setting up of a common language, automatically sets the incidence for exploration and survey in the fields of judgments, values, and other programs less isolated from the realities of modern society.

There are two sides to this dilemma. One is the assumption that the sociological approach to problems of adjustment in such fields as labor-management, race and cultural contacts, personality and culture, individuation and socialization, would be more mature and permanent than the moral imperatives and the political directives so powerfully projected through societal pressures and coercive legislation. The other is the alternative situation in which the tendencies may so easily trend toward irresponsible positions, taken on the assumption of objective specialization but resulting in ideological dogmatizing. This may be illustrated by situations in which sociologists assume for themselves the role of specialists because they happen to be the only authors who have written on a particular specialism. On the mere evidence of titles they not only assume to be specialists but they are so documented by other authors for the simple reason that their titles are exclusive. Thus it may easily come to pass that anyone may set himself up as a specialist by choosing an undeveloped area and writing on it regardless of the scientific quality of his work or the amount of testing of his hypothesis and conclusions. Some evidence of this can be found in the *Dictionary of Sociology* where partisan statements are made under the guise of definitions. Evidence may also be found in current discussions of themes dogmatically presented without documented reference to the same themes, which have often been developed by other authors, or in the dogmatic negation of concepts and theories of such earlier sociologists as Sumner, Ward, Giddings, without the authors' ever having read or understood those authors.

Fortunately, however, the trend seems to be toward a better balanced sociology in which sound theory becomes essentially the most practical thing in the whole scientific realm and practical problems constitute the field from which empirical specialisms form the basis for concrete research and special frames of reference. Hazards may arise, of course, from the multiplicity of specialisms and consequent dogmatic assumptions of specific values in them as ends and in the general tropism toward presenting something new and better than anyone else has done in a polarity of ideology and definition.

In Chapter 15 we have quoted Robert Merton in critical appraisal of social theory and social research. His discussions of both trends and goals may well serve as preview and premise of our continuing discussion of trends and prospects of American sociology in 1950. Thus, one of his facile statements affords a departure for re-examining briefly both contrasts between the earlier and later sociology and for pointing the way toward new directions. Writing on "The Bearing of Empirical Research upon the Development of Social Theory" on page 505 of the *American Sociological Review* for October, 1948, and on page 97 of his *Social Theory and Social Structure,* Merton says, "The stereotype of the social theorist high in the empyrean of pure ideas uncontaminated by mundane facts is fast becoming no less outmoded than the stereotype of the social researcher equipped with questionnaire and pencil and hot on the chase of the isolated and meaningless statistic. For in building the mansion of sociology during the last decades, theorist and empiricist have learned to work together."

This, then, does reflect the new status and may well constitute the framework for new trends to be well stabilized in increasingly effective programs of research and theory set in the framework of realistic contemporary society. In the larger perspective, however, concerning the Merton characterization, two observations are important. The first is that the stalwarts of early American sociology — Sumner, Ward, Giddings, Small, Ross, Cooley — whatever else they may have been, were pretty well contaminated by worldly affairs, although the nature of the problems which they "tackled" were different from those of 1950. Also the pad-and-pencil statistic-hunter never quite came to be the chief mode of sociology from the 1930's to the 1950's. The second observation is that one of the hazards of the new empiricism, developing through the multiplication of specialisms, is that of another kind of stereotype which might substitute isolated empirical reference for realistic empirical study integrated in sound theoretical structure.

We come next, therefore, to the crucial task of estimating the status of the current sociology of 1950 with the logical trends that constitute an essential part of any appraisal of promise and prospect. It is possible to give adequate samplings of published estimates of contrasts and trends and of goals set and methods recommended as found in the sociological periodical literature and in the introductions to new textbooks. Yet it will be more accurate, realistic, and comprehensive to let certain facts speak for themselves, if the several sets of facts may be viewed in their interrelation to each other and to the total situation. These facts include the catalogues of the extraordinarily rich and numerous categories of specialisms now reflecting the work and moods of American sociologists; the actual literature as published in the sociological journals and books; catalogues of current and recent definitions, concepts and constructs as contrasted with earlier sociology; summaries and trends presented by sociologists in encyclopedias; and special summaries on special anniversary occasions.

If we seek to arrive at the newest authentic sources for characterizing contemporary sociology, the best verdict would appear to be a product of several. First of all, there is no substitute for the total facts presented in the previous chapters of this book. They cannot be summarized except in a sort of descriptive review in perspective to changes and trends now continuously in process. Next, there is the study of actual specialisms submitted by the American sociologists who are making the main contributions to research and writing, presented as a whole and in such detailed perspective as each sociologist interprets his own work and method. And third, there are the estimates of representative authors concerning the meaning of the multiple specialisms in the framework of consensus and trend.

Here again, Merton's verdict appears relevant as a framework for looking at the more than four hundred concrete specialisms sufficiently distinctive in their wording to justify a separate cataloguing and sufficiently chaotic to emphasize the need for an over-all systematization of the fields of sociology. Merton is characterizing sociology in 1950 as different from earlier sociology in that, through empirical study in selected limited areas or specialisms, its major concern is developing what he calls theories of the middle range. "I believe," he says on page 9 of his *Social Theory and Social Structure,* "that our major task today is to develop special theories applicable to limited ranges of data — theories, for example, of class dynamics, of conflicting group pressures, of the flow of power and the exercise of interpersonal influence — rather than to seek at once the 'integrated' conceptual structure adequate to derive all these and other theories." In support of the Merton appraisal are the specialisms reported by more than four hundred sociologists whose work represents both the core and the trend of contemporary sociology in America and its increasing influence abroad. In these specialisms may be found measures, not of what someone believes is a trend, nor of selected areas being brought to the attention of the critics, but of what is being done on the broad scale of majority reporting. Other trends will be summarized and other examples of what is being done will be cited, but, after all, the catalogue of specialisms, selected and worded by the participants themselves, can give the best picture of the content and methods of present-day sociology. It is not that these measures contradict the several diagnoses and summaries of trends made by selected sociologists in recent years but that they transcend the more limited specialized descriptions and reports.

Of the more than a thousand specialisms reported by more than four hundred sociologists, it is possible to group enough of them together to indicate prevailing preferences for fields in which many sociologists feel they can contribute more to the increasing scientific nature of sociological research as it tends to conform more nearly to the whole field of scientific inquiry. The total tableland of specialisms has perhaps not been very carefully explored; the selections have often been incidental and partial; the wording of topics individualistic; but in general the continuing story of American sociology may be found in these catalogues and their contexts.

Of the more than one thousand specialisms listed, more than five hundred were so distinctively worded as to require separate cataloguing.

Of those that could be clustered together, however, the largest number, or nearly one hundred, could be classified as "social theory" and the next largest number, seventy-five, was in the category of race and ethnic groups, including minority groups and race relations. In the order of numerical priority the specialisms listed by as many as twenty or more conform to the same ratio as the recent contributions to the sociological journals and in general to the titles of doctors' dissertations catalogued in the last decade. These first twenty might suggest the basis for a conference on the delineation of tools and methods.

Social theory
Race—Race relations
The Family, not including Marriage
Population
Crime-Delinquency
Social psychology
Rural sociology
Industrial sociology
Urban sociology
Methodology

Ecology
The Community
Social planning
Personality
Educational sociology
Disorganization
Social problems
Public opinion
Social change
Foreign cultures

Others indicating ten or more in the general order of priority include a considerable list with many variations. *Social structure,* for instance, included "structure and dynamics of small groups," "theory of social structure," "social structure of India," "social structure of Latin America," "moral integration and social structure," "character and social structure." *Personality* included such variations in terminology as "personality and culture," "primary interaction and personal behavior," "sociology of personality," "social factors in personality development and conflict," "sociological and psychological factors affecting personality," "interpersonal systems and processes," "social psychology of personality." *Communication, mass communication, public opinion* were often closely associated with "community," "group dynamics," "intergroup relations." *Urban sociology* has many variations such as "urban planning," "urbanism and planning," "urban ecology," "ecology and urbanism," "urban-rural sociology." The next priority group includes:

Statistics
Marriage
Intergroup relations

Stratification
Political sociology
Communication

Regionalism
Social movements
Standard of living
Old age
Collective behavior
Culture
Sociometry
Social work
Demography
Institutions
Social structure

Propaganda
Public opinion
Psychiatry
Social organization
Social control
Sociology of religion
Socio drama
Acculturation
Sex
Group dynamics
Political sociology

An unpublished investigation by C. M. Grigg into the specialisms listed by the entire membership of the American Sociological Society, including student membership, revealed a total of 4594. These fell into 409 categories. The first ten categories in order of their importance are as follows:

Social psychology
Social theory
Demography and Population
Criminology and Penology
Marriage and Family

Rural sociology
Family
Race relations
Urban sociology
Industrial sociology

Such samplings of these more recent specialisms will be adequate to indicate the trend toward the selection of concrete problems in specific fields as well as to indicate the range of subjects. How these specialisms are related to methodology may be seen from an examination of recent literature in the sociological journals and in special monographs and books.

One of the best indices of similarities, contrasts, and trends of current contemporary sociology as compared with earlier sociology may be found in the published articles of the two official sociological journals: *The American Journal of Sociology* and the *American Sociological Review*. More specifically, comparison of the first hundred articles with the last hundred in *The American Journal* and in the *Review* will give a fair indication of differences, as will the first hundred of the *Review* compared with the first hundred of *The Journal* or the total catalogue of subjects in the fourteen years of the *Review* compared with the contents of *The Journal's* first fourteen years. For instance, twenty-five distinguished senior authors contributed the bulk of the first hundred main articles in *The American Journal of Sociology,* whereas more than ninety authors, primarily representing the younger research students and teachers, contributed the bulk of the last hundred. Of these earliest contributors, beginning in July, 1895, Lester F. Ward contributed no less than 14 articles; E. A. Ross, 13; Albion W. Small, 10. Four or five each were contributed by C. A. Henderson, Paul Monroe, Shailer Mathews, Ira Howerth, H. A. Millis, W. I. Thomas, Georg Simmel. John R. Commons, H. L. Bliss, E. Muensterberg, Walter Rauschenbusch, Friedrich Ratzel, each contributed more than one article. Other senior authors of that era included James Tufts, Carroll Wright, George Vincent, Hastings Hart, Jane Addams, Charles Zeublin, Josiah Strong, Walter F. Willcox, Jeremiah Jenks, A. G. Warner, F. W. Blackmar, C. A. Ellwood, Florence Kelley.

The nature of the earlier contributions conformed to the general needs and patterns of earlier sociological literature, namely, general themes and over-all discussions together with the role of sociology in America and in Europe and its relation to other social sciences and to philosophy and religion. Ward wrote on the place, the role, the contributions, and the data of sociology, as well as on special aspects of genesis and telesis. Ross contributed a dozen chapters of his forthcoming *Social Control.* Small wrote on the sociological point of view, the meaning of the social movement, sociology and pedagogy, the era of sociology, and other "educational" topics. Shailer Mathews and Rauschenbusch wrote on aspects of sociology and religion. Millis, interestingly enough, wrote four articles on "Law Relating to the Relief and Care of Dependents," while John R. Commons was still the social reformer, writing on "The Junior Republic." Carroll D. Wright and Walter F. Willcox were the pioneers writing on the contributions of the United States Census to the study of specific problems. Other authors included: Harry P. Judson, G. Fiamingo, Arnold Tompkins, J. D. Forrest, Franklin McVeagh, C. F. Beach, Jr., Frédéric Passy, F. C. Sharp, Marion Talbot, A. W. Tourage, S. T. Wood, R. C. Bates, W. A. King, A. M. Simons, Frederick Starr, W. M. Stuart, and C. R. Woodruff.

In contrast to that first hundred articles in *The American Journal of Sociology* is the last hundred up to 1950, with quite a different catalogue of nearly a hundred authors for the first hundred articles. A bare half dozen authors had more than one article including Lee, Ichheiser,

Turner, Nimkoff and Timasheff. The only senior sociologists represented were Ogburn and Burgess writing special articles in a special edition on The Family.

If we make a similar catalogue of the *American Sociological Review,* beginning in December, 1949, and cataloguing backward, for a hundred articles the general result appears very much the same. There are relatively few authors with more than one contribution, and these include W. E. Moore, P. C. Glick, A. B. Hollingshead, R. Bierstedt, R. Mukerjee.

On the other hand, if we begin with the first issues of the *American Sociological Review* in 1936 and catalogue forward, we find quite a different story insofar as the number of authors contributing two or more articles is concerned. At least a score of authors have contributed five or more articles, including Read Bain, Howard Becker, James H. S. Bossard, F. Stuart Chapin, Leonard S. Cottrell, Jr., Kingsley Davis, Hornell Hart, Philip M. Hauser, Norman S. Hayner, August B. Hollingshead, Clifford Kirkpatrick, George Lundberg, Thomas C. McCormick, Robert K. Merton, Delbert C. Miller, Wilbert E. Moore, Talcott Parsons, Joseph Schneider, Mapheus Smith, Bernhard J. Stern, and Carl C. Taylor.

We have already pointed out in Chapter 23 something of a turning point in the publications of American sociology with the founding of the *American Sociological Review* in 1936 as the official organ of the American Sociological Society. Although the trend toward more research and writing on specific fields, more after the manner of the natural sciences, had been well under way since the 1920's, the contents of the *American Sociological Review* afford probably the best measured index of the change. Of approximately eight hundred articles published from 1936 through 1949, more than three-fourths were in the leading categories reported in the catalogues of specialisms given previously in this chapter. These are history and social theory, statistics and research methodology, marriage and the family, social problems, population sociology, criminology, race and ethnic groups, and social psychology. Other leads indicating the same trend were in industrial sociology, ecology, social planning. Rural sociology had become a specialty of its own with its own journal and a consequent low priority, while some of the contributions on urban sociology were in the category of ecology, with history and theory totaling nearly a third of the total articles. The numerical order of the other categories were: statistics and methodology, marriage and the family, social problems, population, social psychology, criminology, race relations and ethnic problems, ecology, social planning, educational sociology, industrial sociology, housing, teaching of sociology, social pathology, urban sociology, rural sociology, with scattered articles on bibliography, introductory sociology and biography.

Although definitions and concepts should not be taken too seriously as indices of either total sociology or trends, we had originally prepared as a terminal chapter a review of some of the prevailing definitions as essential to the understanding of American sociology. Although the length requirements of this book necessitated the omission of this chapter, the review is important both because of the nature of the definitions and the methods by which they have been constructed. A study of definitions, concepts, and constructs from the beginnings of sociology to the present time also affords one of the best bases for comparisons between the earlier and later sociology. These definitions afford certain measures of both status and trends not available from other sources. Thus, certain concepts and definitions in the later theoretical contributions of sociologists, so popular as modes for many sociologists and as objects of criticism for others, indicate indubitably a clear-cut breakaway from the earlier pioneers. This may be seen from the catalogue of concepts or from the fact that in the main contributions of none of the latest sociological theorists just before 1950 is there any textual reference to Ward, Giddings, Small, Ross, Cooley, or to more than a half dozen of any of the presidents of the American Sociological Society.

Next, a new level of definitions in sociology, as in psychology, economics, labor, political science, philosophy, was inaugurated with the coming of the *Dictionary of Sociology* in 1944, edited by Henry Pratt Fairchild but long since outmoded as reflected in the prevailing literature. Samplings from the *Dictionary* and comparison with some of the other dictionaries will indicate the range of definitions and the trend toward "defining." Although the preoccupation of making definitions and of debating methodology and inventing new terms and formulae for their own sake may well be accepted as traits of immature disciplines, nevertheless, the recording and checking of definitions and concepts may also be accepted as signs of maturity. And, although preoccupation of propaganda for "empirical" research may sometimes indicate a lack of it, nevertheless, the trend toward testing assumptions with reality must surely be rated as both progress in a direction and as breakaway from the earlier armchair sociology, except insofar as emphasis is primarily upon definition of definitions; empiricism takes the form primarily of hypotheses; and analysis gets no farther than description and illustrative analogy.

The general consensus would probably justify the conclusion that the shift from the definitions that were primarily about general sociology and society to the emphasis upon new concepts and methodological procedures could be associated with several influences, perhaps "eras." Perhaps the Chicago emphasis upon "the frame of reference" was first, with Thomas' "definition of the situation" next. Lundberg, Bain, and Dodd were eloquent and insistent upon operational definitions. In between and all along, the statistical and objective method as emphasized by Ogburn and as illustrated in *Recent Social Trends* set new levels of definition of problems. Finally the Parsons-Merton sweeping exposition of empiricism and the interrelationship of theory and method set the incidence for a powerful trend in that direction. In general the later trends were primarily breakaways from the earlier elders of American sociology.

And yet Sumner would find himself in doubt whether to "snort" or to smile when the latest sociology text before 1950 defined his folkways as "the hardest core of the normative system," or in terms of the old analogical "the protoplasm of the cell"; or still more when "each *mos* is believed to be essential to social welfare," and "each folkway is considered fundamentally important." There is, of course, no such thing as a *"mos"* or a *"folkway,"* for the concept of *folkways* and *mores* stems from the collective social forces articulate in plurality and integration. Sumner could satirize few things more than the naïveté of "a *mos*," and, to satire, Keller could add eloquent profanity.

Nor would Giddings consider as a great improvement upon his clear-cut definitions and analytical catalogues and steps in a process of methodology, the operational "profile" with which Read Bain summarizes the Blumer critique of *The Polish Peasant*. He concludes that "the specific researches make imperative the revision of organizing concepts and general theories, and such revision by logico systematic analysis sets new problems for further empirical research which requires the development of new or improved precision procedures which depend upon the intention of new or improvement of old technological devices of observation, recording, and manipulation along with new or improved methodological fields and procedures."

Once again Cooley might not consider Parsons' social role definition a very clear-cut simplification of his role of the person in the group, when Parsons, in his presidential address in 1949, says, "Thus what sociologically is called universalism in a social role definition can be psychologically interpreted as the impact of the mechanism of generalization in obect-orientation and object choice. Correspondingly, what on the sociological level has been called the institutionalization of 'affective neutrality' turns out to be essentially the same as the imposition of renunciation of immediate gratification in the interests of the disciplined organization and longer-run goals of the personality."

CHAPTER 25

Hazards and Limitations, Promise and Prospect

In the light of American sociology's extraordinary record and of the convulsive changes that have made 1950 societal situations different from previous societies, and in the light of the communicable knowledge of so many divergent cultural traditions and social organizations and the consequent intercultural relations and conflict, the story of sociology in review and in prospect must be considerably more than the simply stated objective of making the mid-century an anniversary occasion for inventory and catalogue of achievements. Although the main focus is still upon American sociology, our total task is manifestly to envisage sociology as a dynamic science in the setting of turbulent changes and powerful forces at work and of specific factors that now make its role both problematic and incomparably more significant than ever before. These factors may well be symbolized in two major technical events at the halfway mark of an incredibly tumultuous century. One is global and general, namely, the United States' world leadership in a new role as guardian of change; the other is American and concrete, namely, the enactment of Public Law 507, of the Eighty-first Congress of the United States.

The creation of the National Science Foundation, epochal in symbolizing a new governmental premium upon science and the potential control and direction of research, poses sociology's major obligation and opportunity to orient itself in the company of sciences and more specifically to assume responsibility and a certain boldness in making sociology come of age in an era when human relations will surely be more inseparably geared to survival and richness of living than ever before in recorded history. The functions of the Foundation, not only as stated in the legislation, but even more powerfully implied, include the unprecedented urge "to place the highly intricate and technical problems of our complex society in the hands of competent experts" and "to reconcile intellectual authority with public responsibility." The two main aspects of these functions are the support of scientific basic research and the discovery, recruiting, and development of the nation's man power resources for research. Included alongside the policy of endowing youth and supplying techniques and materials will be the defining of areas and problems of research, the use and control of results, and the role of science in the total human picture. Implied also are the definitions of science and the operational procedures that may reject or give precedence to sociology's role in the living society of the future.

Implied in all this then, is first of all sociology's multiple role of maturing itself as a science, of recruiting and training personnel, of developing its capacity to participate in realistic non-isolated research in human relations and its capacity to develop leadership in America commensurate with current and impending needs. Implied in this intercultural dichotomy of conflict, on the one hand, and more intimate world relationships, on the other, are the opportunities and obligations for a more dynamic leadership in international sociology to find a common approach to human problems. This may be symbolized more specifically in the September, 1950, Congress of the International Association of Sociologists under the auspices of UNESCO; some subsequent conferences symbolizing the uniting of East and West; and subsequent working interregional conferences in the Americas and elsewhere.

This, it seems to me, is the minimum framework within which we should envisage the promise and prospect, the hazards and limitations of American sociology as it enters the second half of the twentieth century, even more momentous than the first: (1) the reviewed situation through which sociology has achieved (2) its present status which in turn reflects (3) certain major trends, the understanding of which is basic to (4) a critique of promise and prospect in the light of (5) what is empirically demonstrable and authentically accepted as the newest era, in terms of the dynamics of change and crisis, that human society has ever faced. Yet, such a critique finds *its main focus upon sociology primarily as a very special social science as such and not as just a general social science* seeking cooperation and integration with the other social sciences as a part of a social science movement, for, in order to cooperate effectively and to contribute powerfully to the integration of the sciences, sociology must itself first be strong and have a distinctive scientific contribution to make.

In earlier chapters we have recorded much of the total story of American sociology's achievement in general and in special areas. In Chapter 24 we have continued the story in a general appraisal and critique of status and current tendencies. Our next approach to the continuing appraisal of American sociology as of 1950, therefore, will be found in the catalogue of current trends as indications of direction and capacity and as reflecting also past achievements and current status. And perhaps the first in priority, exclusive of the over-all changes in systematic theory and methodology, which we have already described and to which we shall return, is the strong movement toward closer cooperation and integration with psychology and anthropology. This movement, both on its own account, and as part of the more general tropism toward the integration of the social sciences in the approach to the study of human problems, requires special examination for several reasons. One is to ascertain the degree to which the movement is a new or a continuing one and to determine whether the movement constitutes a trend. Another is to inquire into the effects of this movement upon the specific scientific methods being developed and utilized by sociology and to compare the basic scientific procedures most appropriate for each of the disciplines involved. Still another is to inquire into the limitations of relative degrees of cooperation and integration as they may have a bearing upon the more rigorous science of society as symbolized by sociology at its best. There is no criticism of the laudable ends of cooperative endeavor everywhere appraised as of definitive value. Caution is registered only when integration might be substituted for more vigorous scientific method in sociology itself.

We begin with psychology, in which the increasing role and range of cooperation are indicated in the catalogued specialisms, in the main contributed articles in the sociological journals, in the subject matter and methodology reported in current doctoral dissertations, and in the prevailing estimates by sociologists who undertake to diagnose current sociology. The general close relation between psychology and sociology is, however, not new. The present manifestation is different primarily in the methodology and the kind of psychology and social psychology that forms the basis of the new research and cooperation with psychologists themselves. Indeed, American sociology from the beginning has leaned heavily upon the psychology of its day, not long removed from "mental philosophy." Giddings was early characterized as belonging to the "psychological school"; and his last book, *The Scientific Study of Human Society* had as a part of its descriptive title "The Psychology of Society"; Ward wrote the *Psychic Factors of Civilization*; Sumner's *Folkways* was essentially cultural or folk psychology; Ross wrote the first book on "social psychology"; Cooley's trilogy, *Human Nature and the Social Order, Social Process,* and *Social Organization* were often termed the real forerunners of American social psychology; Small's "interests," Thomas' "wishes," were all reflections of the psychological approach. All told, American sociologists have published a score of books that may be classified as social psychology. Moreover, their European forerunners were strong in the psychological approach: Tarde's "imitation"; Fouillée's "idea forces"; Ratzenhofer's "interests"; Gumplowicz's "race struggle"; Le Bon's "crowds"; and later Durkheim, Weber, Pareto, were influences in the psychological gains.

Among the special aspects of recent American social psychology are the emphasis upon personality, culture and culture patterns, races and groups, intelligence and character tests, folk psychology and the study of political leadership, gestalt psychology, psychopathology and psychiatry, together with many concrete social problems through which the psychological approach assumes a role of first importance. Thus personality has become a key to the interrelation between individual and society, between organic physical backgrounds and social development. In more recent years American sociologists have utilized and contributed to social psychology on three main levels. The first is the over-all textbook approach under the title social psychology itself. In the second place, personality and adjustment have become increasingly important in the study of human behavior. In the third place, they have tended to utilize the Freudian principles more widely and, somewhat earlier, the behavioristic psychology. A fourth level might be characterized as that of culture psychology in the sense that the increasing emphasis upon culture and the closer alignment with anthropology necessarily emphasize more of the interrelationships and interaction processes.

In Chapter 14 we have given a general chronological catalogue of books on social psychology written by American sociologists and have pointed out the dichotomy of "sociological" and "psychological" "social psychologies" as recognized by both sociologists and psychologists. But the newer trend in which sociology draws heavily upon social psychology is something more than merely getting nearer together with the psychologists. It is a combination of adopting several of the many methodologies employed by the psychologists and of appraising the prestige of psychology as more scientific than that of sociology, as well as of seeking to make social psychology a main bridgehead of empirical research and operational methodology. Something of the hazards involved will be discussed subsequently; our assumption here is that, whatever else may be true, the movement sets the incidence for much of what sociology is in 1950 as well as for its potential for the future.

As early as 1941, Leonard Cottrell wrote on page 58 of *Developments in Social Psychology 1930–1940* that "we might venture a prediction about the kind of review a trend-finder would write in 1950. His criterion will be neither a theoretical one nor a methodological one. It will be both. The main theme of his work will point to the growing convergence of concept and operation in social psychology, and it will underscore the advances in precision and insight made possible by this convergence. We hope that he may underscore yet another kind of progress, made possible by this first: namely, a clear definition of the role of social psychology in relation to the other social sciences. We suspect that out of a decade in which social psychologists have patiently tilled their own garden will come the sort of product which other social scientists can use. Eventually, we feel, social psychology will be the bio-chemistry of the social sciences, and somehow we hope that this role will become clear enough in the forties to make the deadline for the 1950 review."

Then, in 1950, in his presidential address before the American Sociological Society, while discussing the limitations of current social psychology, he gave evidence that his prediction was not far away from the reality of 1950. So too, Cottrell's "The Case Study Method in Prediction" in lecture form, and his "The Analysis of the Situational Fields in Social Psychology," published in the *American Sociological Review* for June, 1942, give evidence of contemporary validity as compared with what many workers in the field are just finding out for themselves about the processes of interpersonal interaction and the nature of insight and understanding and communication among human beings. Something of the same sort of evidence of contemporary validity of the dynamics of interpersonal interaction may be found in Chapter XII of Volume I of *The American Soldier.*

Other samplings of many verdicts concerning this movement toward closer cooperation and integration with pyschology indicate that it may be a major trend. Howard Becker in his "Ten Eventful Years" of sociology in the *Encyclopaedia Britannica, 1946,* characterizes as "one of the most striking manifestations, . . . the fusing of selected aspects of sociology, social psychology, social and cultural anthropology, and social psychiatry into a reasonably well integrated whole." Yet he introduces his story with the statement that "the course of sociology during the past decade has been one of consolidation and expansion rather than of innovation." Merton interpreted the situation on page 9 of his *Social Theory and Social Structure* by saying that "the gradual convergence of some streams of theory in social psychology, social anthropology and sociology promises large theoretic gains. Yet, having said this, one must admit that a large part of what is now called sociological theory consists of *general orientations toward data."*

While the current practice features social psychology more specifically than psychology in general, it is not easy to forget the manifestation reflected in the 1920's and 1930's in which "extreme behaviorism threatened to dominate the sociological scene" or the specialized studies of personality in which psychology and anthropology teamed together to tempt the sociologists to all-out generalizations. With reference to the verdict on whether the present reflects a major permanent trend or a temporary manifestation, certain limitations of the present situation may well indicate what will be needed if the movement is to materialize into a measured trend.

For instance, the field of psychology comprehends such a broad base, such diversities and special divisions and methods and such an abundance of periodical literature and published sources that the danger of superficial assumptions by scholars who are not acquainted with the scope and techniques of psychology might well negate many of the desirable facets of fusion. Psychology lists itself primarily as a natural science in the trilogy of natural sciences, social sciences, and humanities. It is compounded of both the biological and physical sciences and the American Psychological Association has a professional enrollment perhaps three times that of the American Sociological Society, a larger proportion of whom are not on faculties of educational institutions. The catalogue of journals includes no less than ten official publications and more than that many other accredited journals, exclusive of the separate field of psychiatry so freely drawn upon by many students. The official publications of the American Psychological Association include: *American Psychologist*; *Journal of Abnormal and Social Psychology*; *Journal of Applied Psychology*; *Journal of Comparative and Physiological Psychology*; *Journal of Consulting Psychology*; *Journal of Experimental Psychology*; *Psychological Abstracts*; *Psychological Bulletin*; *Psychological Monographs: General and Applied*; *Psychological Review*. Other prominent psychology journals in special fields include: *Journal of Genetic Psychology*; *Journal of General Psychology*; *Journal of Social Psychology*; *American Journal of Psychology*; *Journal of Clinical Psychology*; *Journal of Consulting Psychology*; *Personnel Journal*; *Psychometrika*; *Personnel Psychology*; *Rorschach Research Exchange; Journal of Personality; Character and Personality; Psychological Book Previews*.

Other manifestations of sociology's recent tendencies to draw heavily upon psychology are evident in the interrelations between sociology and anthropology and anthropology and psychology to which we have already referred. The tendencies may be specifically measured primarily in two ways. One is the actual closer cooperation and consolidation of sociology and anthropology in departmental arrangements in universities and the general appraisals of the movement by both sociologists and anthropologists. The other is to explore sociology's recent tendency to draw heavily upon studies of personality, community behavior, stratification, differences in social status and ethnic groupings, made by anthropologists who, in turn, lean heavily upon psychology and psychiatry. In each of these may be found adequate specific measures of tendency to justify the need for critical appraisal.

In the case of sociology and anthropology the newer tendency toward integration reflects a different type of cooperation from that with psychology. That is, more than twenty-five leading colleges and universities have now consolidated the two disciplines into a single department of sociology and anthropology or anthropology and sociology. This is a reverse trend from the mode in other social sciences where joint departments of economics and sociology, for instance, have given inadequate scope to one or both disciplines.

Three authors who have dated the newer fusion tendencies from Harvard's reorganization of its sociology department in 1946–47 include Howard Becker in his Encyclopedia article, "Ten Eventful Years," Edward Shils' *The Present State of American Sociology,* and Talcott Parsons and Bernard Barber's "Sociology, 1941–1944," in *The American Journal of Sociology* for January, 1948. Becker wrote that "The tendency toward a science of social relations coordinating social psychology, social psychiatry, social and cultural anthropology, and sociology, was made more clearly manifest by the establishment in 1946 of a Department of Social Relations at Harvard." Shils wrote on page 55 "At Harvard, in the newly formed Department of Social Relations, the collaboration of Talcott Parsons, Henry Murray, Clyde Kluckhohn, Samuel Stouffer and others, provides an important opportunity to synthesize technical virtuosity, analytical vigor, historical breadth, psychological imagination and a value directed sense of relevance in the selection of problems." Parsons and Barber, assuming that "The present position of sociology as a science is best stated in relation to the other social sciences, particularly social anthropology and psychology," wrote "That interdisciplinary co-operation in social science research is increasingly shown by recent changes in the organization of university departments and research programs," and, more specifically, "At Harvard University what is in some respects the most radical experiment in interdisciplinary organization yet attempted in a major university was begun in 1946. It consisted in the establishment of a single comprehensive Department of Social Relations, as a regular unit of the Faculty of Arts and Sciences, combining all the previous department of sociology and the work in social and clinical psychology and in social anthropology." Sorokin had undertaken something of the same objective with, however, integration featuring history, economics, political science, philosophy, and social ethics.

The other measure of tendency with reference to anthropology and sociology may perhaps be best reflected in the very substantial number of community studies in which the methods of anthropology have been applied to the study of the modern community with particular reference to social stratification; to the integration and disintegration of group structures; and to the application of psychoanalytic hypotheses in ethnic relations. Most of these studies have been catalogued in Chapter 17 and will be discussed further in relation to the current tendency toward the integration of other social sciences than psychology and anthropology. Here, again, although there is generous criticism of methodology and content and although the current tendencies and emphasis have not had time enough for adequate testing, it seems likely that the anthropological community studies will continue to exert a considerable influence upon the directions of American sociology.

This fusion of sociology, social psychology, and cultural anthropology may also be appraised as a part of the still wider advocacy of integration in the social sciences. This movement, while new only in its revivification, manifests considerable power, which may be indicated in a number of ways. We have already called attention to the increasingly wider use of non-sociological literature as basic source materials for sociology. This has a number of facets. In the first place references cited in indexes and bibliographies in current source books, in new texts by younger sociologists, and in the more recent discussion of sociological theory, as well as in the books on history and theory, include a relatively small number of sociologists in comparison with authors from other disciplines. There is the protest of the popularizers against sociology's semantics and a consequent extraordinary attempt to translate all the social sciences into common language. The hazard here is that under the guise of the scientific study of man there might grow up an amazing series of abortive efforts that would retard the full birth of creative sociology. There are those who feel that sociology has failed to do as much as was expected and that the answer is to be found in the substitution of something else by non-sociological contributors. There are new programs of promising exploration of such varied fields as area studies, communications, public opinion, psychodrama, group dynamics.

There is, finally, both the necessity and the tendency to utilize, increasingly, wide non-sociological sources that have to do with the contemporary scene in which the widening range of new problems and social tensions challenge every manner of writing and research to seek solutions to current dilemmas. In the accelerating tempo of social change there are increasingly large numbers of dilemmas brought on by technological civilization in contemporary society. Here are multiplied materials, of which whole segments, such as the publications and researches of the UN and UNESCO, are new in the world. Sociology must study facts of all sorts and relationships, as brought out from many divergent sources, and cannot only not be isolated but, for its own increasing scientific work, it must seek all possible means of social interpretation.

It is not necessary that these changes and manifestations of directions be new in order to be fruitful and significant or to contribute to the formation of stable trends. Nor does newness or distinctiveness necessarily insure effectiveness or permanence in the increase and stabilization of social science gains. American sociology was nurtured in the tropism toward a general science of society and there may still be heard the faint echoes of John R. Commons, Richard T. Ely, John Bates Clark, G. Stanley Hall, William James, and a host of economic-philanthropists who somehow failed to set the incidence for an integrated science of society in the drift of the newly developing separate social science disciplines to break away. Albion W. Small was an eloquent advocate of the working together of the several social sciences. Giddings was editor, writer, student, and worker in political science and economics, as well as sociology, and he drew heavily upon psychology and anthropology in his logical systems of evolutionary process and in his theory of European Man. Just before Giddings' final retirement he had proposed that sociology, statistics, and anthropology at Columbia University be consolidated into a single department. The suggestion was sometimes ascribed to Giddings' eagerness to regain and consolidate the early prestige of the two notable departments of sociology and anthropology.

Sumner was nothing less than powerful in his economic and political interpretations, and his sociology was also substantially conditioned by the anthropology of his time. Sumner's challenge to cultural psychology may be just now being accepted in the fusion of sociology, psychology, and anthropology, as witness many samplings such as Murdock's *Social Structure,* Lowie's *Social Organization,* Cottrell's definitions of social and cultural anthropology, and others. Lester Ward's sociology, political science, and psychology were reflected not only in his monumental work, appraised by American historians as crucial in the shaping of American culture and education, but by his amazing proposal to offer a course of instruction on all knowledge. There are other examples of later sociologists whose work in two or more disciplines, as, for example, in statistics and sociology, sociology and social work, sociology and psychology and anthropology, might be cited as symbolic of the search for better integration.

We have pointed out in Chapter 22 something of the influence of Beardsley Ruml and Sydnor Walker, of the Laura Spelman Rockefeller Memorial, through which many million dollars were appropriated for cooperative research and interdisciplinary coordination, at Harvard, Columbia, Yale, North Carolina, and other universities. The history of the movement reflects no success story and Ruml himself retired from Chicago's consolidated deanship to Macy's in New York. Yet, to this day the building and dedication in the 1920's of the University of Chicago Social Science Building appears to have been the most memorable occasion of its kind in the light of the promise and prospect stated and implied in its integrated program. And although no such dreams came to full reality, it would be difficult to find a better illustration of the basic possibilities of cooperative endeavor than Quincy Wright's *The Study of War* which might have been studied more by many social scientists alongside the conceptualization of integration.

Now the task of appraising the promise and prospect, the hazards and limitations involved in new directions must somehow be effective in proportion as it is based upon the observation of experience rather than upon opinion or moral directives. And in the light of experience there are serious limitations and dangers in the over-simplified movement toward integration that are themselves a part of the essential definition of the 1950 situation. In running catalogue, here are samplings: In the first place, the movement might lack knowledge, maturity, specifications, unity, and leadership. For such a profound objective, there will be required well-equipped scholars and strong leaders in relatively large numbers working together in consensus with a more thorough knowledge and longer training than is exemplified in the recent tendency toward narrow specialization for empirical research. In the next place, a superficial trend toward general integration might negate the integrity of sociology itself, which requires, above everything now, a strengthening commensurate with its extraordinary past record of achievement and its new obligations and opportunities. The assumptions of integration, let us say, of the sciences of mathematics, physics, chemistry, engineering, in solving problems of invention, construction, or production, are, first of all, that each science must be concretely adequate.

The supreme task of sociology is to concentrate on its own development through the varying vicissitudes, even as physics and chemistry have concentrated mightily upon themselves and so have wrought unprecedented changes both within and without their own specialisms. Out of such concentration and skill they have emerged as powerful constituent sciences competent to be utilized in genuine integration. Popular advocacy of general integration might also constitute a sort of flight from reality, the reality being the hard task of doing scientific sociological research and translating the results into usable techniques and sound theory. Frustration, which may come from the conflict between complex conceptualization of the methodology of integration and the simple process of doing scientific research, might go hand in hand with certain assumptions by sociologists that other social sciences are perhaps more scientific or have more sophistication and, therefore, more prestige, than sociology. The counter-assumption is that sociology's prestige will grow out of its own achievements and that sophistication may not be a prime requisite. From outside the ranks of sociology there might be the advocacy of integration on the part of those who hold sociology in lesser esteem, and therefore, consciously and unconsciously, minimize it whenever occasion arises. This again is nothing new and often stems from well-motivated objectives. On the more general level the very effective integration of varied materials in source books of sociology, with selections from other social sciences and general knowledge predominating, need not constitute a substitution of what is not sociology for sociology itself in which there are ample resources, both in source materials and in the facility to conceptualize theory or problems upon which the varied source materials focus. Indeed such utilization of relevant materials and the consequent adequate conceptualization may well prove to be among the best fruit of the new sociology now so ambitiously conceived by the host of promising younger scholars.

Yet questions asked by Rupert Vance in 1950 appear peculiarly relevant to the current caution suggested here in the formation of trends. Vance says, "I, too, feel that, while social science is many sciences, sociology must achieve the dignity and integrity of *one science*. Specialisms will continue to develop in our field; to reach maturity and the distinction of achievement; and then to assert their independence and drop out. This poses a serious question: is the content of *general sociology* to be determined by a process of attrition, so that what we have left are things no one has wished to cart off to the new domains of mass communications, social anthropology of contemporary communities, rural sociology, etc., etc.? If we are to have this one science, not some but many of us will have to devote ourselves to the cultivation of general sociology and at a higher level than the synthesis of the introductory course."

The dangers inherent in promiscuous group research or in the attempt to integrate the actual research processes of more than one science may be illustrated in the case of the natural sciences. What they do is to specialize more and more and then make available their findings and acquaint kindred sciences with their knowledge so that waste may be avoided and collaboration achieved in the final stages of attacking a problem. Sometimes sociologists attempting to emulate the natural sciences might adopt methods long since discarded by the sciences themselves. No one except the expert can utilize specialized methods, as witness the crisis and revolution in physics.

Coming more specifically to the tendencies to fuse anthropology, psychology, and sociology in empirical studies of concrete societies from which unified science, scientific methodology, and valid conceptualizations are assumed, we find special limitations that need to be examined as an essential part of this new structure. First are the questions about the main assumptions themselves. Samplings of selected laboratory communities may represent great heterogeneity of cultures, limited in total perspective and adequacy with reference to area, time quality, and ethnic cultural relations. All of America, and especially all of the fabric of universal cultural processes, may not be found in isolated local societies of such diverse regional fabric as to appear almost distinctive from a thousand other communities in all parts of the world under different cultural, spatial, and time conditioning. To assume that the powerful processes of urbanization or of social technology and intellectualism may be studied in a rural-town society of the Middle States or of New England, or that biracial culture may be examined in the southern regions of the United States or in the hinterlands of many communities in other continents, except in the aggregate which can come from adequate numbers of diverse studies well integrated in analysis and conceptualization, is to negate the tenets of sociology's gains in scientific method.

Some limitations in methodology are inherent in segmental approaches in which inquiries may be made by immature, narrowly specialized research personnel, equipped with over-simplified frames of reference, formal psychological tests, or limited assumptions of anthropological techniques, in which the value judgments of the inquirers, but not of the cultures studied, are powerfully manifest. There are two facets to these limitations. In the first place, the investigators may report what they see rather than what is, the shortcomings being in both accuracy and adequacy. In the second place, the communities are alerted to inadequate or hostile reaction more than to cooperative endeavor and the full resources of its laboratory are not explored.

A third caution has to do with the main assumptions of fused or integrated efforts and with the gathering of masses of facts themselves. One is the assumption that masses of facts constitute scientific studies and that empirical studies are automatically susceptible to unified conceptualization. For one thing, the danger may be that the results will not be integrated but segmental; not really fused but compartmental. There is still the prevailing polarity of disciplinary priority and the conflict of vested methodologies in process.

In the earlier anthropological works it was complained that knowledge of primitive cultures was obtained from many different parts of the globe, from multiple divergent cultures, by reporters with varied skills and value viewpoints, and that generalizations were made without reference to structure and function in respect to specific area, time, culture. Now, in somewhat the same way in which it was assumed that because traits and behavior patterns of a kind were reported in different parts of the world, they were therefore universal to all cultures, so in isolation it might be assumed that because certain traits and behavior patterns are found in abundance and consistency in selected communities, they are therefore exclusively the traits of those cultures. A simple checking of the folkways and folklore of a hundred other cultures or the study of cultural backgrounds and history would constitute relevant inquiries basic to generalizations just as tests of cultural experience would be more important than simple elementary tests of intelligence.

These limitations are suggested not in the spirit of criticism but in the light of the extraordinary enthusiasm and resources of an increasing army of able young sociologists who can go far in the new reaches of sociology in the new era if they avoid many of the popular pitfalls of immature methodologies and too easy acceptance of what is often plausible commonplace offered as novelty. It now appears to be the consensus on the part of a majority of American sociologists that it is possible for a few of the present tendencies and practices to assume the proportions of fadism or of methodological ends in themselves where, on the other hand, they might well afford opportunities now so much needed. The fields and areas cited include the specialized community studies mentioned, the various facets of psychometry and psychodrama, some of the techniques of communications research, and group dynamics. It is pointed out that their genesis and direction have often been primarily in the backgrounds and methodologies from European psychology, rather than from a matured methodology consistent with the new American sociology. This has significance in relation to two points: the use to which social science was put in Hitler Germany, and the sweep toward the commercialization of communications research and psychology in certain centers in the United States.

One of the main criticisms most often raised by the presidents of the American Sociological Society was the relative ease with which loose generalizations in print are often accepted without critical examination. Surprisingly, they say, the old folk habit prevails: "If it's printed, it's true." In a half dozen main published appraisals of American sociology and in the presentation of special methodologies, there are sometimes limited perspective, incidental cataloguing of trends, compartmental selection, dogmatic advocacy, incompleteness of survey, and downright misstatements that appear to be accepted primarily because they are published in the official journals and encyclopedias and because there are no others available. On the other hand, it is almost the unanimous conclusion that sociologists do not read carefully enough the main works of other sociologists and that adequate reviews would contribute greatly to the general status of sociological literature. In the case of a number of major contributions and textbooks no reviews at all appeared in *The American Journal*. And there was a period when the *Review* instructed reviewers to emphasize the negative criticisms. There was manifest what Claude Bowman describes as "polarities and the impairment of science" when reviews featured criticism clustering about some opposing viewpoint vested in the reviewers. The catalogue here could be impressive. MacIver wrote good-naturedly about "my grievance," namely, "I ventured on a book entitled *Social Causation*. The only reviews of any scale or critical judgment which I received came from economists, political scientists, and philosophers and not a single one from any sociologists." And Bernard was discouraged "since almost no sociologist reads the contemporaneous writings of other sociologists." The complaint of the critics does not stop here, however; it goes farther and protests judgments given by reviewers without understanding what is written in the works reviewed.

Other criticisms and cautions offered by leading American sociologists have to do with teaching. One has already been voiced by a number of leaders when they regret the tendencies to ignore the task of preparation for teaching. By the same token they decry the tendency to teach undergraduates primarily conceptualizations rather than to teach them the main facts about human society. This, they say, produces a sterility not only for the hundreds of thousands of students who will not become sociologists, but retards even the students who aim to specialize in the field. How, they inquire, can sociology achieve maturity in giving the American citizen an understanding of science and society in a day when this is a supreme need in all sciences? Another criticism is directed toward the adoption of textbooks where it is demonstrated that what is popular in the quick adoption of elementary texts is predigested pabulum, worded in the semantics of what appears to be sophisticated new sociology. It is possible, they say, to adopt a half dozen new introductory sociology texts in which there is very little sociology of a comprehensive or mature nature. By the same token the criticism extends to the point of registering grave dissatisfaction within texts and, consequently again, to the need for a systematization of fields and methods before sociology can take off unhampered in the next period of development.

One of the prevailing criticisms of general practices is that emphasis has been placed by too many critics in too many places upon the short-comings of sociology and the negative aspects of its rise and develop-ment. A part of this is inherent in the multiple discussions on whether or not sociology is a science and in the perennial flow of discussions on methodology and empiricism. The contrary suggestion is that sociology has long since developed beyond the need for that sort of major criti-cism and that much of the criticism stems from an incomplete inven-tory of the picture. An example of general negative interpretation may be found in two appraisals of the status of American sociology. One writes that "The emergence of sociology has largely resulted from growing dissatisfaction with certain features of tradition, with the for-malism of the logic approach, the individualism and rationalism of economics, the individualism and biological orientation of psychol-ogy. . . . The primary emphases of developing sociology have been set by its position relative to these other disciplines." And yet sociology was well on its way when psychology was still "mental philosophy," a discipline attached to departments and schools of education in the uni-versity curriculum, or when it was reflected in the notable educational and general psychology of G. Stanley Hall and William James. Sociol-ogy was not, as another wrote, primarily a breakaway from the past but rather a growth and emergence as a sort of powerful structural dynamics in an inevitable succession of cultural and educational devel-opment in the United States.

The hazard of allocating sociology's genesis to a negative interrela-tionship to other social sciences, coupled with the newer assumptions that its future must be conditioned by another sort of dependent inter-relationship, is one of the main cautions offered by American sociolo-gists who are critical of the promise and prospect of the next period of development. A facet of this criticism might be found in a possible tendency in three or four main manifestations to make sociology de-pendent upon German psychology transferred to America from its tragic impotence and prostitution in the Hitler state civilization. There was a danger, it was pointed out, that a facile transfer to America under the guise of sociology, for the measurement of popular reactions wanted by commercial organizations and political groups, or susceptible to popular drama and emotional reactions, might not only not be scientific sociology but might be next door to the same sort of functions performed in Germany. More than this, it might mean a breakaway from university research and learning and afford but a poor substitute for the broad training, profound scholarship, and comprehensive knowledge that are commensurate with the requisites of sociological leadership.

Some of the dangers inherent in communications study, which combines a miscellany of methods and personnel with endowment from commercial organizations, are implied in a criticism by Elliot E. Cohen in *Commentary* for December, 1948. Characterizing the opinion-molding communications research as a profession, he says, "[it] has burgeoned to include, also, the technicians and executives of advertising, publicity, public relations, merchandising, 'exploitation,' market research, scientific communications, and polling — and the 'media' have multiplied — radio, film, book clubs, television, etc. As might have been anticipated in what is essentially a commercial operation, 'business brains' have won the larger institutional weight and rewards, as against the members of the 'creative' craft."

Alongside the inventory of the extraordinary development of American sociology and the current tendencies, practices, and manifestations that appear as possible trends, one can note a substantial catalogue of neglected opportunities, which, however, by the same token, now may become promising areas of achievement. That is, the answer to the question of what have been some of the principal fields that have been most neglected may be the answer to the companion question: What are some of the sure tasks immediately ahead in sociology's maturing program? For instance, it is not too late for sociology and sociologists to correct the deficiency in which sociology has not achieved a framework in which the main map of its fields and areas of study was projected on a practical basis whereby many universities and departments of sociology might have pursued the same fields of study, utilizing relatively the same methods, subsequently to be checked and compared for further study and testing; this, in contrast to the trend for every department to do something different with different methods with rarely ever a coming-together for consolidating or testing.

Nor is it too late to undertake another immediate task, with a sort of twofold objective of correcting the limitations mentioned above and of moving toward the sure goal of matured research. The first objective would be to recruit for sociology a proportionate ratio of the best students and to provide for their adequate direction and financing over a period of years sufficient to insure maturity and creative research. Two corollary needs might provide for ways of meeting the first need. The first would be a systematization of the field of sociology adapted to uniform research. The second would be to provide for a long-time period of research undertaken more or less uniformly by many departments of sociology and insuring adequate support and maturity for many students in training.

With reference to the first problem, there would be the objective to recruit and to train the best personnel in increasing numbers, commensurate with the urgent need of sociology and comparable to what is being done in the natural sciences. This is particularly important because of the general agreement that the world shows its greatest deficiency at the point of its greatest need, namely, research in the field of social relations. It is especially urgent, also, because of the trend everywhere for increasing endowments for scholarships for research in the natural sciences over against the relative decrease in the field of the social sciences.

The systematization of the field of sociology could represent a framework in which sociology might attain more uniformity and effectiveness in both research and teaching. More specifically, the systematic arrangement of areas of sociological teaching and research should provide two things. One would be the special planning for long-time research over a period of years through which experiments in uniformities in research and systematic presentation of results can be made the basis for endowment of fellowships and for the constant training of younger social scientists. Another criterion for such a systematic field would be to be sure that the catalogue of projects would fall within the range of strictly scientific sociology and yet would set up a systematic group that would focus upon what seem to be the elementary or organic phenomena characteristic of the changing social structure.

Such a systematization of the field of sociological research, far from negating the tendencies toward specialisms and integration, would contribute to both methodology and theory in an increasingly stabilized program in which other neglected areas might well be developed. It would, for instance, give perspective to the neglected field that Roscoe Pound called "sociological jurisprudence" and the whole specialism of law and society. Sociological jurisprudence was both a method and a program of sound theoretical content. There were three great Americans who laid foundations for sociological achievement here, namely, Roscoe Pound, Oliver Wendell Holmes, and Louis Brandeis. Yet, with the exception of a few articles by Pound on "Law and Morals" and his collaboration on two sociological texts, and the special sociological implications of justice and bigness and complexity by Brandeis, sociology has appeared to sense little of the powerful significance of law and society.

How concrete and scientific, as well as comprehensive, the sociological task could be, may be seen from a careful examination of the monumental work, *Law and Society,* published in 1949. In some twenty-four hundred pages Sydney Simpson, Julius Stone, and M. Magdalena Schoch have contributed an extraordinary case book of selections from authentic sociologists, anthropologists, psychologists, historians, political scientists, in three volumes, namely "Law and Society in Evolution," "Law in Modern Democratic Society," and "Law, Totalitarianism, and Democracy." Starting with kin-organized society and moving on to emergent political society and the rise of commerce and industrialization, the continuum of societal development is followed through the more complex economically organized society into contemporary politics and ideologies on up to the rise of totalitarian ideologies and practices. Here are found institutional facets, exploring the fascistic and communistic totalitarianism and examining political, domestic, and religious institutions, social welfare and the utilization of human resources, with adequate analyses and systematization of hundreds of specialisms, basic to a more adequate understanding and direction of contemporary society.

Some tendencies toward accelerating the sociology of religion and toward the recognition of the major place of values and value systems in the total framework of sociology indicate the possibilities of making up deficiencies that have grown out of neglect of the scientific studies of the functional role of religion and morality, areas that have too often been relegated to philosophy and history. The neglect of religion has been reflected not only in the limited exploration of the "sociology of religion" but of the general role of religion in the societal continuum and in the secularization of religion itself. The neglect of values has been reflected, not only in the limited follow-up of the studies of value systems as suggested by such authors as Durkheim, Tönnies, Pareto, Simmel, Cooley, Ellwood, Hayes, but in the frank exploration of the systematics of normative society and the principles of social planning through which specified objectives may be reached. Sociology, through its systematized fields, first and last, finds its main foci upon human relationship in the setting of process, structure, function, and institutional modes of control in a continuum of social and cultural change the normal curve of which is greatly skewed by technology and state civiliaztion.

Social planning represents essentially a broader framework of social theory at its best. The assumptions of social planning are that it reflects an integrated process involving a definite orientation toward value systems. Such theory, however, assumes a knowledge of how societies have developed from their earlier bottoming in nature and primitive groups, conditioned by the circumstantial pressure of environment and the social pressure of culture, and have grown and developed into later more complex, urban, industrial, and state civilization, more powerfully conditioned by physical factors and technology than by general cultural environment and tradition. The understanding of the relations between people and resources, between culture and geographic environment, between races and other ethnic groups, and between diversities of powerful cultures, and the impact of change and technology upon the individual and upon culture — the understanding of all this is essential to the understanding of what problems are and what needs to be planned in terms of social achievements and social values. So, too, the understanding of the essential elements of modern civilization in terms of the state, of industry, of urbanism, of organization, of technology, and of the resulting rise of modern technicways becomes basic to the understanding of what planning means and what sort of planning may be assumed for modern contemporary society.

Other areas of reference to values in which limitations and hazards appear might be found in the promising trend that Howard Becker has called "one of the most interesting recent developments," namely, "the full realization of the significance of values in social life." Examples might be chosen from two of the fields ranking highest in the catalogue of specialisms reported by American sociologists in 1950, namely, race and ethnic relationship, and methodology and research. The hazards are found primarily in the assumptions of objectivity and scientific neutrality but set in the framework of inflexible value judgments and crusading patterns of exposition. In the field of race and ethnic groups it is the consensus of specialists who have kept in touch with recent contributions, including sociologists, anthropologists, and psychologists, that, alongside the magnificent sweep of notable contributions on race and ethnic group relations, the mode has been to neglect substantial empirical research in the basic elemental factors involved. Further hazards may be found in the tendency to select areas of research, theoretical frames of reference, personnel, materials to be used and rejected, and conceptualizations to be attempted, within the framework of pre-research constructs in a scale of "liberal" or "non-liberal" variations or, in the words of many critics, in the framework "of what is proved rather than what is known." Now the need is for a more impressive record of concrete achievements, tested and proved, commensurate with both the efforts expended and the major area involved.

Another major field in which great promise is indicated is that of the continuum of social change in which theoretical conceptualizations grow out of both empirical research and broader historical and descriptive studies. Sociologists have been extremely critical of the magnificent generalizations of Spengler, Toynbee, Sorokin, Mumford, Ortega y Gasset, but have been less critical of sociology's failure to function in this area. On the other side, Ogburn's *Social Change* pioneered a long way back and there have been innumerable studies and assumptions based on his cultural lag, while scores of new contributions to the study of social problems have been set with social change as the frame of reference. Redfield in anthropology has set exploratory modes that are bearing fruit. Many studies of "acculturation" have been started and many programs for the study of the impact of technology on culture have been prepared. Yet there is no technique available nor a single definitive study for analyzing realistically the role and rates of change in a contemporary society characterized primarily by tumultuous change yet frustrated powerfully because of its resistance to change and its conditioning in the values of tradition and survival.

More specifically, in the two fields of communications and of intercultural relations there has accumulated a mighty backlog of needs in the field of conflict which are now basic to the major tensions and dilemmas of human relations all the way from communities and regional hinterlands to the multiplied cultures and ideologies in what is called "one world," yet which abound in greater dynamic differences than have been hitherto recorded. In 1930 the author of this volume in his presidential address on "Folk and Regional Conflict as a Field of Sociological Study," wrote urgently about the neglect of the study of conflict yet did little about it. He quoted Russell Smith, " 'social conflict is sociologically an unexplored field. . . . In short, the sociology of conflict has yet to be written.' Whether, because this is true, or whether, because of the significance and character of conflict, processes in modern technological society, or in the breaking-up of old cultures in the new world, it would seem quite important for sociology to attack the problem as one peculiarly within its own domain; for instance, the Cooley concept of sociology as a means of interpreting life situations, or Ogburn's adaptive culture in social change, or Giddings' equilibrium between folk society and state society. Yet the problem of social conflict in a modern world of technology is different from that in an old world of primary conflict, and the developments of social science have been considerable, outgrowing, to some extent, old theories, so that it becomes necessary to attack the problem from various new approaches."

Now, as late as July, 1950, in *The American Journal of Sociology,* Jessie Bernard wrote, "The theory of conflict and of competition particularly has suffered in the hands of recent American sociologists; since the time of such early pioneers as Small, Park, and Ross, little progress has been made. Where, for example — to limit our discussion to the neglect of a theory of conflict — are the American sociological analyses and scientific measures of sabotage, boring from within, the use of 'fronts,' the Trojan horse technique, the manipulation of parliamentary debate, the use of *agents provocateurs,* the war of nerves, espionage, fifth columns, deceit, fraud? We have excellent descriptions and analyses of lynchings, strikes, riots, and war. But the most important modern conflicts are not necessarily fought on the level of overt violence. Yet American sociologists in recent years have been content to leave the scientific study of conflict where Simmel left it."

With reference to the systematization of the sociological field, the American Sociological Society is moving toward increasingly more specific and dynamic leadership as opposed to an earlier incidental and fortuitous organization and service. In the past the Society has built the structure of its annual meetings, and often its special publications, upon sections and divisions that reflected the cumulative, but incidental, judgment of what the main fields of sociology are. The present indications are that, as is the case in many of the sciences, including economics and political science, the Society may set itself the task, through strong committees, of adopting a classification of fifteen or twenty areas with appropriate sub-areas for the purpose of classifying members, accelerating research, strengthening specialisms, integrating studies, and systematizing the whole field. The need for this is reflected vividly in the miscellaneous and promiscuous cataloging and wording of specialisms by sociologists. One of the main criticisms made by a number of leading sociologists has been that the multiplication of "abstruse subjects and semantics has confused many promising young sociologists . . . [and driven them] away from the real job of sociology." Bernard's *Fields and Methods of Sociology* was the result of one year's effort in the right direction and awaits an authentic and stabilized follow-up.

The current planning of the American Sociological Society points toward a study of its membership, including their specific interests in the framework of the society's systematized subjects, and an adequate classification through which more accurate definitions of the sociologists would follow. In the past it has often been urged that membership in the Society be limited to scholars who have achieved a certain amount of research; yet a common result might be to classify as a sociologist of distinction a research associate in psychology, for instance, none of whose work, interest, or background could be defined as sociology. Manifestly, this is not a sure way to raise the definitive standards of sociology as a distinct science. The present tendency to increase the membership, to classify the members, and to move toward more definite qualifications that will strengthen sociology and encourage a host of younger members will contribute powerfully to the next period of development.

The Society can be moving toward other composite services of great importance in the planning of a substantial budget, a staff of permanent tenure, and continued contact with departments, students, and faculties. One of the most rigorous criticisms of American sociology has been gradually gaining momentum on the part of graduate students who complain that faculties give grudgingly or scarcely at all of time and counsel in the stages of training when creative work is needed and when "speed up" rather than "drag out" is a requisite for the best original work. It is protested that the number of years required to get a degree is often an index in reverse of exceptional ability and high standards. On the other hand, faculties are so crowded with work and their own writing, and outside demands to represent their universities and to contribute to public causes are so great, that the dilemmas become increasingly difficult. The Society could make an important contribution in the study of common problems involved. Another special effort that promises much would be a first-class monograph devoted entirely to the study of the American Sociological Society itself, and the dozen neglected and unknown facets of its record. All in all, the interest and cooperation of all the members in increasing numbers, well organized and integrated by a permanent staff, promises a new era for both the American Sociological Society and sociology as a whole.

As symbol and reality of American sociology's record and prospect are many expressions of high esteem and of confident expectations by hundreds of sociologists in leading roles and in creative writing. Appropriate to the challenge of the second half of the twentieth century are the simple and eloquent statements of two earlier and two later senior sociologists, reflecting the spirit and mastery of sociology today. Ward wrote, "We see, then, the high place which sociology, properly defined, should hold among the sciences and how clear and incisive are the boundaries which mark it off from all other branches of learning." This estimate, on page 20 of his *Outlines,* harmonizes with a different sort of hope of Giddings when he said in his presidential address of 1910, "The great superiorities that now preclude effective government by discussion throughout the world are: (1) technical proficiency based on scientific knowledge, and (2) concentrated economic power. If we sincerely wish for peace, we must be willing to see a vast equalizing of industrial efficiency between the East and the West. We must also welcome every change that tends to bring about a fairer apportionment of natural resources among nations and within them, and a more equal distribution of wealth. If these conditions can be met, there will be a Parliament of Man."

Then, as late as 1949, Parsons identified sociology's role as one commensurate with the new frontiers, when he wrote, "As a professional group we are committed to a venture which is in many ways without precedent and which, indeed, the pessimists freely predict to be impossible. It is a challenge worthy of the finest traditions of the American spirit of enterprise." Again, on page 221 of the November, 1950, *American Journal of Sociology,* Florian Znaniecki wrote, "Thus at the middle of the century, sociology faces a tremendous task — but not an impossible one . . . To be a science, sociology must deal specifically and exclusively with social systems. This is enough to make it more important from the humanistic viewpoint than any other science; for social systems constitute that category of cultural systems on which the very existence of all culture, including science itself, and, indeed, the existence of all mankind, depend." And, referring to the "younger generation" of sociologists he concluded, "And, most of all, may they be fully aware of their great responsibility to mankind, not merely as active participants in social life but primarily as scientists."

Yet, looking both ways, mid-century American sociologists need most of all to work rather than to inventory and regret or reflect optimism or discouragement or even satisfaction. For any incipient sociological anxiety the best therapy must surely be work and the minimization of the egocentric mood or self-appraisal. And if sociology at mid-century is still many things to many men, it must be remembered that the best new methodology and motivation of science is to meet the needs of a changing world in the sense of strengthening whatever differential sciences may be needed for adequacy.

Acknowledgments

Greetings and special acknowledgments go to all those younger sociologists, as yet not so well known, whose enthusiasm and success in hard work and research exploration have contributed powerfully to the hard core of current American sociology and will likely add even more to the promise of the next half century.

Special appreciation is expressed for those presidents of the American Sociological Society who took time out from busy days to write down for use in this book something of their own contributions first hand — definitions, concepts, impressions and convictions — and, by special request, something autobiographical. If some of the best in each chronicle had to be omitted for lack of space, the authors may be assured that the material will still be used in the continuing appraisal of American sociology.

Thanks are due to all of the four hundred and more who so promptly answered inquiries about themselves and their work for a limited "Who's Who" which logically grew too big for *American Sociology*. The subsequent publication of this preliminary "Who's Who," together with the directory of the membership of the American Sociological Society, will serve the purposes for which the original publication was planned.

In a book like *American Sociology* the cumulative obligations are such that it is not possible to identify and to thank all those who helped indirectly and directly. For instance, to the baker's dozen colleagues in the Department of Sociology at Chapel Hill and to the generations of students over the years, one wishes to express appreciation, recognition, affectionate esteem. Among those who have read parts of the manuscript and offered criticisms, special thanks are expressed to Rupert Vance, Gordon Blackwell, Lee Brooks, Katharine Jocher, Dan Price, Robert Merton. Among research assistants special thanks are due to Leslie Syron for reading parts of the manuscript and to C. M. Grigg for standing by for emergency checking and reference. Thanks also go to many in the several regions of America who have written letters, answered inquiries, given opinions, since our first inquiries began in the early 1930's. All these were constituent elements in the abundant evidence that gave us our high esteem for American sociology and are almost as varied as the membership itself.

In the name index alone there were several thousand cross checkings to be made with the possibilities of what sometimes seemed countless simple errors of letters, punctuation, initials, identification, classification. Special acknowledgment, something much more than routine thanks, is expressed to Katharine Jocher, who, although she had no opportunity to check the main facets of the work, nevertheless in her busy schedule as editor and scholar, read proofs and was insistent that we check over and over again all details. In so far as this was done, special appreciation is expressed to Marjorie Tallant for checking names, references, titles, and helping with the proofs and index. To Elizabeth Henderson go special thanks for the seemingly endless task of copying the multiple revisions and for processing the two indexes and the "Who's Who."

Thanks are also due all those who helped with those other unfinished tasks that had to be omitted because of lack of space in any elementary presentation of the story of American Sociology. These included the segments on definition, concepts, and specialisms; critical appraisals of special "theories" of individual sociologists; the rich periodical literature; the bibliography of borderline sociology; and the history of sociology in specific institutions.

H. W. O.

Chapel Hill, N.C.
May, 1951

Index of Names

Index of Agencies, Publications, Societies, including Universities

Index of Subject Matter

DATE DUE